REVOLUTIONARY
INDUSTRIAL UNIONISM

REVOLUTIONARY INDUSTRIAL UNIONISM

The Industrial Workers of the World in Australia

VERITY BURGMANN

Department of Political Science
University of Melbourne

CAMBRIDGE
UNIVERSITY PRESS

Published by the Press Syndicate of the University of Cambridge
The Pitt Building, Trumpington Street, Cambridge CB2 1RP, UK
40 West 20th Street, New York, NY 10011–4211, USA
10 Stamford Road, Oakleigh, Melbourne 3166, Australia

Printed in Australia by Brown Prior Anderson

National Library of Australia cataloguing-in-publication data
Burgmann, Verity.
Revolutionary industrial unionism: the Industrial
Workers of the World in Australia.
Bibliography.
Includes index.
1. Industrial Workers of the World – History.
2. Trade-unions – Australia – Political activity – History.
I. Title.
331.886

Library of Congress cataloguing-in-publication data
Burgmann, Verity.
Revolutionary industrial unionism: the industrial
workers of the world in Australia/Verity Burgmann.
p.   cm.
Includes bibliographical references and index.
1. Trade-unions – Australia – History – 20th century. 2. Labor
movement – Australia – History – 20th century. 3. Industrial Workers
of the World – History. I. Title.
HD6892.B87 1995
331.88'6'0994–dc20   95–3722

A catalogue record for this book is available from the British Library.

ISBN 0 521 47123 0 Hardback

Contents

List of Illustrations

Acknowledgements and Dedication

Publication of this book was assisted by a special publications grant from the University of Melbourne.

The book was researched and written over a seventeen-year period but with many long interruptions caused by childbearing three times over, other books and teaching commitments. Only during a Deakin University research fellowship in 1984-85 and study leave from the University of Melbourne in 1992 did work proceed relatively unimpeded. Several institutions supported the research financially, enabling travel to overseas and inter-State archives, and some limited research assistance: Deakin University ($4000 in 1984-85); the Australian Research Council ($4150 in 1987); the Faculty of Arts at the University of Melbourne ($2000 in 1987 and $500 in 1994); and the Political Science Department at the University of Melbourne ($300 in 1994). Deakin University Library also provided an excellent inter-library loans service.

Many people have helped in various ways, especially Joy Damousi, Stuart Macintyre and Naomi Segal. As a research assistant for three months in 1987, Joy Damousi covered more ground than a normal researcher would in twice the time; as a colleague, she generously continued to feed me research titbits and recently made constructive comments on the final draft. Stuart Macintyre, a longtime lender of obscure tomes, also looked over the final draft and parts of an earlier one, then kindly provided the encouragement and resources necessary to respond to his helpful suggestions. Naomi Segal allowed me to refer extensively to her unpublished paper on the IWW in Western Australia.

Activists, mostly now deceased, gave generously of their time in interviews; their names appear in the bibliography. Other people helped with advice, information, inspiration, hospitality, permissions or in other ways: Paul Adams, Jon Bekken (IWW, Chicago), Tony Birch, Brad Bowden, Sally Bowen, Lorna Burgmann, Meredith Burgmann, David Carment, Robert Corcoran, Drew Cottle, Dick Curlewis, Miriam Dixson, Ray Evans, Beverley Firth, Charlie Fox, Eric Fry, Andrew Gill, Bob Gollan, Roy Hay, Agnes Hickey (formerly Seamer), Jakob Ikerath, Mrs

Bill Ivey, Deborah Jordan, Leo Kelly, Bill Laidler, Michael Long, Peter Love, Fiona Macdonald, Clem Macintyre, Pat Mackie, Marie McFarlane, Peter McGregor, Ken Mansell, Michael Matteson, Andrew Metcalfe, Pavla Miller, Pat Morrigan (formerly Gowland), Mr and Mrs Jim Moss, Stephen O'Brien, Tom O'Lincoln, Laurie Parkes, John Playford, Andrew Reeves, John Sendy, Peter Sheldon, Tom Sheridan, John Shields, Carmel Shute, Martin Sullivan, Stuart Svensen, the late Fred Thompson (Chicago), Ann Turner, Kosmas Tsokhas, Nadia Wheatley, Peter Wright and Steve Wright. Colleagues in my department provided technical assistance, especially Craig Lonsdale, and also Rita De Amicis, Jan Souter and Wendy Ruffles. The Cambridge University Press team involved in the production of this book were efficient and professional.

My three sons – David, James and Robert – persistently obstructed my research and writing, their effect slightly mitigated by Andrew Milner. For this and for support during the long gestation period of this book, I dedicate it to him.

Abbreviations

AA	Australian Archives
ABL	Noel Butlin Archives (formerly Archives of Business and Labour), ANU
ACTU	Australian Council of Trade Unions
A Comm	*Australian Communist*
AFL	American Federation of Labor
ALHUA	Archives of Labor History and Urban Affairs, Wayne State University, Detroit
ALF	Australian Labour Federation
ALP	Australian Labor Party
AMA	Amalgamated Miners' Association
AMIEU	Australian Meat Industry Employees' Union
ANU	Australian National University
ARTSA	Amalgamated Railway and Tramway Servants' Association
ASP	Australian Socialist Party
AWU	Australian Workers' Union
BDT	*Barrier Daily Truth*
BHP	Broken Hill Proprietary
CEF	Colliery Employees Federation
CGT	Confédération générale du travail
CIB	Criminal Investigation Branch
CIO	Congress of Industrial Organizations
Comm	*Communist*
CPA	Communist Party of Australia
CPD	*Commonwealth Parliamentary Debates*
CPGB	Communist Party of Great Britain
CUC	Combined Unions Committee
DT	*Daily Telegraph*
FBI	Federal Bureau of Investigation
FEDFA	Federated Engine Drivers and Firemen's Association
I Comm	*International Communist*
Ind Sol (A)	*Industrial Solidarity* (Adelaide)

Ind Sol (M)	*Industrial Solidarity* (Melbourne)
IIW	*International Industrial Workers*
IS	*International Socialist*
ISR	*International Socialist Review*
IUPG	Industrial Union Propaganda Group
IUPL	Industrial Union Propaganda League
IWW	Industrial Workers of the World
KC	King's Counsel
L	Editorial
LT	La Trobe Library, State Library of Victoria
MHR	Member of the House of Representatives
ML	Mitchell Library, State Library of NSW
MLA	Member of the Legislative Assembly
NL	National Library of Australia
NSWBLF	New South Wales Builders Labourers' Federation
NSWPD	*New South Wales Parliamentary Debates*
OBU	One Big Union
OBUPL	One Big Union Propaganda League
OBUU	One Big Union of Unemployed
P	*People*
PLC	Political Labor Council
PLL	Political Labour League
Prol	*Proletariat*
QRU	Queensland Railways Union
RILU	Red International of Labour Unions
SANSW	State Archives of New South Wales
SFA	Socialist Federation of Australasia
SLP	Socialist Labor Party
Sol	*Solidarity*
SMH	*Sydney Morning Herald*
TLC	Trades and Labor Council
TUC	Trades Union Congress
UAA	Unlawful Associations Act
VSP	Victorian Socialist Party
WASP	Western Australian Socialist Party
WIIU	Workers International Industrial Union
WIUA	Workers' Industrial Union of Australia
WW	*Workers Weekly*
WWF	Waterside Workers Federation

CHAPTER 1

'Flowers to the Rebels Failed'

Nearly eight decades have passed since the Bolshevik Revolution shook the world, and nine since the formation of the first federal Labor government in Australia. In that time we have witnessed the final dashing of the hopes born of the attempt to replace the authoritarian and hierarchical practices of Czarism with an egalitarian communist regime, and the failure of the Labor Party to render Australian society significantly more equitable by parliamentary means. In the first instance, the apparatchiks of the Communist Party redefined for their own purposes the goals of the Revolution and the manner of achieving them, imposing on the Russian people the authoritarian and hierarchical practices of Stalinist Communism. In the second instance, those elected to abolish extremes of wealth and want have lacked either the will to seek the changes from which they would no longer benefit or have been pleased to find insuperable obstacles placed in their way by those who would suffer most from policies of redistributive intent.

However, there exists in Australia an alternative tradition of revolution from below, trusting neither the Bolshevik style of revolution from above nor the Labor one of reform from above. It is exemplified most spectacularly in the tragically short career of the Industrial Workers of the World, the Wobblies as they were known, before and during the Great War of 1914–18. Based on a premise fundamentally different from both Communism and Laborism, the IWW represented a revolutionary working-class politics intent upon self-emancipation, dedicated as it was to the principle that there are none better to break the chains than those who actually wear them. The significance of this alternative radical tradition, as recently as the post-Second World War period, can be demonstrated by examining a novel, an industrial dispute, a movement and a union: Frank Hardy's *Power Without Glory* (1950), the Mount Isa dispute

1

(1964–65), the draft resisters of the anti-Vietnam movement (1967–72) and the New South Wales Builders Labourers' Federation (1970–74).

There are various Wobbly characters in the novels of Frank Hardy, inspired in the main by his Wobbly father and his friends.[1] However, *Power Without Glory* is more than a novel with Wobbly characters; it is a Wobbly novel. Hardy explains that part of his political motivation in writing *Power Without Glory* was his father's Wobbly attitude, hence the invisible narrator is the voice of the militant working class with his father's responses towards the Labor Party. His father

> used to interject more loudly at Labor meetings than Conservative meetings on the basis of the fact that the boneheads . . . were awake up to the Nationalists but not the Labor party . . . He said 'It's not a Labor party. John Wren owns it lock, stock and fucking barrel . . . Join it if you like but don't think you're joining the workers' party because you're not.' That always stuck in my mind when I arrived in Melbourne from the Bush.[2]

Hardy's John West is 'out of his depth' when confronted with Jock Somerton, 'the last of the "Wobbly" trade union leaders'. To West, Somerton was 'a riddle', because he 'could not be bought or even intimidated'. The invisible narrator explains the solution to the riddle was not Somerton's anti-Catholicism, which West blamed, but his Wobbly heritage. 'The IWW had lived long enough to change the old set-up in the Australian unions. Its class-conscious propaganda, vigour and crude militancy had paved the way for the more scientific and better organised Communists who were to rise in the next decade.'[3] The style of the Wobblies is captured by Hardy in the hilarious interjections, 'too radically political to come from casual observers', of the 'two shabby bystanders' at West's patriotic recruiting meeting, who finally introduce themselves as Wobblies and are forcibly removed from the meeting as they sing the Wobblies' Doxology:

> Praise 'Fat' when morning work bells chime,
> Praise him for scraps of overtime,
> Praise him whose bloody wars we fight,
> Praise 'Fat', the leech and parasite . . . AW HELL![4]

A member of the Communist Party when he wrote *Power Without Glory*, Hardy subsumed the Wobbly legacy under that of the Communist. It was in later years that Hardy acknowledged *Power Without Glory* as 'a Wobbly novel', 'a book the Wobblies would have appreciated', rather than a Communist one, pointing out that Roly Farrall and other ex-Wobblies were the most enthusiastic in helping with the binding of the first copies

of *Power Without Glory* while the leaders of the Communist Party were bitterly hostile.[5] He describes himself as an anarcho-syndicalist who acci-
dentally joined the Communist Party; 'the CPA was fucked but there was
nowhere else to go'.[6]

Pat Mackie, like Hardy, became a notorious public figure, the whip-
ping-boy of the conservative Australian media, as Chairman of the
Mount Isa Section of the Australian Workers Union (AWU) during
the infamous lock-out of 1964–65, which divided both the nation and
the labour movement. The workers of Mount Isa elected Mackie to lead
them in the confrontation with Mount Isa Mines, which locked them out
in order to impose contract work and abolish hourly rates: 'The hard-
headed left wing old timers wanted me, knowing of my industrially
militant, non-political "Wobbly" inclinations.'[7] Mackie had joined the
IWW as a merchant seaman on the North American coast in 1934 and
remains a member to this day, 'the accredited Delegate for the IWW in
Australia'.[8]

Mackie was popular with the miners, but the AWU officials, happy to
play the game by company-made rules, expelled him from the Union.[9]
When Mackie toured Broken Hill in the midst of the dispute, an old
man of about 80 approached him in the street and took his hand. He
held it to his heart and told Mackie: 'I'm an old miner, by God! I fought
through the 1916 anti-conscription thing with the Wobblies, and it's the
happiest day in my life that I meet a real honest-to-God Union fighter
like we had then!' Tears were running down his face, he was shaking with
emotion: 'Keep up the good fight!' he said.[10] Since company stubborn-
ness was matched by the men at Mount Isa, consultation ultimately
replaced confrontation as the company's method of operation.[11]

During the Vietnam War, an anti-conscription pamphlet produced by
the Draft Resisters Union reprinted on its front page the famous Wobbly
poster 'To arms!!', that earned Tom Barker a stretch in jail in 1915.[12]
Michael Matteson, one of the first draft resisters, who refused to register
in January 1967 and was accordingly jailed, was inspired by his knowledge of the IWW free-speech fights; he recalls buying the 1965
cyclostyled *Tom Barker and the I.W.W.* from Bob Gould's bookshop and
had become interested in the IWW as early as 1964, when he heard Col
Pollard and Bert Armstrong speaking in the Domain and selling the
American IWW paper, *Industrial Worker*. He was prompted by the
Wobblies' example to think about the impact of similar mass resistance,
which could turn the ethical stand of many individuals into practical politics, and he claims others within the anti-war movement were similarly
moved. Matteson argues that the success of the draft resisters showed
that people inspired by IWW tactics could be considerably more
effective than if they had been imbued with Leninist principles.[13]

Around the same time, the New South Wales branch of the Builders Labourers' Federation (NSWBLF) began to rock the foundations not only of the Sydney building industry but of the trade union movement, imposing green bans that saved Sydney from billions of dollars of 'development' while presenting a new form of union structure that, like the IWW before it, constituted a serious threat to the officials of other unions. The NSWBLF espoused as a matter of principle, and practised, limited tenure of office for union officials, a dramatic departure from normal trade union practice. Jack Mundey explained in 1978 that: 'The driving force that made me suggest limited tenure was my own experience of seeing modern, contemporary unionism and seeing the need for some inbuilt guarantee for limiting power and having inbuilt renewal.'[14] Though a member of the Communist Party, Mundey found that the idea of limited tenure was 'unpopular' with the Party leadership and that it 'alienated' the Party's leading union officials such as Laurie Carmichael. It was, he admits, a Wobbly idea.[15]

In other ways, too, the NSWBLF displayed a Wobbly temper, in its penchant for direct action at the point of production, in its distrust of the pretensions of vanguard parties to lead workers in struggle, in its belief that trade unions themselves could and should educate workers to a class-conscious viewpoint, in its dislike of dogma and doctrinal hair-splitting, in the imaginative and inventive tactics it deployed, in its larrikinism and good-humoured anti-intellectualism. When one of its organisers was asked about Lenin's view that revolutionary consciousness had to be brought to the workers by a separate party, he replied simply 'bollocks'. The NSWBLF held in benign contempt the more dogmatic and serious members of the left-wing political sects that hung around their fringes. While a student Maoist was addressing one of their meetings, they nailed his briefcase to the floor.[16] The Wobblies might have done the same.

Even within the mainstream of society, a legend persists, in increasingly muted form, about the IWW. 'The Wobblies', as Peter Rushton avers, 'cannot be confined to labour history; they are part of a larger legend'.[17] The Wobblies were the terrible infants of the First World War, who tried to overthrow capitalism by burning down Sydney and debasing the currency with forged banknotes. The 1983 *Vedgymight History of Australia* explains that the Wobblies 'tried to set fire to Sydney, but it was damp and wouldn't light properly'.[18] Some of the pieces of more substantial information upon which the versions of the legend are based have been provided by historians; yet historians have played only a minor role in reciting the legend, formed as it is in large part by reminiscence and anecdote, handed down orally through the generations and enshrined in literature.[19]

The influence of old Wobblies has persisted almost to this day, making their impression upon subsequent generations of writers and activists only recently departed. Jack Lindsay in *Life Rarely Tells* reminisces about the impact upon him in the 1920s of the Wobbly, Jim Quinton, a 'cool clear-eyed fighter, rock solid'. He would listen intrigued as Quinton and his friend, another Wobbly, discussed the goings-on at Cloncurry and its copper mines: 'Here was a new world for me.'[20] Tom Payne recalls of his early working life:

> A man named Mark Anthony influenced me greatly at this time. He was a miner who worked at Broken Hill but used to come home to Clunes periodically. He was a Wobbly, a member of the IWW. I used to follow him around like a fox terrier pup. He'd read quite a bit and talked about the working class and its struggles for a better life . . . Mark Anthony was mainly responsible for me taking an interest in the labour movement.[21]

Judah Waten was greatly impressed by a former Wobbly, Joe Shelley, upon whom he based the character of the IWW member, George Feathers, in *The Unbending*.[22] First published in 1954, this engrossing novel about wartime life in a town near Perth is remarkable for its sensitive and accurate portrayal of the courage and suffering of Feathers and his fellow Wobblies. Alan Marshall bears testimony to this: 'I admired the I.W.W. One of its old members was a member of the Writers' League and used to talk to me about his experiences. It was this great faith though, this faith in the future, bright with promise, that was approaching us. Victory was in sight, so we thought.'[23] Ian Bedford's novel, *The Shell of the Old*, though set in the mid-1960s in north-eastern Australia, suggests through one of its characters that the IWW Preamble was 'the closest thing to a Declaration of Human Rights that we've ever had in this country'.[24]

Stories about the Wobblies' exploits still circulate. The son of a labourer who worked on Melbourne building sites in the years after the First World War recalls that his father's workmates believed the war had been caused, in part, by powerful international commercial interests who had become afraid of the growing strength of the IWW throughout the world; the Wobblies, unwittingly, had been responsible for the war.[25] According to Fred Coombe, a former Wobbly, Dr Mannix 'got into trouble with the Pope' for sharing an anti-conscription platform at Melbourne Town Hall with the IWW.[26] Frank Hardy's father told him the Wobblies' £5 notes were not forgeries but real notes stolen from the mint: 'you couldn't pick them'.[27] Tom Audley, May Brodney and Bertha Walker relate the story of the Melbourne Wobblies' frantic attempt to burn the forged notes, only to find they were escaping up the

chimney of Andrade's bookshop, only partially burnt, and out into
Bourke Street.[28]

A striking feature of these references back to a lost tradition is that
many of those who invoked the Wobblies were themselves caught up in
another form of working-class politics. Lindsay, Quinton, Waten, Shelley,
Hardy and even, briefly, Brodney, were all members of the Communist
Party. Communism succeeded the IWW, following the First World War,
as the chief expression of revolutionary activism both here and elsewhere. Echoing Lenin and Trotsky, the Australian Communists claimed
to carry the militant legacy of the Wobblies on to a higher plane of doctrinal purity and organisational discipline. Communism was at once the
historical descendant of the IWW and its political antithesis, maintain-
ing the tradition of heroic defiance and yet ultimately subordinating it to
the authoritarian demands of Stalinism. It is therefore hardly surprising
that when Communists registered dissatisfaction with the stultifying
effects of Party discipline they should reach back to an earlier alternative. And now that Communism has itself passed, we can better appreci-
ate the attractions of its predecessor.

The stories, whether first-hand or second-hand, are now almost gone
with those who carry them; they are relatively few, now, who can tell tales,
approving or disapproving, accurate or inaccurate, of the Wobblies and
their antics. The legend is fading and was, in any case, of dubious value
to the memory of the IWW. Exciting though the Wobblies' alleged
involvement in arson and forgery might be, and though it forms the
heart of the legend, the undue emphasis placed on these cases always
obscured the serious political identity of the IWW. It is the purpose of
this book to extract that identity, to rescue the Wobblies from the good-
humoured condescension of posterity, and to suggest ways in which their
political principles and methods are of enduring significance.

If the Wobblies failed because they were framed on arson charges and
hounded out of existence by vindictive governments, there seems
nonetheless little likelihood that, had they succeeded in their ambitious
attempt to persuade workers to emancipate themselves, this would have
resulted in the despotic excesses of Stalinist Communism. In any case,
failure before the event hardly constitutes the proven political bankruptcy of failure after the event; the years cannot condemn the
Wobblies. Coming from below and innocent of success, the Wobblies
could provide new inspiration to contemporary Australian radicals
crushed between the mill-stones of the disintegration of Communism
world-wide and the disappointment of Laborism at home. As Ian
Bedford wrote in 1967, in praise of the IWW's militancy on the job and
anti-authoritarian forms of organisation, in remembrance of those who
witnessed the beginning of the long hike of organised labour down a

blind alley: 'The example of the I.W.W., who fought when they had no chance of winning, may one day be remembered with gratitude by those looking for a sign.'[29]

Unfortunately, the legend also obscures the potential importance of the IWW to a new form of politics in its tendency either to sentimentalise and sensationalise or, in the case of hostile story-tellers, to belittle and revile the IWW. In their role as partial mediators of the legend, historians too have naturally brought their own particular prejudices to bear upon the matter.

On the right, IWW stood for 'I Won't Work' and its disreputable coterie represented all that was most repugnant within the working class.[30] Small children, in the later years of the First World War and for some time after, were warned that, if they did not behave the IWW would 'get them'.[31] Or, to the right within the labour movement itself, the IWW is deemed to be better placed 'in a history of Australian crime rather than of Australian labour'.[32]

The mainstream labour movement version, still recited by trade union officials and Labor MPs, deems the IWW foolish extremists who cried for help, in their hour of need, to the movement's elected representatives they had derided. Bill Hayden maintains that the IWW was 'impossibly idealistic', its tactics 'self-destructive'. His father, a merchant seaman, was a Wobbly in the United States, where brutal employment conditions explain the rise of the Wobblies. 'Direct action appeared justified.' In Australia, on the other hand, where unionism was well established and Labor governments a periodic reality, the arbitration system avoided the 'industrial excesses' of the American system.[33]

The implication here, common to the moderate Labor perspective on the IWW, is that the achievements of the labour movement rendered an Australian IWW unnecessary. However, the Wobblies of the time maintained that it was precisely the dismal performance of Labor in government and the failure of the well-entrenched craft unions that demanded a rejection of parliamentary strategies and the formation of revolutionary industrial unions; the unusually advanced nature of the labour movement in Australia explains the appeal of the Australian IWW to the most militant within this well-organised labour movement. It explains, too, the distinctive attributes of the Australian IWW that differentiated it from its American progenitor. Patrick Renshaw has commented that the IWW Locals which appeared in countries like Canada, Britain and Australia 'slavishly followed all the American trends, debates, and schisms'.[34] On the contrary, there were significant differences between the American IWW and the Australian that render the Australian IWW more modern and relevant to the experiences of working-class and other radical activists today.

The significance of the IWW is that it represents a truly different form of working-class politics: more democratic than the Communist and Labor Parties in its disavowal of hierarchy and bureaucracy, its insistence on the self-emancipation of the working class through its own direct action; more modern in its internationalism and vehement anti-racism, its belief in equal pay for women workers, its interest in civil liberties, its concern for the waifs and strays of society such as recent immigrants and the unemployed; more relevant in its trenchant critique of the wasted benefits of new technology, as widespread unemployment continues because reduction of working hours has been waived in favour of pre-serving profits; and, funnier by far than the Old Left, with a better singing voice and a greater flair for entertainment. The Wobblies had panache. Lloyd Ross recalls the IWW as 'much more colourful' than the 'humourless Communists'.[35]

The New Left was inclined to agree. In Australia, as in the United States, the IWW held a fascination for radical activists in the 1960s and 1970s. Copies of *Songs to fan the Flames of Discontent* were easily available in left-wing bookshops. These songs, such as 'Solidarity Forever', were heard on demonstrations and included on the official song sheets of May Day marches, and often enlivened or terminated in maudlin emotionalism many a New Left party.[36] For two decades, from 1970 to 1990, the newspaper of the Socialist Workers Party was named *Direct Action* after the Wobbly one, replaced only recently by *Green Left Weekly*.

In the American context, William Preston argues that the Wobblies spoke for a continuing phenomenon, a deprived and permanent American underclass.[37] In Australia, with its much higher levels of union-isation, the Wobblies in their time represented the moods and inclina-tions of the most belligerent section of this organised working class. As late as 1963 Ian Bedford claimed that:

> The descendants of the I.W.W. are to be found nowadays among the rank and file in some unions. . . . Now this situation too is being brought to an end, with the connivance of the union officials. Yet it would be premature to suppose that the spirit of direct action will be thoroughly extinguished among Australian workers.[38]

Long after the collapse of the One Big Union movement in 1924, the ideal of one big union lingered amongst the militant rank and file and continued to be felt in areas of Australian trade unionism for another half-century.[39] Though it would be preposterous to claim, in the 1990s, that there remains within the union movement a Wobbly legacy, an informed and deliberate imitation of IWW principles and methods, the militant temper that was once articulated so charismatically by the IWW, still remains.[40]

The tenacity of the legacy, the influence of IWW-type ideas, and the existence in the first place of the IWW, focusses attention on working-class attitudes, a vast unchartered historical wasteland.[41] John Saville claims it is mental rather than physical chains that bind people to their social order in advanced industrial societies; and yet, the complex relationships between social reality and social consciousness, as well as the role and place of myth and illusion in political thinking, are matters largely neglected by historians.[42] Why are some workers so greatly attracted by the vision of reality drawn by the IWW and others, whom the Wobblies themselves would unkindly and patronisingly term 'bone-heads', so repelled by it and obstructive of these vital efforts to criticise and transform society? To examine the ideas and practices of the IWW, which represented a most determined and articulate refusal of the belligerent section of the working class to accept the terms of existence imposed on that class, may make some imprints on the uncharted wasteland, offer some tentative suggestions about the way in which the ideas motivating different classes or sections of classes develop out of the circumstances in which they find themselves.

Some of the circumstances, of international war and of a union movement as yet imperfectly incorporated into the system, have changed. However, many of the circumstances – of employers anxious to secure the highest returns from the labour of others and of Labor governments unwilling to challenge employer prerogatives – are still with us. If the IWW was, in the words of Vere Gordon Childe, 'the first body to offer effectively to the Australian workers an ideal of emancipation alternative to the somewhat threadbare Fabianism of the Labour Party',[43] that ideal merits re-examination. Most significantly, the collapse of Communism and the disarray in the ranks of its erstwhile believers must surely turn attention to those, like the IWW, who, in their ideas and actions, offered an immanent critique of the entire Communist project.

In the United States the IWW has been derogated in Communist historiography as an infantile disorder that became a victim of its own anti-political syndicalism.[44] Australian Communist historians such as E.E. Campbell, L.L. Sharkey and Edgar Ross have written similarly pejorative accounts, reflecting the Party's own mythology about the relationship between the earlier, unscientific, IWW and the later, more sophisticated Communist Party, which absorbed Wobblies and changed them for the better.[45]

On the other hand, historians from the Communist Party stable that broke to varying degrees with their background, have been intrigued by the movement that prefigured some of their own reservations about the Party from which they sprang. To Eric Fry, we owe the recording of Tom Barker's memoirs. Ian Turner deems the IWW 'the most significant revolutionary movement the Australian working class had yet known'.[46] In 1967 his *Sydney's Burning* both articulated and reinforced the most sensationalist aspects of the mythology about the IWW. Bob Gollan commends the IWW as 'a reaction both against the class collaborationism of the mass labour movement and the remoteness of the socialist sects' that was for a few years 'a significant force within the labour movement'. Writing in 1970 he added pertinently that the previous fifty years of the Communist Party's central concern with power at the expense of both class struggle and forms of social structure made the IWW something more than a mere antecedent in an inevitable process towards the true revolutionary party.[47]

This book seeks to restore an understanding of the IWW in Australia. It draws mainly on the personal papers and memoirs of Wobblies and close contemporaries, interviews with some of these in their very old age, the relevant newspapers and pamphlets of the time, the assiduous records maintained by the police and military intelligence, and the valuable research of other scholars in the same or adjacent territory. Some of the primary sources used have only recently emerged, such as Ted Moyle's notebooks in Adelaide; the letters written from prison by Charlie Reeve, inherited fortuitously in 1990 by the workmate of a friend in Melbourne and now in the Mitchell Library; and a Wobbly scrapbook unearthed from a garage in Sydney around the same time. From such rich archival material this book reconstructs the origins of the IWW, and traces its organisation, activities, doctrines and methods.

CHAPTER 2

'On the Industrial as well as on the Political Field': The IWW Clubs, 1905–1910

Early this century a Colorado copper mine owner was asked why he had not installed safety devices to reduce the high number of fatalities amongst his employees. He replied: 'Dagos are cheaper than props.'[1] Workplaces like these had goaded the Western Federation of Miners under 'Big' Bill Haywood into establishing more effective trade union organisation than that offered at this time by the American Federation of Labor (AFL). At the same time, leading socialists such as Daniel De Leon of the Socialist Labor Party and Eugene Debs of the Socialist Party of America saw in the new movement an opportunity for socialists to forge better links with working-class militants. Accordingly, the convention of socialists and trade unionists that met for eleven days in Chicago from 27 June 1905 founded the Industrial Workers of the World (IWW) and adopted this Preamble on 3 July:

> The working class and the employing class have nothing in common. There can be no peace as long as hunger and want are found among millions of working people and the few, who make up the employing class, have all the good things of life.
>
> Between these two classes a struggle must go on until all the toilers come together on the political as well as on the industrial field, and take and hold that which they produce by their labor through an economic organization of the working class without affiliation with any political party.
>
> The rapid gathering of wealth and the centering of the management of industry into fewer and fewer hands makes trades unions unable to cope with the ever-growing power of the employing class because the trades unions foster a state of things which allows one set of workers to be pitted against another set of workers in the same industry, thereby helping to defeat one another in wage wars. The trade unions aid the employing class to mislead the workers into the belief that the working class have interests in common with their employers.

11

These sad conditions can be changed and the interests of the working class upheld only by an organization formed in such a way that all its members in any one industry, or in all industries, if necessary, cease work whenever a strike or lockout is on in any department thereof, thus making an injury to one an injury to all.[2]

In 1908 the IWW movement split: those most contemptuous of political parties and resentful of the SLP's attempts to dominate the IWW packed the convention, successfully moving a resolution that deleted from the Preamble 'until all the toilers come together on the political as well as on the industrial field' and substituted in its place 'until the workers of the world organise as a class, take possession of the earth and the machinery of production, and abolish the wage system'. Rather than remain in a minority position, the SLP section under De Leon withdrew and established separate headquarters in Detroit; the larger 'non-political' section remained based in Chicago.

Although the movement drew some of its ideas and much of its revolutionary vocabulary from the European syndicalist movements, the development of the IWW was rooted in American experience and shaped by American events. Its emergence was an intelligent response from within the labour movement to the increasing centralisation of American capital and industry, a concentration of labour power to meet a concentration of ownership. The AFL was deemed the 'American Separation of Labor' by those who presumed to replace this cautious and clumsy confederation of autonomous craft unions with industry-based unions that would in time become mere departments of one big union for all workers.[3]

The AFL was scathing about the IWW and it was the AFL perspective that was first heard within the Australian labour movement. On 15 July 1905 the *Worker* printed a letter from the San Francisco *Coast Seamen's Journal* that insisted the movement, which would 'amount to nothing', was led by men notorious for their 'unreasonable opposition' to the AFL and its officials. Firmly aligned with those forces in the United States whose conservatism and elitism had helped call into being the fledgling organisation they now feared, trade union officials and Labor MPs in Australia were chilled by the appearance of the IWW: if it were taken seriously by a large number of workers, it would challenge their claim to represent the working class, threatening their very livelihoods as well-paid delegates of that class. A few weeks before the Chicago Convention, American IWW theorist, W.E. Trautmann, had circularised the Trades and Labor Councils and Trades Halls of Australia expounding the ideas motivating the formation of the IWW. F.S. Wallis of the Adelaide TLC had replied: 'We in Australia have our own method of improving relations between employers and employees – endeavouring to abolish strikes and lockouts and put an end to sweating . . .' Unfortunately for prosperity, he did not expound further.[4]

It was from socialist organisations in Australia that a positive response to the IWW first came. Since October 1905 meetings of the Australian Socialist League, which had lived a precarious existence in Sydney and the Newcastle area since 1887, had discussed with interest the idea of industrial unionism. Its newspaper, the *People*, announced in November 1905: 'The I.W.W. has a grand ideal and magnificent tactics as its theory.'[5] On 28 March 1907 the League, now called the Socialist Labor Party (SLP), decided to establish Clubs of the IWW in Australia.[6]

In June 1907 in Melbourne, a conference of socialist organisations unanimously resolved 'that the time has arrived for the re-organisation of the Australian working-class on the lines of the Industrial Workers of the World', and adopted the Preamble.[7] This was proposed by the Barrier Socialist Propaganda Group, from the mining town of Broken Hill in far western New South Wales. From deserts the prophets come. More particularly, it was moved by the Secretary of the Barrier Group, Horace J. Hawkins, one of its two delegates to this conference.

Hawkins had recently arrived in Australia from England, where he had been, successively, a member of the Independent Labour Party, the Social Democratic Federation and the Socialist Party of Great Britain. His peripatetic political career had been prompted by his desire 'to find an organisation sound in principle and straight in tactics'. From early in 1907 Hawkins had been introducing the ideas of the IWW to the Broken Hill Group. Its newspaper, the *Flame*, argued that industrial unionism was both 'flawless in theory and correct and undeniable in practice', so it was the unionism for those workers 'seeking foundational change rather than cyclic palliation'.[9] On his way home to Broken Hill from Melbourne, Hawkins continued his IWW proselytising at the Adelaide Democratic Club. He described the scene to a Melbourne comrade: 'you should have seen the audience warm up as I gave them I.W.W. and "no compromise". The rank and file are ripe – the "leaders" hang behind and drag them back.'[10]

Endorsement of the IWW was one of the few principles upon which those who had gathered together in Melbourne, ostensibly to form a unified Australian socialist party, could agree. Indeed, support for the IWW could have formed the basis for a greater unity than that ultimately achieved by this conference, if the organisations had not argued instead about which of them was the most committed to the IWW. The SLP withdrew from the proposed unified party when the other groups refused to accept the SLP programme in its entirety; its rationale for this tendentious behaviour was that because it was the only group that had already advocated working-class organisation along IWW lines, the only 'scientific' basis for unity was for the other socialist bodies to accept the revolutionary principles, methods, and tactics of the SLP.[11] As the other organisations would not accede to such a request, the Socialist Federation of Australasia (SFA) that resulted from this conference comprised only the Victorian Socialist Party in Melbourne, the International Socialists in Sydney and the Barrier Socialist Propaganda Group in Broken Hill. Outside this fold, the SLP remained, implacably dedicated to the destruction of both capitalism and the Socialist Federation of Australasia.

As part of this project, the SLP at last embarked on the programme of establishing IWW Clubs, but not before Horace Hawkins left Broken Hill for Sydney and joined the SLP in September 1907.[12] Hawkins' defection goaded the SLP into acting on its formal resolution to found Clubs, and he became the Clubs' general secretary. Possibly alone in the SLP, he hoped to break down the sectarian animosities between the SFA and SLP through the joint activity of their members within the IWW Club movement. However, most of his comrades saw the SLP as the necessary and only true political guide of the IWW Clubs, taking their cues in this matter from De Leon.

De Leon had declared that the SLP, like all Truth, could bide its time, and proceed serenely along its orbit. The SLP in Australia likewise revelled in its purity, in the fact that it was 'as narrow as science and as intolerant as truth'.[13] De Leon demanded iron discipline within the party, rejected the Marxist concept of a mass party, favoured a small elite party in a superior position of authority over the working class for the purpose of thwarting proletarian spontaneity, and insisted on the party guiding the industrial movement. All these political traits derived from the assumption that truth and goodness inhered in a very select few.[14] His Australian followers displayed all the worst excesses of De Leonite sectarianism and were accordingly resented by others within the labour movement. Thus, as we shall see, the SLP's sponsorship of the political, De Leonite, Detroit IWW Clubs based on the original 1905 Preamble ultimately worked to the advantage of those in Australia who preferred the non-political position adopted in 1908.

The IWW Clubs urged the working class 'to vigorously prosecute its emancipatory mission on the political as well as on the industrial field'. De Leon had enunciated the 'sword and shield' concept of working-class emancipation: industrial action would wrest control of industry from the capitalists, while political action, by neutralising the state apparatus, would defend this action.[15] The Clubs therefore maintained the necessity of revolutionary political action, 'not to endeavour the absurd and impossible task of gradually ending exploitation by reform legislation;

but in order to attack the possessing class in its Parliamentary strong-hold, and to use the political arena for the purpose of legalising the workers' industrial struggle'.[16] To take and hold the means of production as collective property required both the political and industrial arms of the movement.[17] Apart, then, from voting for the SLP, workers should join the IWW Clubs, which would continue as a propaganda and educa-tive force until the IWW could become launched as an Industrial Union with a minimum membership of 5000.[18]

Although the SLP claimed that the IWW Clubs 'control their own affairs and are not affiliated with the Socialist Labor Party',[19] the SLP in fact endeavoured to subordinate these Clubs to the SLP, to ensure the eradication of any independent thinking on the part of Club members that might challenge SLP control of the Clubs. According to the Constitution, absolute conformity was demanded of Club members and the National Executive Committee was to exercise 'a supervising control' over all Club business. Officers abounded and this bureaucratic hierarchy was costly to the rank-and-file member, who was levied twopence 'susten-tation fee' per month to maintain it. The order of business for meetings, which had to open at 8 p.m. and close at 10 p.m., was laid down in detail in the Constitution, and the conduct of these meetings was to be strictly controlled by the chairman.[20] Doctrinally rigid and organisationally authoritarian, the Clubs had therefore little appeal to those whom they might otherwise have recruited: the disaffected, wayward spirits of the labour movement whom the non-political IWW later attracted.

The first IWW Club was established in Sydney on 22 October 1907 with forty-two members. Some International Socialists became active Club members, notably Harry Holland, President of the Tailoresses' Union, and Harry Scott Bennett, ex-Labor member of the Victorian Parliament and Secretary of the Sydney International Socialists. However, their involvement was not welcomed by the SLP, more inter-ested in control of the Club than its growth. In September 1908 the Club changed its meeting times, to clash with the traditional Sunday night gatherings of the International Socialists, and passed a resolution that any member taking part in a meeting in opposition to an IWW Club meeting would be expelled. This forced the International Socialists in the Club to make a choice: Harry Holland and Harry Scott Bennett, for two, opted for the International Socialists, complaining in writing to the Club about the incompatibility of meeting times and the restriction placed on International Socialists retaining membership of both organ-isations.[21] Ironically, the Club motion had to be rescinded in April 1909 so that the SLP could continue its Domain meetings. In Brisbane, the SLP branch did not even engage in subterfuge but simply became the IWW Club in August 1910 by changing its name.[22]

On 10 November 1907 a Club was established in Cobar, a copper-mining centre in north-western New South Wales that had been the scene of concerted strike activity in the spring of 1907. Of the twenty workers who joined this Club in its first five weeks, at least seven were members of the SLP. However, by December 1908 the Cobar Club had collapsed.[23] More successful were the Clubs formed in the Hunter Valley mining districts of West Wallsend, Cessnock and Kurri Kurri, by local militants such as Tom 'Bondy' Hoare and Dave McNeil. These Clubs flourished between 1908 and the outbreak of war, carrying out extensive propaganda work throughout the northern mining region. In October 1909 a Club was formed in the western mining district of Lithgow.[24]

The Melbourne IWW Club was formed in February 1908 with a 'live membership' of fifty, largely the work of SLP stalwarts, but many of the original number were members of the Victorian Socialist Party (VSP) and the VSP co-operated with the Club throughout 1908, distributing its literature and granting it free use of its hall for functions.[25] Mark Feinberg and A.G. Roth from the SLP and Monty O'Dowd of the VSP had held a preliminary meeting in January 1908, which appointed O'Dowd secretary. O'Dowd hoped that the Club would 'afford earnest industrialists of all parties an opportunity of working together harmoniously in the advancement of this great principle'.[26] Apart from addressing union branches, it held open-air meetings regularly at the Richmond and Yarra Parks and occasionally on street corners. Its first chairman was Eureka Stockade veteran Monty Miller, 'the darling of the ladies of the Club'.[27]

Union membership trebled between 1901 and 1909, while the number of unions doubled. Demarcation disputes and sectional fights were frequent, as more than one union catered for the same category of worker in many situations. Employers, on the other hand, were forming industry-wide associations.[28] This rapid organisational growth was shaped by new institutional forms. The federation of the Australian colonies into a Commonwealth in 1901 removed the trade barriers that had restricted industrial organisation. The creation of a Commonwealth Court of Conciliation and Arbitration in 1904 supplemented the new industrial tribunals of the States to foster union growth. But the system of union registration, the granting of preference to existing craft unions, and the limits that arbitration imposed on industrial action all restricted the capacity of unions for effective representation of working-class needs.

Activists in the labour movement felt that the existing union structure needed serious overhauling to cope with the new circumstances. IWW Club correspondence files contain many letters from unions requesting a speaker to address them about the IWW and explain the Constitution and

Preamble. There was a ready audience for the message that craft unionism was obsolete, that only in industrial unionism could the real embodi-
ment of the solidarity of labour be presented, 'the power of the closed fist
of class unionism as opposite to the weakness of the limp and open hand
of class disunity – craft unionism'.[29] By 1908 the IWW was beginning to
provide a focus and a philosophy for the left-wing elements in the labour
movement, giving form, slogans, and sometimes leadership to the existing discontent.[30] In March 1908 Monty O'Dowd observed that the
Melbourne Trades Hall was 'moving in a remarkable direction towards
I.W.W.-ism'.[31] The West Wallsend Club secretary wrote to the Sydney Club
secretary in November 1909 that arbitration was 'a thing of the past' as far
as the miners were concerned: 'They recognise the efficacy of the I.W.W.
form of waging the class struggle . . . they are beginning to adopt all of our
arguments, and they talk as if they allways [sic.] knew it was right.'[32]

Australian unionists, according to Childe, seized upon the IWW's
point about the futility of the 'organised scabbery' of craft unionism,
which divided the workers up into small sections, each out for their own
hands and regardless of their mates.[33] The IWW, as Gollan points out,
raised important organisational issues: where the American IWW was
seen as an alternative to existing unions, the influence on Australia was
to suggest a reorganisation of existing unions by the linking of separate
unions within the same industry and the diminishing of the influence of
the numerous small craft unions. Bedford maintains the IWW ideas circulating in the labour movement after 1907 were the expression of two
principal tendencies: first, the inclination on the part of unskilled and
semi-skilled workers towards the reorganisation of existing unions, partly
along industrial union lines; second, the rejection of the political party
and arbitration courts.[34]

Discontent with the experiment of industrial arbitration, from 1900 in
Western Australia, from 1901 in New South Wales and from 1904 in the
Commonwealth, was mounting.[35] The frustrations unions experienced
with the slow and costly procedures, the frequent defeats of the workers,
the penalties prescribed for strikes, the use of coercion by employers in
contempt of arbitral procedures, and the fact that the slight wage
increases awarded had not compensated workers for the higher cost of
living, seemed to confirm the dire prognoses of the militants within the
labour movement who had opposed the system from its inception. They
had argued, typically, that the organised working class should rely only
on its industrial strength; that arbitration court judges would be drawn
from the class of people who favoured employer interests; that the
principle of arbitration sanctioned the right of employers to extract surplus value from their employees; that the system would operate to the
advantage of employers by ensuring that labour power would be the one

commodity whose price was not determined by the market, restraining the power of the unions when times were good yet imposing upon unions the full force of employer power when times were bad.

The practice of arbitration was beginning, however, to create a trade union movement in its own image. While resistance was real, so also was the process by which unions were being tamed, immured to the new process of industrial relations that shifted the centre of gravity from the stop-work meeting to the court, and from the union membership to the secretary who represented the union in court. But these were early days. As Fitzpatrick notes: 'For though now small unions in small industries, and the adherence to them of workers new to unionism, might build up a new unionism which was, as it were, the child of the court, the old militant unions, veterans of the struggles of the 'nineties, were at best troublesome wards of the court.'[36]

IWW Club recruits were typically unskilled or semi-skilled male workers. The Clubs gained their greatest popularity on the coalfields to the north and south of Sydney, amongst miners prepared by generations of industrial struggle for IWW ideas, who had observed on the coalfields 'the centring of the management of industries into fewer and fewer hands' and who had long maintained that 'an injury to one is an injury to all'. The decision of the 1907 socialist unity conference that this area was the most suitable locality for the SFA to propagate IWW theories was not, as Gollan points out, a mission to the heathen, for IWW ideas were already being propagated to miners by miners, especially by Peter Bowling, president of the Colliery Employees Federation (CEF), whose aggressive and militant leadership had improved pay and conditions on the coalfields.[37] The mine-owners, according to Sydney *Truth*, 'raged most furiously about the I.W.W.'. The letters IWW 'came to have a sort of cabalistic signification', as there had been 'much talk' concerning the IWW during the northern district coalminers' strike of 1907.[38]

Bowling had established contact with the Western Federation of Miners in the USA. In August 1907 the northern district miners adopted the IWW Preamble, after deleting the reference to political action, arguing that, if all the workers came together on the industrial field they could, in any case, control events on the political field.[39] In February 1908 Newcastle miners voted on the proposition: 'Are you in favour of the basic principles of the I.W.W. or the Australian Labor Federation?' The Preamble placed before them was identical in spirit with the non-political one adopted by the American IWW nine months later. A majority of Newcastle miners favoured the Labor Federation; but 2154 of the 6054 who voted preferred the IWW.[40]

Also in February 1908, the Melbourne Trades Hall Council Executive was asked to report on a motion: 'That in view of the fact that Arbitration Courts and Wages Boards have failed to give the protection to the workers that they so much desire, the Trades Hall Council be requested to consider the advisability of organising on the lines of the I.W.W.' The response was a detailed report, which stated: 'To cope with this mighty industrial octopus, unionism must come closer together, weld its force and become militant in the interest of the whole industrial movement, they are our enemies who preach peace. There is a class war clear cut and must eventuate sooner or later, the sooner the better.'[41] It condemned the divisive effects of craft unionism and recommended a central fighting fund for the union movement, and, while it did not specifically endorse the programme of the IWW, it intimated that it represented 'another phase of the unionist movement', when the millions of unionists would be disciplined, undivided, and mobile towards achieving their ends: 'That this is possible your Executive is assured.'[42]

Late in April 1908 the NSW Trade Union Congress in Sydney debated at length the resolution moved by the Newcastle Labour Council:

> That whereas it has been demonstrated that our present system of craft unionism is hopelessly impotent to prevent the exactions of concentrated capital; and whereas the position of the workers is year by year becoming more insecure; and whereas it is absolutely necessary that the workers should be organised industrially in order to cope successfully with combinations of capitalists, be it therefore resolved that this meeting adopts the constitution and preamble of the I.W.W.[43]

This proposal to transform fundamentally the organisations to which those voting belonged was rejected by only 55 votes to 23, a serious indictment of much they had previously sponsored.[44]

In the meantime, the Sydney IWW Club was assuming a leading role in resistance to the New South Wales Liberal government's Industrial Disputes Act of 1908, designed to replace the Industrial Arbitration Act of 1901 with a Wages Boards system even more conducive to employer interests. The Club emphasised the Act was aimed primarily at the right to strike and would 'put the working class into the hands of anti-working class judges'.[45] As soon as the details of the Bill were made public, the Tailoresses' Union under Harry Holland resolved:

> That this Union, recognising in Mr Wade's Wages Boards proposal a premeditated outrage against industrial unionism, urges that in the event of the Bill becoming law all unions should refuse to recognise its provisions or to obey its awards, and further urges immediate re-organisation on the scientific lines of the Industrial Workers of the World.[46]

On 30 October 1909 a conference of trade unions was held in Melbourne with the object of more closely combining the wage workers of Australia. Similar conferences had been held earlier in Adelaide and Sydney. In a paraphrase of the non-political IWW Preamble, the Melbourne conference resolved:

> That this conference strongly urges all trade unions and wage workers to organize industrially with the object of obtaining possession of the fruits of their industry, recognizing that the employing class and working class have nothing in common, and that poverty and want will continue until the wage workers unite on the industrial field as a class to abolish the wage system. . . .[47]

Unfortunately for the IWW movement, a committee was appointed to draw up a constitution and report to conference. It appears nothing further happened.

The debates within the labour movement over industrial unionism focused attention on the behaviour of Labor politicians and trade union officials. Time and again, disputes between the IWW Club movement and the rest of the labour movement were expressed in coded form, in accusation and counter-accusation about the integrity of the representatives of the labour movement. To the IWW Club, trade union bureaucrats occupied 'comfortable positions on the backs of the workers'. The corruption of the labour movement that had produced these 'manipulators' began with the founding of the Labor Parties: these had contained both bona fide socialists who thought, wrongly, that they could lead the workers to socialism by means of political action alone; and 'those who saw in the attempt to turn the workers towards political channels, the great opportunity for personal pelf and ambitious advance'. By such a process, 'the Unions were converted into feeders for the politicians'.[48]

Some unions and their officials were not fully incorporated into the Labor world vision and the Club was dependent upon these unions for the opportunity to spread its ideas, dependent therefore upon the existence of unions whose political outlook defied the generalisations made by the Club about unions. Many unions were happy, at least initially, to hear speakers from the Club or to pass IWW resolutions condemning Labor government betrayals. The United Labourers Society, with Club member George Waite as its president, was a Club stronghold within the union movement. But many other unions refused immediately to hear speakers or support Club initiatives, some expressing distaste for the contempt with which the Club held Labor politicians. The secretary of the Goldfields Federated Miners' Union, Kalgoorlie and Boulder branch, informed Hawkins in August 1911 that his union held Mr Fisher 'in such high esteem' that it refused to approve the Club's criticism of him, and 'we resent the bitter and unmanly tone of the correspondence'.[49]

The polarisation within the labour movement between Laborism and industrial unionism was shown clearly in the Sydney tramway strike of July 1908, which Labor parliamentarians attributed to IWW plotting. Aghast at the damage being done to Labor's public image, they were bitter in their denunciations of the IWW.[50] Such allegations were rendered plausible as militant socialist propaganda in the course of this strike (which ended ignominiously with Labor MPs inducing the men to return to work) urged the value of revolutionary industrial unionism.[51] An SFA pamphlet, *The Strike-breakers. The Truth about the Tramway Fiasco*, drew a hard-hitting lesson from the Labor Party's apostasy. Mick Considine, who had been a member of the Sydney IWW Club in 1908 until the International Socialists were forced out, wrote: 'let the present catastrophe prove to you the necessity of keeping the Politician at arm's length, whatever his "label" may be'.[52]

In fact, the IWW Club had not supported the tramway strike. Across the left/right divide within the labour movement lay the ghastly division emerging within the left over the issue of the IWW Club and the SLP's role within it. Relations between the Club and the International Socialists of the SFA, always tense, had soured further as a result of the International Socialists' more militant position during this strike. They had offended the Club by holding propaganda meetings in conjunction with some tramway employees; the Club rebuked Holland for his role in rallying support for this abortive strike.[53] O'Farrell contends that the friction between the SLP and Holland reflected a fundamental difference of temper: 'The S.L.P. thought of the I.W.W. as a formal plan; Holland saw it as an imperative to action.'[54] This pattern of Club inactivity and sectarian back-biting continued in subsequent industrial confrontations.

However, the Club did not need to be militant in practice to be condemned by the Labor Party. Labor politicians rejected on principle the Clubs' revolutionary theories and resented what they regarded as an attempt to seize control of the labour movement.[55] Accordingly, those who benefited most from the continuing obeisance of the working class towards Labor politicians were concerned to discredit the new movement. W.M. Hughes alleged in 1908 that: 'The contempt of the I.W.W. for methods which do not reek with the promise of much violence and at least a promise of bloodshed is overwhelming.'[56] In blaming the IWW for the 1908 and 1909 turmoil in Broken Hill, W.A. Holman declared: 'The whole trouble is due to two or three men belonging to the Industrial Workers of the World.' In a thoroughly vicious attack, he added: 'What they want to see is, not a victorious body of strikers, but a defeated body of strikers.' The IWW had taken upon itself 'the immense moral responsibility of causing loss and suffering to thousands of their fellow-workers'.[57] In fact, the Clubs had demurred on the Broken Hill lockout, as we shall see.

On 27 August 1908 Holman addressed the Sydney Labor Council, expressing his regret that members of the IWW 'by activity and constant attention to Union affairs' had attained positions as delegates to the Council: 'There is no doubt that a certain percentage . . . consists of proclaimed I.W.W. followers.' A delegate interjected: 'That is true.' Another delegate objected: 'No, it is absolutely untrue.' A 'chorus' of Council members shouted: 'It is true.' Holman blamed this IWW presence for the friction that had developed between the Council and the Labor Party.[58] In September 1908 the secretary of the Labor Council informed the IWW Club that, 'owing to the large amount of business engaging the Council's attention', it had been decided that the Club's request to address the Council could not be acceded to 'at this juncture'.[59]

Clearly, the tide was turning against the IWW Club within the Council; the Club's sectarian stance towards other socialists made it easier for the more conservative forces within the labour movement to mobilise against it. Late in 1908, the pro-Labor sections of the Council successfully moved a resolution that delegates belonging to other political bodies should be debarred from the annual conference of the Political Labour League. Mr Brock of the Wharf Labourers referred to Mr Keegan of the Bridge-painters and Dockers and other IWW-minded delegates as 'snakes in the grass'.[60] In Melbourne, too, the Trades Hall Council resolved on 10 February 1910 that: 'The unions affiliated with this Council abstain in future from allowing any speakers at any union functions to deprecate the value of Labor in politics.' The IWW Club was refused use of a room at the Trades Hall.[61]

The lines of conflict within the labour movement, between left and right, and within the left, were seen clearly in the Broken Hill dispute early in 1909 when miners were locked out for two months for refusing to accept a wage cut, the companies refusing to abide by a decision of the Commonwealth arbitration court. During the struggle, police interfered with pickets and several union leaders were arrested.[62] Before this confrontation, many miners had responded to the Socialist Propaganda Group's enthusiasm about the IWW; but there was also resistance to IWW influence from the officials of the Amalgamated Miners' Association (AMA). The Socialist Group had printed 500 copies of the IWW Preamble for distribution at the AMA meeting of 9 February 1908, at which a deputation from the Group urged the AMA to adopt the Preamble. They were met with a firm rebuff.[63] On 18 November 1908 the AMA's newspaper, the *Barrier Daily Truth*, attacked the Group as 'dogmaticians of the most virulent kind', who were attempting to replace the AMA with an IWW-type organisation.[64]

However, in August 1908, when the Combined Unions Committee (CUC) was formed in Broken Hill to fight the battle the miners could see looming, an IWW sympathiser and AMA delegate to this CUC, William Rosser, persuaded the CUC to appoint VSP secretary Tom Mann as its organiser. The appointment of Mann, known by this stage as an enthusiast for industrial unionism, indicated the local unions' dissatisfaction with legislative approaches to the problem of achieving better conditions.[65] On 3 April 1909 the *Barrier Daily Truth* conceded that

> a reaction is setting in against the absolute reliance upon political action as a means to obtain the objective of Labor. The belief is growing that perfect industrial organisation is of more value than anything else, and that politics, to be of any use at all to the workers, must be based upon, and rise out of, industrial unionism.[66]

In September 1909 Mann reported that 'a growing proportion of the intelligent pioneers of economic changes are expressing more and more dissatisfaction with Parliament and all its works'.[67]

Mann and Harry Holland, who also played a prominent agitational role in Broken Hill at this time, were members of the SFA, which condemned them in the eyes of the SLP. Thus, when the lawyers of the ruling class, then its jailers, came for Mann and Holland, the IWW Club allowed sectarian considerations to temper its support for the campaign to release them.[68] As Chas. H. Green, a socialist activist in Broken Hill, complained: 'where the S.F.A. or its members have taken up the cudgels for the working class in industrial upheavals the S.L.P. has laid low and barked'. He recalled its supine role compared with the SFA in earlier confrontations such as the rockchoppers and tramway strikes in Sydney, the Newcastle strike and the Free Speech Fight in Prahran in Melbourne. Green charged the SLP:

> You said that the men who went to jail were fakirs with axes to grind. You sat there, like so many mollycoddle philosophers – criticising and damaging – while the plutes got the leg irons ready, issued warrants, packed juries and silenced the only men who had pluck and grit enough to lay their liberty for a while on the altar of the working class.

The Crown, he pointed out, had used the SLP's newspaper in preparing its court cases.[69]

Mann's commitment to industrial unionism and his hostility to arbitration was strengthened as a result of his Broken Hill experience.[70] He argued that the Broken Hill miners could have won their battle in a fortnight had they not applied to the arbitration court, which took more than twenty weeks to decide the matter.[71] 'As things were, leaving undone the vital work of scientific industrial organisation was playing the fool.' He had come to Australasia, he later maintained, to see whether, in countries with broader franchises, 'a drastic modification of capitalism could be made'. He found, rather, that the emphasis on political action in these advanced democracies had encouraged 'slowness'. He pointed to the bad conditions of the Ballarat miners. 'Yet Ballarat and the adjacent division are represented in the State Parliament by Labour men who believe in Socialism; but they with their colleagues are powerless to achieve a change in the absence of sound economic organisation.' The situation was the same for South Australian miners, he noted, and with a Labor Premier.[72]

He became convinced of the need for the kind of union organisation advocated by the IWW, while remaining aloof from the actual IWW movement in Australia, associated as it was with the SLP. He recalled of this time: 'I was in keen sympathy with the I.W.W. which at that time was growing vigorously in the U.S.A. and also with Syndicalism then growing rapidly in Italy and France.'[73] He attempted to convert his comrades in the VSP and trade unionists generally to industrial unionist methods, recommending that politics be dropped for a time in order to improve industrial organisation.[74] He regretted that 'undue importance has been attached to political action' and that 'to listen to the speeches of the typical Labor politician it is clear that he is surfeited with the idea that that which is of paramount importance is the return to the legislative bodies of an additional number of Labor men, and that all else is secondary and relatively trifling'. Mann considered the very opposite was the case: 'Experience in all countries shows most conclusively that industrial organisation, intelligently conducted, is of much more moment than political action, for entirely irrespective as to which school of politicians is in power, capable and courageous industrial activity forces from the politicians proportionate concessions.' He insisted that 'reliance on parliamentary action would never bring freedom'.[75] Though he rejoined the Social Democratic Federation on arrival back in England in 1910, within a year he had resigned, because he 'differed materially re the State and their reliance upon it whilst I was definitely a Syndicalist'. By 1912 British conservatives were blaming Mann's Australian experience for the importation into Britain of 'the squalid and melancholy doctrine of Syndicalism'.[76]

Graeme Osborne believes Tom Mann's campaign on behalf of industrial unionism was essentially negative, that he was not swayed by the vision of one big union but instead saw in it an opportunity to press for the abandonment of parliamentary aspirations.[77] On the contrary,

Mann's response was a positive reaffirmation of the revolutionary principle that the emancipation of the working class must be the act of the
workers themselves. On this point Mann's syndicalism and the IWW's
revolutionary industrial unionism coincided.

Osborne stresses the strength of the opposition to the IWW within the
VSP, suggesting in effect that the VSP's formal support for the IWW was
a one-Mann campaign, with R.S. Ross openly critical of the IWW Clubs.[78]
Where Mann's experience in Broken Hill had cast him firmly on the side
of the IWW, Ross' period in Broken Hill before the 1908 lockout had seen
him firmly aligned with forces hostile to the IWW. Ross had been instrumental in securing the 1908 SFA resolution to withdraw support from
the IWW Clubs and to promote the principles of revolutionary industrial
unionism through SFA branches instead, arguing this would comply
with the logic of Australian labour development, which was towards political power, not, as in America, towards industrial organisation.[79]

The Barrier Group was torn asunder in 1908 over the issue of the formation of an IWW Club. The majority, led by William Rosser, opposed
Ross' position and wished to form a Club in Broken Hill, 'on the lines
laid down by the S.L.P.'. Though they had the numbers, their attempt to
establish a Club in Broken Hill under Group auspices was ruled out of
order, because the Group was formally part of the SFA which, thanks to
Ross, was officially opposed to the formation of IWW Clubs.[80] In August,
Ross wrote to Mann that 'I.W.W.-ism has lost us Rosser, who has
resigned'; he regretted that the Group contained 'two diverse tempera-
ments' and referred in veiled terms to 'the menace of De Leonism'.[81]
Rosser was scathing about Ross' arguments in a letter to the SLP: 'the
same old spook is being held up to us, of wrecking organisations which
have taken such time and trouble to build up, and it makes one wild with
these people, when they talk in such strains, seeing that they are the
wreckers and misleaders . . .'[82]

However, the SLP had done its share of wrecking within the socialist
movement, its IWW Clubs discouraging rather than encouraging greater
unity amongst socialists, becoming a focus for heated disputes between
socialists. Accordingly, the components of the SFA, especially the
International Socialists, became centres for IWW ideas independent
from, and increasingly in opposition to, the SLP. The *International
Socialist Review* featured many articles on industrial unionism; and all
pamphlets published under SFA auspices in this period argued vehemently in favour of revolutionary industrial unionism, on the lines laid
down by the IWW.[83] At a meeting of the Kalgoorlie Social Democratic
Association in July 1910 several comrades, objecting to the nationally
oriented reformism of the Labor Party, declared their support for the
International Socialists in Sydney and recommended their support for

revolutionary industrial unionism. In Broken Hill the International Socialist Club, which had succeeded the Group in 1910, began distributing industrial unionist literature once more. In Melbourne, VSP members left the IWW Club and, from 1910, propagated industrial unionist ideas to the trade union movement through the VSP's Industrial Committee, directed by Percy Laidler.[84]

Despite the limited support offered them by the Australian working class, the SLP's IWW Clubs remained confident in their work, insisting that the existing unions had been 'shaken fundamentally', that the question of industrial reorganisation had been brought prominently to the fore by the ardent propaganda of the IWW Clubs. Club documents in 1911 and 1912 assured members it was only a matter of time before the working class became sufficiently intelligent and revolutionary to join the Clubs in numbers sufficient to take and hold the means of production from the employing class, 'the end of Capitalism'.[85]

The problem for the IWW Clubs, however, was not so much an insufficiency of class consciousness but a surfeit of it. The militant working class had come to despise the SLP; the threat to the established institutions of the labour movement was contained, in the final analysis, by the sectarian outlook of those who made the challenge. Chas. Green, admittedly a member of the SFA, wrote to the SLP in August 1911 that the working class knew the SLP for what it really was:

> It knows it for a muckraking party. It knows that it concerns itself more with slating persons than with smashing principialities; that it has developed a spleeny mania for fastening on to every man or woman outside the pale of its own party, who mounts a soap-box or writes a line or in any way sees the limelight. Its members segregate themselves from the rest of their class because their own intellectual cocksure conceit hampers them from effectively boring within the proletariat.[86]

Condemned by their association with the SLP, the IWW Clubs could not capture the imagination of the disaffected within the union movement; these militants showed a decided preference for action over abstract philosophising, solidarity over sectarian mud-slinging, and for uniting only on the industrial field and leaving the political field well alone. As these discontented workers had developed spontaneously their own non-political versions of the IWW Preamble, it is hardly surprising that they subsequently gravitated instead towards the representatives in Australia of the other IWW.

CHAPTER 3

'Wild Men from Yankeeland':
the Arrival of the Chicago IWW,
1910–1914

When the issue of political action was debated in the Melbourne IWW Club soon after its formation in 1908, Monty Miller stormed out of the meeting, objecting to the Club's continuing commitment to political action. Though Miller had worked to build the infant labour parties, he had witnessed, with what he described as 'sorrow and shame', the defection of Labor politicians, who 'betrayed the best interests of workers, and in many cases played the part of traitors to large bodies of workers in strike conflict with capitalism'. As he left the meeting, Phil Halfpenny remarked: 'Let him go, he wants to go.'[1]

Monty Miller subsequently joined the Chicago non-political IWW that adhered to the revised 1908 Preamble. As in the United States, it was this IWW that was known popularly as 'the IWW' in Australia and achieved the more spectacular success, eclipsing the Detroit political version of IWW ideology and practice that had established itself before 1911. The formation of Locals (branches) of the non-political IWW was, according to Childe in 1923, the most momentous event in the political industrial history of Australian labour since the historic decision in favour of political action in 1890. 'No body has exercised a more profound influence on the whole outlook of labour in Australia.'[2]

In the Australian circumstances, there was one very strong argument on the side of the non-politicals: socialist interventions in lower house elections had been disastrous. Late in 1908 the VSP ran two candidates in the State election: Percy Laidler received a derisory 85 votes in Collingwood and Angus McDonnell a worse score of 82 in Melbourne. Harry Holland for the SFA fared badly against the Labor candidate, W.M. Hughes, in the West Sydney federal electorate in April 1910; in the ensuing parliament Hughes became federal Attorney-General. Had the electoral system been preferential, as it is today, the socialist results would undoubtedly have been better; in the first-past-the-post system then used for lower house elections very few socialists were prepared to waste their votes by voting exactly as they really pleased rather than for the Labor Party, by that stage well entrenched as the only viable representative of labour in the formation of governments. Only in elections for the Senate and State upper houses were socialist election results less demoralising. Ultimately, doubts about the possibility of socialist electoral success worked to the advantage of the Chicago school of IWW thought and hastened the demise of the IWW Clubs.

It was the peculiarly advanced nature of the political labour movement in Australia, its precocity in the 1890s and its subsequent fall from grace by the second decade of the new century, the fact that it had been tried in ways not experienced elsewhere and accordingly found wanting, that explains the appeal of the Chicago IWW to militant workers in this period. The Labor Parties had been given sufficient time in which to reveal their shortcomings, especially in government. 'So far as the worker is concerned the Labor Party is a calamitous failure', wrote John Dawson to the British *Socialist Standard* after the South Australian Verran Labor government had crushed an asphalters' strike late in 1910. Tom Barker explained his adherence to industrial unionism: 'I was absolutely convinced, particularly after seeing [Labor] politicians in both New Zealand and Australia that a strong and even ruthless working-class body was necessary to see that people were properly protected and properly paid.'[3] The experience of the first majority federal Labor government from April 1910 and the first New South Wales Labor government from October 1910 undoubtedly aided the early growth of the Chicago IWW.

In Britain, on the other hand, the Chicago IWW never attained even the limited following enjoyed by the De Leonite Industrial Workers of Great Britain; the experiment of labour-in-politics had only just begun and there was no Labour government until 1924. In the United States, the situation was radically different from either Britain or Australia: the huge underclass of unskilled and largely immigrant workers were often disenfranchised, so the Detroit strategy made no sense to those to whom political action was impossible.

Renshaw draws inappropriate comparisons between the American and Australian circumstances to conclude that the strength of the movement in both continents can be attributed to the closing of the frontier, 'producing a unique type of post-frontier radicalism'. He argues that, while few European working men could remember any other system than wage-labour, 'the vision of a more decent life was still very vivid to many Americans living close to the frontier'. The same experience, he maintains, held in Australia 'where the frontier situation was also just being replaced by a wage system for the first time'.[4]

In fact, the Australian frontier had always relied heavily on wage-labour, which had encouraged the emergence of new unions of unskilled workers that assisted the unusually early formation of Labor Parties. The impact of the IWW here can be attributed, not to economic backwardness but to political forwardness, the labour movement's precocious parliamentary debut and unprecedented formation of governments, in stark contrast to the American situation. The two movements, as we shall see, were consequently different in important respects, though the American IWW remained an important influence on the Australian, and the contacts between them, especially through American merchant seamen, were always significant.[5]

The wild men from Yankeeland also brought with them a distinctive vocabulary. They denounced plutocrats and extolled bums, reviled limelighters and scorned the fakirs who smoodged for the support of the wage slaves. The calculated iconoclasm of this diction appealed to the restless young men who made up the core of Wobbly recruits. It contrasted with the stilted formality of Labor politicians, and carried with it a racy disrespect for the established hierarchy of esteem. 'Hallelujah, I'm a Bum', the Wobblies boasted. At a time when American popular culture had significant currency in Australia – the popular theatre of the black and white minstrels, the pulp fiction and even the flickering images of the cinema – the provenance of the Wobblies was readily acceptable. The romanticisation of the drifter or hobo struck a chord with the local figure of the Lone Hand, a single male untrammelled by ties to family or place who was free to roam. 'Unemployed at last', rejoiced Tom Collins in the opening words of Joseph Furphy's novel *Such Is Life* in 1903, anticipating the defiant reversal of conventional values that the Wobblies would turn into a political credo.

The appeal of the Chicago IWW in this period in Australia was based on political factors. In the years immediately before the First World War, the Australian economy grew significantly, yet wage increases lagged behind the increased level of prosperity. Working-class discontent with wage levels became, in the context of Labor governments, highly political. In the period before 1910, dissatisfaction with traditional craft union organisation and the workings of the arbitration courts had worked to the advantage of the Detroit IWW. After 1910, discontent with the performance of Labor politicians became especially marked, adding force to the arguments of the Chicago IWW against political activity. The failure of arbitration to meet workers' expectations, in a period when Labor was in government, did not endear militant workers to the Detroit argument that a political party could act as the shield of the revolution; but it did incline many of these workers to the Chicago view that the parliamentary process had nothing to offer a revolutionary working-class movement.

In New South Wales, trade union activists saw Labor MPs as complicit in the passage of the 1908 Industrial Disputes Act of the Wade Liberal government that replaced the Industrial Arbitration Act of 1901 with a system of compulsory arbitration and Wages Boards, which to their mind was even more obviously weighted in the employers' favour than the original legislation. Although the Labor Party had formally opposed this Act, it had strongly urged the trade unions to accept it and used all its influence within the movement to break down the industrial wing's boycott in opposition to the Act. When the miners, influenced by IWW ideas and led by Peter Bowling, engaged in strike action late in 1909 to resist this Act, Hughes did much to ensure that neither the waterside workers nor the transport workers joined the strike movement. While Bowling and the militants worked assiduously to extend solidarity, Hughes and the moderates complained about IWW influence and effectively subverted the strike. Other Labor politicians denounced the strike as an IWW conspiracy and persuaded the Strike Congress to dissolve and rely upon a Labor government to repeal the Wade government's Coercion Act of December 1909, which had declared unlawful strikes or lockouts in connection with the production or distribution of a necessary commodity; to nationalise the coal industry; and to establish a State-owned steelworks.[6] By 1910, shortly before the first Labor government in New South Wales, the Trades Union Congress and the Labor Council had been beaten into submission by the parliamentary party, accepting the principle that the Industrial Disputes Act should be amended rather than repealed by those who had at one time promised to make and unmake social conditions.

However, the McGowen Labor government that assumed office in New South Wales in 1910 did not keep these promises. The amendments to the Industrial Disputes Act left the penalty clauses intact, which provided for fines and imprisonment for assisting in unlawful strikes. Labor MPs had decided that arbitration was unworkable unless compulsory – that is, unless strikes were punished.[7] The coal mines were left in private hands and, instead of starting a State-owned steel works, the McGowen government provided assistance to BHP to establish a steel industry.[8] Although the politicians, led by Hughes, had scored a distinct victory over the Detroit IWW in defeating the coal strike and securing the election of a Labor government, the subsequent behaviour of this government confirmed the dire warnings of the Chicago IWW against parliamentarism.

The tensions between Labor politicians and the workers who elected them grew; Labor governments had demonstrated their incompetence at fulfilling their own promises. It was the IWW that rallied the remaining elements of working-class resistance to the corruption of Labor MPs and the incorporation of many trade union officials to the MPs' point of view. Just as it attracted the sympathy and support of the left wing of the unions, so it also aroused the open antagonism of the rest of the movement. The Labor MPs and many union bureaucrats feared the IWW. Senator Pearce urged 'all trade unionists and all connected with the labor party not to let this section acquire influence or use the labor press or platform to put forward its doctrine'.[9] As Ernie Lane recalls: 'The I.W.W. comprising the vanguard of working class revolt, was regarded – and treated – by this latter section of Labour as a deadly enemy'.[10] Undoubtedly, the IWW appealed only to a minority of working-class activists in this period, but it represented the most articulate and effective reaction to the moderation of the majority ever seen. Thus the conditions for the comparative success of the Chicago IWW were provided by those within the labour movement to whom they opposed themselves.

The Chicago IWW developed within the shell of the old IWW Clubs because working-class socialist activists, many of them associated with the SFA, felt that the Detroit strategy for revolution would repeat the mistake made when militant workers forsook industrial action and founded the Labor Party. Moreover, the IWW Clubs were increasingly the domain of the SLP; they had become propagandist bodies more concerned with upholding formally correct positions than engaging in militant activity to promote industrial unionism. Horace Hawkins' original vision of the Clubs as a place where sectarian animosities could be laid aside, where all might work together in the cause of promoting revolutionary industrial unionist ideas, could not be achieved by a Party so habituated to denigrating the ideas and integrity of others. Indeed, by 1911 Hawkins himself had become well trained in the SLP school of sectarian abuse. In a letter to the Lithgow branch of the SFA, he referred to the SFA as 'a mere fakir organised parasitic growth sponging upon the working-class movement'.[11]

Accordingly, while adhering to the principles of revolutionary industrial unionism, the SFA had become disenchanted with the Clubs. In 1909 the SFA Conference withdrew its endorsement of the 1905 Preamble and declared support only for the 'broad principles of Industrial Unionism',[12] taking in effect a neutral position on the split between Chicago and Detroit. Well before the formal establishment of the Chicago IWW in Australia, news of the 1908 split had reached these shores, informing the growing opposition within and without the Clubs to the De Leonite version of the IWW. During the Broken Hill lockout early in 1909 about twenty miners went fruit-picking in Mildura, camping on the bend in the Murray River where they entertained themselves of a Sunday afternoon with Chicago IWW songs such as 'Pie in the Sky' and 'Hallelujah I'm a Bum' and militant speeches recommending direct action. On Saturday evenings, as the Mildura people went about their shopping, these Broken

Hill miners expounded Chicago IWW theories from a soapbox in the main street.[13] Within the IWW Clubs, too, dissension was widespread from late in 1910 and throughout 1911.[14]

Hawkins, as general secretary of the IWW Clubs, felt obliged to respond to this discontent. In March 1911 he issued an open statement to the socialist movement in Australasia, warning it was threatened with a 'hindrance to progress' in the shape of the 'non-politicals', who:

> whilst speaking in the name of Socialism and particularly professing to advocate industrial unionism, are declaiming against political action and with the zeal of the convert and the naive enthusiasm of the uninformed are proclaiming as new-found truths the oft exploded fallacies of the anarchists. . . . Political action is stated to be always and necessarily reactionary and political representatives to be necessarily corrupted by their environments . . . It is also urged by some that . . . political action . . . emasculates the virility of the movement and impedes the growth of revolutionary industrial organisations.

This 'extreme anti-parliamentarism' resulted, understandably, from 'disgust at the antics of the so-called Labor parties'. However, such a response was dangerous. 'Why deliberately leave the other side in undisturbed possession of the public powers, ready and organised to attempt counter-revolutionary measures?' Parliament need not always corrupt politicians:

> if men are elected by a revolutionary working class constituency who vote consciously for, not reform, but revolution – that is a different matter. A sell out in such a case would mean political extinction, scorn, hatred and contempt. The representatives themselves will be revolutionists: men who have fought an uphill fight for years against odds: scorning compromise, declining to budge an inch from principle for votes or position. Such men, elected by a class-conscious majority, will be unbuyable.[15]

Militant trade unionists were not impressed by these arguments: the uncompromising socialist politician was a familiar sight, as was his subsequent apostasy; and these Clubs were the province of the SLP, subordinated to its dogma and prone to the sectarian behaviour attendant upon its political tunnel vision. The Chicago IWW, by comparison with the IWW Clubs, promised freedom from political entanglements with either the Labor Party or the SLP, both distrusted for different reasons by militant workers; and, in place of the doctrinal hairsplitting that had driven many out of the Clubs, it promised solidarity and activism.

On May Day 1909 the *International Socialist* published the new 1908 Chicago Preamble. On 10 September 1910 it urged the formation of the IWW in Australia, claiming that the present Australian organisation that bore its name was not connected with it, as proved by its repudiation of the 1908 Preamble. This statement was written by Harry Denford of the United Laborers' Union, now working on the Adelaide sewerage works, who had been blacklisted on the Barrier for his militant role in Port Pirie and Broken Hill during the 1909 dispute.[16] In December 1910 Denford argued that political movements, as they became more powerful, necessarily grew less revolutionary and were captured by opportunists: 'It is folly to hope for the transformation of society by political action . . . The emancipation of the working class must be the act of themselves alone, not by proxies and ballot boxes . . . It is industrial unionism which is the decisive weapon.'[17] Articles extolling the virtues of industrial sabotage, a tactic lauded in Chicago and deplored in Detroit, started appearing, and the International Socialists began distributing Chicago literature.[18] With the SLP controlling the strings of the IWW Clubs, the revolutionary industrial unionists within the SFA found that the logic of the situation inclined them towards the other IWW.

Ironically, it was out of efforts made to launch a political IWW Club in Adelaide that the non-political IWW first established itself in Australia, because SFA members wished to align themselves with an IWW that was not De Leonite. (A parallel process prompted the emergence of the Chicago IWW in New Zealand.) The Sydney IWW Club had despatched Fellow-Worker Peter Christensen to Adelaide in mid-1910 to spread ideas and literature to further the politicals' cause.[19] Christensen attended a lecture on the IWW Preamble at the SFA headquarters on Sunday 2 October 1910, delivered by Ted Moyle, who had recently arrived from England and was a Carpenters' Union delegate to the United Trades and Labor Council and South Australian representative on the SFA National Executive. Christensen moved that the meeting write to IWW Club headquarters in Sydney with a view to forming a Club in Adelaide. Harry Clarke moved an amendment that information first be procured from America. Neither resolution nor amendment were put; instead, it was agreed that Clarke and Christensen were to obtain both versions of the Preamble for further discussion.[20]

Christensen procured copies of the political 1905 version from the Sydney Club, proceeded 'to work quietly' with his propaganda and eventually had the 'sublime satisfaction' of being asked, around March 1911, to lecture on industrial unionism. There was a 'record attendance' but Clarke appeared with huge quantities of Chicago literature and Christensen's hopes for the immediate formation of a Detroit-line Club were dashed, because a further meeting was called to discuss the two alternatives. Hawkins in Sydney contemptuously dismissed these moves to set up a Chicago Local in Adelaide as 'coquetting' with the 'I-am-a-Bum anarchistic hoboe crowd'. At the subsequent meeting, Clarke moved that a Chicago-line Local be formed; Christensen, to his 'amazement and chagrin', could not get a seconder to his amendment to form a Club, which made him 'sick, sad and sorry'. Chairman Moyle, acknowledged by Christensen to have been fair and impartial, adjourned the meeting for a fortnight to enable Christensen to find a seconder.[21]

Christensen was unable to produce a seconder at the adjourned meeting on 6 May 1911, attended by ten people; the principal objection raised to the formation of a Club was that the SLP would thereby dominate the IWW. The numbers in favour of a Local were provided by members of the SFA, determined to avoid SLP control of another Club, and the meeting resolved in favour of forming a Local, which they did with eight members on 24 May. Christensen admitted to Hawkins that the seeds he had sown had fallen on 'very stony ground' because of 'prejudice against the S.L.P. and consequently anything endorsed by the S.L.P. stinks and is rotten'.[22] Following proper IWW nomenclature, Ted Moyle became General Secretary-Treasurer and Harry Clarke became General Organiser.[23] Membership doubled to sixteen by June and to twenty-four by July; and this Adelaide Local became the 'Australian Administration' of the Chicago IWW, with the right to charter further Locals on the continent of Australia.[24] It remained convinced, as it informed fellow workers in Sydney in September 1911, that 'any industrial movement that is bossed by any political movement cannot live'.[25]

In the second half of 1911 two groups in Sydney attracted to the Chicago line, or at least hostile to the Detroit line, corresponded with the Adelaide Local, which issued a charter to one of these groups as the Sydney Local on 13 October 1911. After announcing in a letter to Moyle that 'the Sydney I.W.W. is an accomplished fact', John Dwyer of the Sydney Local commented of the Labor government's recent strike-breaking action against the Lithgow miners that 'a party that can send up trainloads of armed Police to Lithgow is a queer crowd to carry the flag of emancipation'.[26] The two Sydney groups subsequently amalgamated under the charter at a joint meeting on 25 November 1911 attended by twenty-three people, including Donald Grant and Joe Fagin, which started at the home of Mr and Mrs Ferdinand Harris in Surry Hills then adjourned to the Queens Hall in Pitt St for a more public meeting; a list was signed and sent to Moyle in Adelaide. Another meeting in the Queens Hall the following evening attracted fifty-one people, five of whom were women. Although numbers attending meetings continued to rise, eighty-nine being present at the meeting on 27 December 1911 when the charter received from Chicago was exhibited, there were only fourteen fully financial members in April 1912.[27]

This Sydney Local published its own version of the Preamble, with a significant addition: 'knowing that all attempts to bring Emancipation of the Proletariat about, by means of any kind of political party has and must end in failure, therefore we reject parliamentary action . . .' Moyle responded with Adelaide's understanding of the 1908 Chicago Preamble: 'the I.W.W. does not concern itself about political action, either for or against it'.[28] Denford, the secretary of the Sydney Local early in 1912, denied that the IWW was violently opposed to all forms of political action, claiming it was neither pro-political nor anti-political. Another stalwart of the Local and secretary-treasurer for most of 1912, George Reeve, insisted that adherence to the 1908 Preamble did not entail the belief that 'acts of physical violence, the preaching of theft, and the cracking of skulls, both individually and collectively, were a means of education to dispossess the ruling class'.[29] The Local was clearly becoming divided on the issue. On 10 June 1912, at a meeting chaired by Donald Grant, Fellow-Workers Fagin and Johnson moved that the ASP be informed that the Local wished to have printed under its label in each issue of the *International Socialist* that 'This organisation stands for Industrial Action only, and is not affiliated with any parliamentary Party whatsoever, nor with any body other than an industrial organisation.' After Grant vacated the chair to speak and 'a great amount of discussion' took place, the resolution was carried.[30]

The SFA continued for a time to support the Chicago IWW, 'the only true international industrial organisation which is worthy of the workers' attention', providing it with meeting facilities until June 1912 when the Local deemed the room too small for its meetings.[31] In 1912, after the VSP split away, the SFA renamed itself the Australian Socialist Party (ASP). It began to promote IWW ideas in the West, to build upon the discontent with the reformist orientation of the Western Australian Socialist Party (WASP) that had expressed itself in 1910. Within a few months, the Perth branch of the WASP split, with the issue of the IWW as one of the bones of contention; the militant supporters of revolutionary industrial unionism formed a Perth branch of the ASP in opposition to their erstwhile comrades remaining in the WASP. This left breakaway took fourteen members initially, including two subsequent stalwarts of the Chicago IWW in the West: Monty Miller, who had recently arrived in the West, and his daughter, Annie Westbrook. This group then merged with the thirty-four members of the Industrial Branch of German Workers.[32]

The SLP, loyal to the last to the original 1905 Preamble and the De Leonite IWW, clearly resented the ASP's involvement with what it contemptuously referred to as 'the Bummery', characterising its action as 'a crime against the working-class' and harping upon the apparent absurdity of a political organisation such as the SFA lending support to the 'anti-political' IWW.[33] The ASP retort was that the Chicago IWW was not anti-political but merely non-political and that an IWW member could therefore also belong to a political organisation which endorsed IWW principles. In reality, the SLP had provoked the SFA/ASP into support for the Chicago IWW. However, in 1912 the ASP and SLP embarked on negotiations aimed at unifying their organisations, and ASP support for Chicago was clearly detrimental to the success of these negotiations. During 1913, in the interests of rapprochement with the SLP, the ASP discarded its attachment to the Chicago IWW, a stark reversal of attitude much encouraged by events within the Sydney Local.[34]

Tom Glynn had arrived from South Africa late in 1912 and organised around him a more classically 'Bummery' element, which included Joe Fagin, J.B. King and Andy Macpherson, to gain control of the Local from those who still had some residual beliefs in political action.[35] Glynn, born in Galway in Ireland in 1881, had arrived in Australia in 1900, served as a trooper with the Victorian Bushmen in the Boer War and remained in South Africa as a sergeant in the Transvaal Police. By 1907 he was active in New Zealand's left politics, leaving the Wellington SLP, small and sectarian, to join the larger Socialist Party with a view to encouraging the splitting off of its 'revolutionary element'. By 1910 he was back in Johannesburg in the tramway service, becoming general secretary of the South African Industrial Workers Union. He played a leading part in a tramway strike in 1911 for which he was jailed. After becoming prominent in radical journalism in South Africa he left for Ireland and the USA, where he joined the IWW, and finally worked his way back to Australia in 1912 as a stoker, after which he worked mainly as a tramway conductor in Sydney.[36]

In January 1913 the Glynn group succeeded in expelling George Reeve from the IWW for 'failing to hand over the property of the Sydney Local'.[37] Reeve refused to recognise his expulsion, continued to sign himself secretary-treasurer of the Sydney Local and displayed a letter from Vincent St John endorsing his position and version of the events. He even contemplated legal action against those espousing 'the Serfs' methods of physical force only', whose 'crazy actions will inflict untold suffering on the ill-informed'. Reeve later found his natural home in the De Leonite Club. According to Reeve, when Moyle visited Sydney at Easter 1913 he permitted the Glynn group to take over at a meeting he chaired that was packed with new members because he was 'intimidated' by the 'physical force element'.[38]

A different account would stress that the takeover, which had the numbers, expressed the determination of the majority of the Local to have nothing to do with political action. The Local's new position was not in favour of the advocacy of physical force, as Reeve caricatured it, for such a position would declare that the organisation was 'too intellectually weak to carry out its mission'; it merely rejected political action.[39] From this point on, the Sydney Local grew, and spectacularly. The Australian

Administration was shifted from Adelaide to Sydney. By November 1913 there were 199 members 'in good standing'.[40] On 31 January 1914 the Sydney Local began publication of *Direct Action*, the official organ of the Australian Administration. Three years of Labor government in the Commonwealth had exhausted the patience of many militant workers and made the arguments of those who defended the record of Labor-in-politics seem ever more specious. And exiles from South Africa and New Zealand, in the wake of strike defeats in those countries, swelled the ranks; the principal speakers for the IWW in this formative period – Donald Grant, J.B. King and Charles Reeve – were, like Glynn, recent immigrants.

These global patterns of movement are a distinctive feature of the Wobbly phenomenon. The decades around the turn of the century marked a period of international capitalist development that in turn

Donald Grant speaking in the Sydney Domain. (Donald Grant, *Through Six Gaols*)

fostered an international labour market. During the Indian summer of free trade and imperial expansion, the European-settler economies of the New World offered higher wages than were available at home. Patterns of movement were freer then than they would become after the First World War, when trade barriers and immigration restrictions became more systematic. Mining, construction and heavy industry provided employment opportunities for footloose single men in search of adventure; cheap sea travel linked Britain, North America and the white dominions, while an efficient mail service and print capitalism allowed ready communication from one worksite to another.

Grant, born in 1888 in Inverness, Scotland, migrated to Australia in 1910 where he found work in a paper mill, later as a dental mechanic. Leaving the International Socialists for the IWW, he became undoubtedly the IWW's most gifted speaker. Tall, with his thick red hair brushed back, and retaining a strong Scottish accent, he attracted huge crowds to the Sunday meetings in the Sydney Domain.[41] Betsy Matthias recalls him with admiration as 'Curly-headed, Scotch, poetic Donald!' whose speeches eclipsed all others.[42] Fred Farrall claims he was:

> an orator that could hold his own with anybody in the country, anybody. The average politician wouldn't be in the race. His command of the language and the way he could use it could be devastating. He could humiliate anyone. And he could recite yards of Robert Burns and Shelley and those poets who upheld the rights of the common people.[43]

Henry Boote, writing in 1917 when Grant had been jailed for his oratorical powers, noted:

> For years he was the most popular orator of the Sydney Domain. Sunday after Sunday thousands surrounded the stump from which he spoke. His pungent satires upon capitalistic society evoked the laughter and applause of vast audiences. His eloquent appeals for working-class solidarity stirred them to the depths of their being.[44]

Detective Moore respected and feared his ability to inspire his listeners, describing him as 'the most dangerous speaker in Australia'.[45]

John Benjamin King, a hefty Canadian born in 1870, who had worked as a miner, teamster, stoker and engine-driver, had been an IWW organiser in both Vancouver and Auckland before arriving in Sydney in 1911. The police assumed, wrongly, that he had been sent in an official capacity by the Chicago headquarters, but, like the increasing number of American seamen they noticed speaking from the IWW platform, King had come of his own accord. Though not in Grant's league, he was a fine orator with a boisterous and aggressive style. There were many baseless rumours about King: that he had a considerable private income; that he had blown up a newspaper office in Los Angeles; and that he was wanted for murder in the USA.[46]

Reeve, a thickset Cockney, with straight, well-oiled, long dark hair pushed back, was, according to his security file, only 5ft.1in. and 'very much tattooed on the arms, hands and fingers'. Born in 1887, he arrived in Sydney in 1907 after experience in the IWW in the USA, and worked as a bricklayer. The police regarded him as 'one of the most aggressive speakers of the I.W.W.'; his fellow members, according to Donald Grant in later life, considered he was 'a bloody madman' who 'would fight the whole world – so long as it was looking on'. Tony McGillick remembers a more poignant side to Reeve, that he was a master at painting word-pictures of the sad lot of the worker: 'He would describe a cold morning when it was still dark, when the worker would awaken to the shrill peal of the alarm-clock, with the prospect of a day of weary toil for little reward.'[47]

After the Glynn group took over the Sydney Local, it appealed to socialists to drop all attachment to revolutionary political action, to join the IWW in organising industrial unions to achieve industrial democracy by direct action.[48] The ASP was not interested. Rather, it became decidedly antagonistic towards the Chicago IWW during 1913, and towards the Sydney Local in particular. In July an *International Socialist* editorial launched a ferocious attack on this Local: 'certain cantankerous and disruptive elements' had assumed control, declared war against Socialists, denounced all political action, instituted a boycott against the *International Socialist*, withdrawn its label and column from it and circulated the lie that the paper was benefiting from its appearance; a leading member had absconded with funds; and it was plagued with individual antagonisms. In September the ASP announced that events had shown that the ASP had more in common with the Detroit IWW and that, with the Chicago IWW's growing hostility to socialism (by which it meant parliamentary socialism), there was added impetus to its desire for unity with the SLP. To facilitate the moves towards unification, which foundered ultimately over arguments about printing plants, the ASP formally endorsed the Detroit IWW on 10 November 1913.[49]

On the left, two distinct blocs had formed by the time the winds of war were felt. On the one hand, there was the Chicago IWW, loud and energetic, calling on militant workers to abandon all faith in politicians, Labor or socialist; on the other, there was the Detroit IWW and its close allies in the SLP and the ASP, small but smug, denouncing 'the Bummery' at every opportunity and imploring the working class to send them, as true socialists, to parliament in the place of Labor MPs.[50] There were no growth prospects for the ASP in fixing its hopes on the Clubs. By

March 1914, according to one long-standing member, they were 'stagnating through inactivity'. The Clubs gave 'unlimited opportunities for the exercise of philosophy' but they did 'not create that stamina which comes only from participation in the work of a concrete union'.[51] Clearly, the action was now with the Chicago Locals. The ASP's attachment to the Clubs indicated serious reservations about the aims and methods of the Chicago IWW.

The bitterness of the ASP's disillusionment with the Chicago IWW, with its representatives in Australia, is revealed in the *International Socialist* editorial of September 1913:

> The more one listens to non-political I.W.W. speakers the more disgusted he becomes at the barbarous crudeness of their views.
>
> They are an impossible lot, and the end of their story is brute force and transparent cunning. Their view of sabotage would be amusing if it was not so dangerous to the workers themselves . . . The anarchist is sane and sound compared with the I.W.W.-ite whose interference in labour disputes generally leads to disaster . . . the workers ought to know by this time that the armed forces of capitalism are not to be played with by those who sing 'Hallelujah I'm a Bum' and throw brick-bats.
>
> The working class here will never be led by wild men from Yankeeland, but must be convinced by reason and argument . . .[52]

However, the Australian adherents of the Chicago IWW showed that during the First World War a significant section of the working class was prepared to be led by these 'wild men from Yankeeland' and that in many cases IWW 'interference in labour disputes' resulted in workers securing a better deal than the established union would have won. Moreover, the 'armed forces of capitalism' revealed they were considerably more concerned about the sabotage, singing and brick-bat throwing of the IWW than they were by the 'reason and argument' of the socialist sects. As for 'the barbarous crudeness of their views', it is to this allegation that we now turn.

CHAPTER 4

'Education, Organisation, Emancipation':
the Revolutionary Project

The IWW was one aspect of the general dissatisfaction with the existing forms of socialist doctrine and working-class organisation that became apparent in the early years of the twentieth century. Capitalism had survived the mass discontent associated with its birthpangs: the initial disruption of economic relations, and the social misery of an uncontrolled market in all commodities. This revolutionary new mode of production had spread to encompass the globe, it had generated new organisational forms, including the large-scale company, and it enjoyed the support of a vastly expanded state apparatus. The principal working-class response in the English-speaking countries, the trade union, accepted the reality of the capitalist labour market and simply sought a larger slice of the cake. On the continent of Europe the socialist parties and their industrial wings espoused a purely formal antagonism to a class order they were unable to contest – a fact recognised in the socialist Second International between 1889 and 1914 in the debate between the revisionists and the custodians of Marxist orthodoxy. The debate turned on the undeniable fact that Marx's prediction of a growing immiseration of the proletariat leading to a breakdown of capitalism had not occurred. To the orthodox, material conditions were expected to create class-conscious workers and the socialist millennium must wait until this necessary process was complete.

In response to this apparent impasse there emerged a number of new departures. One was syndicalism, which eschewed parliamentary strategies and emphasised struggle at the point of production. Strongest in France, Spain and Italy, the IWW was commonly deemed an Anglophone variant of this phenomenon. Another was guild socialism, which sought to redefine socialism to encompass consumers as well as producers. In central and eastern Europe, where workers' parties operated in conditions of semi-legality, a restatement of Marxism occurred that placed new emphasis on the party as the catalyst of working-class consciousness and the vanguard of revolution. This process began with Lenin's *What Is To Be Done?* in 1902, but it was not until 1917 that his Bolshevism became more generally known as Communism.

Formulated in response to particular conditions and drawing on particular cultural traditions, the boundaries that separated these doctrines were at first indistinct. The Englishman, Tom Mann, came to Australia in 1902 as a trade unionist and an ethical socialist of the Independent Labour Party. As a socialist and trade union organiser in Victoria and Broken Hill, he became increasingly dissatisfied with the limitations of craft unionism, parliamentary activity and arbitration, and in 1909 published a pamphlet, *Industrial Unionism*, as a manifesto of militant industrial action. In the following year he launched the *Industrial Socialist* in London and in 1920 he became a founder-member of the Communist Party of Great Britain. He had left Australia just as the IWW was established, yet it expressed many of his concerns and attitudes. While the IWW responded to the fatalism of the Second International with a new emphasis on industrial organisation, in other respects it retained a conventional socialist doctrine. As we shall see, it affirmed an orthodox Marxist critique of capitalism and expected an understanding of Marxism to catalyse the experience of workers; its particular novelty lay in the temper with which it expounded Marxism. Wobblies had little patience with the laggardly progress of history. Instead, they employed a calculated effrontery to unmask the capitalist lie, and their educational effort was conducted not just in study circles but also in humour, denunciation, iconoclasm. The stock figure of the boneheaded wage slave was at once an acknowledgement of the immensity of their task and a reassurance that they would prevail.

Academic commentators have tried in varying ways to squeeze the IWW into the pre-existing doctrinal pigeon-holes. The result has been a degree of confusion that has obscured the true identity of the IWW and its distinctive contribution to left-wing theory and practice. Syndicalist one minute, anarchist the next, sometimes anarcho-syndicalist, very occasionally Marxist – such a schizophrenic political personality as the IWW hardly merits serious investigation.

Most commonly the Wobblies are classified as syndicalists or anarcho-syndicalists, because they shared with this movement a belief that socialism was the administration of industry directly by the workers themselves and was not a form of government or state. Moreover, socialism, to Wobblies and syndicalists alike, could only be achieved by workers acting in their capacity as workers and through their unions or syndicats, and not by proxy either through representatives in parliament or a revolutionary seizure of state power.[1] This similarity notwithstanding, the Australian IWW maintained a critical distance from syndicalism and anarcho-syndicalism. Though it attacked the *Age* for a hostile review of Sorel's *Reflections on Violence*, most references to the syndicalist movement were at best ambivalent. One article in *Direct Action* lumped the French syndicalists of the *Confédération générale du travail* with the ALP and the German Social Democrats, because, on the outbreak of war, they 'combined their inefficiency with the blackest treachery'. Another piece referred to the 'bankruptcy of French syndicalism', which indulged in 'theoretical declarations' while neglecting the 'practical revolutionary fight'.[2] Yet the syndicalists were clearly the closest political relatives of the IWW. Bill Genery, who joined the Melbourne Local in 1916, conceded in a 1969 interview that Wobblies regarded the IWW as 'an offshoot' of the syndicalists.[3]

In their alleged espousal of sabotage and valorisation of spontaneity and in their real hostility to hierarchical and bureaucratic forms of organisation, the IWW is occasionally deemed anarchist, an accusation also made in the form of abuse by political opponents, both conservative and socialist, at the time.[4] Norman Rancie, one-time editor of *Direct Action*, responded to the comparison in 1957:

> Anarchists believe in complete individual freedom and each man a law unto himself. They refuse to recognise any form of organisation or authority. This is the very antithesis of all the principles of the I.W.W. which believes in organisation, discipline, and not 'every many a law unto himself', but every member responsible to his organisation which has a book of rules and a constitution, which of course is the very negation of anarchism.

Anarchists, he was adamant, 'would never by any standard fit into the I.W.W.'[5] When asked by a New Left student whether the Wobblies considered themselves anarchists, Bill Genery replied quite definitely that they did not.[6] The real anarchists of the time agreed. Distressed by the tendency in some quarters to confuse the IWW with anarchists, a purist anarchist sect published an attack on the IWW in 1916, 'that rotten mass of rules', in order 'to clear Anarchism and to disqualify I.W.W-ists as Anarchists'.[7] A perceived similarity with anarchism existed primarily in the minds of the IWW's detractors and cannot be detected in any serious analysis of its political practice, which emphasised collectivity, unity, organisation and centralisation.

In many ways the IWW was more classically Marxist than syndicalist, anarcho-syndicalist or anarchist; it frequently and fulsomely acknowledged the profound influence of Marx on its outlook and strategies. The IWW Manifesto, a much longer and more analytical piece than the punchy Preamble, clearly reflected a Marxist world vision, which IWW theorists such as Trautmann and Hagerty had derived from books, and American workers from experience of what seemed the classic Marxian pattern of monopoly capitalist development.[8] In Australia, in addition to the Marxist mould brought in from the American organisation, the cast of the ASP remained with the Chicago Locals, and fresh Marxist imprints were made by the new breed of leaders after 1913, notably Tom Glynn and Tom Barker.

Yet the Wobblies were not Marxists, pure and simple. A more obscure nomenclature is needed, that which they used themselves: they were revolutionary industrial unionists. This term is used to refer both to the organisational procedure of the IWW – methods of obtaining a uniform structure for the entire labour movement – and to the attitudes and philosophy of members. It refers also to the means by which the IWW hoped workers would attain control of production. Only wage-workers were eligible for membership, because only wage-workers, through revolutionary industrial unionism, could achieve the transition to socialism; non-wage-workers, having different economic interests, would subvert the purposes of the organisation.[9]

The IWW's three-stage strategy for social transformation was: education, organisation, emancipation. It aimed, firstly, to educate the working class into an understanding of its exploited position in capitalist society and to inspire workers with a class-conscious determination to end this wage slavery; secondly, it aspired to organise the working class, now educated, into industrial unions, not craft unions, ultimately joined together in the One Big Union, containing all the country's workers; finally, it planned that this One Big Union, the ultimate attainment of proletarian solidarity, would emancipate the working class, and bring freedom from wage slavery, by assuming control of the means of production, distribution and exchange. In the content of its education, the form of its organisation and its concept of emancipation, the IWW developed its own unique and coherent approach of revolutionary industrial unionism, while owing its greatest philosophical debt to Marx.

Education

The IWW was concerned, first of all, to change the ways in which the working class comprehended the world. In waging this propaganda war, Marxist ideas were foremost, especially Marx's theories about the nature and dynamics of the capitalist mode of production. Enamoured of Marxist theory in general, the IWW was especially convinced of its ability to clarify workers' thinking by exposing the exploitative relationship of which they were the unfortunate half. Former Wobbly, Guido Baracchi, maintained in a 1968 poem about the Wobblies that, in spite of their 'unseemly larks', they 'kept a high regard for Marx'.[13]

Marxist terms such as 'surplus value' and 'ruling class' were the standard vocabulary of IWW propagandists. One of these, Alf Wilson, insisted: 'Marx is undisputed and he is my intellectual master.' J.B. King, during his 1914 speaking tour as General Organiser, was billed as 'a convincing and earnest expositor of scientific organization, and Marxian Economics'.[11] In *Industrial Efficiency and its Antidote*, one of the first indigenous productions of the Australian IWW, Tom Glynn referred and deferred frequently to *Capital*, where Marx revealed how 'the history of the capitalist system affords many illustrations of how blind competition amongst capitalists, with the resultant phenomenon of over-production, affects the economic and social well-being of the workers'. Articles expounding Marx's ideas appeared in most issues of *Direct Action*. Many Locals held regular classes in Marxist economics; the Sydney Local explained this was necessary to spread knowledge of the structure of capitalism among the working class to help speed the day when, by their knowledge, the workers would be able to abolish the wage system and rear in its place a newer and saner form of society.[12] Amongst the regular items of literature distributed by the Australian Administration were *Capital* in three volumes, *Value, Price and Profit* (6d.), *Wage Labour and Capital* (1d.) and a *Summary of Marx's Capital* (2d.).

Capitalism was not only a system of exploitation but one of ideological domination that secured the consent of the exploited to their own exploitation. Well before Gramsci wrestled with the problem, the IWW groped towards some formulation of the problem of hegemony: 'The proletariat holds the same opinions as the capitalist class in spite of the fact that their interests are not identical.' While the ruling class controlled schools, churches, and press, it was impossible for most workers to think for themselves.[13] Late in 1913 the Australian Administration published and distributed an American IWW pamphlet, *How Capital has Hypnotised Society*, which noted the inconsistency between working-class reality and working-class consciousness:

> The working class, as a class, is compelled to be at war with the capitalist class almost continuously. At every point, their interests are exactly opposite . . . And yet, the mass of workers act, when it comes to the test, as if the system of mastership and slavery were a sacred system, and any violation of it a criminal and blasphemous thing.[14]

Every ruling class, *Direct Action* noted, sought to impose its interpretation of moral tenets upon the subject class, and every ruling class justified its overlordship by appealing to the prevalent moral code. One of the chief functions of the propagandists, therefore, was to destroy the belief held by the great mass of workers in the absolute nature of capitalist morality, for whilst such a belief existed, the work of revolutionary unionism was sorely handicapped.[15] Essentially, the IWW sought to challenge the hegemony of the capitalist class, to undermine by audacious and iconoclastic means the consent given by the masses to the authority of the ruling class, and establish instead its own hegemony.

The backwardness of the Australian working class was, according to *Direct Action*, because they were at best only job-conscious, not class-conscious. Until the workers understood the fundamental facts of their existence there could be no cohesion, purpose or collective will; knowledge was the key to power. Part of the Wobbly indictment against trade unionism was that it had not combined class education with organisation and had even promoted ideas which prevented the development of class consciousness. Mick Sawtell explained in *Direct Action* that, until there was an understanding of economic laws and the capitalist system of production, there could be no class-conscious working-class movement that would seize the industries of the world and run them in the interests of the workers; there would merely be purposeless revolt.[16]

It was the mission of the IWW to foster the necessary spirit of class consciousness. *Direct Action* announced:

> It is the function of the I.W.W. to educate the workers of the world into right ideas concerning the economic relationship of the workers of the world . . . The workers can never be emancipated without first being inspired and permeated with new ideas . . . First, education; second, organisation; and finally, emancipation.[17]

The IWW emphasised the importance for revolutionary action of a subjective, as well as an objective, common interest: 'The economic laws can only be modified or mitigated in favor of the workers by themselves through scientific economic organisation, combined with a conscious knowledge of their slave status under Capitalism . . .'[18] Capitalist class consciousness had to be countered before the capitalist system could be challenged.

> We can do nothing, absolutely nothing, TILL WE UNDERSTAND . . . .
> We must destroy capitalism, and close the class struggle.
> This will surely take place when the conscious workers successfully explain capitalism with all its ramifications to the . . . deluded workers. The class war will cease when we have explained the national and international conspiracy of the capitalist class. The class war will cease when we rouse the workers of the world by explaining . . . Explain till our class becomes class-conscious; till it sees itself, sees itself and its class power.[19]

Syndicat members, on the other hand, were not expected to subscribe to any particular political philosophy; in syndicalist thought, common economic interest alone was the unifying force, not comprehension of this common interest and its significance. The IWW was an association of choice, a group of workers with a common set of political beliefs; the syndicat was merely an association of necessity, of workers in a common industrial situation.

Unlike the syndicalists, then, the IWW did not consider objective economic interests as a sufficient basis for proletarian organisation. A change in consciousness was also essential; the working class had to become, in Marxist terms, a class for itself.[20] Indeed, the projected One Big Union, with its rallying cry of 'an injury to one an injury to all', could be seen as the ultimate realisation of the working class as a class for itself. Marx allocated the important role of bringing revolutionary ideas to the working class, encouraging its transformation from a class in itself to a class for itself, to the Communists, the 'advanced and resolute' workers who clearly understood 'the line of march, the conditions, and the ultimate general results of the proletarian movement'.[21]

The IWW believed it could fulfil this function, that it could teach revolutionary, Marxist, ideas to the rest of the working class but from within that working-class movement. It did not, like the Detroit IWW, place its own organisation in a superior position of authority over the working class; rather it hoped that the One Big Union would become coterminous with the class and that no decisive revolutionary action would occur before that moment. De Leonism, and later Bolshevism, interpreted the role of Marx's Communists in a more restricted way, replacing the Marxist trust in the proletariat with an approach which reposed confidence in a vanguard party organised separately from the working class itself.[22] The IWW, on the other hand, shared Marx's and Engels' faith in the revolutionary potential, with the goading of the revolutionaries amongst them, of the great mass of workers organised as workers. The IWW depicted its part in the working-class movement in much the same way that Marx described the role of the Communists as being merely the most class-conscious section of the wider movement.[23]

Education had necessarily to precede organisation and emancipation: 'We have not penetrated . . . far enough into the enemy's country to overthrow capitalism. The ignorant worker is the soldier we have to overcome; him we conquer by the appeal of reason . . .'[24] Impatient to proceed with its revolutionary project, the IWW frequently expressed its irritation with the level of development of those whose minds had first to be changed. Despite its commitment to non-hierarchical and democratic organisational forms, the peculiarly insulting nature of Wobbly vocabulary made the IWW seem even more patronising and elitist towards

'ignorant' workers than the other left groups of the time or revolutionary organisations generally. It regretted that

> the few who step out are held back . . . by the BONEHEAD, who succumbs to
> his fear and instead of awakening and grasping fraternal workers' hands, and
> taking the step in advance, he rushes back to his old familiar sensations –
> doped – weakened and hypnotised . . . they who hold the reins of the Earth's
> Government, WITH THE BONEHEAD'S DUMB PERMISSION, PUT THE
> LASH ON THE FEW, WHO HAVE STRIVEN TO GO FORWARD AND
> THEY CRUCIFY, HANG, SHOOT, OR JAIL THEM.[25]

A regular cartoon strip entitled 'The Amazing Adventures of Mr Simple'
cruelly ridiculed the worker who was easily duped by the bosses because
he trusted them. Mr Simple was the Australian IWW equivalent of the
American IWW's Mr Block, whose head, according to the song, was
made of lumber and was as solid as a rock.[26] The stultifying effects of capitalism on the mentality of the working class was a continual theme in
Direct Action.

However, revolutionary industrial organisation, and therefore emancipation, would not be possible until all the boneheads were educated.
In this sense, IWW elitism differed significantly from other forms of van-
guardism, such as Bolshevism's emphasis on the leading role of the party
of professional revolutionaries in the revolutionary act and syndicalism's
reliance on the activities of the class-conscious minority who would,
when the moment came, 'goad the inert mass to action'.[27] IWW elitism
took a different, merely temporary, form: the boneheads, and boneheads it insisted they were, had to be made to interpret the world differently so all, together, could change it. The IWW relied on both economic
necessity and the enlightening effects, not of 'dogmas and theories' but
of correct ideas tested in practice, to persuade all workers into revolutionary industrial unionism:

> the worker's mind is too untrained to grasp a plan for a world-wide and revo-
> lutionary reconstruction of society. *He will gradually wake up to that later on.* But
> the appeal to his sense of solidarity is apt to be most successful if it is made to
> the stomach first, then to his intelligence . . . The big mass are 'gross materi-
> alists' who move only in obedience to economic necessity, like a herd of
> buffaloes, and can only gradually acquire the power of unselfish social vision
> by class education . . .[28]

So, while often arrogant and intolerant in the meantime with boneheads, the IWW believed ultimately in the inherent wisdom of all workers, their capacity to become class-conscious. Thus, the IWW was more
classically Marxist in this respect than syndicalist: it would and must
bring revolutionary ideas to the working class in order to build the One

Big Union, for emancipation was not possible if only the minority were class-conscious and organised.

Organisation

Direct Action claimed that Marx's theory was never clearly established in practice until the IWW Convention in 1905. Tom Glynn argued that Marx realised the vital need of the working class for thorough organisation instead of 'futile grasping' at a collection of ballot papers thrown together every three or four years, only to go up in smoke with the first whiff of grapeshot.[29] The IWW saw itself as the true heir and interpreter of Marx, who turned his ideas into action, his philosophy into practice; by so doing, it believed it was acting in the real, revolutionary spirit of the Marxist tradition, in contrast with both the reformism of the mainstream labour movements and the abstract philosophising of many Marxist intellectuals.

Because of its rejection of parliamentarism, the basic strategy of labour and social democratic parties, the IWW did have much in common with syndicalism in its emphasis on direct industrial action as opposed to parliamentary action and its associated endeavours. However, the two movements differed substantially in their responses to the question of how best to organise the working class in the extra-parliamentary, industrial arena.

In the first place, syndicalists were 'borers from within', a tactic contemptuously dismissed in Wobbly propaganda. Just as the IWW did not consider that working within the Labor Party could bring any revolutionary returns, so also did it reject all arguments that gaining positions of power within the existing craft-based trade union movement would advance the cause. Syndicalists, however, were mostly active within craft-union oriented labour movements. Peter Stearns acknowledges that syndicalism had a 'special appeal to craftsmen' and deems French syndicalism 'antimodern in its appeal to craft traditions'. Though not hostile to industrial unionism, syndicalism had emerged from the existing craft unions and remained reasonably content with the old form of organisation; it was militant but nonetheless sectional unionism and based its conception of present organisation and future society on craft autonomy.[30]

The organisational form of the IWW was a response to the perceived inadequacies, from both a reformist and a revolutionary viewpoint, of trade union organisation. *Direct Action* explained the historical processes that prompted its formation. The industrial revolution of the nineteenth century rendered obsolete the craft form of organisation, based upon particular skills. With the centralising of a large body of workers into one factory, craft unionism became disunion, because those workers, slaves of the same capitalist, should have been organised together, instead of which they were divided into probably a dozen or more separate trade unions, each with its own narrow craft interests, and without regard to the interests of the working class as a whole.[31] Recognising the sectional nature of craft unions, which followed the occupational divisions of capitalism rather than uniting workers as a class, the IWW aimed at creating a new kind of unionism that would weld workers so tightly together that they would be in a position to overthrow capitalist society by assuming control of the means of production: 'By organising industrially into one big union of all workers, regardless of sex, creed, or color, we will be able to attain that solidarity which alone can abolish wage-slavery and usher in the new society.'[32] Revolutionary industrial unionist organisation, unlike craft unionism, could and would result in working-class emancipation; in the meantime, its superior organisational methods would better enable workers to defend their immediate interests.

Direct Action claimed that craft unionism, which necessarily involved a hierarchy of unionists, with skilled workers jealously guarding their status and privileges in relation to unskilled and semi-skilled workers, fostered division within working-class ranks, hindering solidarity; it bred systematic, organised scabbery and upheld capitalist society. Industrial unionism, on the other hand, was 'scientific'; and its tactics were not met with approval by the boss, for it aimed to make 'an injury to one an injury to all'.[33] The IWW would organise workers on a solid basis, on the lines of the class struggle, where the workers would not fight in sections, but as a class: 'Trade unionism has got to go, industrial unionism must take its place . . . Link up into the fighting union of the working class, which recognises no peace between the master and the slave.'[34]

Syndicalism also favoured highly decentralised, even disorganised, patterns of protest, which reflected the decentralised status of industry in France and southern Europe.[35] The syndicalist militants within the CGT protected vehemently the autonomy of the syndicats, the lowest units of the movement, and opposed centralisation as an evil in itself.[36] The spontaneous activity of the class-conscious elite, 'the minorities which sow and propagate new ideas',[37] would, according to these syndicalists, be jeopardised by disciplined mass proletarian action; moreover, the self-conscious action of this elite was, they believed, the motor-force of change, not economic laws such as those laid down by Marx and accepted, to a large extent, by the IWW. Activism to syndicalists was not so much a means to an end as an end in itself.

The Wobblies disagreed with this decentralised, spontaneist approach. They preferred mass not minority militancy, solidarity rather than spontaneity, discipline not disarray in industrial action. The structure of the

IWW clearly indicated a recognition of the 'centering of industry into fewer and fewer hands', the tendency towards monopolisation occurring in both the United States and Australia. The indictment against craft unionism in the Preamble of the IWW could as easily be directed against the syndicalists. Syndicalism relied on a coincidence of militancy which, when it failed, resulted in scabbery. As Childe points out, instead of the chaos of warring interests which seems possible under syndicalism proper, the IWW offered a highly centralised organisation of society transcending the limits of individual industries just as it overleapt craft divisions.[38] It believed in fighting like with like, the ruthlessly efficient capitalist system with a well-organised and unified counter-force, a disciplined proletarian army. In aspiration at least, the IWW was highly centralised; whatever the actual level of organisation achieved in practice, it believed in the need for organisation.

No more elaborate blueprint for the future, no more detailed 'fanciful picture in the air' was ever devised than Father Hagerty's 'Wheel of Fortune', the Chicago IWW's diagrammatic vision of the One Big Union, its departments and sub-departments, that would form the basis of the IWW's new, intricately centralised and highly organised world order. Revolutionary industrial unionism aimed at substituting industrial government for political government; syndicalism had no use for government of any sort. The ramblings of syndicalist 'theorists' such as Georges Sorel have little coherence when compared with the very concrete programme of the IWW.

Early in 1914 *Direct Action* serialised B.H. Williams' *The Constructive Programme of the I.W.W.* The lowest unit in the structure of the IWW was the shop branch, enabling workers to confront the boss directly; but, for the purpose of local unity in a given industry, all shop branches were to be bound together in a local industrial union. General local unity of all industries would be ensured by the industrial district council of representatives from each local industrial union. Local industrial unions would be linked to form national industrial unions, such as railwaymen, to enable workers in a given industry to maintain the nation-wide unity and solidarity considered essential for defence and aggression against the capitalist enemy. These national industrial unions would then be grouped into six huge departments: agriculture; mining; transport and communication; manufacturing and general production; construction; and public service. Ultimately these departments would be brought together in one general union of the entire working class, to bind together all workers of all industries into one cooperative commonwealth. In reiterating this elaborate plan in 1917, Frank Callanan boasted of the IWW's determination to match the level of organisation of the capitalists, to 'meet the requirements of a highly centralised industrial system'.[39] In stark contrast to syndicalism's faith in the industrial efficacy of the lowest and smallest units, the One Big Union was premised on the organisational advantages of centralisation.

Emancipation

The 1906 Convention had inserted a new phrase into the Preamble: 'By organizing industrially, we are forming the structure of the new society within the shell of the old.' The IWW was to be both the embryo of the new society and the revolutionary instrument for achieving it.[40] Crucial to the successful realisation of the new order was a rejection of state-based means for achieving social change.

The IWW lamented that many workers looked upon the state as a social saviour, whereas the function of the class state was simply to perpetuate plutocratic power, the state being one gigantic scheme of oppression and exploitation. All governments in modern society, Tom Barker argued, existed for the purpose of protecting private property and the interests of the propertied class; whether the politicians were Socialists or Conservatives, they could only safeguard and perpetuate the system. All institutions of the state had one end in view, the maintenance of bourgeois property and power: education, for instance, made the workers more efficient slaves. 'The State does not represent society, but only tries to administer things in the interests of the ruling minority', *Direct Action* explained; 'all established institutions are adjuncts to the scheme of exploitation which is centred and functions in and through the medium of the State'.[41]

Whatever the form of the capitalist state, the IWW insisted it was primarily an organ of class rule; the working class could not therefore lay hold of the state machinery and wield it for its own purpose but must instead seize power where it really existed – at the point of production. The IWW's rejection of political action in the parliamentary sense stemmed from this classically Marxist analysis of where the locus of power lay in capitalist society:

> Political action at best only attacks a reflex of property, re-shuffles the cards, while direct action from below aims straight at the foundation of exploitation – private property . . .
> The power of the master class does not rest on legality or Christianity . . . This power is essentially economic, and rests on Force . . .[42]

Political institutions, according to the IWW, were a reflex of economic forces; there was no point appealing to a reflex. 'The class struggle is fought between the worker and the capitalist – not between the politician and the capitalist.' It took place in 'fields, factories, workshops, mines and in every other sphere of economic production and distribution, and not in Parliament House'. Reliance on the ballot box to effect change was pointless, because the control of industry lay in the Chambers of Commerce and the Stock Exchanges of the world.[43]

The real business of the state was performed behind the scenes. Parliament, according to the IWW, was akin to the games and circuses of ancient Rome 'by means of which the Roman rabble were kept in a good humour and out of mischief'.[44] It was an arena in which the working class dissipated much energy in struggling for the assumed power that parliament offered.

> It isn't the shame and it isn't the blame
> That stings like a white hot brand,
> It's the cussed foolishness of a jay
> Who'll work ten hours for two hours pay,
> And vote for the thing on election day,
> And will not understand.[45]

The Immediate Demands of the I.W.W. insisted 'it is a waste of time for the workers to attack or capture capitalist government'. *Direct Action* argued that parliamentary activity, 'political action', was a played-out weapon of the working class and that the place for action was at the point of production – on the job.[46]

Unlike parliamentary socialists, the IWW did not regard the state as a potential sphere of opposition to capital: 'Parliament is a failure, as no worker has any say in placing laws on the Statute book, unless it is suitable to the capitalist class, and if the boss favours it, then it must be useless to the working-class.' Under capitalism, 'legislation leads to exploitation of the poor, *never to economic salvation.*' The hope for the future, it contended, the way to emancipation, lay in industrial organisation on the lines of revolutionary militant action, not the 'supine, cowardly subterfuge of revolution by proxies'. Political action was irrelevant to the conduct of the class struggle and the ultimate emancipation of the working class; the IWW was convinced that, given the requisite solidarity on the industrial field, the attainment of the One Big Union, the working class could get all it wanted without the aid of parliament.[47]

'The I.W.W. is not anti-political, but simply non-parliamentary', *Direct Action* explained.[48] Its stance was indeed a highly political rejection of state-based means for achieving socialism, an implacable anti-parliamentary posture, an expression of unmitigated contempt for the Labor Party and similar reformist parties, and a declaration of wariness also about the aims and ambitions of revolutionary political parties. The

IWW's notion of revolution was different: the emancipation of the work-ing class had to be achieved by the workers themselves, acting as workers, through the One Big Union assuming control of the means of produc-tion, distribution and exchange. Parties, whether reformist or revolu-tionary in intent, could not achieve change on the workers' behalf. *Direct Action* frequently sported above its front-page logo Marx's famous maxim: 'The Emancipation of the Workers Must be Achieved by the Working Class Itself.'[49] It took extremely seriously Marx's advice that there was none better to break the chains than those who wore them.

Revolutionary parliamentary political parties were an impossibility: 'Politicians must, of absolute necessity, become conservative. Their very jobs demand it. Their very lives prove it . . .' A revolutionary party, the IWW insisted, would, if engaged in parliamentary activity, 'become as conservative and corrupt as all their predecessors'.[50] The very fact of a socialist party getting into office would convince the capitalists that the older parties were no longer competent to protect business interests; property owners would transfer their support to the new party in office and the Socialist Party would in consequence become the party of a united capitalism, and would have to protect the interests and solve the problems of capitalism. The Socialist Party was destined to go the same way as the Labor Party, destined to become the sport and plaything of middle-class property owners and exploiters, its 'revolutionary' spirit becoming smothered in reforms and palliatives.[51] Socialist parties were no exception to the iron law of conservatism for political parties: all political parties become less radical as they begin to capture political offices, 'and when they really capture political power they are always conservative'.[52]

This categorical rejection of the role of political parties in the revolu-tionary process was informed also by the IWW's own experience with attempts by organised revolutionary groups to 'capture' the IWW as their industrial wing. The IWW not only guarded its independence jeal-ously, ferociously even, but clearly resented the inference that could be made from parties' attempts to use the IWW for their own purposes that the IWW did not cover all the needs of the working class.[53] On the con-trary, only the IWW was all-sufficient, because it combined the propaga-tion of correct political ideas with practical industrial organisation. The IWW was, as Mick Sawtell pointed out, something more than a mere pro-paganda group.[54] The IWW hoped to persuade workers not to listen to those who saw salvation in parliament or party, but to trust to themselves alone, through the One Big Union, the task of ending capitalism and establishing the cooperative commonwealth.

Direct Action commented scornfully that socialist parties often accused the IWW of reformism because it advocated a six-hour working day. The

SLP, in particular, disputed the value to workers of reforms under capitalism; the IWW, on the other hand, insisted that, while it was a revolutionary movement, it nevertheless believed in reform, even petty reform,
'but the reform we stand for starts with the pay envelope and job conditions and winds up with the whole works. . . . the full product of our
labor'. Reforms, the IWW warned, could not be won from within the parliamentary process; where reforms were conceded by politicians it was
due to pressure, militant working-class activity, at the point of production.[55] *The Immediate Demands of the I.W.W.* maintained that the first step in
the revolutionary process was to make immediate demands in regard to
wages, hours and conditions and to fight for them; and the building of
industrial unions to serve as organs of production and distribution in
the new society, the ultimate function of the IWW, was the second step.[56]

This strategy marked an important difference between the two wings
of the IWW and helps explain the greater success of the Chicago section.
For the De Leonite IWW rejected the struggle for immediate demands,
'mere palliatives', and insisted instead on raising the necessarily rather
abstract demand for the immediate realisation of socialism. To the
Chicago IWW, starting with material issues was common sense because
'the easiest and most natural way to begin the attack upon the employers
is to demand the abolition of abuses which even the dullest worker cannot fail to see'. Memory of this victory would provoke new demands and
each little battle strengthen the organisation and build a revolutionary
movement by the changing consciousness of the workers in struggle.
These immediate demands for improved conditions, shorter hours and
better pay were the rallying cries by means of which the IWW could wake
up the dormant mind of the average worker, educating and mobilising
him for efforts of a higher order such as building the new society.[57]

The importance of gaining reforms lay in the relief obtained, however
slight, from the effects of exploitation and the psychological effects such
advances had on the workers concerned. The amelioration, even under
capitalism, of the material exploitation of the proletariat was regarded as
progress. Any diminution in surplus value extracted, any betterment of
pay and conditions, was an advance and a step towards ultimate victory.
Similarly, any deterioration was a set-back, because 'exploitation in its
manifold insidious forms, goes on sucking the life blood of the workers,
crippling the men, ruining the women, and slowly murdering the children'. The crushing experience of exploitation was the key to all forms of
oppression endured by the working class. All social evils, such as drink,
crime, prostitution, poverty, disease and war, the IWW insisted, could be
traced ultimately to the fact of exploitation of one class by another. Such
evils helped keep the working class in subjection, so any economic reform was both a material and social benefit that would aid proletarian

self-activity. Revolutions, the IWW insisted, were not made by a demoralised and beaten working class, but by a working class on the offensive, continually making demands on their employers. The winning of reforms was both valuable in itself and valuable as a morale-booster.[58] The IWW, then, was not hostile to reforms as reforms, as long as these were not regarded as sufficient palliative, these crumbs not viewed as the entire loaf.

The tactical emphasis on reforms notwithstanding, the IWW remained adamant that a 'world set free' could only be achieved through a revolutionary reconstruction of society. It could be argued that it was only the tactics of the syndicalists, illegal direct action, that were revolutionary; their aims fell far short of the elaborate IWW plans for the complete reconstruction of society. As the Adelaide Local's sticker declared: 'One Enemy: The Employing Class. One Goal: Complete Industrial Control.'[59] It was, in fact, the IWW's concept of how this revolution would occur that made the battle for reforms an important component in the revolutionary process. For this battle for immediate demands, for reforms achieved through industrial action, was 'the cement which gradually binds us together into the unions forming that structure', the One Big Union, which would form the framework of the new society within the shell of the old.[60]

Reform and revolution were intimately connected for the IWW, precisely because the revolution was to be the result, not of a forcible seizure of state power nor the winning of an election, but of mass proletarian organisation. The building of the One Big Union presupposed the formation of the proletariat as a class for itself, a process dependent upon the propagation of class-conscious ideas and their successful application in class struggle. An insistence on the mutual interdependence of class consciousness and class struggle lay at the heart of the IWW strategy for revolution. Correct theory and successful practice in the winning of reforms encouraged the organisation of the workers into One Big Union, and this One Big Union was, in essence, the revolution itself. The general strike, during which the working class would calmly assume control of the means of production, distribution and exchange, merely celebrated the completion of the revolution; it would prove that the proletariat had reached the ultimate stage of organisation, the One Big Union, and was thus ready and able to take control of society. For the syndicalists, the general strike would produce the revolution; for the IWW, the revolution, the successful organisation of the class into the One Big Union, would produce the general strike. Thus, IWW theory, like that of Rosa Luxemburg,[61] did not accord the general strike the cataclysmic role apportioned it in syndicalist theory. Of far greater importance was the necessary attainment first of absolute working-class unity in the One Big Union.

The revolution was therefore the outcome of organisation – at all levels:

> the workers can drive away the shirkers and take real possession and control of the world's resources only by beginning at the bottom, that is, by *organizing on the job*, by making one immediate demand on top of another, and thus gradually *growing into control* of the industries and throwing off the control of the shirkers . . .
>
> The road to our emancipation is paved with 'immediate demands' successfully fought for, and not 'revolutionary' phrases or political dogmas. Real control of the industries is gained, not by means of bayonets held by our hands, but by means of knowledge held by our brains and by intelligently organized and co-ordinated industrial action . . .[62]

The additional and final paragraph of the Chicago 1908 Preamble declared:

> It is the historic mission of the working class to do away with capitalism. The army of production must be organised, not only for the every-day struggle with capitalists, but also to carry on production when capitalism shall have been overthrown. By organising industrially we are forming the structure of the new society within the shell of the old.[63]

The hope of the future lay in industrial organisation, not the activity of a few representatives in parliament. Only one big union of all workers regardless of sex, creed or colour, would guarantee the abolition of wage slavery and the ushering in of the new society.[64] The IWW 'seeks the abolition of the present system of production and distribution, with all its misery and suffering for the millions who toil, introducing in its place an Industrial Democracy of peace and plenty for all'.[65]

The central administration of the One Big Union would form the future central government of this Industrial Democracy; the departments and locals were the future subordinate governing agencies.[66] Does it not follow, the IWW asserted rhetorically, that after the workers have secured control of industry, their organisation will provide them with all the necessary machinery to handle the problems of the new society?[67] Rushton argues that the IWW was 'blissfully ignorant that the implementation of such an administrative structure would have demanded a bureaucracy surpassing in size and complexity any state structure which then existed'.[68] On the contrary, the IWW argued forcefully that the organisation of the future would be relatively simple because the exploitation of one class by another would be ended, and so the systematic repression of the majority, the main purpose of the state in capitalist society, would not be necessary.

The new society would replace the government of people with the administration of things; the Industrial Unions, the nucleus of the future society, required in its leaders *administrative abilities* only.[69] Tom Glynn explained: 'The I.W.W. does not seek to "rule", that is, it has no ambition to govern people; but we desire to establish the administration and government of the economic resources which were meant by nature, not for the enrichment of the few, but the welfare of all.'[70] The future society would require comparatively little organisation, since it would be devoid of the exploitative relationships that necessitated elaborate systems of control in the present society. With the war of the classes over, society would be able to revert back to communism, its natural state:

> Authority, with its costly machinery, parasitism, oppression, incompetence, and injustice, must then rapidly dwindle into insignificance. No longer will we need huge penal establishments and judicial bludgers . . . the domination of one section of the community will not be possible, and society will be just, because it is lawless.[71]

The future parliaments would be the union meetings.[72] In these days of the One Big Union there would be democracy, majority rule, for differences of opinion would always exist; in fact, there would be more rather than less democracy after the organisation of society along OBU lines:

> In the new order of society . . . workers can afford the utmost divergence and difference of opinion; every view-point may have free play: so long as all agree on this one vital principle, namely: That Production shall continue to be carried on for the use and benefit of the working class, and not for the profit of a few capitalists, as at present.

But, *Direct Action*, acknowledged, in the unlikely event that the majority wished to revert to capitalism, it would be open for them to do so.[73]

In this new society, there would be a place for former capitalists; it was the 'historical mission' of the IWW 'to put the Australian boss into hobnails and overalls'.[74] The Wobbly response to the argument that the capitalist contributed to the production of wealth was: 'The Capitalist produces nothing and should get all he produces.' Some 'brainwork' was necessary in industry, the IWW conceded, but this could in the future society be provided by true experts, properly qualified people suited to oversee certain tasks such as engineers and other technical experts whose skills deserved respect, whose temporary, invited authority in a workplace would be based on something substantial, unlike the arbitrary, imposed and unnecessary authority of the boss in capitalist society.[75] In making this distinction between spurious authority and real authority, the IWW reasoned like Bakunin in *God and the State*.[76]

Ideally, the transition to this lawless, because classless, society would be effected peaceably since the level of organisation reached in the One Big Union should ensure that violence would not be necessary. As a prisoner on trial in Western Australia in 1916, Mick Sawtell insisted: 'By revolution we do not mean bloodshed. We workers have seen enough of that business in the French Revolution and in the Commune.' Revolutions could be of a peaceful order, without any violence. Sawtell maintained this position not only for public consumption but in private correspondence.[77] *Direct Action* was adamant:

> A working class organisation which depends upon the use of violence for the furthering of its objects is unscientific, antiquated and dangerous.
> . . . Far mightier than the might of the master class, with all their machinery of oppression, is the power the working class possess in Industrial Organisation. Better far than the bomb and the bullet, is the war of the folded arms. In this battle no life need be lost, no blood need be spilt. The power of One Big Union of the working class can stop all capitalist violence and bring the captains of industry to their knees . . .[78]

If, however, the employers dismissed from their posts retaliated with armed resistance, then the revolution would be defended by a brief dictatorship of the proletariat; but it would be a dictatorship exercised not through a central committee of a revolutionary party but by the workers themselves. In this situation the One Big Union would become, at its moment of triumph only, the ruling class: 'it will only be a "ruling" class for a moment – just long enough to make sure of victory'. This temporary formation of the proletariat as ruling class would then abolish classes altogether, and let the former capitalists, defeated, come into the industries – to work.[79]

The IWW definitively abjured Bolshevik activity, a forcible seizure of state power by a revolutionary party. And it rejected such a strategy in the name of historical materialism, basing its position on classically Marxist lines. In a remarkably prescient passage, *The Immediate Demands of the I.W.W.* warned:

> the law of economic necessity is such a vital factor in our life that *no limited group of men or political party can abolish wage slavery by merely conspiring or co-operating to capture the political offices and the government buildings.* Such procedure would only give the people *a new master, a bureaucratic autocracy* . . .

It deplored the very notion of revolution from above: 'the dogma and theory-bound movements of political socialism which would reconstruct society from the top downward in accordance with programs expressing the special economic urge of the would-be leaders of the working class in revolution, instead of the economic urge behind the mass of the workers . . .'[80]

The IWW, unlike the Bolsheviks, did not believe that the vanguard could give history a push. It wished to act upon industrial and social conditions, but only in accord with the general tendency of economic development and only with the workers themselves, not their delegates, actively involved in the revolutionary process: the formation of One Big Union.

CHAPTER 5

'We, the Hoboes': who were the Wobblies?

There are many theories about the origin of the term 'Wobbly'. One legend ascribes it to a Chinese restaurant-keeper on the American West Coast who agreed to feed some IWW strikers. When he tried to ask: 'Are you IWW?' the nearest he could manage was: 'All loo eye wobble wobble?' Thereafter the laughing term among them was 'I Wobbly Wobbly'. Another authority argues that a possible derivation is from the 'wobble saw', a circular saw mounted askew to cut a groove wider than its own thickness. Whatever its precise etymology, it has been used to imply, literally, wobblyness.[1] Similarly, the character of the Wobbly has been impugned by the wilful misinterpretations placed upon the acronym, such as 'I Won't Work', 'I Want Whiskey' and 'Irresponsible Wholesale Wreckers'. Unstable, disreputable, work-shy was the assessment of the movement's denigrators; the Wobblies themselves replied with the refrain, 'Hallelujah, I'm a Bum', and embraced the hobo stereotype of themselves.

However, the characteristics of the Wobbly that to their enemies signified instability meant to the Wobblies themselves the steadiness of solidarity and class consciousness. Tom Barker, after attacking the spinelessness of the Second International, wrote:

> Let us get to work, we of the Industrial Workers of the World, we, the countryless, the pariahs, the hobos, the migratory workers. Let us throw off . . . the pusillanimity of political sentimentalists . . . Economic conditions are bringing us together in spite of ourselves . . . We, the workers of the world, are dependent upon one another.[2]

To Barker, the nomadic male worker, in the fact that he had really nothing to lose, epitomised strength not weakness, steadfastness not wobblyness.

A long historiographical tradition has drawn a picture of the Wobblies as homeless drifters, migratory unskilled labourers, a caricature sketched as early as 1917 by Wobbly historian, Vincent St John.[3] To the Wobblies and their sympathisers in the academy, their social standing, their outcast status, was in itself indictment of the society that produced them and the IWW's very good reason for political being; to liberal historians the temptation to romanticise via caricature was great and the end-product similar to that also drawn by conservative historians, to whom the Wobbly as social flotsam and jetsam was a convenient image to obscure the point of their political protest. The hobo stereotype has persisted because it has served varied purposes: to belittle the Wobbly and to dismiss their criticism; or to proclaim that in the dispossessed status of the membership, in the essential accuracy of the hobo caricature, lay the true strength and vitality of the movement and the source of its distinctive morality and incorruptibility.

From the establishment viewpoint, the hobo image was used to discredit the IWW, to obviate any need to respond to its criticisms of an unjust status quo. If the Wobblies can be classified as bums, less attention need be paid to their protest, just as modern-day urban riots can be ignored if those responsible are deemed 'riff-raff'. The result is to stereotype dissent as criminal or pointless and thereby to neutralise its impact.[4] Refusing to concede the point of any protest, Perlman argued in 1922 that the IWW was a sort of pathology, interesting but essentially aberrant.[5] Similarly, but from a more tolerant perspective, Carleton Parker concluded that whatever success the IWW enjoyed could be explained primarily in terms of its providing camaraderie and status for socially and psychologically alienated and isolated workers:

> To the great wandering rank and file, the I.W.W. is simply the only social break in the harsh search for work they have ever had, its headquarters the only competitor of the saloon in which they are welcome . . . The American I.W.W. is a neglected and lonely hobo worker, usually malnourished and in need of medical care.[6]

Dubofsky refined this 'culture of poverty' theory. IWW recruits in America were Marx's *Lumpenproletariat*, 'individuals who felt marginal, helpless, dependent, inferior'. These disinherited joined the IWW because it promised the 'social break' identified by Parker. More importantly, it promised its followers also a way out of their 'culture of poverty', offering them identification with larger social groups that might destroy the psychological and social core of their marginality, dependence and impotence.[7]

Historians of the Wobblies elsewhere tend towards similar conclusions. Walter Galenson's work on the Scandinavian IWWs argues they made inroads in these countries, especially Norway, which was being transformed from an agricultural into an industrial economy, because its uprooted workers were similar to the migrating workers of the American IWW, 'men divorced from the stabilizing influence of permanent employment, property ownership, home life, social status, and the conventional forms of approbation, men who saw no reason why they should feel indebted to the established order of things and were ready to fight capitalism with the first weapons to hand'.[8] In New Zealand, Erik Olssen describes the IWW audience as living in the mining towns, the timber camps, the flax mills, the shearing sheds, on the coalfields and on the wharves. The IWW's growth in Auckland, he explains, owed much to that city's uniqueness: its disproportionately male, young and single population. 'Auckland shared with the mining towns the demographic characteristics of a rapidly expanding frontier. The pubs, brothels, gambling dens, and street life of the inner-city reflect the predominance of single young men.'[9]

Much that has been written about the Australian Wobblies echoes American literature, and, like the American literature, draws heavily on the local Wobblies' own accounts, which confirm to a large extent the hobo stereotype. Bill Beattie claims: 'The bulk of our membership was composed of bush and construction workers who travelled by necessity.'[10] Tom Barker explained:

> We had the Home Guard, from Sydney, but most of the members worked in the country, came into Sydney from time to time, took out their card, and would take a bundle of papers and sell them wherever they went. Often they worked as miners until the shearing season came, then went up to North Queensland, started to shear and followed the sun until they got down to Victoria, which was quite a long time . . . The same applied to gold miners from the West. They'd come over and perhaps go to Broken Hill, Broken Hill was a strong I.W.W. town. In North Queensland from Cloncurry to the copper belt the bulk of working people were indoctrinated or associated with the I.W.W. philosophy.

Reminiscent of the 'social break' argument, Barker argued that the IWW could be said to have come about in a time when it was absolutely essential:

> That was a time of great unemployment, backward industry and vast movements of working people, especially single men. Migratory people looked for support when they came to a new place and if they found an I.W.W. branch they knew they were amongst friends, and that created a solidarity of spirit that was something more than words. It was the fact that wherever there was an I.W.W. branch you could go there for friendship and help and also to get on to a job.[11]

Here, he recalls the IWW as a kind of politicised substitute, in a period of social turmoil, for the traditional masculine fraternity of the bush. The IWW rooms, Childe concedes, offered members the advantages of a club.[12]

Childe notes that the programme of the IWW was drawn up to meet the needs of the semi-skilled nomadic worker of the western United States; in Australia there was a precisely similar class, the unskilled worker who roved about the bush to mines or railway-construction works, harvesting cane and grain or picking fruit, or taking casual employment in meatworks or shearing sheds. Childe suggests that, whereas workers with a relative certainty of regular employment, with opportunities for material acquisition, were not likely to be the revolutionaries Marx assumed, the itinerant class of worker approximated more closely to the ideal proletarian described by Marx, who 'has almost literally nothing to lose but the chains that bind him, and nothing to sell but his simple labour-power'.[13] Churchward, too, stresses that, though there was no section of the Australian workforce equivalent to the disenfranchised immigrant workers of the United States, there were similar economic conditions experienced by many Australians in mining and outback occupations such as timber-getting and construction works. And it was amongst such workers that the IWW achieved its greatest support in both countries.[14] Military intelligence observed that IWW influence in the Queensland meatworks was strongest in the freezing departments, the less skilled areas of employment that hired itinerant workers; the more skilled workers in the killing departments, engaged every season and domiciled in the district, were comparatively untainted by IWW ideas.[15]

Rushton incorporates the Wobblies into the Australian Legend. Russel Ward had argued that the mores of the nomadic rural proletariat worked upwards and outwards until they became the principal ingredient of a national mystique: contempt for middle-class virtues such as sobriety, industry, formal education and religious observance; loyalty to one's mates; and antagonism towards authority. The Australian Wobblies, Rushton claims, not only recruited many of their members from amongst the descendants of these 'nomadic tribesmen', but manifested many of the attitudes and values of the national culture-heroes: Ned Kelly, the jolly swagman camped by the billabong, Peter Lalor, Private Simpson and Henry Lawson. 'A predominantly masculine society the I.W.W. adopted a consistent pose of extreme toughness, was possessed of a biting humour and developed a strong in-group loyalty. Mateship was highly regarded; the scab and the pimp were detested.'[16] Tom McMillan wrote of the Port Pirie free speech fight:

We are hoboes and scamps and tired tramps,
But we love our Union well;
Our spirit won't fail, we will die in gaol,
And smile in the flames of hell.[17]

Alf Wilson commented to a friend concerned that his Wobbly views would bring him into trouble with the authorities: 'when they attack me I will let them know that I lived for a while in the Kelly country'.[18]

The peripatetic Wobbly was undoubtedly real. Tom Audley recalls that Bill Casey, who wrote 'Bump Me Into Parliament', was 'a real hobo type'.[19] Bill Jackson's nickname was Hobo.[20] Guido Baracchi explained in 1941 that, in living with her fellow-Wobbly Pat Harford, Lesbia Keogh assisted him to 'more stable living conditions which, having passed through a period of "hoboing", she felt he urgently needed'.[21] *Direct Action* ran frequent reports from Wobblies 'on the track', which typically contained tales of a cowed boss quickly conceding the demands of the group of Wobblies he had unwittingly hired: 'The boss started to squeal. We all told him to go to hell. So he left us in peace. We also demanded a half-hour for crib instead of twenty minutes.'[22]

Wobblies did not last long on jobs, with the result that they and their propaganda became dispersed and circulated all over the continent. When Jimmy Seamer, a union activist during the First World War, was asked whether the Wobblies moved about a lot, he commented: 'Yeah, and they was pushed about, too.'[23] Most Wobblies had little to lose and were immured to such loss. The IWW recognised necessity:

To be 'fired' simply means a change of jobs, and a change is good for all. It is not good to be in one job too many years. It has a tendency to make one too contented. The more one roams around, the more experience he gets, and he is more fitted to fight the industrial battle.[24]

Unemployment, too, the search for a master, had a similar effect. For instance, early in 1916, some Wobblies left Broken Hill for the Mildura area in search of fruit-picking work. They reported that: 'At every fair sized camp along the road, animated discussions took place upon the I.W.W., its methods, principles and objective, and many wise guys, of many years standing in many unions, freely expressed their disapproval of the A.W.U. and labour politicians and endorsed the direct action policy of the I.W.W.' All along the route, stickers and IWW mottoes appeared. 'The I.W.W. has sure got some live supporters and barrackers in the back country.'[25]

Military intelligence stressed the nuisance value of the wandering Wobbly, the peculiar advantages of the hobo as agitator fomenting discontent: 'Quinton, being a canvasser for insurance business (State Insurance Office) travels over a considerable area of the Darling Downs country; therefore has special opportunities for spreading the teachings of the I.W.W.'[26] Reporting on trouble in the northern canefields in 1918, the censor noted: 'Shepard and others of the I.W.W. gang appear to carry a good stock of literature with them – they are always on the move and they disseminate their criminal doctrines at every halting place.' The censor referred to Norman Jeffery as one of the many members of the IWW 'touring the country disseminating, by their soap box orations, the doctrine which our Government . . . has thought fit to denounce'.[27] There are, indeed, numerous examples of the mobile Wobbly agitator, fanning the flames of discontent the length and breadth of the continent, roaming because their limited skills could not secure them stable, urban employment.[28]

May Brodney claims the IWW appealed particularly to the carefree characteristics of Australian seasonal workers. It was for this reason, according to Bertha Walker, that the IWW was comparatively weak in Melbourne. 'Melbourne & its revolutionaries were rather too respectable for the IWW. Sydney & Brisbane were centres for itinerant workers that worked all over the State. They were of a more restless & less staid character.' Writing from the perspective of the staid and respectable Melbourne socialist movement, Walker avers that the weakness of the IWW was that its members were mainly nomadic, 'not closely knit to trade unions and industry in any consolidating way'. The lack of such association encouraged the popularity of adventurist ideas such as sabotage and currency debasement.[29]

Bertha Walker exaggerates the alienation of the Wobbly hobo from, and his atypicality within, the labour movement of the time. The Australian Wobblies, whether hobo or otherwise, were ordinary. Whether the American accounts are right or wrong, factually, in stressing the hobo characteristics of the Wobblies, they all tend to have in mind a social aberration, whether revered, mythologised or despised. In Australian society in the second decade of this century, hoboes were still commonplace, normal; the itinerant worker was the stuff of union politics, not neglected by it, his demands accepted as legitimate as those made by less itinerant and more formally skilled sections of the workforce.

Far from being neglected by Australian unionism as their American equivalents were by the AFL, these nomads were amongst its strongest supporters and were especially active in the new unions formed around the turn of the century. If they died on the track, their union cards identified their remains. Within the context of the labour movement, the type from which many Wobblies came was more mainstream than in the

United States. As Jack Crampton declared to the Third Annual State Conference of the Queensland branch of the AMIEU in 1914:

> Even today we find the nomad assisting to carve out the destiny of the more militant of our industrial associations. The strength of many a union to-day is the result of the work of the rambler . . . It is farcical to speak to these of the loss sustained by a stoppage of work. They are always stopping, their work is intermittent; being such, they become independent and self-reliant.[30]

The nomad had a revered standing within the Australian labour movement; his American equivalent was an outcast and cast out by the institutions of the labour movement there.

In any case, the stereotype, caricatured so heavily in the literature and revered also in song and story by Wobblies themselves, deserves qualification. Examination of the minute books of the Broken Hill Local reveals that this Local, composed of miners settled at least for the moment, flourished as a solid and stable institutional form: for instance, one of the duties of the management committee was to go to the local hospital every alternate Sunday to visit sick fellow workers and deliver their copies of *Direct Action*.[31] Shor has argued that the Broken Hill Local affords a corrective to those who saw the IWW as a loose affiliation of migratory militants; he draws a picture of a more extensive and community-based membership, albeit in a rather intensive and, perhaps, atypical setting of working-class solidarity and militancy. By the end of 1916 the Broken Hill Local included over one hundred members; even after the jailing of a significant portion of its membership, the Broken Hill IWW had both an organisational life and identity that guaranteed its social significance.[32]

Apart from a signalman from Port Kembla, all those who formed the Sydney Local in 1911, who attended the first meeting and signed the list going to Adelaide, gave inner-city addresses: sixteen in the central business district (one of these in an hotel), two in Darlinghurst, two in Paddington and one in Surry Hills.[33] When the police raided the Sydney Local headquarters on 23 September 1916 they obtained 'documentary evidence' with which they compiled a list of 1091 members of the IWW, with addresses and occupations, which they duly forwarded to military intelligence. From studying the residential addresses on this list it is evident that there are two common categories of Wobbly: the itinerant worker; and the stationary worker living in the inner city. Of the 1091 on the list, 102 appeared to be of no fixed abode, giving country or city post offices as their address or declining to give any address at all. In addition, many gave vague addresses such as the twelve who were from 'Linda Valley, Tasmania'. Others gave more definite country, country town or inter-State addresses. Moreover, it is likely that many of the urban addresses proffered were boarding houses for transients in town for a while. Otherwise, it is apparent that most Wobblies lived in the inner-most suburbs, such as Redfern, Woolloomooloo, Surry Hills, Glebe, Newtown, Annandale and Balmain, and many in the city area itself. Four lived in the IWW hall in Castlereagh Street. Only a smattering lived further afield in places such as Strathfield and Bondi.[34] Many Wobblies would have been lost in the bush, as useless with green hide and stringy bark as city-bred craft unionists.

These qualifications notwithstanding, the itinerant Wobbly formed a real and significant portion of the membership for the simple reason that this membership was drawn disproportionately from the less skilled of the working class. The IWW, *Direct Action* announced,

> carries on its agitation principally amongst the unskilled workers. By organis-ing the lowest paid workers and gaining better conditions for them, it has the tendency to force the higher paid grades and 'aristocrats of labor' to get busy and fight for more concessions if they would keep ahead of the 'common labourer'.[35]

Fred Coombe claims that it was from 'right amongst the working class' that the IWW gained its support, from 'the hard workers', such as labour-ers and miners.[36]

Of those who formed the Sydney Local in 1911, there were nine labourers, four wharfies, three miners, two wireworkers, one gardener, one shearer, one glazier and one signalman.[37] By the end of 1911, this Local had eighty-nine signed-up members, of the following occupa-tional groupings: thirty-five labourers, eight miners, seven seamen, five wharfies, three gardeners, three timber-getters, two carpenters, two engineers, two stonemasons, two bakers, two shearers, and one painter, canvasser, tinsmith, signalman, glazier, wireworker, dental mechanic, boilermaker, painter and docker, engine-driver, conductor, automobile-driver, carter, fitter, elevator operator and hairdresser.[38] Though the list compiled by police after the September 1916 raid used broader cate-gories than the earlier lists, it is apparent nonetheless that the occupa-tional breakdown is similar, the vast majority being in unskilled or semi-skilled employment. Well over a third of the men (375) classified themselves as a labourer. There were 42 wharfies, 66 miners, 56 seamen, 44 firemen (including ship and railway firemen), 35 factory workers, 69 building workers, 55 metal workers, 71 transport workers, 55 hotel and retail trade workers, 13 rural workers and 8 postal workers. There were 92 skilled workers, such as fitters, electricians, plumbers, mechanics, printers and cabinet-makers. There was a sculptor, a musician and two vaudeville artists and a few non-manual workers – a school teacher, six public servants, seven clerks and one draughtsman. Of the twenty females on this list, seven were employed in the clothing trade, two were public servants, there was one laundress, one typist, one governess, one housekeeper, one labourer and one clerk; two gave their occupation as 'married woman', and three others, presumably of a similar calling, declined to give any occupation.[39]

It is the predominantly unskilled calling of IWW workers, rather than the category of itineracy, that most clearly defines the membership. All unskilled workers were subject to the threat, at least, of enforced instability, of the possible need to go up-country to find work. The extent to which they could afford to stay in the cities and towns depended on the availability of work there or the amount of money they could save from their previous employment in the country. Most preferred the urban environment but were resigned to stints of varying length in the country. The occupation of 'labourer', so common in Wobbly records, denoted precisely the kind of worker who could be forced to work wherever it was available: a migratory worker by necessity but often also finding work of a more settled kind, a wandering fruit-picker in the summer, a navvy on a Sydney building site in winter. It was the vagaries of employment, the uncertainties determining the life of unskilled workers generally in this period, that give substance to the hobo stereotype.

Another distinctive characteristic was the Wobbly as foreigner. A stereotype grossly exaggerated during the war years by those to whom the IWW now meant Imperial Wilhelm's Warriors, it bore nonetheless a relationship to reality. If a significant proportion of the membership in general belonged to the nomads of the domestic labour movement, a significant proportion of the most public propagandists of the movement hailed from another geographically dispossessed tribe, the internationally itinerant, the globe-trotting troublemaker, who featured prominently also in the socialist groups of the time.

However, where Tom Mann and Ben Tillett had become public figures via their activity as trade union officials before migration, Wobbly 'leaders' such as Charlie Reeve, Tom Barker, J.B. King and Tom Glynn were simply trade union activists experienced in the labour movements of other Anglophone parts of the planet, thanks to the lack of restrictions on movement within the British Empire. These were men whose principal reference point was, in theory and in practice, the world and its workers. In jail in 1921, Reeve confessed how his thoughts always strayed to the Domain at 3 o'clock on Sundays: 'I am there with you, at my beloved meetings, rubbing shoulders with Men from all parts of the World, and can feel the unspoken wish and determination to strive for a better world. With all their faults, I love my class.'[40]

Tom Barker, one of the globetrotting agitators who helped the IWW achieve notoriety in Australian society. (Brodney Collection, LT10882/2)

Reeve, King and Glynn we have already met. Tom Barker was born at Crosthwaite in Westmoreland, England, in 1887, of Lakeland farming stock. He went to work as a farm worker at 11, then to Liverpool at about 14 to work in a milkhouse. In 1905 he joined the army, training young horses, took an army certificate of education and became a lance corporal. Invalided with slight heart trouble in 1908, he worked on the Liverpool railways, 60 hours a week, for 25 shillings. In June 1909 he emigrated to New Zealand, joining the tramway company in Auckland as a conductor. In 1911 he became secretary of the branch of the New Zealand Socialist Party, but left around New Year 1912/13. Sacked from the tramways, he went organising for the IWW and became involved in the general strike of 1913, three charges of sedition being laid against him. Regarded as the key figure of the IWW, he was imprisoned in Wellington in January 1914 then placed under a £1500 bond. He came to Sydney in February 1914.[41]

Of the seventy-five Wobblies prosecuted under the Unlawful Associations Act during September 1917, twenty-seven were born overseas, mostly in the British Isles. Of the Sydney Twelve, whose arrest and trial are described in chapter 13, only John Hamilton from Victoria and Bill Teen from Tasmania had been born in Australia. Three were from England (Reeve, Besant, Beatty); two from Ireland (Glynn, Larkin); two from Scotland (McPherson, Grant); one from New Zealand (Moore); one from Canada (King); and one from Russia (Fagin). In addition to Fagin, a glazier who arrived in Sydney in 1910 via Wales and the United States and had been a member of the Socialist Party of America, there were many other continental Europeans. Russians, Bulgarians and Italians in particular formed ethnic networks within the IWW; there were a number of German- or Austrian-born members, too, some of whom were interned enemy aliens, a matter of considerable concern to the authorities.[42]

The Wobblies were proud of their polyglot membership. Fellow-Worker Shannessey declared at a meeting on the beach at Townsville in August 1917: 'We are accused of being foreigners and I can tell you we have some very good foreigners amongst us too. . . .'[43] Non-Anglophone Wobblies were clearly a minority nonetheless. Of the eighty-nine members in the Sydney Local by the end of 1911, fifteen had continental European names. Three presented American dues cards; another three had transferred from Auckland Local. Most of the surnames and given names on the list of 1091 obtained in 1916 were Anglo-Celtic names, including fifty-six 'Mac' or 'Mc' names and sixteen 'O' names and many other clearly Irish ones such as Maloney or Murphy; there were eighty-four names signifying the bearers were likely to be of continental European origin, mainly Scandinavian or German, of whom ten gave their occupation as seaman.[44]

Wobblies were less likely than other labour movement activists to be religious. Against the prevailing orthodoxy, Donald Winters contends that religious impulses were significant amongst American Wobblies; whatever the truth of the matter, Winters' revisionist arguments certainly do not apply to the Australian Wobblies. Of the Sydney Twelve, five said they had no religion (Reeve, Hamilton, McPherson, Fagin, King); four said they were Roman Catholic (Glynn, Larkin, Besant, Teen); two said they were Church of England (Beatty, Moore); one said he was Presbyterian

(Grant). Of the eight Wobblies arrested initially in Perth and subsequently tried, seven were agnostic, atheistic or of no religion; Alex Horrocks was Church of England.[45] There is no evidence, however, that those who gave themselves a denominational category were anything other than lapsed. Fred Coombe, who joined before the First World War, confirms that Wobblies were suspicious of religion and believed it was 'getting workers on the wrong track'. Reeve, in particular, was an aggressive atheist with the utmost contempt for ministers of religion: 'If priests and parsons wore their trousers back to front as they do their collars, there would be less illegitimates in the world.'[46]

As an organisation, the IWW was hostile to the churches. *Direct Action* denounced the 'coquetting' of Labor MPs with the Catholic Church.[47] When the Presbyterian Moderator in New South Wales assured workers that their real wages would yet be paid by God, Tom Glynn commented that 'the mission of the Church is pretty well now what it was in the beginning, and ever shall be: To induce the workers to accept a blank cheque on eternity. THEY'LL GET PIE IN THE SKY WHEN THEY DIE.'[48] It was a lie, the Wobblies protested. When the Victorian Labor Party objected to the *Direct Action* cartoon depicting the worker crucified on a gun, the editor complained that it was more easily offended by a travesty upon the crucifixion of a religious fanatic 2000 years ago than by the present-day crucifixion of millions of wages slaves.[49] Occasionally, like socialist groups of the time, the IWW made a distinction between Christianity and Churchianity. The Broken Hill Local resolved to purchase for its library *Life of Jesus* for 2 shillings but also *That Great Lying Church of England* for 2/6d.[50] In 1917, Fellow-Worker Randolph declared from a stump in Broken Hill that, if Jesus were around, he would be in the IWW and not in the Salvation Army; he was arrested and charged with 'shocking expression'.

Norman Rancie preferred a neutral position on religion, fearing division would otherwise be introduced into the ranks of the labour movement. Religion, he insisted, was a question for the individual, having as much connection with the working-class movement as the man in the moon:

> The I.W.W. does not attack religion – it never did and it never intends to – it has something more important to do . . . The I.W.W. as an organisation does not interfere with the private beliefs of any member, so long as they do not conflict with the principles of industrial solidarity. The battles of the working class will never be won under the banner of any religious sect, neither can victory be achieved under the flag of atheism.[51]

In practice, the IWW did attack religion, at least in its institutional forms. Its derisive parodying of religious musical forms clearly signalled rejection of the religious content. It was not difficult for the enemies of the IWW to brand it as godless, and few Wobblies shared Rancie's concern about this image. Rancie is right, however, that the IWW did not expend inordinate energy in attacking religion. More specifically, as we shall see in chapter 9, it waged war against bourgeois notions of respectability, the unwritten codes of social conduct that contained and constrained working-class behaviour, defining what was right and wrong in terms that suited the exploiters of that class.

Many Wobblies, like the socialists of the time, were readers. P.J. O'Farrell writes of the Australian IWW that it recruited 'the self educated workman with his elementary library of books on history and philosophy, his enthusiasm for "useful learning", his dislike of authority, and his sanguine or emotional belief in the perfectability of man'. Fred Coombe confirms that the other Wobblies he encountered were 'all well-read', that they had read Marx and Engels in particular. Charlie Reeve, according to Bluey Howells, 'revealed a love for and knowledge of the Humanities' and 'was capable of giving faithful résumés of the writings of Carlyle, Tolstoy, Voltaire, William Morris, Thomas Paine . . .' Alf Wilson's memoirs depict his obsession with building a library. However, due to their straitened and often less than stable circumstances, Wobblies were often restricted in their access to literature, obliged to share their reading matter or use public libraries extensively. Tom Payne recalls the autodidactic nature of Mark Anthony, a Wobbly who had left Clunes to work in Broken Hill: 'Mark Anthony was a very brilliant intellectual though he came from a working-class family. If anyone wanted him they would try the Broken Hill library.'[52]

Most Locals had a library of appropriate books and newspapers on their premises. The Fremantle Local, for instance, boasted 'a library of up-to-date revolutionary economic working class literature . . . , and all rebels after some mental dynamite are invited to blow in and help swell the ranks of the rebel army'.[53] The rebels blowing in would come across left-wing classics such as Paul Lafargue, *The Right to be Lazy*; various works by Karl Marx, including *Capital* (in three volumes); Emile Pouget, *Sabotage*; Joseph Dietzgen, *The Positive Outcome of Philosophy*; August Bebel, *Woman and Socialism*; and Karl Kautsky, *The Class Struggle*. Specifically Wobbly mental dynamite included: Vincent St John, *The I.W.W. Its History, Structure and Methods*; G.H. Perry, *The Revolutionary I.W.W.*; B.H. Williams, *Eleven Blind Leaders*; W.E. Trautmann, *Industrial Union Methods*; Father T.J. Hagerty, *Economic Discontent and its Remedy*; A.E. Brown, *The Shorter Working Day*; and Tom Glynn, *Industrial Efficiency and its Antidote*. More general or abstruse works would also feature in these libraries, such as Morgan's *Ancient Society* and Gibbons' *Industrial History of England.*[54] *Direct Action* deplored the lack of attention given in other newspapers to scientific discoveries, art, and intellectualism: 'Reading matter which might elevate and instruct is rigorously tabooed; rather is there a tendency to pander to the morbid tastes and brutish instincts of the ignorant.'[55] *Direct Action* and the American papers the IWW circulated, *Solidarity* and *The Industrial Worker*, contained, in addition to news of industrial activities, serious articles on economics and politics.

Like the American IWW, the Australian IWW encouraged workers to become intellectuals themselves as a necessary step in their emancipation.[56] Bill Beattie insists the IWW was an important instruction for unskilled workers:

> As many workers after leaving school read very little but the newspaper headlines (and perhaps the racing news), the results of these classes were astonishing. After a month or two of this system of study most of them became keen readers and soon developed a confidence of speech and thought undreamed of a few months – in some cases even weeks – earlier.

He recalls:

> When two or more members found themselves on a job together they organised study and reading classes – all workers welcome. We used *Value, Price and Profit*, or some such work on economics, and maybe some other good type of book with a popular appeal. The method would be to assemble in a private tent or camp. Each man might read a few paragraphs and then pass the book to the others in turn. Difficult passages were always a subject for discussion until the matter was clear to all.[57]

There were IWW discussion groups, too, amongst the unemployed.[58]

Nor did wandering deter Wobblies and others of their kind. At Borroloola in the Northern Territory, Mick Sawtell attended what the local wags called the University of the Northern Territory: the collection of 3000 books housed at the police lock-up, available to anyone who wanted to borrow them, the gift of Lord Hopetoun, Governor of Victoria, to a local officer. It was here that Sawtell first became enamoured of the American philosopher, Ralph Waldo Emerson. Thanks to this library, erudition was the fashion in Borroloola. In the pub, with books under their arms, stockmen, drovers, prospectors, sundowners and mission-educated Aborigines would argue about everything from Homer to Oscar Wilde. It was on the track, too, on a 900-mile droving expedition from Darwin to Derby in 1908, that Sawtell came across a copy of Robert Blatchford's *Merrie England* at an abandoned camp, from which he dates his conversion to socialism.[59]

Rushton insists nonetheless that Wobblies were woefully uninformed about the ideas of the movement to which they adhered; despite lectures, classes and study groups the bulk of rank-and-file members were profoundly ignorant of the basic tenets of their faith. As evidence he cites lack of knowledge amongst them of Hagerty's 'Wheel of Fortune', the plan to reorganise society into six industrial departments: in almost half the applications for membership the category 'Industry' was left blank or incorrectly completed.[60] Possibly many of those who left the blank were unemployed; in other cases, inability to recall the precise details of an esoteric blueprint hardly constitutes evidence of profound ignorance. Moreover, applicants for membership would naturally be less well informed on average than members already enrolled. The IWW recruiting card issued to these raw recruits listed 'Pamphlets You Should Read': *Advancing Proletariat, The Social Evil, The Immediate Demands of the I.W.W., Industrial Union Methods, Arbitration and the Strike, Job Control, Direct Action.*[61] The Preamble on this card served, at the very least, as a concise expression of IWW ideology and was undoubtedly known well by the vast majority of members, off by heart by many. Included in everything the IWW published, this Preamble, in its hardhitting and blunt terminology, which nonetheless embodied a world of Marxian theory and proletarian wisdom, was considered better by far than all the sacred texts of the socialist sects.

The IWW consciously prized its rather less academic leanings as a proletarian virtue that intimated incorruptibility in the practical struggle. It despised the 'scientific socialist' who could, according to *Direct Action*, quote *Capital* by the page, who had the theory of socialism down pat but lived the life of one of the boss's stool pigeons, who was all right in theory but nobody at home in practice:

> Glib-tongued theory is of little help in the class struggle unless it is backed by class loyalty and class action . . . A man is not what he thinks, but what he does. It is easy to think war, or think strike, or to theorise on tactics, but it takes real manhood and real womanhood to back up these theories and these thoughts in the actual everyday battle of the working class.

Talk and education were necessary, *Direct Action* argued, but class activity and loyalty were most important. Better a non-theoretical activist than a theoretical non-activist. 'The capitalist system cannot be theorised out of existence, nor can it be effaced by a plentiful supply of platitudinous piffle'; it was necessary to avoid 'an over-indulgence in the brain-storming, action-destroying, mental dope dished up by the superior persons'. The fact remains, the IWW argued: 'that analysis of the capitalist system of exploitation is only more or less of academic interest; the matter of vital importance is the remedy for putting a stop to that exploitation, which the worker, consciously or unconsciously, knows to be a fact irrespective of its causes'. Experience had proven that the members worth having in a

Local were those whose understanding was of a practical bent, suited for revolutionary action, those with 'an intelligent conception of the industrial form of organisation and the tactics which go with it'.[62]

In its preference for activity over theory, the IWW located its hostility to the doctrinal rigidity typical of the De Leonites: 'Certain organisations in the past have been more concerned in perpetuating particular dogmas than in seeking the most efficient and practicable method of achieving the goal of militant endeavor.' The IWW was no rigid institution 'which sets up a dogma and compels all its units to accept such in all humility and faith' but was the logical outcome of working-class experience: 'It is a live body, and, being alive, acts.'[63] Activism and theoreticism are here cast in the Wobbly mind as polar opposites. To the Wobblies, as Rushton notes, it seemed that so much of the energy of socialist bodies was expended in doctrinal exegesis that they had but little time to spare for action.[64]

The activist temper that defined the typical Wobbly has encouraged academic commentators to characterise the IWW as irrationalist, crudely materialist, anti-intellectual. C.H. Parker has written that the American IWW was a 'stomach philosophy' and its politico-industrial revolt was a hunger riot.[65] Rushton stresses what he regards as the irrationalism of the Australian movement:

> The significance of I.W.W. ideology lay not in its content but in its function. Activity was paramount; ideology served to rationalize what was fundamentally a non-rational movement. Essentially the I.W.W. represents a complex of attitudes, emotional reactions and neurotic adjustments to a particular socio-economic system by men drawn in the main from the lowest economic and social strata.[66]

Endorsing, in effect, the 'social sore' explanation for radicalism, he argues that, being 'essentially non-rational', the Wobblies were 'impervious to reason' because their reaction to capitalist society was intuitive.[67] The Wobblies themselves would undoubtedly dispute such value judgements, insisting that theirs was a proletarian rationality, not a capitalist one, and on that basis no less rational.

Commentators have often assessed the membership by categories the Wobblies would themselves reject: thus there are the deserving and the undeserving, worthy Wobblies and unworthy Wobblies. Childe, for instance, explains that the organisation was not without ideals, but in order to arouse the class consciousness necessary to make its ideals real, it harped freely on the negative aspects of the class struggle.

> Thus it attracted to itself, besides those who were in glorious revolt against the injustices heaped upon themselves and their fellow wage-slaves, others

actuated by motives intellectually lower. Loafing on the job appealed to man's natural inertia. 'The Right to be Lazy' had an attractive sound. Sabotage provided a relatively safe means of venting one's spleen on the boss or his hirelings, and gave a spice of excitement to the dreary monotony of daily toil, without exposing one to unreasonable risks. . . . But it must not for an instant be thought that the members of the I.W.W. were all or even largely recruited from loafers, cowards, or criminals. They displayed enthusiastic and unflinching energy.[68]

Rushton also distinguishes between the good, the bad and the ugly Wobbly: 'The organization attracted the disgruntled, the larrikin, the army dodger, the criminal, and those who joined merely for companionship. It also appealed to the idealist . . .'[69]

Admittedly some Wobblies made similar classifications. Alf Wilson insisted the Melbourne Local was 'scarcely connected with the Sydney lot and their methods'. In writing of this Local, the Sydney one clearly served as a negative role model for Wilson: 'Our party in Melbourne was a good little party and kept well away from anything that might savour of criminality. Some members might have advocated sabotage, but Laidler and I kept strictly to Industrial Union propaganda. Our little hall was the home of a happy little party.'[70]

Other Wobblies have varying descriptions of their fellow workers. Norman Rancie remembers: 'We had amongst our members men and women of high ideals, intellectuals, men holding responsible positions, men of integrity, clean living family men and home lovers.' Tom Payne notes that Mark Anthony was 'a man with a big heart', who returned regularly to Clunes to look after his mother and family, filling up their larder before returning to Broken Hill. There were heroes too: Tom Glynn had been suspended from the South African police force for refusing to shoot a Zulu boy during a drive of rebel blacks; Alexander Horrocks had lost one eye from a fall of earth while waiting to save a mate in a mine accident. Fred Farrall, on the other hand, described his Wobbly cousin, Roly Farrall, as being in his everyday life a contradiction of his political views, having no respect for other people, least of all his wife, Jean, who was frequently a victim of Roly's drunkenness: 'But he was a character.'[71]

That the Wobblies were 'characters' is indisputable. Most writers on the subject have attempted to impart to readers something of the panache of these people and the extent to which the organisation had style. Brooks has written of the American IWW that all the drudgeries and enduring strain demanded by reforms were wan and colourless compared to the inscrutable pageantry of an IWW attack, which, like the stroke of a suffragette's hammer upon plate glass, got instant attention. Conlin argues that, if the Wobblies had planned for nothing but a

posterity, they could not have done better: 'The movement was spontaneously colorful.'[72]

May Brodney, who disliked the 'exhibitionism' of the IWW and dismisses it for making 'a cheap appeal to emotionalism rather than logic',
writes nonetheless: 'And give them their due they were most entertaining.
. . . The language was colourful & speakers were fluent & had their
following.'[73] The *Sydney Morning Herald* conceded reluctantly on 30
September 1916 of the Wobbly: 'He has an enthusiasm in his ideas which
gives him an almost fearful impetus in the promulgation of his views,
and the infection of others with his doctrines.' The *Bulletin* of 14
December 1916 commented: 'Misguided they are, of course, and all
that; but how the enthusiasm of these I.W.W. people shames Liberals
and Laborites.' Rushton believes the source of the Wobblies' invincible
optimism and boisterous energy was their conviction of ultimate victory.
He quotes *Direct Action* of 1 July 1914: 'The most pitiless and cruel struggle the world has ever known . . . can only conclude with the extermina-
tion of one of the warring classes.'[74]

Rushton exaggerates the optimism of the IWW. As the extract clearly
indicates, Wobblies were not sure of ultimate victory, aware as they were
of the many obstacles in the way of proletarian solidarity. If working-class
organisation did not adapt to economic changes, the ruling class would
become ever more invincible. Workers had a choice: the OBU or
Barbarism. Wobbly energy levels were rather an indication of the vehe-
mence with which they adhered to their class-struggle philosophy, the
extent to which they were formed from that section of the working class
with the most radical chains of all, which lost no time reflecting on what
they might lose in seeking to change the world.

CHAPTER 6

'No Barriers of Race': the Challenge to Working-class Racism

Amongst the first words uttered by Bill Haywood, in calling the first IWW Convention in 1905 to order, were words of criticism of AFL unions for refusing membership to 'a colored man' or 'foreigners'.[1] Fundamental to the Wobbly notion of industrial organisation was the inclusion of those whom the AFL spurned; in fact, those traditionally overlooked or excluded in many AFL unions, such as immigrants, Negroes, and women, became an IWW priority. The new working class, the IWW argued, differed essentially from the craftsman, as the idea of an exclusive property in skill had disappeared and along with it the notion of an aristocracy of labour; the new unionism, organising on the basis of the machine, welcomed every improvement and development in industry, excluded no worker from these machines on any grounds of undesirability, such as race, creed, colour, sex, age or skill.[2]

Despite the strength of new unions within the labour movement in Australia, the movement was far closer in both its industrial and political aspects to the racial values of the AFL than the IWW. The Federal Labour Conference of 1905 adopted as the first of its two main objectives: 'The cultivation of an Australian sentiment based on the maintenance of racial purity.' In 1908 it added 'Maintenance of White Australia' as first item on its fighting platform.[3] Racism was deep-rooted in the practices and ideologies of the labour movement at this time. Operating within this movement that enthusiastically endorsed the ruling racial ideas of the age, socialists in the late nineteenth and early twentieth centuries had generally ignored the internationalist imperatives of socialism for to embrace these traditions in the Australian context appeared to them to be a policy calculated to ensure loss of support for socialists amongst workers. 'Workers of the World, Unite!' was the advice from Karl Marx that these socialists had found most difficult to

79

apply. Though acknowledging that racial attitudes and practices weakened working-class resistance to exploitation, they did not oppose these attitudes and practices.[4]

Furthermore, the White Australia Policy was a core element of the means whereby Labor leaders and conservative union officials sought to 'civilise capitalism' in Australia. Immigration restriction, along with the protective tariff, industrial arbitration and other protective devices were intended to insulate the domestic economy and allow the maintenance of living standards. So just as non-British immigrants were excluded along with foreign products, women were excluded from many occupations and men were awarded wages calculated on the basis of family needs in order that they should fulfil their responsibilities as breadwinners. Racism, along with sexism, was a foundation-stone of the Antipodean wage-earners' welfare state.

The IWW, on the other hand, inherited the American IWW's hostility to racism as an ideology that divided workers at the point of production. Anti-racism was essential to the revolutionary method of the IWW: workers could take and hold the means of production only if the ultimate form of solidarity, the One Big Union, had been reached; this was a strategy dependent upon the breaking down of all divisions between workers. Opposition to racism was crucial to the formation of the One Big Union; and the One Big Union would not be complete without the workers of all nationalities and races.

Both factions of the IWW agreed on the importance of countering racism in the working-class movement, for both emphasised the importance of absolute solidarity in the industrial arena, the need for better organisation culminating in the One Big Union; their disagreement centred on the utility of political action in addition to industrial. This difference did not affect their respective standings on the issue of racism. Both adhered firmly to internationalism, in theory and practice, as a fundamental principle of revolutionary industrial unionism. As the Sydney IWW Club announced in January 1911: 'The I.W.W. knows no distinction of race, creed, or colour. Its policy is one of international working-class solidarity.'[5]

It was the IWW Clubs, as the first exponents of revolutionary industrial unionism in Australia, who first confronted in any concerted way the racism of the labour movement and argued that it was indeed the particular duty of the most forward sections of the movement so to do. The Chicago IWW continued this role with even greater energy, with even more scorn and contempt for those within the movement whose concept of solidarity was circumscribed by racial boundaries. Boneheads were invariably portrayed as racial bigots, patriotic mugs and boss-lovers. It criticised the Labor Party, consistently and persistently, for pandering to nationalist and racial prejudices in enunciating its White Australia policies; and it regularly berated trade unions for their racially restrictive practices and policies.

A debate in 1912 between Mr Edgar of the Carpenters' and Joiners' Union and Fellow-Worker Halfpenny of the Melbourne IWW Club revealed the gap on such issues between revolutionary industrial union-ism and traditional unionism. In reply to Edgar's support for the White Australia Policy, Halfpenny commented that it was the workers of the whole human race, not a section of it, that would bring about the eman-cipation of their class.[6] The Labor Party was roundly abused for its racism by Club propagandists. At a meeting in Cessnock in 1911 Fellow-Worker Mackenzie claimed the Labor Party, through its support for the White Australia Policy, was 'keeping the workers of one country at the throats of the workers of another country, and by appealing to racial prejudices kept them divided'.[7] When Western Australian Labor Premier Scadden proposed legislation to exclude Italians from the mining industry, the Sydney Club wrote him a public letter of protest saying that such a bar-baric and unjust proposal should not be countenanced by the workers of Western Australia

> who are misled by unscrupulous politicians misruling in Labor's name, delud-ing their unthinking dupes by appeals to racial hatreds and ignorant preju-dices, instead of showing that the bad conditions prevailing in the mines of W.A., as in South Africa, lie at the door of the mining magnates and cosmopolitan financiers, combined with the defective organization of the mining industry.[8]

In a pamphlet, *The Two Wars*, the national executive of the IWW Clubs called on Australian workers to

> organise under the banner of the I.W.W. and fight the real working-class battle against capitalism and wage-slavery. Lay aside national prejudices, crush race hatred beneath your heel, join in true comradeship with the workers of all lands into One Great Union, for, in the words of Karl Marx: 'You have nothing to lose but your chains (economic poverty and servitude), and a World to Gain.'[9]

It boasted that it was taking every opportunity to stem the tide of racial hatred being promulgated by vulgar politicians and superficial press-men.[10] The ideas of the IWW prompted Australian socialists to recon-sider their attitude to working-class racism, encouraging for the first time the development within the labour movement of a coherent anti-racist viewpoint.

In the 1901 election campaign in the new Commonwealth, the SLP had portrayed itself as the only true champion of working-class interests, because of its especially hard line on immigration: 'To vote, then, for a White Australia, is to vote for the Socialist Labor Party. This party alone stands for a White Australia, owned and controlled by white workers.' It admitted that racism was a capitalist device used to divide workers, but argued that the 'race problem' would simply disappear under socialism: the best way for workers to prevent race antagonism was to abolish the capitalist system and its evils at the ballot box. For the SLP, statist and elitist, socialism was not a prize to be earned in struggle but a gift that would be handed down from above: workers would be given collective ownership of the means of production after they had used their vote wisely, as a reward for intelligent electoral behaviour.[11] Racism would prove no obstacle to the achievement of socialism by parliamentary fiat, the granting of socialism to passive workers who had done nothing more energetic towards their own emancipation than to vote, as individual citizens, for the SLP. Industrial action, the power of workers in combination, had virtually no role to play in this process. Because it was in open competition with the Labor Party for working-class votes, it was liable to pander to any popular prejudice it did not consider obstructive of its efforts to end capitalism. Before its conversion to IWW principles, the SLP did not regard racism as a hindrance to its particular method for achieving socialism; a strategy based on atomised electoral support would not be jeopardised by racial divisions in the working class.

In a dramatic turnabout in 1907, the SLP decided that reliance on the electoral process alone was inadequate, that the ballot had to be backed up by 'the organised economic might of the working class' as set forth in the 1905 Preamble of the IWW.[12] As a consequence, it at last considered racism a problem: 'The I.W.W. is right; it is the true economic organisation. It embraces all workers – skilled and unskilled – black, white, brown, or yellow. Its door is open to all honest wageworkers.'[13] It noted that capitalists had no prejudice of race, creed, colour, age, or sex, being always ready to combine with other capitalists of any race in the congenial act of robbing the workers of all races. It asked why the workers should not profit by the example set by their betters:

> Why should not they too eschew questions of race, color, or creed, when the question is one of the material interests of ALL workers? Is not every worker whether black, white, brown or tawny, entitled to the whole value of what he produces by his labor? Do you say Yes? Then up with the Industrial Workers of the World.[14]

The SLP's new-found interest in promoting the practical organisation of the working class at the point of production, the Wobbly strategy for emancipation, caused the SLP to admit that there was a race question, and that it was not a question that could be shelved, pending the revolution.[15] It was an obstacle to be overcome in order that socialism might be achieved.

Rejecting its previous commitment to the belief that the White Australia Policy was necessary under capitalist conditions, the SLP now advocated not restrictive immigration legislation but the organisation of all workers, wherever or whoever they might be. It claimed that racial propaganda was disgracing the Labor Party and that revolutionary industrial unionism and revolutionary political action, without regard to race, creed, or colour, were the present need of the working class. IWW jargon became an integral part of the SLP's new anti-Labor Party, anti-racist vocabulary. It despised the Labor Party for encouraging working-class racism, for ingratiating itself with all sorts of reactionary elements in the community in its scramble for votes.[16] The SLP now believed that socialism had to be created also from below, by revolutionary industrial unionism, as well as from above, through revolutionary political action. Socialism could only be achieved by workers acting as workers and in unison. Such a scheme for the regeneration of society depended on the breaking down of all barriers to working-class solidarity.

The influence of the IWW also changed dramatically the Barrier Socialist Propaganda Group's response to the question of race. The Group had started life in 1906 as a state socialist grouping, which supported the White Australia Policy and all other vestiges of labour racism. However, early in 1907, as we have seen, H.J. Hawkins persuaded his comrades that the IWW was the organisation of the future. The Group became, accordingly, a revolutionary industrial unionist propaganda organisation, hostile to the Labor Party and to any signs of racism in the workers of Broken Hill or elsewhere. The Group stressed the necessity for working-class solidarity against the class enemy rather than national solidarity against the imagined enemy; it recommended that workers embrace industrial unionism as outlined by the IWW.[17] The transition to confrontation of working-class racism, effected by the Group, was a necessary part of this new commitment to IWW methods.

The IWW had a similar impact on the Sydney International Socialists and, through them, on the ASP, its federal organisation from 1912. Before this adoption of IWW ideas, the International Socialists were mis-named: their internationalism extended not much further than expressions of solidarity with all other sections of the Second International.[18] Working-class solidarity was conceived, not in absolute and objective terms, but in partial and subjective terms, as a sentiment to be shared only with the elect of the proletariat. By May 1908, as they became involved in IWW Club activity, the International Socialists had clearly changed their mind on the race issue.[19] In April 1910 they referred contemptuously to the Labor Party's demand for a White Australia as 'a clap trap election cry' and despaired of those in the labour movement who could not see the dangers in stirring up racial hatred: 'Was ever the need of industrial organisation more plainly shown?'[20] By 1911, when the ASP was establishing the Chicago IWW, it announced: 'Industrial unionism, which is the only organisation that can successfully fight the combination of the masters, recognises neither sex nor color line.' The ASP considered it was the duty of every working-class man or woman to study the principles of Industrial Socialism as advocated by the IWW, which organised all workers, whatever their race, colour, creed, sex, or calling. It opposed all restrictions on immigration and advocated instead a general vigilance over wages and conditions.[21] Only by industrial unionist methods would capitalism be overthrown, and industrial unionism demanded absolute solidarity. When the ASP contested the 1913 State elections, Mick Considine, candidate for Sturt, declared that the ASP stood for industrial unionism on the lines of the IWW, as it was essential for the working class to sink all differences of craft, creed, or colour.[22]

The sections of the VSP most sympathetic to revolutionary industrial unionism were also those most hostile to the racism of the labour movement. Tom Mann, the principal enthusiast for industrial unionist ideas, was the prime mover in attempts to bring the Party to a more decidedly anti-racist position. However, after Mann's return to England in 1910, the state socialists gained control. Basing its strategy on winning the Labor Party over to socialism, the VSP remained impervious to the ideas of revolutionary industrial unionism and did not, therefore, embrace the vehement anti-racism that accompanied genuine commitment to IWW methods. Many of Mann's allies left the VSP to become the Melbourne branch of the ASP in opposition to the reformism and racially limited cosmopolitanism of the majority in the VSP. R.S. Ross, wary of both sections of the IWW and a firm supporter of the White Australia Policy, became the leading figure in the VSP. The ASP scorned the VSP for falling prey to White Australian ideas. It rebuked Ross for using the White Australia legislation as proof that political action could help workers: it claimed this was rejecting the materialist conception of history, the internationality of the working class, the necessity for industrial unionism, and the commodity status of labour power.[23]

In Western Australia, too, tensions between anti-racist, IWW-influenced socialists and racist, Labor-oriented socialists caused regrouping. In 1912 the WASP split. Some comrades declared their support for revolutionary industrial unionism, objected to the nationally oriented reformism of the Labor Party, and announced themselves the Perth branch of the ASP. The remainder, who retained the title WASP, re-affirmed their support for the Labor Party and through their paper, *Dawnward*, continued to espouse, in the words of the Perth ASP, 'a white Australia, Conscription, Arbitration, "a step at a time", and other Stone Age principles'.[24]

No spontaneous, indigenous socialist opposition to working-class racism had developed. Only under the influence of the 'foreign' idea of revolutionary industrial unionism were socialists finally persuaded that racism was a problem that could not be ignored, that it was an obstacle that had to be overcome if they were to achieve their aims. From 1907 on, the extent to which socialist groups accepted IWW ideas – that socialism would be achieved by workers in combined struggle in the industrial sphere and not by representation in parliament – explains their reactions to racism. Those who preferred parliamentary strategies remained trapped within the racial world vision of the Labor Party, for racism did not endanger such a tactic; those who embraced revolutionary industrial unionism, where socialism was to be achieved by workers acting as workers and together, discovered a new world of racial tolerance. While it had been largely the efforts of the IWW Clubs which caused the drastic reorientation towards anti-racism on the part of the Australian socialist movement, it was the Chicago IWW, through its greater popularity and capacity for propaganda, that reached the racialised hearts and minds of the wider labour movement.

In calling on workers to join, the IWW explained in *The Immediate Demands of the I.W.W.* that it was composed of wage-workers only, but that these were of all nationalities, speaking all tongues, yet all of one nation, the working class: 'There are no barriers of race, creed, color, sex, age or skill, to entrance into its fighting ranks.' Its members paid allegiance to no imaginary boundary lines and claimed no country except the world; being propertyless and landless, they had no patriotism nor reason for patriotism. It announced that the time had arrived when it became imperative, in the interests of all workers, young and old, skilled and unskilled, black, brown, or brindle, to organise on the lines which capitalist development and economic conditions dictated.[25]

Because it shared the popular assumption of the time that the Aboriginal race was dying out and because its principal point of reference was the male worker in paid employment, IWW anti-racism centred on the issue of immigrant workers. *Direct Action* referred to the 'original possessors of the soil' as having been 'driven off, exterminated by war and decimated by famine and disease, or enslaved . . .'[26] Apart from expressing sincere regret at the plight of the Aborigines and indicting British imperialism for its hand in this, *Direct Action* otherwise ignored the Aboriginal issue; the IWW wrongly judged it as lacking industrial significance.

The IWW recruiting stickers stressed unity, solidarity and organisation as
necessary prerequisites for victory. All workers were welcome to join.
The IWW despised unions with racially restrictive membership qualifications.
(R.S. Ross Collection, NL3222/6)

For the same reason that it rejected racism, so too did the IWW oppose
other divisive ideologies such as imperial patriotism and nationalism.
Direct Action referred to Labor MPs as patriotic parasites and heaped scorn
on the Labor objective of cultivating 'national sentiment'. In rejecting
Australian nationalism, the IWW was distancing itself from the other
source of opposition to imperial patriotism within the labour movement,
that mounted by the Irish-Australian nationalism of the Catholics, though
the IWW, like the labour movement generally, included many Irish
Catholics.[27] This influence notwithstanding, the IWW was critical not only
of Australian labour nationalism but of Irish nationalism. *Direct Action*
attributed the 1916 Easter Rebellion's failure to advance the workers'
cause to the nationalist elements in the movement: 'many of the leaders
were purely and simply nationalist politicians, having no enthusiasm for
working class emancipation, but simply wishing to emancipate the Irish
from British domination; so that, as far as the movement was nationalistic,
we could not expect economic results.'[28]

It used local interest in Irish events to put forward its arguments.
James Larkin's brother Peter, a stockier, more grizzled, squat-nosed edition of his famous brother, had joined the Sydney Local when he arrived
from Ireland in 1915 and lectured to enormous meetings in Sydney and
Melbourne in the wake of the Easter Rebellion. But Larkin was no propagandist for Irish nationalism: he desired to see an Ireland belonging,
not to 'the Irish' but to 'Irish workers'.[29]

In its pamphlet, *Direct Action*, the IWW argued: 'The antagonisms between races and nationalities can only be abolished when the idea of class solidarity has been accepted by the workers. In the task of promoting that idea, the I.W.W. is the only organization that is meeting the needs of the times.'[30] This claim is justified: no organisation was as vociferously anti-racist as the IWW. Article 1, section 1 of its by-laws stipulated: 'No working man or woman shall be excluded from membership in local unions because of creed or color.'[31] In *Direct Action*'s life-span of little over three and a half years, there were forty-four lengthy articles on the evil effects of racism in the working-class movement, as well as numerous short anti-racist asides, such as 'Let us rally the forces, which no language or creed can divide' and 'Labor cannot emancipate itself in the white skin where in the black it is branded'.[32]

Direct Action explained that, as capitalism was international and the master class internationally organised, the working class must also be internationally organised. The cry amongst the workers should be: 'What are you, worker or parasite?' and not that inane cry of 'Where do you come from?' In confronting the racism of those around them in the labour movement, the IWW recommended, as a superior world vision from a working-class standpoint, the internationalism inherent in classical Marxist ideology: 'Contrast the narrow parochial outlook evidenced by the "white Australia" policy with the world-oriented outlook of Karl Marx, when he sent his famous cry ringing down the ages: "Workers of all countries, Unite!"'[33] It argued against immigration restriction:

> The arrival in this country every year, of thousands of immigrants, is thought by the average wage-slave to be the cause of unemployment, but they forget that this curse is world-wide, and that these workers have themselves been forced to leave the land of their birth by the unemployment existing there . . . The real cause of unemployment is because the workers have not reduced the hours of their labor in proportion to the productivity of the machine.[34]

The solution was industrial unionism: to organise wage workers so they could shorten hours, slow down on the job, and restrict output by systematic sabotage, and so provide more work for the jobless, which would automatically raise wages and better conditions of all workers.[35]

The IWW did not discount the difficulties in surmounting racial prejudice. It conceded that, in organising all workers into One Big Union, the chief difficulty lay in racial antipathy, as capitalist exploiters were crafty enough to use racial differences to promote dissension and check, if not prevent, the world-wide union necessary for the existence of a stable, united, and happy society. Craft unionism was largely to blame for racial prejudice. *Direct Action* noted that the craft unionist stupidly did not object to being robbed by a white employer, only a coloured one, and while disliking coloured labour, refused to organise in the only way that would give him power to control at any time an influx of the coloured labour to which he objected. A working class organised upon industrial union lines, *Direct Action* explained, would be able to so control industry as to check a sudden inflow of coloured labour not so organised, if necessary, and to secure by concerted action the immediate reception of coloured workers into the unions of their respective industry. Tom Glynn considered that the worker in Australia who was deluded with the belief that his material progress would be endangered by, for example, Japanese immigration, would do well to realise the fact that Japanese competition in the labour market was just as much a reality as if the Japanese were rubbing elbows with him at the factory gates or factories were established throughout Australia in which none but Japanese were employed. Such was the tendency of capitalism with the development of faster and cheaper methods of transportation, and the only solution was class organisation, irrespective of colour or creed.[36]

To counter Anglo-Celtic industrial chauvinism, the IWW frequently mentioned 'foreign' militancy. For instance, when thousands went on strike on May Day in Russia and Italian workers staged a general strike, *Direct Action* commented that the despised foreigner was showing some points in class fighting to his supercilious brethren in more 'civilised' countries: 'If the patriotic British and Australian slave would condescend to learn a point or two from the "ignorant foreigner", there would be fewer fines and broken heads after strikes.' When the employees, mostly Spanish and Italian, conducted a successful strike at the Mourilyan sugar mill at Innisfail, *Direct Action* stressed that these men knew how to stick together and were good direct actionists. On 1 July 1915 *Direct Action* published a heartfelt obituary, in its usual editorial space, to a Chinese anarchist communist, Sifo, who had translated much IWW literature into Chinese, who had done so much 'to place before the workers of Asia, the principles and tactics of the One Big Union'. The IWW had been communicating with Chinese anarchist communist groups since at least September 1914.[37]

Its refusal to discriminate against them and its determination to embrace them, earned the IWW a significant following amongst non-English-speaking immigrants. In the Broken Hill Local, the ethnic members joined as a group; Shor suggests that their pre-existing ethnic network pulled them together into the IWW.[38] This Local seriously considered that fellow workers should learn Esperanto to facilitate communication; in September 1916 it appointed organisers to work amongst the Italian, Russian and Bulgarian members and acquired stocks of literature 'for members of other nationalities'; and in May 1917 it aspired to raise funds to translate the trial proceedings of the Sydney Twelve for its Russian members.[39] The Sydney Local, too, had an active Russian following. The 600 Russian books housed in the IWW hall in Sydney were, according to Detective Moore, 'for the use of Russian members'.[40] More spectactular still in the organisation of non-English-speaking militants was the all-Russian Local (no. 12) formed in Cairns, which operated as a focal point for Russian workers in several parts of Australia who, according to *Direct Action*, showed 'a decided tendency towards the One Big Union idea'. Joe Fagin at the Sydney headquarters organised the distribution to these Russian workers of *Golos Truda*, *Rabochaya Rech* and Russian literature. *Direct Action* regularly contained details, too, of how individuals could subscribe to any of a wide range of American foreign-language publications.[41]

IWW members were especially active amongst the Italian and Slav workers in Western Australia. In response, the Labour Federation started to publish matter in Italian for fear that the Italians would be organised into the IWW. *Direct Action* insisted the Federation was acting too late: 'The I.W.W. is in the West for good, for it is already meeting with a hearty reception from the workers whom at one time were despised and persecuted by the very men who to-day are evidently anxious to collect their dues, if not to organise them.' It imported IWW pamphlets in Italian from the American IWW for distribution in Australia.[42]

The IWW was particularly hostile to the Australian Workers' Union, which it termed the 'One Big Onion'. This aversion was partly because the AWU chose to interpret the One Big Union concept as meaning that all other unions should be swallowed up into a gargantuan AWU; and partly because the AWU was racist. In a pamphlet entitled *Why the A.W.U. Cannot Become An Industrial Union*, the IWW deplored the fact that: 'it refuses to enrol within its ranks all Asiatic workers and natives of the South Sea Islands. Yes, an A.W.U. cocky or carrier is too respectable to belong to the same union as a rebellious Asiatic worker, who is up against the boss on the job.' The AWU could never become an industrial union because it denied the class struggle, the fundamental basis on which industrial unionism and the One Big Union idea was built.[43]

In April 1915 Tom Barker outlined the role of the AWU in the Northern Territory. The 600–700 white workers were organised in the White Australia AWU and the 2500 coloured workers were not allowed to join:

> The A.W.U. stands for the white man alone, and treats all coloured workers with unconcealed contempt. The man of colour, although working for the same skinner and exploiter as the white, is denied the right of organisation, in order to make the demands of his class more effective.

In a recent strike of whites, the coloured workers had consistently refused to scab in spite of tempting proposals made to them by the employers, but were still refused AWU tickets after the strike was broken by white scabs. Barker commented that the AWU was so proud of the chains of wage slavery that it desired a monopoly of them and, in attempting to be exclusive, was playing into the hands of the employers: 'The Class War is a nobler sentiment than the Race War, for it strives for the abolition of chains and not for their perpetuation.' The IWW stood for revolutionary economic international working-class unity. As the coloured workers of the Territory were an economic factor either for or against the working class, they had to be organised for their own class against the employers, and as the AWU had refused to do so, the IWW announced it would.[44]

The AWU not only continued to refuse to allow coloured workers to join its ranks, but refused to permit them to be employed on any work with its unionists, even to recognise their right to employment, though they were long-standing residents of the Territory who had formerly performed all the waterside work. The IWW, which proceeded to organise the coloured workers, was placed in an awkward predicament in a strike amongst AWU waterside workers in Darwin in late August/early September 1915. Though the IWW members were desperate for employment and began unloading cargoes, the IWW organiser did not allow them to continue the work, even though the AWU turned its strike into the issue of 'A White Australia'.[45]

The IWW did achieve some success among coloured workers in tropical Australia. A Fellow-Worker Cubillo in Darwin sent the names and subscriptions of nineteen Malays, Filipinos, Japanese, and Cingalese, who had formed a recruiting Local in Darwin. Cubillo was confident of the prospects for a very powerful branch of the IWW among the coloured workers in the Territory and mentioned that several white fellow workers were giving a hand with the development of the union. A Chinese fellow worker, editor of a Chinese workers' paper in Burma, began translating IWW literature for the Darwin Wobblies, which they aimed to spread 'far and wide' and there were plans for a Chinese organiser to come to Australia to form more recruiting Locals of the IWW among Chinese workers. Though no viable Local was ever established in the Northern Territory, copies of the Preamble in Chinese were widely distributed.[46]

Frank Farrell claims that, in rejecting all the 'benefits' of nationalism, the IWW's 'impractical' approach to the White Australia Policy resolved the 'problem' of applying internationalism to the Australian situation, but in a way that no one in the mainstream labour movement could possibly accept. He dismisses the anti-racism of the IWW as 'crude, emotional, irresponsible, and escapist' – adjectives that could be used to describe the promulgation of racial ideas. Wobbly unwillingness to accept the solid working-class adherence to racist ideas and the White Australia Policy proved, to Farrell, the Wobblies' lack of realism. He writes:

> Their escapism was symptomatic of the enormous problem faced by parties dedicated to dogmatic internationalist purity but operating in an environment in which racialism was strongly entrenched and closely intertwined with the basic aspirations of the working class. The AWU, in championing racialism and exclusionism, was simply continuing to reflect a popular and primitive creed sanctioned by the labour movement's history and experience in Australia; in openly opposing racialism the IWW issued to the labour movement a frontal challenge which, in 1915, had very little appeal to the working masses.[47]

Farrell implies, therefore, that 'dogmatic internationalist purity' was the problem, not working-class racism. He seems to suggest the IWW would have grown more rapidly if it had ignored the race issue. But if the IWW had done so, it would not have been the IWW: anti-racism was a fundamental tenet of its ideology.

Rushton suggests that the anti-racism of the IWW was its only un-Australian characteristic, locating the Wobblies as he does within the legendary masculine bush ethos of mateship and rugged individualism: 'In only one important area did the I.W.W. ethos differ from the tradition that helped to mould it. The I.W.W.'s genuine internationalism provided a marked contrast to the typical Australian nationalism and narrow racist outlook . . .' He claims the IWW's internationalism was derived from its revolutionary ideology.[48] Yet the SLP was racist, though verbally revolutionary, in its early days. The IWW's anti-racism was a consequence of its revolutionary *method* – the organisational principle of industrial unionism.

It was this emphasis on industrial organisation that prompted the ferocity of the Wobbly attack on racism. IWW internationalism was not simply a product of its revolutionism; it was given its impetus by the IWW's particular strategy for revolution, which was essentially an organisational accomplishment. The Wobblies existed to promote the solidarity of the world's workers. In Australia, they had made a start by convincing many militant workers and most socialist groups of the need for combating racial ideas in the labour movement. In so doing, the IWW issued the first effective challenge ever to working-class racism in Australia.

CHAPTER 7

'It's Great to Fight for Freedom with a Rebel Girl': the Answer to the Woman Question

According to American Wobbly propagandist A.E. Woodruff, craft unionists not only made the mistake of looking down on coloured workers, they also considered that 'women were desirable only as satellites to men'; the IWW scorned such intolerance of women in industry and excluded no worker from its ranks on grounds of sex.[1] Ann Schofield's study of 'the Woman Question' in the journals of the IWW and AFL concedes that 'the Wobblies vigorously and effectively organized women' and refers to 'the IWW's sincere inclusion of women in the One Big Union' and how it 'welcomed them in the struggles leading to the millennium'.[2]

The IWW movement in Australia, too, aimed to incorporate women organisationally and to encourage their militancy industrially. Just as there were no barriers of race, neither were there any barriers of sex 'to entrance into its fighting ranks', which were 'ever open for red-blooded men and women of the working class'. Its advertisements did not discriminate: 'WANTED, Recruits, male and female, for the Industrial Workers of the World. Must be determined, unscrupulous, and unafraid of gaol or death.' On a much more patronising note, *Direct Action* commented in November 1914: 'A good sign of the times is that quite a few ladies are attending IWW lectures. Bring your women folk with you. Seating is now more comfortable.'[3]

However, according to its own rules, the IWW could only recruit women who were wage-workers. On 10 June 1912 the Sydney Local debated whether a woman who was the wife of a wage-slave could be a member; it was held eventually that, according to the Constitution, none but actual wage-workers could be accepted.[4] For the same reason, Bill Jackson, though prominent as a Wobbly propagandist, could not formally join because he sold spectacles for a living, mainly in outback Queensland.

Although the rule occasionally disbarred men from membership, it acted more frequently to deter women not in the paid workforce.

Moreover, the IWW's appeal to women was in any case severely limited for the same reasons that its appeal to certain men was strong. There were no women amongst the eighty-nine people on the Sydney Local's books on 27 December 1911. Of the 1091 names of IWW members compiled by police in September 1916, there were only twenty clearly female names.[5] Fred Coombe, a member for several years before the First World War, said he never met a female Wobbly, while adding that Elizabeth Gurley Flynn of the American IWW was known about and much admired. Tom Barker recalls of the Sydney Local: 'The organisation was masculine. To a great extent they were of the migratory type . . . They would come to Sydney to spend their money and see the lassies, then start and do the same again . . . We had very few women members . . .'[6]

A picture emerges of a masculine fraternity that liked to drink together. Mrs MacDonald's bar in Elizabeth Street was 'the place where many of the things were cooked up while most of the people were in a state of semi-intoxication'. From Adelaide in 1911, Peter Christensen of the Detroit-line Clubs complained to Horace Hawkins that Harry S. Clarke of the Chicago mob had not been sober for several Saturdays in succession and was 'almost too drunk to stand on the stump'. Ted Moyle conceded that, when Clarke was arrested and charged with 'abusive language', he had indeed been abusive because he was drunk. Broken Hill Local minutes for 10 September 1916 refer to the problem of 'intoxicated soap-boxers'. The address of the Mount Morgan Local was the Queensland National Hotel. Wobblies were less likely than the average male wage-earner to be married: only three of the Sydney Twelve and two of the eight Westralian Wobblies initially arrested and tried were married.[7]

At a superficial level, the Wobblies could be seen as a delayed expression in twentieth-century society of an essentially late nineteenth-century version of masculinity, hangovers from an earlier stereotype of true men as irresponsible, family-free and often itinerant. Marilyn Lake has differentiated this earlier model of masculinity from its subsequent replacement by the 1920s by the notion of real men as stable breadwinners.[8] Yet, the Wobblies differ from the earlier type in important respects. Their concept of true masculinity conformed more to the later, feminised version: before assuming control of industry, the virile working man should in the meantime demand higher wages, in order to provide better for his wife and children; so also should he abjure sexual double standards. Moreover, the IWW rejected the worst aspects of the masculinism of the contemporary labour movement as surely as it rejected its racism and its attempts to exclude women and coloured workers from its embrace.

The point at issue, therefore, is the discrepancy between the IWW's overt commitment to sexual egalitarianism and its mode and manner of operation that made women feel decidedly out of place. As Joy Damousi notes of the IWW, its central focus was the male breadwinner and its dominant style was virile industrialism: 'The "public" realm of male-dominated industries, and the tactics of direct action and sabotage, were sites of working-class masculinity, alienating some women.' Moreover, the IWW's rejection of hierarchical and authoritarian structures made it a very loose organisation, which attracted the migratory, itinerant worker – the so-called 'bummery element' – who was usually single and male and associated with a 'rough' style. Andrew Metcalfe's typology is helpful here, in his identification of two types of working-class male activist: rebellious, larrikin sons and respectable, patriarchal fathers.[9] The rebel boys of the IWW fit the larrikin mould, appealing to women in a way irresistible, yet, at the same time, more repelling than the respectable patriarchs of, for example, the VSP. This demeanour of the Wobblies that was so uninviting to women confounded its declared aspiration to recruit rebel girls.

The gendered language of the IWW, which Francis Shor has highlighted, reveals the extent to which it valorised the male and, by default, accorded lower value to the female. Tom Barker promised that the IWW would weld the coloured workers of the Northern Territory into 'a militant, virile organisation'. *Direct Action* brought to the working class a message 'of virility, strength, and unconquerable optimism'. For Glynn, the IWW was a 'virile organisation . . . ready . . . to advance the interests of the working class'.[10] Sabotage was 'the worker's most potent weapon in his struggle for victory in the class war'. Arbitration, on the other hand, meant for workers a system in which they had degraded their manhood.[11] From prison in 1919, Charlie Reeve boasted in a letter to 'Dear Little Mother' that 'others may turn aside, for a less stern life, Real Men; No, the harder the fight, the greater the victory'.[12]

Against conservative propagandists, especially conscriptionists, who used similarly gendered language, the IWW affirmed true working-class masculinity as expressing itself best in bold, defiant actions against the ruling class and the forces of conservatism generally. In the face of the declining real value of wages during the war, *Direct Action* informed the working class there was a way out:

> But it is a Man's way out. It is for MEN, and not hypnotised political serfs . . . Strike, strike, strike, if you are MEN, STRIKE, if you have the attributes of a man. And if you refuse to fight your own battles, don't blame the fat-headed, weak-hearted Labor Parties; blame your spineless, emasculated slavish selves.[14]

One of the favourite songs borrowed from America encapsulates the connection the IWW frequently made between proletarian militancy and masculinity:

> Would you have freedom from wage slavery,
> Then join in the grand Industrial band;
> Would you from mis'ry and hunger be free,
> Then come! Do your share, like a man.[15]

Direct Action reiterated these sentiments: 'Fellow-worker, if you want to be a man and not a slave, get into the I.W.W. and do your share in the Fight for Freedom.'[16]

The masculinism of the IWW reflected in part the extent to which the IWW was more proletarian than the socialist parties or Labor Party of the time which, unlike the IWW, allowed non-wage workers to join. Wobblies, whose collective self-identity was as virile, class-conscious working men, addressed each other as 'fellow-worker'; they despised the term 'comrade', used by socialists, as 'cissy'.[17] Peter Stearns has observed within the working-class male culture of western Europe between 1890 and 1940 a link between gestures of militancy and notions of manhood, that many strikes were 'intense expressions of male bonding'. (This pattern might be set against the earlier forms of collective industrial action such as those depicted in the nineteenth-century French novel of Emile Zola, *Germinal*, set on the northern coalfields at a time when both men and women worked underground: here it is the women who lead the uprising and their castration of the hated mine manager is a symbol of vengeance.) In Erik Olssen's study of New Zealand's 'Red Feds' before the First World War, a 'vision of manhood' animated the new industrial unionist ideology which spread among unskilled workers: the strike represented 'exhilarating militancy' in place of 'submission'; craft unionism produced workers without backbone, whereas industrial unionism encouraged 'manly self-reliance'; arbitration made cowards of workers.[18] The IWW, in its thoroughgoing determination to abolish the cause of all distress rather than alleviate the symptoms, in its emphasis on struggle in the workplace, cast itself as more truly virile than the effete socialist parties or the limp company of Labor MPs.

Indubitably, the virile class warriors of the IWW would have felt uncomfortable with the issue of homosexuality and with homosexuals. Charlie Reeve was homosexual. His letters from prison to his mother express constant anxiety about 'the American boy' and his failure to write. After his term in jail he lived in a homosexual relationship with another Wobbly, a Danish seaman called Carl Jensen, who worked as a labourer on White Bay power station. By the 1930s, at least, Reeve was 'free in his discussions of such things', according to Leo Kelly who knew him then. Such openness would not have been encouraged in the wartime IWW. Donald Grant suggests Reeve was personally unpopular with the others while in prison and was intensely disliked by Glynn in particular.[19] Possibly, this negative reaction to Reeve was prompted by distaste for his sexual orientation, which overturned the shared sexual morality of the Wobblies.

The IWW hoped that the polarity between the sexes would be heightened rather than diminished in the future ideal society; the successful culmination of the class struggle would benefit men and women equally, but as complementarities, as male and female: 'Industrial Democracy will make real manhood and womanhood possible for the whole human race.' Anxiety for masculinity had as its necessary corollary concern for the preservation of femininity. If capitalism emasculated working-class men, who should reaffirm their manhood in resistance to capitalism, it also defeminised working-class women because it produced 'a dehumanised, sexless, anaemic, and sickly individual, known as the factory hand'. The men were complicit in capitalism's unsexing of their womenfolk: 'Have the men ever put up a spirited determined fight against the system, on behalf of the millions of women the world over who have to bear the weight of family raising and suffer the inhuman conditions of a factory sweatshop at the same time?' Betsy Matthias cautioned the working man that if he wanted the woman to be in the home, he must see to it that her home was fit to live in; it was men's fault that woman had surged out into the industrial world, to find there was less value put on her labour power than man's. 'She knows she "scabs" on you, but you, yourselves, are the cause.' She addressed sternly the working men who, in 'ignorant indifference', caused women to suffer. 'Why do you build palaces and brown stone mansions for other women, while your own women live in hovels and even tents?' Male Wobblies agreed: 'We ought to be damned if we don't look after our own dear wives and dear little ones.'[20]

Such utterances suggest a commitment to the notion of separate spheres: men in the paid workforce and women in the home. Certainly, an IWW recruiting sticker declared: '"Democratic Australia" means strong men on the swag, women on starvation wages, children in the factories. ONE BIG UNION means strong men at work, women in their own sphere, children in the playground.'[21] In fact, the IWW position was less traditional. While it clearly subscribed to the belief that women should not be obliged through economic necessity to enter the paid workforce, it argued specifically that women had as much right to paid employment as men.[22] Women working in industry should not be expected to vacate their positions to make way for unemployed men after the war:

> The women will learn that they can live better as self-sustainers than as the dependents of men content with a starvation wage . . . Women have the right to earn their livelihood as they think best for themselves, the idea that her place is in the home is a mere relic of barbarism, but probably comes down to us from a time when the men were spirited enough to provide a decent home for her. Those times have vanished.[23]

Though working men had been complicit, capitalism was the ultimate cause of women's degradation in industry and in the home; revolutionary industrial unionism, bringing about the downfall of capitalism, was the solution to the woman question as well as to all other questions.

Accordingly, the ideal male–female relationship imagined by the IWW was the companionate militancy of the rebel boy and rebel girl:

> That's the Rebel Girl, that's the Rebel Girl!
> To the working class she's a precious pearl.
> She brings courage, pride and joy
> To the fighting Rebel Boy.
> We've had girls before, but we need some more
> In the Industrial Workers of the World.
> For it's great to fight for freedom
> With a Rebel Girl.[24]

The term 'rebel girl' was common amongst Wobblies, who wished to see more of them.[25] Against the prevailing notion that women should occupy a sphere separate from men, the private family-centred realm, it espoused an idealised partnership in the public political arena of the militant proletarian couple; admittedly, this partnership was both heterosexual and based upon the male as principal breadwinner, but the IWW at least encouraged women to participate in activities then deemed inappropriate for them. Matthias urged the working man to rise up with the working woman: 'enter hand in hand, mentality with mentality, on a new era, in a "solid, united struggle for economic equality"'.[26]

Though rebel girls were a rare breed, they did inhabit public space. By contrast, the women in the socialist organisations of the time generally did the Party housekeeping – sewing banners, raising money and organising social functions – and were largely excluded from the public realm of speaking, proselytising and agitating.[27] Within the IWW, there was less oppression in this manner of the female membership; where they existed they were not confined to the private realms of the movement. In part, female Wobblies were protected from such treatment by the rebel girl ideal. More significantly, there was very little in the way of private realm in the IWW, because it was not so enamoured of itself as an organisational form that needed sustaining through dances and bazaars. There was no elaborate hierarchy of full-time paid officials, whose wages had to be raised by collective Party endeavour. IWW women, where they existed, had a better chance of being treated like men.

The Melbourne Local, more respectable and more like a socialist party than other Locals, was something of an exception here. Alf Wilson recalls: 'Every Saturday afternoon one of the girls would buy the requisites for a Sunday tea, and when we came from the Yarra Bank we would find half a dozen girls and some young fellows with a delightful tea ready.' The IWW Clubs too, committed as they were to costly full-time officialdom and bureaucracy, were more traditional in their treatment of women fellow-workers, resembling the socialist groups in the tasks allotted to the women comrades: raffling a dinner set, a tea set, a bed-spread and an opal ring; holding socials; and organising bazaarettes.[28]

Within the Chicago IWW, the women were far too few, but were not, except in Melbourne, relegated to the kitchens of the organisation. In Sydney, Fellow-Worker Mrs Sullivan chaired the crowded May Day meet-ing in the IWW hall in 1915 and women were regular lecturers at the hall, invariably to 'a very large and appreciative crowd': for example, Mrs Katz in September 1914 on 'Woman: Past, Present and Future'; Mrs McDonald in June 1915 on 'The Sex Question'; Mrs Paul in August 1915 on 'Conscription' and Lena Lynch in November 1915 on 'Women and the War'. When the police entered the IWW hall on 22 July 1917 and searched the 500–600 people present, it was a woman who was addressing the meet-ing. The IWW wished its rebel girls to fan the flames of discontent, and in full public view. And yet, its efforts in encouraging rebel girls were, in the final analysis, inadequate. As Annie Westbrook commented in December 1916 in reporting the emergence of two more rebel women in Perth: 'if we could only make rebels of the women, the game is ours', and yet, 'the IWW of Australia has neglected the woman factor much in the past'.[29]

As in the United States, the scarcity value of the rebel girls prompted elaborate praise from the IWW. Annie Westbrook was one such idolised and idealised rebel girl. Monty Miller wrote to *Direct Action* in October 1916 about one of her performances on the Perth Esplanade, how she was 'in full swing with one of her glowing diatribes against the injustice of capitalism and the sufferings of workers, especially women workers', when some boneheads arrived and 'tried to down and out our sister rebel with interjections and abusive accusations'. The regular audience of the IWW 'got indignant, and fairly roared and howled against the opponent of their popular woman speaker'. Mostly, crowds were respon-sive to the woman speaker: one habitual interjector announced at a meeting of Westbrook's that he would not interrupt a woman. Westbrook exploited her novelty value – in the interest of her class: 'women can get in where men cannot . . . this is the best method of pro-paganda', she wrote to a friend.[30]

Under the tutelage of Lena Lynch, May Ewart, a joiner's daughter born in 1893 in Manchester, became active in the Sydney Local. She worked as a barmaid and clerical worker at the 'First and Last' at Circular Quay, unfortunately demolished in 1980, then at the 'Arcadia', until Detective Hawe prevailed upon her employer to dismiss her. His raid of her quarters in North Sydney unearthed evidence of her studies

The 'Rebel Girl', May Ewart Wilson (*third from left*), 13 August 1925 at
Williamstown, Rhondda. (Courtesy of Sally Bowen, Wollongong)

in French and German and her love of Oscar Wilde. She was convicted
under the Unlawful Associations Act in October 1917 but her three
months jail sentence with hard labour was suspended with a twelve-
month good behaviour bond by a magistrate who muttered complaints

about the police sending decent young girls to chokey. Ewart married fellow Wobbly Jock Wilson, born on the Island of Mull in western Scotland in 1884, who had arrived in Australia in 1909. The service was conducted by a Presbyterian minister in Long Bay jail on 4 October 1917, where Wilson was serving a six-month sentence. The bride wore a navy blue coat and skirt. Lena Lynch, also in jail for four months with hard labour, and the prison governor were witnesses; after presenting the bride with a copy of *The Sentimental Bloke* and £1, the Governor showed Mrs Lynch the prison gardens so the newly weds could be alone. Jock recalls: 'We had the marriage ceremony, and I didn't see her again till we were both on the boat on which we were being deported.'[31] A Wobbly couple, a rebel girl and boy.

Another such couple were Lesbia Keogh, born in 1891, and Pat Harford. When Lesbia Harford's poems were published in 1941, Guido Baracchi's address began: 'if I were asked to describe Lesbia Keogh, as I knew her, in two words, I would answer: "Rebel Girl"'. She herself endorsed the Wobbly ideal of companionate militancy in 'Companions':

> The girls who prattle of work and pleasure,
> Of last week's picnic and this week's joys,
> Of past and present, nor heed the future,
> Are lagging comrades for dawnstruck boys.[32]

An unlikely candidate for the rebel girl role, a convent girl with a serious heart problem, Keogh had graduated in Law from Melbourne University in 1916. Refusing to enter the legal profession, 'in which . . . the scales of justice were loaded against the worker', she chose to work in the clothing trade in order to become an IWW member, attracted to it rather than any other socialist group because of her dislike of rigid hierarchies and structures. She was soon at the forefront of union activity in the Clothing and Allied Trades Union: she represented her section of the trade on the union executive and on the Dressmakers' Wages Board and was elected vice-president of the newly formed section of the union.[33] Of her other rebel activities, Baracchi, whom she recruited into the IWW, writes that 'She showed her mettle . . . when, after speaking against conscription night after night at street corners, her exhausted heart and throat finally landed her in a Melbourne hospital . . . However, she . . . silently stole away, only to break the silence the very next night from a soap-box.' Believing that art should reach an audience wider than a gathering of intellectuals, she composed tunes to her poems about revolution, social injustice and the class struggle and sang them. However, her poems and songs were not taken up by the IWW; Modjeska argues they were too modern and female to be accommodated within the working-class masculine orientation of IWW balladry. After Baracchi, her lover from 1916 to 1918, deserted her, she moved to Sydney, 'living her life in the circles of the suppressed I.W.W.', making her living at the clothing trade, 'with intermissions imperatively dictated by the condition of her heart'. There, in 1920, she married Patrick John O'Flaghartie Fingal Harford, an Irish boot trade worker, who was 'charming but irresponsible'. Lesbia was not always happy with her rebel boy, confiding to May Brodney: 'He neglects me badly but I don't like the idea of leaving him because I think he would break up pretty badly if I did. I see nothing but drink, bad health, & probably short periods of jail ahead for him if I leave him.'[34]

With the disappearance into jail of many of the leading male activists a significant number of women at last joined the IWW. The women became more numerous partly because political housekeeping, especially raising money, had for the first time become an organisational priority, indeed necessity. Betsy Matthias wrote in January 1917: 'this month last year there were but few women in the Sydney Local of the I.W.W., but since the persecution started three months ago the women have surged into the organisation and are now as busy in the release, defence and social functions as are the men'. An I.W.W. Women's Committee was formed around this time which became, after suppression, the 'ex-I.W.W. Social Committee'.[35] In part, too, repression encouraged female Wobblies to become rebel girls – but as understudies. Lena Lynch announced in the Domain in September 1917: 'I am busy instructing a class of girl speakers, who will attend the Domain every Sunday to keep the movement alive until the sentenced members are released.' To frustrate her efforts, she was promptly imprisoned for four months with hard labour.[36] Although the men's incarceration pushed female Wobblies to the forefront, it was their perceived role as female supports to virile class warriors that was most clearly being reinforced. When Betsy Matthias' husband Rudolph was sentenced to his six-month term, she recalls standing in the court with

> another wife, who was to become the mother of another little babe the next week, and with streaming eyes and faint heart she turned to me, as the 'six months' hard labor' was given her husband by the court, and said, 'O, Mrs. Rudolph, it's hard, but I must bear it. I know his principle, and I know he is a man, a real man.'[37]

When the town hall was used for a public welcome to the released IWW prisoners in August 1920, a meeting of conservative women assembled at the town hall to protest against its use for such an occasion. Wobbly women disrupted this meeting and great disorder followed. The rebel girls greeted the national anthem with shouts of derision and much argument ensued between the women on the platform and the women on the floor.[38] For Wobblies, male and female alike, notions of sisterhood were nonsense; society moved in grooves of class, not sex.

The most detailed discussion of gender issues in IWW literature was in its pamphlet on *The Social Evil. Prostitution and its Cure*, published around July 1917. 'Throughout the ages man has been the strong, invasive, dominant sex, and women have been more or less weak, dependent, subservient. In various ways, from savagery to modern civilization, women have been subjugated; they have been first captured, beaten, stolen, then bought and cajoled . . .' Probably, in the very beginning, there was a time when the human female was as strong, as swift and capable of self-sustenance as the human male, but once men had gained the upper hand by taking advantage of women's vulnerability when pregnant or lactating, women's physical prowess was discouraged and their subservience to men ensured by brute force and by 'inculcating the idea of duty, and of the honor to be found in faithfulness and virtue'. Man conquered woman before he conquered anyone else and he found her a useful conquest: 'A slave female meant unlimited sexual indulgence. Free and equal females inferred some trouble exercised in winning them.' With the establishment of social inequality between the sexes came the gendered discrepancy in moral standards: 'the all-prevailing idea of man's right to indulge his passions, while his companion is a disgraced and wicked creature'.[39]

Awareness of the long-standing inequality between the sexes notwithstanding, the IWW was concerned primarily to indict capitalism for its role in the subjection of women: 'Perhaps the most revolting feature of modern capitalism is its subjugation and consequent degradation of women.' Capitalism treated woman without any scruples, forcing her to be a wage-slave and to submit to all the indignities of male domination.[40] Not men but capitalism, not a sex but a system was responsible for the condition of women. Accordingly, class organisation was the most appropriate response and class differences between women were stressed persistently.

In vivid contrast to the rebel girls of the working class were 'the parasitical bunch of hussies' in the National Council of Women. These wealthy women, 'Mrs Potts Point, Mrs Mosman', concerned to harness female labour for the war effort by a scheme of national service for women, were a particular hate-object of the IWW.

> The spectacle of this idle, vicious, good-for-nothing clique, who cannot wash their own soiled underwear without having a woman of the working class to

do it for them, discussing the problem of work, is enough to raise a howl of laughter in hell. If one could be sure that they would be taken out of their mansions and motor-cars, placed in the factory, and compelled to house, clothe, and keep themselves on the fifteen shillings a week which statistics show to be the average wage for female labor in Australia, industrial conscription might be justifiable.[41]

Similar hostility was expressed towards the white-feather brigade, the 'terrible recruiting sergeants' of the war. When one argued that every mother risked death to give birth so men should do the same for mothers, *Direct Action* deemed this 'sentimental slush' and used the occasion as an opportunity to stress the significance of class differences in the experience of childbirth: how poor women were forced into the ugly wards of a public hospital run by wealthy women who wished to gain a name as philanthropists, where the hard beds were unpleasant havens for work-worn women risking death in childbirth, who then had to vacate them quickly to make room for others.[42]

Tom Barker seized upon the sensation caused by Edith Cavell's murder at the hands of the Germans to point out the hypocrisy of such concern:

> It ill becomes the garrulous capitalist press of Australia to howl about the murder of one Englishwoman, when it has consistently stood for the exploitation of little girls of fourteen, who have been dragged out of the playground, and pushed into the unhealthy and foetid atmosphere of the ruling class factories . . . working for wages that are not sufficient to house and feed them . . .

One Big Union, he admitted, would not be able to resurrect Miss Cavell, 'but it will be able to abolish the state of society that condemns millions of her sex to laborious toil, and long hours for wages that would not keep Lady Strickland's cat in ribbon'.[43]

The 'unfortunate women of the working class' had nothing in common with 'the pampered, pug-nursing, Potts Point dame'.[44] Lesbia Keogh, working in the clothing trade wrote:

> All day long,
> We sew fine muslin for you to wear . . .
> Just like flames,
> Insatiable, you eat up all our hours,
> And sun and love and tea and talk and flowers,
> Suburban dames.[45]

The IWW insisted that class distinctions between women were as significant as those between men, whatever the relationship between men and women within each class might be. The 'daughters of the working class' have to work, being nothing but human commodities, 'as different from the daughters of the rich as midnight is different from midday'.[46]

The IWW thus took issue with feminist movements that asserted the common interests of all women against all men; the rebel girls' common cause was not with women but with men of their own class. In her writing and speaking, Betsy Matthias always enjoined working-class women to fight alongside their menfolk, and working-class men to encourage the participation of women in the struggle to end the poverty and misery caused by capitalism. Annie Westbrook appealed to the 'women of Australia', to 'wake up and fight the class that robs you of your inheritance, your joy, your love, your children'. In a letter to his mother who worked a ten-hour day as a maid, Charlie Reeve observed: 'how can Liberty become a fact with all Mankind unless Woman is free'; of woman's place, he insisted, 'cannot the blind fatuous Males not see that it is the first shackle to be broken, if they themselves wish for Freedom'. By ignoring the woman question, men were tilting at windmills: 'fools, fools, when, oh, when will that wooden headed, two legged chump say, come on Mate, & together Win a World'.[47]

The IWW regretted that the advanced movements of the day showed a common failing in dealing with the woman question. It was adamant that

> in being a wage slave she stands exactly on the same plane as man – in relation to the employing class, that is, as slave to a master. The I.W.W. stands for the abolition of 'wage slavery', the cause of women's degradation, since the only natural thing for her to do is to join the I.W.W.

The working class, the IWW insisted, 'have everything to gain by acting in unity with their sisters. Theirs is a common battle against adversity, and they should act in unity when fighting against a common foe.' In common with the socialist organisations of the time, the IWW perceived feminism as weakening the class struggle by dividing the unity of workers.[48]

Yet the IWW did not rebuke all feminists or feminist movements: it depended who they were and what they stood for. It approved the strong feminist presence in the anti-conscription movement and promoted Adela Pankhurst and Cecilia John's propaganda tour to Sydney on behalf of the Women's Peace Army in November 1915. It criticised Pankhurst's belief that a set of supermen and superwomen could adjudicate on the division of spoils between the ruling classes and hand down perpetual international peace, but insisted that, in so far as she exposed the economic causes of modern warfare, she deserved the support and assistance of militant workers.[49] When Pankhurst visited Sydney again, in August 1916, she was escorted from the hall after her oration by Donald Grant and Peter Larkin.[50] In March 1917 the Broken Hill Local ordered a bundle of books entitled *The Awakening of Women*. On the other hand, the

IWW had no time for 'that agitation which shrieks for the "economic emancipation of woman," yet bids her scorn the union of her class'.[51]

The IWW supported and approved women's right to vote; where women were not enfranchised, capitalism was even more reprehensible than usual in this denial of equal citizenship rights to women. The women's suffrage movement was, in its own way, composed of rebel girls: 'One attribute which I think women in a great cause possess more than men is that of enthusiasm. The militant suffrage movement proves the truth of that statement . . .'[52] As direct actionists, who believed in the principle of self-emancipation, Wobblies appeared to sympathise with the desire of women to free themselves. After commenting 'what a queer animal that Male is, arrogating to himself the Universe, & then relying on the Woman to keep it going', who then had the temerity to announce that he was 'allowing the Woman the right of entry into all arenas', Reeve observed:

> its not by the grace of HE, but Woman's determination to escape the Pots and Pans, more power too her . . . HE has had the running of things for ages, & what a mess HE has made of it, now HE get out, give SHE a chance, or rather SHE must take the chance, not wait for the conde[s]cension of HE.[53]

Where the American IWW regarded feminist movements as vitiation of the overall struggle for class-based organisation, the Australian movement simply viewed such movements as inadequate for securing permanent improvement in the condition of women. The vote had not emancipated women for it had not even yielded equal pay for equal work.[54] Supportive though it was of the female suffrage movement, the IWW expected as little to come from votes for women as it expected of votes generally.

Of far greater use to women, as far as the IWW was concerned, were battles at the point of production to secure equal pay for women workers. The first issue of *Direct Action* in January 1914 informed its readers that, in Victoria and New South Wales, 65 000 female wage-slaves, 'your sisters', were employed at an average wage of 15 shillings per week. This, it added, was what the Labor Party called 'step at a time' legislation. 'Women have as much right to jobs as the men, but the trades unions should see that equal pay for equal work is received.' *Direct Action* maintained:

> we must work together until we get women as thoroughly organised as men are; together we will see to it that child labour is abolished; there shall be equal pay for equal work . . . Women must be organised into trade unions . . . They must not take any substitute for industrial organisation.[55]

However, strident though the IWW critique of the arbitration system was, it did not, as Joy Damousi notes, point to its crucial role in sanctioning the discrepancy in pay rates and conditions for men and women.[56]

While urging and approving the organisation of women within the mainstream trade union movement to secure equal pay for equal work, the IWW argued that only the One Big Union could really solve the problem of the exploitation of labour power, male and female alike: 'There is one salvation for the women wage-workers – ORGANISATION . . . Like the men, they only have one hope – that is, to join the One Big Union of the working class. The I.W.W. is the only way out for all who toil in the industrial hells of capitalism.' Monty Miller, in his lecture on 'Woman as a Worker' in April 1916, argued that the security of labour could only be attained by a wise combination of male and female labour, by one big union of men and women, and that, although capitalism would foment jealousy and competition, 'for the workers, that way madness lies'.[57]

The IWW stressed that notions of male superiority or prejudices against women workers were dangerous for class organisation and enhanced the position of the ruling class; if the boss could work up an antagonism between male and female workers, he would be safe for a few years longer. The identity of interest of all workers must be understood.

> Let us prove to the master class that we are not as simple as he thinks. Let us show him that he cannot set us fighting SEX AGAINST SEX in the mad scramble for jobs. Let us demonstrate to the boss that we are going to fight him AS A CLASS, and not in sections.

If the toilers united as a class and demanded 'equal pay for equal work' and 'an injury to one an injury to all', the bosses' position would be weakened and that of both male and female workers improved.[58]

It was because women had not been receiving equal pay for equal work that many of them had resorted to prostitution. The IWW argued persistently that the terrible evil of the trade in women was caused by the poor remuneration of women in the paid workforce. Women who chose to sell their bodies rather than starve were not to blame: 'Is it not the capitalist system which is responsible?' Tom Barker commented: 'When one wanders through the streets of Sydney and sees the great and ever-growing army of the night, with its sweet girl recruits, and its broken, battered veterans, he can see the vicious and griping hand of commercialism and low wages.'[59]

However, prostitution was not simply a product of capitalism but of the subordination of women to men, 'of centuries of abuse, oppression, and robbery'. When the sexes were more equal, at the dawn of recorded history, when the male would have nothing to offer the female to induce her to do what her own nature did not prompt, there was no prostitution. As women became less equal with men they could not compete with men in the sale of their labour power in any form; they had only one possession men were willing to pay for. 'It is but natural that the disinherited ones of the earth, placed as they are at such a frightful disadvantage, should think of every device, every possible service, they could render in order to obtain the comforts of life . . . Where there is poverty and destitution there will be prostitution . . .'[60] From a contemporary perspective, this explanation is striking for its denial of agency to females: it employs conventional sexual morality to arraign a social order in which men are dominant.

Not only did the system render women sufficiently desperate to turn to prostitution, the existence of prostitution then helped to keep male wages down: 'Ye make the prostitute, that the young men of to-day may remain single, and remaining single, return more profits to your evil coffers.' The exploitation of male workers made it difficult for them to aspire to married life; the majority of men were condemned to work the greater part of a day for the privilege of patronising a brothel. Thus, the 'sycophantic snuffle about the sacred bonds of matrimony' could only arouse feelings of derision, for these 'pimps of plutocracy' were 'striving strenuously to legitimate bastardy'.[61]

Where references to working-class male use of prostitutes blamed the system that made such visits imperative, the more frequent discussions of ruling-class patronage of prostitutes denounced the men and emphasised the way in which the prostitute-client relationship was unequal in both its gender and its class dimensions. A *Direct Action* columnist wrote bitterly: 'In my slum I have seen wretches of your class come and purchase young virgins of my class for a few pieces of silver. Yes; I have seen pure young maidens sold to rich, syphilitic old derelicts, for the sum of five shillings . . .'[62] Even more despicable were those men who profiteered from the sale of women's bodies, who procured vulnerable and desperate women for the trade under false pretences and then intervened in the transactions so that the poor women were not even paid the full price for their own bodies.[63]

The IWW was outraged that men, pimps and patrons of prostitutes alike, then had the temerity to 'despise and persecute the whore'. So also did it express impatience with the working-class man for his prejudices. The wage-worker, it noted, unreservedly and unprotestingly sells himself to a boss, 'and still he looks with contempt at the woman who sells her sex rather than her labor power'. It preached solidarity with her:

> We are all workers, we of the bottom rung; we, the hoboes, the thieves, the prostitutes, the scabs, the workers. Cast aside this capitalist morality which makes us shatter those battered relics – the women who sell their bodies. These 'poor dumb mouths' need our pity, our love, and our service. To hell with cant![64]

The efforts of crusaders who sought to convert the unfortunate women or regimes who tried to stamp out the trade could amount to nothing: 'A complete change in the institutions of civilisation, and in the prevailing ideas of our attitudes as human beings toward each other, must be brought about before a thorough cure of this monstrous evil can be accomplished.' When men and women stood on an equal footing, general social equality having been established, there would be neither reason nor cause for prostitution: 'Love would come into its own again, and would bless and purify the inborn impulse that has been dragged through the mud and mire of centuries until it is a monster, not a natural attribute of the complete, sane, self-controlled human being.'[65]

Direct Action looked forward to the abolition of prostitution, along with the ending of capitalism:

> Given freedom, production for use instead of for profit; . . . then life and love will be free; no maiden shall sell her body, and no man shall want to buy it. Education, enlightenment, intelligence, clean living, natural sexual relations, will soon wipe out this awful scourge.[66]

The subordination of women to men made 'natural sexual relations' impossible. It deprived her of the right of the disposal of her body, except under bond usually of the most exacting character, imposed upon her misery, shame and disease if she indulged in 'clandestine relationships', or gave her the mentally and physically demoralising alternative of no sex experience whatever. 'Contrast this picture with the ideal of a free society, wherein woman shall be the economic and social equal of man; free to direct her own sex life, aided from childhood by a thorough knowledge of sex functions.' The IWW sold copies of Margaret Sanger's book on birth control, *What Every Mother Should Know*, and stressed the importance of information about family limitation being easily available.[67] Stearns has argued that many working-class men at this time opposed birth control as a threat to their image of masculinity.[68] However, the larrikin Wobblies do not appear to have been affronted by birth control; it was at the point of production, in industrial skirmishes with the boss, that virility or otherwise was proven.

Although the IWW was dismissive of 'pseudo-radical' sexual reform movements which discussed endlessly the question of marriage and divorce while ignoring the issue of industrial exploitation, it defended vehemently the well-known sex reformer, W.J. Chidley, who propounded the notion that men should not be aggressive or even dominant in the sex act. *Direct Action* claimed Chidley had been brought to the grave by the brutal persecution he met with at the hands of the authorities, because his philosophy was 'not acceptable to the leading citizens'. To the over-dressed and over-fed man, saturated with alcohol and nicotine, the stalwart philosopher, Chidley, in his 10 ounces of silk, without alcohol, tobacco, animal food, might seem a crank, a lunatic: 'But the unbiassed, scientific man, could see nothing amiss, either in the man Chidley or his philosophy.' *Direct Action*, ever optimistic, predicted: 'The day will probably dawn when his philosophy will be accepted, but that will be when reason usurps the powers which ignorance holds to-day.'[69]

In the meantime, the capitalist media encouraged the sex perversion created by the system, 'pandering to the perverted sex-instincts of those pitiable bye-products of modern civilisation who morbidly crave for the revolting details of cases of sodomy, bestiality and child-violation'. The capitalist class itself was rendered dissolute by its role in society: 'A little useful labour will give the capitalist class less time and inclination for immorality and wife swopping. The I.W.W. ARE anxious to keep society pure.' Children should have impressed upon them the sacredness of the process of reproduction.

> Teach them that there is a beautiful time to come to them . . . when they can look into a tiny baby face, clasp two tiny baby hands, and feel this wonder and beautiful creation a part of their own being . . . Teach them to keep their minds and bodies clean for this wonderful gift.[70]

Yet the IWW was not sexually puritanical in the conventional sense. The purity to which it aspired was that based on freedom and consent, on complete lack of coercion in sexual relations, denied working-class men and women alike; it despised the professional purity mongers of capitalist society, their hypocrisy and their cruelty towards those denied 'normal sexual relations' by the system these crusaders upheld. Marriage sanctified by such people was, under capitalism, a form of prostitution for the woman, who in dependency sold her body in exchange for the necessities of life provided by the man:

> Why is it that when a man and woman from the pure motive of love, without any stipulated price, give themselves to each other, without a ceremony, we punish them for adultery: but when another man and woman make a distinct bargain, pay a stipulated price, and without any thought of love enter upon sexual relations, after getting the union label from the State, we have not a whisper of criticism for them.[71]

Direct Action fulminated against the moralisers of capitalism, the wowsers and puritans, 'the cold water craze, charity and cadging crusades, the kill joy cliques, social purity brigades', regretting their activity as a social and political force. Puritanism, it noted, assiduously preached industry, sobriety and thrift to the masses: 'Philosophically, Puritanism is antagonistic to reality and life, upholding the doctrines of predestination, pain, renunciation and sex perversion.' Moreover, Puritanism 'vigorously opposed the anti-slavery, feminist, and other progressive movements'.[72]

Commentators such as Shor, who rightly draw attention to the image, style and language of the IWW, which discouraged the full incorporation of women, often overlook more positive features, damning it for its sexist form and ignoring its anti-sexist content. As Charlie Reeve wrote from prison about the condition of women: 'it is not in accord with Our Ideal, that she should be dominated by Man, or that the family she is busy with should absorb all her life'.[73] In the case of the IWW, it is indeed unfortunate that its unconsciously gendered political personality could not attract the rebel girls that it consciously desired.

CHAPTER 8

'A Real Democracy':
Organisation and Practice

The American IWW has been dismissed as incorrigibly anarchic, one commentator observing that 'No one uses the word "organization" oftener or practices it less.' Rushton repeats the charge against the Australian IWW: 'Despite the constant insistence on the need to organize, this amorphous mass was incapable of being organized.' Childe, too, notes that the departments and unions envisaged in the IWW's form of industrial organisation existed only on paper, that no attempt was made in Australia to create them, that only the skeleton of the organisation – the locals and the General Executive Board – ever existed in Australia.[1]

Admittedly, there was a discrepancy in the importance the IWW attached, in theory, to organisation and the extent of organisation achieved in practice. Certainly, the elaborate unity of the Wobbly vision only ever attained the very lowest stages of realisation in the structure of the Australian IWW. However, unlike the anarchists, the Wobblies aspired to be organised. The IWW saw its role as being to impress workers with the need for better organisation, in other words, to use the word 'organisation' frequently: 'The function of the I.W.W. . . . is to point out the lines on which . . . a genuine Labor movement may be formed . . .'[2] Talking about organisation was not the opposite to organising in practice: it was its prerequisite.

Moreover, Wobbly organisational forms were not easily noticed by external observers; they did not consist in full-time office-bearers and neatly kept books of minutes. They differed markedly from the more hierarchical and authoritarian practices in Labor Party branches, trade unions and socialist parties at this time: 'it is the teaching and aim of the I.W.W. that all power be vested in the rank and file'.[3] The internal democracy practised in the IWW might well appear to the outsider and to posterity to be chaos.

The IWW was contemptuous of other labour and left-wing organisations for their varying degrees of elitism and bureaucratism. The Sydney Local's first leaflet in 1911 announced on its banner-head: 'All Power is Centred in the General Membership.'[4] *Direct Action* boasted that 'in complete contradistinction to the trade union movement the IWW organises from the bottom up'. In doing so, it was prefiguring the future society. 'The I.W.W. in organising from the bottom up, and giving full power to the general membership to transact the business of the organisation is laying the foundation of a real democracy.' It was 'impossible for the officers of the I.W.W. to dominate or side-track the organisation as they have no more say than the humblest member'. Thus, 'the I.W.W. is truly democratic and free from all officialdom'.[5] The Adelaide Local decided at its inception that chairmen should have a deliberative vote only, since 'the person fit to exercise the prerogative of two minds has yet to be born'. Rather than allow the chairman a casting vote in the event of a tie, a motion should lapse.[6] Tom Barker stresses:

> We were a very loose organisation . . . We didn't have a paid organiser anywhere . . . virtually everything was done by voluntary, unpaid effort. There were no strap hangers or people who were living on the organisation. I think I was about the only person who was full time . . . thirty shillings a week . . . I lived very simply, as most of us did at that time.[7]

As general secretary-treasurer, Barker was in a position to suggest and guide – but only insofar as the membership consented; he was permitted, for instance, to inspect the speakers before the Domain meetings each Sunday to ensure they were clean, shaved, tidy and sober. During the trial of the Twelve, Wobblies called as defence witnesses were prepared to admit that some of the defendants were more obviously in the public eye than they were themselves, but were adamant that 'they were no more prominent in the organization than any other man'. Bill Genery of the Melbourne Local recalled in a 1969 interview that this Local was 'very democratic', changing its office-bearers at least annually, but that it was also 'well organised'.[8]

The IWW was organised around an openly identifiable chain of responsibility, supposedly preventing the operation of more covert and enduring bases of power: Local officers were responsible to the Local Committee which in turn was responsible to the General Executive Board which was headed by the general secretary-treasurer, all of whom were elected and frequently. So grave was the concern lest one member should dominate the movement that a different chairman was chosen for each weekly business meeting.[9] Here, truly, was limited tenure of office. Mindful, too, of the problem of the 'tyranny of structurelessness'

identified by the women's movement in the 1970s, IWW meetings limited the speaking time of each to ensure greater freedom of speech for
all. The anarchist Groupe D'Etudes Scientifiques roundly denounced
the IWW for its 'jesuitical' attempts to regulate meetings. The Groupe
insisted that 'freedom of speech' and time limits on speech were incon-
sistent: 'Who can determine, in advance', they enquired, 'how long a
speech will last? . . . I.W.W.ists can have a "limited time" for their representatives and bring a "chairman" for them – half a dozen if they wish –
we most decidedly refuse to interfere or deny them their natural
right . . .' It rejected the 'Authoritative Method' of the IWW in the name
of unrestricted individual liberty.[10]

The organisational practices that distinguished the IWW from any
anarchist movement were not achieved at the expense of internal
democracy. The IWW functioned like a participatory democracy, notable
for the high level of participation in its activities by the card-holders. Bill
Beattie insists that 'all decisions were made by majority vote'. Unlike
anarchist groups, these majority decisions were binding on all members;
debate was accordingly vigorous and continual. The binding nature of
majority decisions was justified by the IWW because of unanimity about
the aims of the organisation: the necessity for organisation by the working class on industrial union lines.[11] In practice, there was little dissension. Tom Barker wrote to Tom Glynn from Moscow on 29 February
1921, confessing he was homesick for Australia and the IWW crowd in
Sydney:

> When we remember how little we differed, how little factionism or lime-
> lightism entered in the old wobbly crowd in Sydney, the fights we had, the
> storms we lived through, your own cases, the shootings . . . the deportations,
> and the paper – well, I sometimes feel homesick, and wish that I was back in 403
> with Paddy Quinlan leading the band, and the route marches going to Redfern
> and Botany when the trams were stopped. The I.W.W. fought well . . .[12]

Unity in resolution and action, but only after a democratic process of
arriving at decisions, would achieve IWW ambitions. The Wobblies saw
organisation and democracy as complementary not antagonistic.

Though committed to democratic organisation as the best means to
advance the class struggle and the formation of One Big Union, the
IWW did not tend to itself as an organisation in the way typical of trade
unions and socialist parties. By comparison with these it was an
impecunious vagrant in the world of left-wing politics. Dick Surplus
commented that the Brisbane Local 'didn't need much finance because
it had very little expenditure'. Only the relatively staid Melbourne Local,
more like a VSP branch in many ways than an IWW Local and widely

acknowledged as the most respectable of the IWW organisations, nourished itself financially. When Jock Wilson paid a return visit to Melbourne from Sydney, he castigated the Melbourne Local for not doing all the things they ought to; they defended themselves on the grounds that they had done magnificent work in a few months in straightening the finances.[13] Otherwise, IWW Locals were serious credit risks. Detective Moore reported to military intelligence in June 1916 that the finances of the Sydney Local were 'at a very low ebb, and their funds would appear to hardly meet working expenses . . .'[14]

Drawing its members as it did from the lowest economic strata in the community, Wobbly finances were invariably shaky. Perhaps making a virtue out of necessity, the IWW turned organisational impoverishment into a matter of principle: 'To facilitate the work of organization, large initiation fees and dues are prohibited by the I.W.W.'[15] Beattie emphasises that the Locals financed their activities as much by sales of their newspapers and pamphlets as by dues, which were 'very light'. Cheap membership was justified not only as a necessity for recruiting poorly paid workers, but as a deliberate means to keep the outfit financially lean. Wobblies were wary of organisations that assumed a form independent of the members that comprised them, a process that would be encouraged by the accumulation of assets. It was against principle, Beattie recalls, to amass funds. Members were more inclined to contribute generously to aid specific causes, such as assistance to striking workers and the defence of the Twelve, than to sustain the IWW as an organisation.[16] The Sydney Local's total assets were little more than a printing press (bought in June 1914 with money borrowed from Fellow-Worker Hamilton), a piano, a library and large stocks of literature for sale. Other Locals owned much less, mostly nothing more than a small library and literature for immediate sale.

Unlike the socialist groups of the time and the Communist Party from the 1930s, the IWW never owned any real estate; it rented cheap halls. Initially, the Sydney Local was based in a disused Gospel Hall at 330 Castlereagh Street, a building that disappeared later when the tunnel was put through from Central Station to the Harbour; in May 1916 it moved to an old hall at 403 Sussex Street, formerly used for attempts to rehabilitate prostitutes.[17] If necessary, it hired the town hall for big events, for example, the May Day celebration in 1916. However, to save the additional charge for using the town hall's piano the Wobblies brought their own with them, a dozen fellow workers hauling it up the town hall steps.[18] The Melbourne Local was housed at 243 William Street, moving in August 1916 to a more central location at 197 Russell Street on the south-western corner with Little Bourke Street, where fellow workers climbed especially dingy stairs to the meetings and lectures, the Saturday night dances and the Sunday evening teas. The Trades Hall Council had refused them use of a room at the Trades Hall.[19] The Adelaide Local met at the Oddfellows Hall, Mooltan Street, off Flinders Street. In Broken Hill, the Local's rooms were in the Palace Buildings in Sulphide Street; around May 1916 it also acquired use of a hall at 316 Argent Street. The Fremantle Local rented a hall at 35 Phillimore Street.[20]

Barker maintains the IWW's main sources of income came from sales of *Direct Action* and other newspapers and pamphlets such as *War, What For?* The Sydney Local hauled its 'mental dynamite' to the Domain each Sunday on a hand-cart, sometimes collecting as much as £100 from sales in a single afternoon. Kerr & Co.'s small reprints of such works as Karl Marx's *Value, Price and Profit* were retailed at threepence, having been bought in bulk by Locals for roughly one-third or one-quarter of that price. Capable organisers were often supplied with stocks of literature at wholesale prices or given free, which financed some of the speaking tours.[21]

Direct Action sold for a penny. Four pages long, each with four or five columns of short articles, news and commentary, it was enlivened by Syd Nicholls' superb cartoons and adorned with a bold bannerhead depicting two sturdy working men grasping hands beneath the international IWW logo. Initially monthly, it became fortnightly in May 1914 and weekly in October 1915. Ted Giffney was the manager of the paper, in charge of sales and subscriptions. The editor, the only paid labour, was responsible for preparing sufficient copy for each issue, setting up the paper and running the press in the little alcove at the back of the Sydney office. The authorities were curious about who was editor, for the paper itself announced: 'Editor: Mr. A. Block'. Barker recounts: 'We got a block of wood with a dingy old top hat on it and kept it behind the door in the editorial room. When the detectives came round they got very annoyed when they were introduced to the editor.' Glynn, whose journalistic abilities were greater than his oratorical skills, was in fact the first editor, and for two subsequent stints until arrested as one of the Twelve. Barker, who succeeded him as editor, reckoned Glynn 'had a magnificent fluid style of provocative writing. He had a great flow of English and could reduce things to their essentials . . . It became, in my opinion, one of the most formidable newspapers that have been published . . . compared with the general run of socialist papers at that time . . .'[22] Subsequent editors were Giffney, Reeve, Kinman, A.A. MacInnes and Norman Rancie; but only Barker approached Glynn's editorial skill.

Fellow workers and Locals were invited to send in reports of activities, news and short snappy articles: 'Above all, don't send long, windy articles about nothing in particular . . . The first idea of the organisation is to propagate the tactics and structure of the I.W.W., and, therefore,

VOL. 3, NO. 91.   Registered at the General Post-office Sydney, for Transmission by Post as a newspaper   October 7, 1916.

WORKERS'

Members of Your Class are in Long Bay Gaol for TREASON

Jesus Christ

was Crucified

FOR TREASON

Front page of *Direct Action*, 7 October 1916.

necessarily, this paper will express those ideas primarily.'[23] Its diction was aggressively proletarian:

> This paper is written by slaves for slaves. So long as we are understood by the workers, we do not care whether or not critics criticise, friends approve, or enemies revel in denunciation. . . . We drop our h's in conversation, our composition is faulty, and our punctuation abominable, but fellow slaves will, nevertheless, understand our message. This is not meant to be an apology. It is merely a roundabout, but we hope a polite, method of telling would-be critics to go to h – – l!'[24]

Working mostly as labourers by day, the Wobblies involved in the production of the paper spent their evenings setting type, reading proofs, bundling and addressing. Every copy had to go through the press twice, for it was an old Wharfedale flat press, sixty or seventy years old. This press, which the IWW had bought in the belief that ownership of it would remove all restraints upon 'the expression of clear-cut revolutionary principles' was unregistered and was confiscated on this basis in September 1916, after which *Direct Action* had to be put out to a commercial printer. The moment the paper was ready it had to be packed and posted; enormous quantities of bulk deliveries of *Direct Action* were sent through the post office. It was especially important that the papers caught the posts and boats going west and north, in time for the regular propaganda meetings in the most remote outposts of Wobbly influence, such as Kalgoorlie, Broken Hill and Cairns.[25]

Individual subscriptions were significant but most copies of *Direct Action* were dispensed at meetings. It was not unusual for the Sydney Local to sell 1000 copies at the Sunday afternoon meeting in the Domain; the very first issue of *Direct Action* in January 1914 went that way. A year later, during the Sydney newsboys' strike in 1915, 4500 copies of a single issue were sold by the newsboys alone. In the middle of 1914 the Adelaide Local was expecting soon to sell 1000 copies of the paper each issue. A report from Broken Hill in August 1914 mentioned that seven dozen copies of *Direct Action* were sold 'in a few minutes'.[26]

During 1915 *Direct Action* grew considerably in circulation; and, in the hands of IWW members, a well-travelled section of the working class, it was covering a wide area of the country. Jimmy Seamer recalls that *Direct Action* was 'widely read by militants'. According to Barker's reminiscences with which Childe concurs, *Direct Action* had a regular weekly circulation of 15 000 'in the big days'.[27] Norman Jeffery, then active in the IWW, estimates the maximum circulation as 26 000. These figures are almost certainly exaggerated. The issue for 14 October 1916, 'big days', boasted that circulation had just reached 8000. According to letters from Barker to Glynn, Barker was hoping to reach a circulation of 10 000 shortly before the arrest of the Twelve, the actual maximum circulation being 9000 at the end of October 1916; by mid-1917 circulation figures had dropped to 6000.[28] However, in estimating readership as opposed to circulation, these figures might safely be doubled or even trebled, because of the still pervasive custom of passing on reading matter to a mate; in this way, the inflated estimates might not be so wide of the mark.

A distinctive propaganda tactic of the IWW was the extensive use of stickers. About four times the size of a postage stamp, these were pasted on shop windows, on motor-cars and elsewhere. Dick Surplus claims the IWW produced hundreds of thousands of these, with captions such as: 'Fast workers die young', and that people could not help but notice them because they were placed, dozens at a time, in prominent places.

Also important as a means of communicating with workers were the outdoor meetings, street meetings of an evening and Sunday afternoon meetings at the established venues for radical orators, such as the Domain in Sydney, the Yarra Bank in Melbourne, the Botanic Park in Adelaide, the Esplanade in Perth and Tank Street in Brisbane. Most Locals held a regular speakers' class to train fellow workers for this important activity, to increase the supply of 'able propagandists' who could 'expound and explain the philosophy and methods of the I.W.W. and make more converts, especially on the job'.[29]

The Melbourne Local held Friday-night outdoor meetings at South Melbourne Market or in Brunswick at the corner of Sydney Road and Victoria Street. In Sydney the Local held meetings at the corner of Bathurst and Liverpool Streets every Friday and Saturday evening at 8 p.m. and Sunday evening at 7 p.m., before the meeting inside the hall. As early as February 1914 *Direct Action* was noting that the meetings at Bathurst Street were becoming larger, 'and many are waiting for the message of industrial unionism long before our speakers commence their addresses'. The Broken Hill Local performed at the corner of Chloride and Argent Streets every Sunday 'and the meetings are always attended by a good crowd of wage-workers who are anxious to hear of a better form of organisation than exists on the Barrier to-day'. The outdoor meetings of the Brisbane Local on Wednesday and Saturday evenings were often held in Tank Street. In Adelaide, the Local announced that 'Slaves interested in bettering their conditions should attend our open-air meetings, which are held opposite Cowells, Victoria Square, every Saturday night.'[30]

In an era before cinema and television, good speakers were valued and not only for enlightenment; outdoor oratory was a form of public entertainment. Jimmy Seamer claims the IWW was popular and appreciated because of its many talented speakers. According to Fred Coombe the IWW had 'men that could really talk, colourful men . . . who demanded that you stopped and looked and listened . . . men with a sense of humour'. Lloyd Edmonds maintains that the Wobbly speakers he heard on the Yarra Bank in 1916 were the best open-air speakers ever, remarkable for their clarity and their wit.[31]

Roly Farrall, one of the IWW's renowned orators, always advised the other speakers to 'beef it up'. According to Jim Garvey, although Roly later joined the Communist Party he did not like 'the reduction of the colourful style, to fit in with the jargon as he saw it of the CP, they frowned on use of any emotional appeal to the crowd, they regarded that as demagoguery'. The IWW traded unashamedly on its demagogic talents and used colourful methods to attract crowds, the singing of rousing songs such as 'Solidarity Forever' and 'The Rebel Girl'. In Melbourne the singing was accompanied by a loud busker organ. Nor were Wobbly agitators easily deterred. For instance, when police attempted to disperse an IWW meeting on Townsville's beach on 14 June 1917, Bill Jackson, Gordon Brown and Paul Freeman moved the meeting into the ocean and, with the waves washing around the platform, continued to address the crowd of several hundred on the water's edge. At meetings in the central square in Brisbane, IWW speakers regularly outwitted police by climbing one of the fig-trees and addressing the crowds from a branch so obviously close to breaking that the police did not dare pursue the matter.[32]

Some of the most gifted Wobbly speakers travelled long distances on speaking tours lasting several months. The impact of these visiting propagandists was often dramatic. For instance, in the winter of 1914 Broken Hill Local received a propaganda visit from Charlie Reeve:

> The great audiences listen greedily to his lectures, the wives of the workers and girls being especially prominent and enthusiastic. One can hear many a sweet voice singing cheerfully the songs of the I.W.W., 'pie in the sky' being favoured. Scores of workers, skilled and unskilled, are rolling into the local . . .[33]

Reeve had come to Broken Hill via South Australia. During his stay in Port Pirie, where he held three propaganda meetings at the smelter gates as the workers came off shift, sixty-one new members joined the Local and another large batch was expected the following week, because 'His clear and logical explanations of economics, and the way he has expounded the principles of the I.W.W., has set the slaves thinking round here . . . The workers have been duped, and are fed up with Parliamentary action, although they have drawn it in with their mother's milk.'[34] And yet this Local ceased to function by the middle of the following year. Membership always grew with speaking tours; but Locals, left to their own devices, could not always hold these recruits.

In the United States, free-speech fights were vital to the early efforts of the IWW; these crusades called upon the faithful to journey great distances and face imprisonment.[35] Some similar but less spectacular battles were waged by the Australian Wobblies, notably in Port Pirie, the Sydney Domain and in Newcastle, in which fellow workers were called upon to surrender their liberty in flocks.

Around the middle of June 1914 Reeve was arrested while addressing an IWW meeting in Port Pirie and imprisoned for refusing to move on while addressing a large street meeting. He informed the magistrate: 'I don't care how long a sentence you give me, but I will continue to address the workers of Port Pirie.' The Local, comprising mainly construction workers, announced its preparedness to fill every jail in South Australia and continued to hold street meetings in defiance of the regulations.[36] *Direct Action* issued a call for help.

> We call upon all rebels and lovers of freedom to rally to the cause of Free Speech. Salvation Army ranters and fanatical sky pilots are allowed to make night hideous in the streets of the cities, because their teaching of the cowardly Christian 'virtue' of meekness and servility is calculated to keep the workers' minds in bondage.[37]

Tom McMillan, who travelled from Broken Hill, wrote:

> We came by rail and boat, on bikes, tired legs and blistered feet, to show to the world that our solidarity was not a vain empty boast, and to demonstrate by precept and example that an injury to one is an injury to all . . . They can gaol us or trample our faces in the dirty streets of Port Pirie, but they can never take from us the militant spirit that permeates the breast of every member of the Industrial Workers of the World. We will fight this fight with passionate devotion to our principles, and we mean to win, irrespective of the sacrifices to be made.[38]

The small Port Pirie jail became quite crowded, with about thirty Wobblies inside. Barker recalls: 'When they got into jail these fellows, being well organised, turned it upside-down. They made it such a misery for the staff of the jail and for the authorities that they were only too glad to get rid of them.' Moreover, the numbers of Wobblies and their sympathisers packing the open-air meetings, as many as 3000, were alarming the local police.[39] This capacity to draw on non-members for support was often crucial to the success of Wobbly campaigns. Unlike other left groups, the IWW drew a significant following in addition to its paid-up membership; there were many drawn to the message who could not take out a ticket and accept the level of activity that imposed. If the IWW asked for a commitment that few could make, it was at the same time the most outward-oriented and charismatic of the left groups and evoked a sympathy of an unusual kind.

According to the Sydney *Sun* of 25 and 26 June, 200 members had left Sydney, another 500 were ready to leave and there were 1000 or more Wobblies throughout Australia ready to move. These reports were wildly exaggerated; and, in fact, no such effort was necessary. At least seventeen Wobblies came from Broken Hill and two from Adelaide and it appears these were sufficient to alarm the Port Pirie authorities into a strategic retreat: the town's mayor instructed police that 'no prosecutions be instituted', that the IWW be allowed to hold its meetings.[40] *Direct Action* proclaimed that the authorities were for once compelled to recognise a power greater than themselves, the power of working-class solidarity: 'The fighting spirit, and the unswerving devotion to principle which characterises members of the I.W.W. . . . were something the "powers that be" had not estimated in their calculations.'[41]

Meanwhile, back in Sydney, the State Labor government of W.A. Holman was attempting to prevent Wobblies plying their ideas in the Domain, jailing them for selling literature, taking up collections and 'singing to attract a crowd'. The IWW decided to defy the regulations: 'When they endeavour to suppress our literature or our opinions, instead of being meekly submissive, we are going to retaliate with all the tactics and all the resources at our disposal.' By August 1914 *Direct Action* was claiming that: 'The attempted suppression of our literature has meant a sale and circulation hitherto not thought of by the most optimistic of our members.'[42] Barker recalls what the battle entailed: going to court, a fine and a prison sentence: 'We wouldn't pay fines on principle; we always took it out in the nick.' The itinerant fellow workers who had 'just come into town' were well placed to make trouble, disappearing again if necessary: 'They didn't even go to court.' Barker, on the other hand, spent seven days in Long Bay for not paying his 10-shilling fine.[43]

In the course of this campaign Glynn and Barker went to Macquarie Street to see the relevant Minister, Fred Flowers. After being ushered out of his office when he realised they were not the respectful delegation of Newcastle miners he was expecting, they discovered there was a ladder up to his window, left by workmen, which they climbed. Finding Flowers and two other ministers quietly enjoying cigars and whisky, they told Flowers in no uncertain terms to stop the prohibition on selling papers in the Domain, threatening to return with 10,000 unemployed if he did not put an end to the harassment of Wobblies. A few days later at the Political Labor Leagues' annual conference, Wobblies expressed their grievances then barricaded the doors and pulled out the light switches so the place was in darkness. After much pandemonium, the Labor League delegates broke a window, shouted and were finally rescued by police. 'Out of these various battles', Barker recalls, 'we established the right to sell the paper in the Sydney Domain and cleared every other body for the same thing.'[44]

The Holman Labor government forbade street speaking in Sydney by the IWW. *Direct Action* responded with a cartoon of prominent Labor politicians hanging from the lamp-posts of Macquarie Street. (*Direct Action*, 15 January 1916)

In a similar way, by simply 'singing in the streets' of Sydney in defiance of traffic ordinances, the IWW secured the right accorded to the Salvation Army of speaking in certain streets at night.[45] Barker recalls of this more general free-speech fight in Sydney that their main tactic was simply to outmanoeuvre the police:

> We would start a meeting somewhere and then when the police were gathering around, we'd pack up and clear off to some other place that was already planned. By keeping the police running around, they never knew where we were going to be next . . . The authorities got tired of trying to fight us. They knew we were determined and the jails would be packed with men.[46]

Early in 1915 a similar campaign was conducted in Newcastle. On 5 February Fellow-Workers Reeve and Morgan were jailed for speaking in Perkins Street. *Direct Action* announced: 'Wanted! 1000 Industrialists and Lovers of Freedom to help fill Maitland Jail.' About thirty Wobblies were imprisoned for their turn on the stump in Newcastle. *Direct Action* claimed that the IWW could not be annihilated by suppression, 'it only augments its growth, makes it command public attention'. Up to a point, this was correct; but *Direct Action* added, unpresciently, that the government could not legislate the IWW out of existence, that it was in Australia 'for keeps'. Eventually, when the IWW proceeded with a meeting which had been refused a permit, in Shortland Park on 22 February, the police refrained from stopping either the IWW speakers or the sale of literature.[47]

The behaviour of the Wobblies in Maitland jail had become notorious. Barker recalls: 'They went in and they turned the Maitland jail upside-down . . . Whenever the warder said, "Right turn", they all went left and did everything back to front. That was part of the game.' Crucial to the success of these free-speech fights had been the preparedness of Wobblies to go to jail. Barker explains:

> To a lot of men it wasn't much different being in jail or being out, because there was a lot of unemployment at that time. They enjoyed it, really. They knew they wouldn't be in there for long. That's what created for our organisation, the IWW, a reputation of being a general nuisance to the prison authorities and the police.[48]

These glamorous aspects of agitation aside, the everyday work of the IWW was centred on the Locals, which emerged in most State capitals and some major provincial industrial centres. The Adelaide Local (no.1) and the Sydney Local (no.2) were formed, as we have seen, in 1911; the next, by April 1914, were Broken Hill (no.3) and Port Pirie (no.4) (which ceased to function around the middle of 1915), followed by Fremantle (no.5) and Boulder City (no.6) before the end of the year.

The Brisbane Local (no.7) and the Melbourne Local (no.8) both appeared in January 1915. In country New South Wales, a Local (no.9) was formed at Tottenham in May 1915, but was disbanded in January 1916. Around Christmas 1915 the last three Locals were formed – no.10 in Perth, and two more in Queensland – no.11 at Mount Morgan and no.12, an all-Russian Local, at Cairns.[49]

Mostly these Locals were formed by an explosive mixture of local militants and assistance from some previously established Wobbly stronghold through the movement of Wobblies looking for work or by the visit of an organiser from Sydney headquarters. The Fremantle Local and the Boulder Local were developed largely by the immigration of Broken Hill Wobblies enduring layoffs at the Barrier caused by the wartime disruption to trade. Originally from the West, Tom Macmillan arrived back in September 1914; by October he and Pat Daly, also a Broken Hill Wobbly, were mixing with Fremantle socialists, spreading the IWW message. Amongst local stalwarts, Mick Sawtell and Monty Miller were important in the founding of the Westralian Locals, which then requested help from Sydney to establish themselves firmly. Concerned especially to proselytise within the mining industry, the IWW concentrated efforts in the first half of 1915 on the Boulder Local: J.B. King arrived in January 1915, armed with a huge bundle of Wobbly literature, and the meetings he and Mick Sawtell organised boosted the Local's membership and literature sales; Reeve replaced King in June, introducing a rigorous programme of meetings, lectures and educational and reading classes. Reeve departed coastward in September, where he succeeded in restoring the fortunes of the Fremantle Local and established another Local in Perth with the help of Annie Westbrook and others.[50]

Wobblies became members through joining one of these Locals, either in person or by post, giving their name, occupation, industry and address. The member had to declare that they subscribed to the principles of the Preamble and agreed to 'diligently study' the principles of the IWW and to become acquainted with its purposes. To join the IWW, to participate fully in the activities of a Local, was a demanding commitment; in general, levels of involvement were high. The Broken Hill Local was pleased that a large number of its fellow workers were not merely dues-paying members as in the craft unions, but took an interest in the affairs of the organisation and attended the economic classes held weekly, 'doing their utmost to become acquainted with ways and means to enable them to fight the master class'.[51] Fred Coombe recalls of the Wobblies that 'their organisation was tremendous, they were good organisers on the job, all the time, selling papers, holding meetings, they never let the grass grow under their feet'.[52] These activities, ostensibly outward-oriented and directed towards reaching the uninitiated, also strengthened the distinctive Wobbly subculture that aimed to promote a new, militant identity for the proletariat.

The weekly schedule of some of the Locals, more demanding even than the activities typical of the other left groups, indicates the hectic pace set in building the new. The Sydney Local held an economic class on Monday night, later shifted to Wednesday evenings; a speakers' and reading class on Tuesday night, replaced by a speakers' class on Saturday evenings; a lecture in the hall on Wednesday night; the business meeting on Thursday night and a lecture in the hall on Sunday night. The routine activities of the Melbourne Local were: a business meeting on Monday evening and a speakers' class on Wednesday evening or an educational class, 'Working Class Economics', of a Thursday and an educational lecture in the hall on Saturday evening. A typical schedule for the Boulder Local, which covered the two nearby mining centres of Boulder and Kalgoorlie was: a class meeting on Wednesday evening in the hall; a propaganda meeting outside Boulder Post Office on Friday evening and in Kalgoorlie on Saturday evening; a business meeting at 10.30 a.m. on Sunday in the hall; a lecture at Keane's Goldfields Hotel Athletic Club at 2.30 p.m. on Sunday; and a propaganda meeting on Sunday evening in Boulder. On the Barrier, the Broken Hill Local held an educational class every Wednesday evening and on Sunday evenings there was, alternately, a business meeting and an economic class.[53] These indoor activities, it should be noted, were in addition to the many open-air meetings.

The important question of following remains difficult to answer. Wobbly influence, as opposed to membership, is not easily quantified, for the IWW did not count up its successes in traditional ways such as the election of its members and supporters to positions within the trade union movement or their pre-selection to parliamentary seats. Its influence was at ground level, ebbing and flowing according to local circumstances in the industry concerned, not amenable to precise measurement.

Estimating the extent of Wobbly influence is further complicated by exaggeration on the part of the security forces, the press, the politicians and the Wobblies themselves. A security file on the IWW in the wake of the First World War regretted that: 'Their influence amongst the workers has been very great, in fact altogether disproportionate to their numbers.'[54] The *Sydney Morning Herald* commented on 30 September 1916:

> It is idle to deny the force and rapid spread of the doctrines of the IWW. They are spreading at a rate that is really appalling . . . its more or less constant followers in Sydney alone number between 20,000 and 30,000, and they are in numbers in all the unions – the more dangerous because the I.W.W. man is everywhere the most energetic as a doctrinaire and the most enthusiastic.[55]

Although there was no Local of the IWW in the mining town of Cobar in western New South Wales, the *Argus* reported confidently that the IWW membership there was 150 and 'increasing rapidly'. Politicians of all brands, but especially those on the right-wing of the Labor Party, railed mightily against IWW influence amongst workers. Concerned as they were to mobilise resistance, their statements necessarily exaggerated the seriousness of the IWW offensive. So did the Wobblies. Bill Beattie insists that the IWW 'wielded an influence in trade union circles out of all proportion to its numbers'. Tom Barker claimed IWW responsibility for the defeat of the conscription referenda and refers to the IWW's considerable influence in the unions and even in the army.[56]

Even membership figures are subject to overstatement, especially by the IWW itself. Bill Beattie's memoirs claim a total roll of 55 000, but never exceeding 11 000 at any point in time. Norman Jeffery retrospectively estimated the maximum membership as 4000.[57] What was the reality? At the end of 1913 there were 199 members. In June 1916, according to the police, there were some 300 members in Sydney but membership increased rapidly as conscription became an issue. Rushton's detailed research reveals that Childe's estimate of membership is roughly correct: about 2000 for the whole of Australia, 1500 of whom were associated with the Sydney Local.[58] Percy Laidler likewise reckons the IWW had 2000 activists across the country.[59] These figures are not contradicted by the lists of members compiled by police at the time. Membership in Australia, with a population of 4.5 million at the time, was therefore slightly smaller in proportion to overall population than in the United States.[60]

Few details are available about the growth rates of individual Locals. The only minutes available for the Sydney Local are from 9 September 1915 to 30 December 1915 and for August and September 1916. In the earlier minutes the secretary usually wrote 'new members were admitted'; where actual figures were given they averaged seven to ten per week over the four-month period. During August and September 1916 the total recorded number of new members admitted was 105. At Broken Hill, at least 251 new members were admitted between July 1916 and August 1917, the period where minutes are available.[61] In January 1917 this Local decreed those attending business meetings must show their pence card, unless well known, suggesting a membership in excess of a band of mutual acquaintances. Also indicative of IWW success in Broken Hill was the Local's reported problem with the man using the IWW 'as a means to assist him in ped[d]ling his quack medicine'; it was resolved to let it be known he was not a propagandist of the IWW and to not allow him the stump.[62] A much less successful Local was the Brisbane one, which, according to Dick Surplus, a one-time member, had only 'twenty or so active members'.[63]

In Queensland in particular there was a disparity even more marked than usual between membership and following; here, truly, was an IWW influence entirely disproportionate to its numerical strength. John Armstrong's thesis on the Queensland trade union movement of the time claims that none of the three Locals in that State was very large; certainly, the small number of Queensland addresses in the membership lists held by the Sydney Local support the notion of a small Queensland membership. Yet reports in *Direct Action* by Tom Barker and William Jackson, who paid several visits to the north and western areas during the peak of the seasonal working period, always referred to a large IWW following in that part of the State. Both reported the imminence of establishment of Locals that never eventuated. Townsville was a case in point. Fellow-Worker Shannessey claimed in August 1917 that there were about 100 IWW workers in Townsville alone; about the same time, a police sergeant reported of a meeting in Townsville that 'the attendance was about 150. Mostly all members of the IWW organisation and a large percentage being Russians and Danes.' Yet no Local was ever established in Townsville.[64]

The inability to establish Locals is taken by Doug Hunt as evidence of the IWW's 'insubstantial hold' on Queensland's militant meatworkers and miners, amongst whom, he acknowledges, the IWW enjoyed a significant following. An alternative reading, less inclined to measure influence in terms of organisational accomplishment, would suggest that the non-existence of a Local was no index of lack of Wobbly sentiment in any area. For it would seem that the actual membership of the IWW in Queensland was unremarkable while, at the same time, its influence amongst itinerant workers was considerable. Armstrong concedes that many of the sympathisers, like most of the IWW ticket-holders, could have been transient workers; such people, for whom commitment to anything or anybody was problematic, are not joiners.[65]

Naomi Segal's research reveals the often very precarious nature of Wobbly organisation in the West. The Westralian IWW conducted a major propaganda campaign between late 1914 and October 1916, distributing 5000 copies of *Direct Action* on the goldfields alone and at least 1000 IWW pamphlets. Its amateur proselytisers and professional speakers, she notes, carried the IWW message onto woodlines, along railway lines, into the mines, and to farming districts, shearing sheds and the wharves. In November 1915 Pat Daly wrote from the Corinthian goldmine to Fred Lunn: 'Fancy twelve months ago, the I.W.W. was a mere baby in this land of sin and sand and today it is like the kangaroo, bounding along at each corner of W.A.' Within six months, however, Daly received correspondence from a fellow worker at the Boulder Local indicating that it was 'financially putrid . . . demoralised and shattered'. Mick

Sawtell was not confident the coastal Locals would survive Reeve's departure eastward. 'As an organisation, the I.W.W. in Western Australia exists
on paper only', he wrote to Ted McLoughlin.[66]

The fortunes of the Westralian Locals were mercurial. The Boulder
Local had thirty members by the end of November 1914. By late June
1915, with King's help, it had 117 members and was holding meetings
that attracted crowds of up to 1000. When Reeve replaced King in the
middle of the year, the momentum was maintained. However, after
Reeve's departure for the coast in September 1915 Boulder Local lan-
guished for want of experienced propagandists and could not even provide an IWW speaker when requested by the Lakeside Woodcutters
Union. It ceased its activities in May 1916 and its members rejoined the
Miners' Union. While King was busy in Boulder the Fremantle Local had
dwindled to seven members, but later in the year after Reeve arrived on
the coast and the Boulder Local declined, the Fremantle Local flourished and Local no.10 was formed in Perth. Joint meetings of these two
adjacent Locals attracted large crowds. When Reeve returned to Sydney
in August 1916 the Fremantle and Perth Locals continued the meetings
successfully, until the arrests in October 1916 of Miller, Auwart,
Johnstone and Hanscombe, a blow from which they did not recover.[67]

The Sydney Local was undoubtedly the most successful, both in formal membership, as we have seen, and in the even larger number of supporters. Many of these were female, attracted to the defiantly colourful
Wobblies but unable to join because of family commitments or an inability to identify fully with this band of workingmen. By June 1917 *Direct
Action* was boasting that the 500-capacity IWW hall could never hold one-
quarter of the crowd that rolled up to their Sunday-night lectures, and so
overflow meetings had to be held outside in Sussex Street. This report
argued that the continued persecution was having a stimulating effect:
'The large crowd that marches down George Street on its way to the Hall
every Sunday night, singing our songs, is a sight to inspire even the most
pessimistic.'[68]

Roly Farrall claimed in January 1916 that the IWW had done more in
the previous twelve months to alter the psychological outlook of the
worker towards the present system than all the 'class war theorists' had
done in ten years.[69] To the extent that this comment is justified, it raises
the question: why? Coming from within the ranks of the working class
and from nowhere else, it seems the IWW was able to connect with workers subjected to the daily indignities and privations of the labour process
by stressing the things that mattered to them in their working life; it also
took the wise precaution of refraining from abstract, complicated and
dogmatic rhetoric. This approach appealed to militant workers concerned about wages and conditions. The IWW's doctrines 'spread like

wildfire', according to Childe, constituting 'the most eloquent testimony to the insight into proletarian psychology of its founders and propagators and the direct appeal of its doctrines to the toilers'. To Beattie, the appeal of the IWW 'was due mainly to the simplicity of its policies and its apt and lucid statement of prevailing conditions'. Dick Surplus maintained there was 'a lot of logic in the arguments of the IWW' and that many workers found that 'its basic ideas were correct'. Mick Sawtell insists that, inasmuch as the IWW was successful, it was because its industrial tactics were essentially sound, its ideas tested in practice shown to be correct to those involved in confrontation with employers.[70]

The immediate demands of the IWW, ostensibly a prelude to a revolutionary reconstruction of society, seemed to many militant workers a more sensible strategy for securing *reforms* in the meantime than the activities of those in the labour movement dedicated to the mere attainment of such reforms and resistant to efforts to secure more fundamental change. However, while such workers were impressed by Wobbly ideas and tactics and prepared to try them out in the battle for immediate demands, it was only a small proportion of them that was also willing to join the IWW, to help in the revolutionary task of building a new society within the shell of the old.

Since a new society was indeed the ultimate aim of the IWW, not simply the alleviation of the lot of the worker within the shell of the old, it failed in its own terms. The erratic nature of IWW organisation, the unspectacular record of so many of its Locals even before repression, represents the failure of the IWW itself. And yet, at the same time, the IWW was spectacularly successful as an idea that challenged both the merely reformist aspirations and the hierarchical and bureaucratic organisational forms of the mainstream labour movement. It proved significant as an indefinable movement that could incite hundreds, sometimes thousands, of workers to extremist gestures of solidarity and militancy that might otherwise have been dispelled, discouraged by the elected officials of these workers and their representatives in parliament. In the final analysis, the IWW was a cry of anguish from the far left, the loudest yet heard, at the direction in which the rest of the labour movement was tending.

CHAPTER 9

'A Poor Day's Work for a Poor Day's Pay':
Ethics and Economics

In his presidential address to the 1916 Convention of the AWU, W.G. Spence expressed the revulsion felt by those like him towards all that the IWW symbolised: its 'bastard kind of political philosophy' imported from foreign parts wanted a perpetual state of war; it preached the immoral doctrine of not keeping agreements; it set up 'shibboleths of class-consciousness and economic determinism'; it was a throwback in unionism to the dark ages of the destruction of labour-saving machinery.[1] According to an anonymous Labor pamphleteer, the 'industrial anarchists' of the IWW were a serpent in the new Eden, 'a reptile ready to poison the clear spring of progress, to turn social affection to class hatred, new-born hopes to despair, to preach class solidarity against social unity'.[2] At the same time as the IWW attracted many of the most militant of the rank-and-file activists of the time, it antagonised and repelled other sections of the labour movement. Unabashed, the IWW encouraged this recalcitrant image of itself.

Where the mainstream labour movement of the time was dedicated to the attainment of 'a fair day's pay for a fair day's work', the IWW was determined upon workers providing the capitalists with 'a poor day's work for a poor day's pay'. 'IWW' was often wilfully interpreted by its detractors to mean 'I Won't Work', indicating the extent to which the Wobblies were known to be at odds with the prevailing values of the wider society, upheld to a large extent by this labour movement. The IWW creed encapsulated the rejection of bourgeois values concerning hard work, the dignity of labour, thrift, self-help and respectability:

> I believe in the Class War, the Materialist Conception of History and the
>   Theory of Surplus Value.
> I believe in beating the boss.

I believe in Sabotage.
I believe in getting wise at the boss' expense.
I believe in the 'Right to be Lazy' and in Direct Action.
I believe in doping the Labor fakir with his own dope, and the capitalist
  with his own weapons.
Hallelujah! I'm a bum![3]

Bourgeois values, the Wobblies argued, reinforced the power of the capitalists over the workers, increased the rate of exploitation and inculcated notions in the working class accepting of the capitalist order. In an open letter to W.G. Spence, in his '£600 a year job as a mental prostitute of the master class', *Direct Action* declared: 'You blathered about the immorality of the I.W.W. in breaking agreements; to hell with your morality, it belongs to the filthy, blood-sucking leeches who have lived on us. Too long we, the workers, have been bound by their rotten moral ethics.' The IWW had no use for 'the morals of the masters', which had turned the revolutionist of Nazareth into 'a canting slave philosopher'; the great work before the IWW was 'to give to the working class a philosophy for the basis of an ethical code that will be working class in character'.[4]

For instance, in attacking the popular notion of thrift *Direct Action* explained that the man who scrapes and saves all the time was a drawback to the working class: 'If everybody becomes thrifty, thousands of men and women workers would have to be dispensed with . . . thrift is one of the most plausible and dangerous things that the working class has got to fear . . .' Thrift was a clever ruse of capitalist economists that had two objectives: to increase unemployment by reducing the amount of money in circulation, creating a larger excess labour pool to facilitate exploitation; and to accustom the proletariat to a lower standard of living which could, if necessary, be made permanent by a reduction in wages.[5]

Popular notions sanctioning hard work and upholding the dignity of labour were similarly capitalist constructs. *How Capital has Hypnotised Society* likened the working class of the world to a person under the spell of a hypnotist, under the control of another person, whose standards of right and wrong were 'determined by the demands of the industrially and politically ruling class'. The author inquired: why does the working class consent to become hoboes, paupers, outcasts, mere rubbish and waste in a world whose whole output they themselves have created? Why is it that, even when they are organised into unions or a political party, they do not dare to touch the product of their own toil which has been stolen from them? 'To take what they have produced, to enjoy the fruits of their labor, is as natural for the working class as any function of the body is natural. It is the only ethics Labor has: TO THE LABORER HIS PRODUCT.'[6]

The IWW republished Paul Lafargue's *The Right to be Lazy* in which he argued that the proletariat must trample under foot the prejudices of capitalist ethics, that it was necessary to curb the extravagant passion of the labourers for work to oblige them instead to consume the goods they produced.

> It must return to its natural instincts, it must proclaim the Rights of Laziness, a thousand times more noble and more sacred than the anaemic Rights of Man concocted by the metaphysical lawyers of the bourgeois revolution. It must accustom itself to working but three hours a day, reserving the rest of the day and night for leisure and feasting.[7]

As Ernie Lane recalls, the IWW's promulgation of Lafargue's brilliant exposition of the workers' right to discard the old shibboleths regarding eternal toil 'came like a burst of sunlight through a black and murky sky'.[8]

The Wobblies were engaging in a transvaluation of bourgeois values. *How Capital has Hypnotised Society* argued 'it is just as imperative that the working class create its own civilization, its own morals, ethics, religion and industrial and economic order, as it was that the capitalist class should'. In order to make bourgeois values, such as self-reliance, serviceable, workers should take such advice not as individuals but as a collectivity. *Direct Action* explained its adaptation of Nietzschean philosophy: Nietzsche had shown the way for the favoured few; it was necessary to do likewise for the many, to teach the masses 'the will to power'. The weakness of labour organisations lay in the psychology of the units, therefore Nietzsche was badly needed to clarify the workers' vision, to transvalue all capitalist values, thus rejuvenating the ranks of labour with a new hope and a definite goal.[9] The IWW rejected categorically the ethics of the exploiters and proposed instead the adoption of an alternative moral code: the ethics of the producers. Just as economics and ethics were intimately connected for the exploiters, each reinforcing the other in the interests of the ruling class, so also were they connected in the alternative morality of the IWW, which purported to express the true interests of the working class. However, because IWW definitions of 'work' embraced merely public, industrial labour, its ethical position found no resonance with the women of this class who worked for 'loved ones' rather than for a boss; its appeal was limited to those who could resent the surplus value they created for strangers.

This distinctive IWW code of ethics was expressed cogently in its peculiarly insulting vocabulary, a new discourse for a new morality. A worker who lacked class-consciousness was a 'Block'; clergymen were 'black-coated vultures'; capitalists were 'parasites', 'boodlers' or 'Mr Fat'; temperance fanatics were the 'cold tea brigade'; the ALP was the 'Hard Labor Party'; Labor MPs were 'Labor Fakirs'; Christians were 'Fire Escapers'; the craft union movement was 'Organised Scabbery'; the New South Wales parliament was the 'Macquarie Street Gas House'; professionals who supported the system, such as academics, judges and journalists, were 'mental prostitutes'; the Salvation Army was the 'Starvation Army'; and a foreman was a 'straw boss'.[10] Some of these epithets were not new – Mr Fat was a stock figure in the *Bulletin* of the 1890s – but collectively they made up a gallery of comic-ridiculous proportions. The Wobblies were never intimidated by the guardians of respectable orthodoxy: they challenged the hierarchies of knowledge and authority by ridicule.

Especially important to the alternative cultural world of the IWW was the song. When American Wobbly song-writer Joe Hill was executed on 19 November 1915 there was a huge demonstration of protest in the Sydney Domain, arranged by the IWW. These IWW songs, according to May Brodney, had a bravado which appealed to the young revolutionist.[11] Childe describes their voice:

> The I.W.W. took a leaf out of the Salvation Army's book and used crude songs with catchy tunes to draw a crowd and attract converts. Their songs are remarkable for their courseness and brutality, but are all the more proletarian for that; they take their diction from the real everyday life of the camp, the factory and the mine . . .[12]

Barker concedes the analogy: 'We had the I.W.W. song-book . . . These had a tremendous effect and we used to have some really good singing at our meetings. In some ways we were like the Salvation Army.'[13]

One American Wobbly song, particularly well-suited to Australian diction and predispositions, which entered the local radical canon and later became especially popular during the Depression years of the 1930s, was 'Hallelujah, I'm a Bum', in which the Wobblies celebrated their rejection of the capitalist work ethic:

> Oh, why don't you work
> Like other men do?
> How the hell can I work
> When there's no work to do?
> Hallelujah! I'm a bum!
> Hallelujah! Bum again!
> Hallelujah! give us a hand out,
> To revive us again![14]

Adapted for Australian purposes and very popular, too, was 'Mr Block', the worker whose acceptance of bourgeois values constituted a drag on working-class organisation:

> Please give me your attention, I'll introduce to you,
> A man who is a credit to our red, white and blue;
> His head is made of lumber and as solid as a rock,

He is a common worker, and his name is Mr Block.
  And Block, he thinks he may
  Be premier some day.

Oh, Mr Block, you were born by mistake,
  You take the cake,
  You make me ache.
Tie a rock on your block, and then jump in the lake;
Kindly do this for liberty's sake![15]

The American IWW, in Robert Tyler's view, were more than disgruntled victims of industrialisation; they were antagonists in a climactic cultural conflict. His *Rebels of the Woods* has emphasised the culture of the IWW and the system of values that sustained it, values outrageously at odds with those of compromise, cooperation, hard work and Christian piety.[16] The Australian IWW, too, used alternative cultural forms – slang, song and spectacle – as an aid to practical proletarian solidarity. It created for a time a self-conscious and self-confident revolutionary ambience radically out of temper with other moods within the labour movement. The class-consciousness of revolutionary industrial unionism was embodied in new traditions, new words, new songs and new ideas. And it was expressed most forcibly in the propaganda about, and practice of, offering a poor day's work for a poor day's pay.

This emphasis on working less, on shorter hours and the go-slow, was central to the IWW's political economy, which was closely linked with its alternative moral code. Stickers produced by the Sydney Local declared: 'Slow Down. Respect yourselves. Protect yourselves. The hours are long. The pay is small. So take your time. And buck them all.'; 'If you are unemployed, it is because some bonehead is doing two men's work. Unemployment means more competition for jobs, less wages, slum life, and gaol. Only fools and horses work hard.'[17]

The IWW argued, ostensibly following Marx's theory of surplus value, that the work day was divided into two, very unequal, parts: necessary labour, the short time needed to produce the equivalent in commodities to the wage earned; and surplus labour, in which the labourer was working, in effect, 'free' for the capitalist, thereby providing profit. 'Surplus labor is the basis of capitalism, therefore the I.W.W. very logically argue that by reducing this unnecessary toil we will strike at the very base of things.' Shortening the hours of labour would not, it assured workers, reduce wages, because they were already as low as they could be to maintain the supply of labour for the capitalist; rather, it would reduce the profits of the boss. Moreover, shortening hours would make it necessary for him to employ more workers, so the army of unemployed would be decreased. Since unemployment made 'suckers' of the employed (the fear of the sack causing them to work to the utmost limits of their endurance) and scabs of the unemployed, reduction in the supply of unemployed labour would raise the level of wages.[18] With blissful disregard for Marx's own analysis of the working day in *Value, Price and Profit* and the competitive laws of capitalism, this argument established the basis of the go-slow.

A.E. Brown's *The Case for a Six-Hour Day*, produced by the Sydney Local, argued that, with a shorter working day, the relative wage (the proportion between what workers produced and what they received) would increase; and with this reduction in surplus value, the power, influence and domination of the master class would be lessened.

> When it is remembered that out of Surplus Value – the unpaid wages of labor – are maintained standing armies, navies and police, and vast hordes of non-producers and middlemen of various kinds; and that it is the source of the wasteful and riotous living of the rich; it will be seen how important it is to lessen the amount of Surplus Value produced, and thereby the amount of its appropriation by the capitalist class.

Although a six-hour day would not completely absorb the unemployed, it would considerably lessen competition in the labour market, enabling improvements in working conditions and organising power and ability. A sticker issued by the Adelaide Local declared: 'WORKERS! The Boss determines the hours you shall work to-day. Organise in The Industrial Workers of the World, and determine the hours yourselves. Agitate for the Shorter Working Day.' In anticipating the post-war situation of closed munitions' factories and thousands returning from the front, *Direct Action* argued that a radical curtailment of the working day, to increase the demand for labour, was the only measure likely to mitigate economic conditions for the workers after the war.[19]

The IWW insisted that shorter working hours and slowing down on the job, because it reduced unemployment, would automatically raise wages and better the conditions of all workers. Wages were not raised or lowered as the productivity of the worker ebbed and flowed; wages were simply the market price of the commodity called labour power.[20] This price was based on the minimal means of subsistence for the worker:

> It may rise above this minimum, according to the standard of social development, the degree of organised resistance to exploitaiton, or it may fall below, as in times of industrial depression, when unemployment is rife. . . . the means of subsistence is the determining factor, the starting point from which all fluctuations in wages must be explained.[21]

With the unemployed around, the market price of labour power tended to the lowest possible minimum; with fewer men competing for jobs, the workers would be in a position to demand higher wages. Thus, according to the Wobblies, shorter hours and higher pay always ran together.[22]

The IWW scorned notions that wage levels were determined by profit levels or labour productivity. When Justice Heydon declared in the arbitration court early in 1914 that workers should make things easier for employers because increased profits would enable employers to pay higher wages, *Direct Action* turned the arguments of arbitration back on the judge. If wages were determined by profit levels, why was the learned judge at such pains to ascertain what was a 'living wage' for the worker? When the *Sun* of 17 July 1914 suggested that the bigger the total yield of an industry the bigger the fund of profit into which the workman could dip, Glynn commented sarcastically: 'Happy workman! Imagine him going into the boss's strong room at the end of the year and helping himself without hindrance as a consequence of his industrious habits.'[23] If wages were determined by the productivity of the labourer, why, asked Glynn in *Industrial Efficiency and its Antidote*, were workers still getting but the bare means of subsistence, when new inventions had dramatically increased labour productivity in the past half-century? Why was the Australian worker receiving a smaller proportion of his product than ten years ago, despite the fact that his productivy had increased enormously?[24]

This did not mean that only shorter hours were worth fighting for. Workers were forced also to demand higher wages in an effort to keep pace with the ever-soaring prices of commodities. In any case, it was desirable to make a bold bid for more wages, to take back some of the loot that had been stolen, to struggle continually for a better standard of living, to make some of the so-called luxuries of life necessities, precisely because the wages of the working class were determined not by output but regulated according to the price of things deemed the necessities of life.[25]

The very concept of the 'living wage', enshrined in the arbitration system, was proof that wages were determined not by profits or productivity but by the perceived minimum amount necessary to maintain the workforce; for workers to exist, in the words of the court, in frugal comfort. When Judge Heydon called for some method of raising or lowering the living wage with the rise and fall in the cost of living, *Direct Action* pointed out that statistics showed that the total wealth production had grown larger and larger, and yet the workers who had created this wealth were calmly being told that their share was to be just barely sufficient to keep body and soul together. Moreover, in its careful calculations of how little workers could eat and still work, its deliberations on how few rooms a worker's house could contain and still preserve decency, the arbitration court stood as a standing insult to workers.[26]

Arbitration did not even stick to its own avowed principles. Under the heading 'ARBITRATION CHUCKED OVERBOARD. ONLY USEFUL

TO THE BOSS IN GOOD TIMES', *Direct Action* noted in August 1914 that the Holman Labor government was bringing down legislation to cancel all industrial awards, which would give employers unlimited opportunity to take advantage of the unprecedented and rapidly increasing army of unemployed. In a mock obituary in November 1915, *Direct Action* recorded the death of the 'living wage' in a decision by Justice Heydon. 'So this is where the arbitration principle, so loved by labor leaders, has landed the workers.' It commented that wages boards and courts were handy institutions for preventing the workers bettering their conditions at times when competition for jobs was less keen, but that when conditions produced an abundance of slaves, 'then to hell with the living wage and such humane balderdash'.[27]

Slowing down had a beneficial effect similar to shorter hours: 'Slow work means more jobs for the unemployed. Less unemployment means less competition for jobs. Less competition means more wages. More wages means a higher standard of living.' The IWW was particularly anxious to discourage workers employed by small capitalists, who worked alongside their employees, from working hard; these 'cockroach exploiters' often extracted extra effort from workers by their matey behaviour. It was important for workers to remember that these employers, like larger ones, 'must be treated as one would a noxious reptile, which must be exterminated as soon as possible'.[28] The IWW insisted it was time the worker recognised that the slow-down policy and tactics of an allied nature were the only methods by which he could counter the strangle-hold of his exploiters: 'The only "fair" day's work for him is that which he can perform with the least possible effort, consistent with the holding down of his job.' According to Dick Surplus, Brisbane Wobblies achieved a slow-down rate of about 10 per cent in many workplaces without the boss retaliating.[29]

Increasing automation made shorter hours and slowing down all the more imperative. The IWW welcomed the potential benefits of machinery: 'We, the industrialists, welcome the ever improving machine; we hate laborious toil with a bitter hatred.' However, it deplored the effects on workers of the introduction of machinery under capitalist relations of production, which ensured that machinery increased unemployment because, being owned privately rather than collectively, its labour-saving benefits were used to increase profits rather than reduce working hours. J.B. King wrote: 'It must be obvious to all that as the machine reaches a greater state of automation, even fewer men will be required, which means that the unemployed will continue to increase, and our position will become ever and ever more insecure.'[30] In its critique of the overemployment of many in long working hours and the accompanying unemployment of others, the IWW's political economy seems pertinent, peculiarly modern and relevant, to an era subject to the dramatic effects of computer-based technological change, of chronic unemployment occasioned by new technology. Its political economy and its alternative moral code challenged not only capitalist ethics but also capitalist rationality; implicit in the IWW treatment of such matters was always the suggestion that capitalist forms of organisation were deeply irrational, because wasteful of human resources and disruptive of social relations.

Tom Glynn was scathing about a lecture at the Trades Hall by Professor Meredith Atkinson, university teacher of economics to the Workers' Educational Association, who argued that the introduction of machinery only caused short-term unemployment because the increased demand for goods made cheaper by automation soon created more employment. Everybody but a professor, Glynn insisted, could see that the problem of unemployment was continuing and growing with the introduction of machinery. Glynn informed Atkinson: 'Unemployment is not going to be solved by dialectical humbug. It will be solved by the "ignorant", "unwashed", mob: the working-class, whom you and your class despise.'[31]

The solution to unemployment and low wages lay in the hands of the workers themselves: 'there are thousands of unemployed in Australia, because there are thousands of boneheads working too hard'. Workers had to insist on reducing the hours of their labour in proportion to the productivity of the machine.[32] Thus, Wobbly political economy accorded with its direct action philosophy. Workers should puncture the ruling-class rhetoric about thrift at the same time as they raised wages and reduced unemployment by their own industrial action:

> In short, if the boss expects you to be thrifty, or pays you only wages enough to be thrifty, be thrifty with your work, work slower . . . Practice thrift with your work, but be a spendthrift with your wages and demand the best; and YOU HAVE THE POWER TO TAKE IT, when you understand the methods and economics of the I.W.W.[33]

The crisis tendencies of capitalism were manipulable by proletarian activity, for better or for worse – here, at any rate, the Wobblies relaxed the fatalist economic analysis of the Second International. The IWW believed that boneheaded workers, through working too hard, exacerbated the recurrent problem of overproduction. *Direct Action* noted that when a boom was on, the workers were speeded up to the limit of their physical endurance in order to supply the demand, which boom produced in its turn the inevitable oversupply with the resultant depression and unemployment. The workers, as well as blind economic forces, were to blame for this situation, for consenting to the ideology of hard work. 'There is only one logical solution to over-production and that is slowing down on the job. Produce less and make the job last longer . . .'[34]

Especially dear to the IWW, as a way of decreasing output, was industrial sabotage: either the deliberate destruction of employers' property or concerted efforts to perform an extremely poor day's work for a poor day's pay.[35] *Direct Action* was full of short comments, ominous from the employer viewpoint: 'Fast workers die young'; 'A little sugar in the concrete will make a few more jobs for the unemployed'; 'Remain on the Job and Study Sabotage. It pays YOU, Damn the Boss.'[36] IWW stickers, too, advertised the concept: 'Sabotage. The Boss's Nightmare' and 'WHY dabble in Arbitration Courts and Sectional Strikes when you have such a powerful weapon as **sabotage** . . .'[37] Bill Genery of the Melbourne Local insisted in 1969 that, in practice, sabotage did not involve destruction but simply 'the conscious withdrawal of industrial efficiency'. Dick Surplus admitted some Brisbane Wobblies destroyed machinery but that IWW propaganda always stressed that sabotage need not entail destruction. Either way, the IWW saw sabotage as 'a brake upon the wheels of capitalist exploitation', for it impeded and retarded the accumulation of surplus value.[38] Sabotage had the advantage, too, of anonymity: 'Sabotage is the smokeless powder of the social war. It scores a hit, while its source is seldom detected.' Though allegations of IWW sabotage were many, rarely were IWW culprits brought to trial.

According to the IWW's proletarian morality, sabotage was justified by the continual sabotage of workers' lives and health by capitalists. Tom Payne recalls Mark Anthony responding to the way in which the 'imperialist war-mongers' expressed outrage at the prospect of Wobblies placing emery dust in the more delicate wheels of industry: 'They should talk of emery dust! Why, the cemetery at Broken Hill is a resting place for scores of miners who went to an early grave because of dusted lungs.'[39] Adulterated food and cheap substitutes were the lot of workers under capitalism. *Direct Action* advised: 'Give adulterated work for adulterated food, and show the masters that sabotage can be returned for sabotage.' Monty Miller considered that sabotage by workers on capitalism was a fitting response to sabotage by capitalists, the cause of much suffering and misery; it was 'a fulfilment of the law of cause and effect'.[40]

Though the IWW believed that individual acts of sabotage helped reduce output and deepened the individual worker's sense of class solidarity,[41] it generally stressed the much greater value of collective forms of sabotage. Walker C. Smith's pamphlet *Sabotage*, reproduced by the Australian Administration, specifically rejected the anarchists' apotheosis of sabotage as 'the main weapon of industrial warfare, overshadowing mass solidarity, industrial formation, and disciplined action'. Some people, it regretted, 'even go so far as to claim that sabotage can usher in the new social order'. The IWW conception of sabotage severely restricted its meaning and applications, and emphasised its use as an

occasional tactic only. It might mean the destroying of raw materials destined for a scab factory, the spoiling of a finished product, the dis-
arrangement of machinery, working slow, giving overweight to
customers and pointing out defects in goods, using the best of materials
where the employer desired adulteration, and the telling of trade
secrets. It was not intended to inconvenience the consumer, only the
capitalist. Walker C. Smith insisted that:

> Sabotage is the destruction of profits to gain a definite, revolutionary, eco-
> nomic end . . . SABOTAGE DOES NOT SEEK NOR DESIRE TO TAKE
> HUMAN LIFE. . . . sabotage is simply one of the many weapons in labour's
> arsenal. It is by no means the greatest one. Solidaric action is mightier than
> the greatest acts of a few. Industrial class formation gives a strength not to be
> obtained by mere tactics. Self-discipline and co-operative action are necessary
> if we are to build a new social order as well as destroy the old.

The IWW preferred mass, rather than individual, forms of sabotage:
'The concerted withdrawal of efficiency, by slowing down or other
means, is sure to bind the workers closer together.'[42]

In the practice of industrial sabotage, Wobbly ethics and economics
were neatly expressed in one blow, in one direct action. Neither the
moderate Laborites nor the socialist parties of the time approved of sabotage; to them it epitomised the Wobblies' dangerous disrespect for the
existing laws and ethics of society, based upon a tendentious understanding of capitalist economics. In general, others on the left and
within the labour movement accused the IWW of a lack of theoretical
sophistication and neglect of 'the inner man', of a jesuitical 'ends-justi-
fies-the-means' approach to social change.

Against such charges, the Wobblies defended themselves. *Direct Action*
explained that, although the IWW was a material organisation fighting a
material struggle over material goods, it had ethics and ideals as beauti-
ful as any other organisation. But the exploited millions needed something immediately, as they might otherwise be crushed and mangled in
some industrial hell; and the realisation of ideals was dependent on
material forces:

> We believe that by organizing on the lines laid down by the I.W.W., we are
> helping to bring nearer the day when slums, squalor, misery, poverty, and
> crime will be things of the past, and the whole human family will enjoy the glo-
> rious benefits of a world set free where there will be neither master nor slave.[43]

Only when the industrially organised workers had obtained control of
industry would it be possible for art and literature to reach their fullest
and freest development. Then, the IWW promised, none would have to

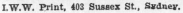

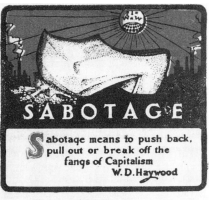

The ethics of the IWW and its poor opinion of 'crawlers' were depicted in its recruiting stickers. (R.S. Ross Collection, NL3222/6)

smother their talent or curb their pen in order to cater for the ruling class: 'With industrially organized workers in control of industry, the inventive genius of the human race can be enabled to blossom forth as never before in the history of mankind.'[44]

Revolution from below would unleash proletarian creativity in ways unimaginable by those who counselled reform from above, who necessarily restricted the aesthetic capabilities of workers. In the Wobbly mind, the pragmatism of the mainstream labour movement, which accommodated itself so readily to capitalism's utilitarian mores, was accompanied by a philistinism that feared the unrealised artistic talents of workers just as it dreaded their potential power to change the world that these representatives of the labour movement found increasingly congenial. The distinctive ethics and economics of the IWW, as we shall see next, informed its especially cogent critique of the Laborism that had flourished in the preceding decades.

CHAPTER 10

'Bump Me into Parliament':
the Critique of Laborism

Less than quarter of a century before the appearance of the IWW, the Labor Party in New South Wales had vowed to 'make and unmake social conditions'; the memory of this promise was still fresh in the mind of many workers, who had lived to see the undertaking woefully unfulfilled. Hughes acknowledged in federal parliament early in 1917 that the strength of the IWW represented 'the revolt of the people against the chicanery of legislatures', which had not relieved their suffering: 'The best remedy for syndicalism is effective political action.'[1] The IWW had decided the reverse was the case: that the best remedy for ineffective political action was revolutionary industrial unionism. It expressed and reinforced the strong feelings of resentment felt by many militant workers towards their elected representatives. Accordingly, it was widely resented by Labor apologists for its 'determination to make workers believe their representatives in Parliament are all unmitigated scoundrels'; concern was also expressed that the IWW was encouraging workers to avoid registration under the Commonwealth Electoral Act.[2]

To the American IWW, political action was not a possible practice to be rejected as a matter of principle but an irrelevancy, because those to whom it appealed, the disenfranchised itinerant workers, had no political means, estranged as they were from the electoral process by the racial, linguistic and residency requirements for voter registration. Accordingly, the American IWW, while rejecting *control* by political parties, never expressly condemned political action and many American Wobblies were active members of parties such as the Socialist Party. Too much has been made, Conlin insists, of the deletion of the political clause in 1908; equally significant was the rejection without discussion by the 1911 Convention of an amendment to the Preamble that referred to 'the futility of political action'.[3] The strength of the IWW in the United

143

States stemmed not from disillusion with parliamentary politics, which had never been seriously tried, but from discontent with the especially conservative and ineffective nature of American trade unionism.

In Australia, with a comparatively democratic franchise and reasonably fair access to electoral registration, the IWW was more expressly and truly anti-political. The Australian IWW's determined rebuttal of political action was informed by the experience, peculiar to Australasia, of the duplicity of Labor, the betrayal of working-class interests by Labor governments. While individual Wobblies may occasionally have voted in elections, the IWW itself was insistent that political action had nothing to offer: 'The I.W.W. does not say that the workers must not vote at Parliamentary elections; but that such voting is of no use to the proletariat in the great class struggle.'[4] *Direct Action* explained: 'Our members are not pledged to do one thing or the other on election day. They simply please themselves. They can vote if they wish, or they can "strike at the ballot box with an axe." It matters not to the organisation.' In fact, many Wobblies chose to avoid electoral registration (which was then compulsory though voting was not compulsory until 1924) and for this some were fined under the Commonwealth Electoral Act.[5] Disenfranchisement was here their choice; it was not imposed upon them by circumstances, as in the United States.

The ballot, the IWW argued, was 'the greatest fraud ever perpetrated upon a long-suffering and over-patient working class'. Hundreds of thousands of workers were living in a fools' paradise because of 'insidious teaching on the part of those whom the workers themselves have raised to positions of privilege and of others aspiring to such positions'.[6] The best-known indigenous Wobbly creation was the song of the Labor MP, 'Bump Me Into Parliament', written by Bill Casey in Melbourne, to the tune of 'Yankee Doodle':

> Come listen, all kind friends of mine,
> I want to move a motion,
> To build an El Dorado here,
> I've got a bonzer notion.
>
> *Chorus:*
> Bump me into Parliament,
> Bounce me any way,
> Bang me into Parliament,
> On next election day.
>
> Some very wealthy friends I know
> Declare I am most clever,
> While some may talk for an hour or so
> Why, I can talk for ever.

I know the Arbitration Act
As a sailor knows his 'riggins',
So if you want a small advance,
I'll talk to Justice Higgins.

Oh yes I am a Labor man,
And believe in revolution;
The quickest way to bring it on
Is talking constitution.

I've read my Bible ten times through,
And Jesus justifies me,
The man who does not vote for me,
By Christ he crucifies me.

So bump them into Parliament,
Bounce them any way,
Bung them into Parliament,
Don't let the Court decay.[7]

When Labor was victorious in the Queensland election of 1915, *Direct Action* was pleased:

the accession of Labor Socialists to the plums of office will, we hope, clear the
working-class mind of another deep-rooted superstition, when they see the
futility of expecting things through the methods of the ballot-box. It will clear
the ground for the I.W.W. propaganda. [8]

In its very first editorial *Direct Action* maintained that faith in Labor politicians, the age-long tendency of putting trust in princes, was a most
potent factor in the continued enslavement of the workers. The Labor
MP would naturally put his own material interests before those of the
working class, 'since economic determinism is such a powerful factor',
and his interests were not compatible with the workers' welfare.[9] Also to
'Yankee Doodle' was another Australian IWW song, 'Hey! Polly':

The politician prowls around,
For workers' votes entreating;
He claims to know the slickest way
To give the boss a beating.

Chorus:
Polly, we can't use you, dear,
To lead us into clover;
This fight is ours, and as for you,
Clear out or get run over.

He claims to be the bosses' foe,
On workers' friendship doting,
He says, 'Don't fight while on the job,
But do it all by voting.

Elect ME to the office, boys,
Let all your rage pass o'er you;
Don't bother with your countless wrongs –
I'll do your fighting for you.'

He says that slowing down won't do,
(It isn't to his liking),
And that without HIS mighty aid
There is no use in striking.

He says that he can lead us all
To some fair El Dorado;
But he's of such a yellow hue
He'd cast a golden shadow!

He begs and coaxes, threatens, yells,
For shallow glory thirsting,
In fact he's just a bag of wind
That's swollen up to bursting.

The smiling bosses think he'd like
To boodle from their manger;
And as he never mentions STRIKE,
They know there is no danger.

And all the while he spouts and spiels,
He's musing undetected,
On what a lovely snap he'll have
When once he is elected.[10]

Labor MPs, the IWW argued, had too congenial an atmosphere in parliament to waste their time standing up for workers in struggle: 'they would rather drink champagne with the boss'. Though physical violence was definitely rejected as a tactic by the IWW, a caveat was attached in the case of Labor MPs: 'the law of self-preservation will eventually compel the workers to treat such atavistic abortions as they would treat a mad dog that would bite the hand that fed it'.[11]

This formal position apart, good relations otherwise existed between Wobblies and a tiny number of MPs; the IWW was capable of distinguishing between parliament and some of the people in it, between those interested only in emancipating themselves and those still concerned with the working class. Tom Barker and Frank Anstey were friends and remained in touch for many years after Barker's deportation. Percy Brookfield is discussed with considerable affection as 'Brooky' in Charlie Reeve's letters from prison. The Broken Hill IWW had very good relations with Brookfield and, to a lesser extent, with Mick Considine.[12] Consequently, Brookfield was expelled from Caucus for his IWW sympathies and Considine's selection for the Barrier seat was endorsed only after he signed a letter announcing he was not and never

had been a member of the IWW and that he did not agree with its policy or methods.[13]

The IWW pointed out both the sins of commission and of omission
on the part of Labor. After carefully enumerating the recent strike-breaking record of the New South Wales McGowen government, it claimed
the doings of this Labor government should 'serve as a warning to the
working-class, not alone of this country but of the whole world. The capitalistic State, no matter by whom its institutions are manned, must function as the protector of the economic system which gave it birth.'[14] The
much-vaunted social laboratory of *fin de siècle* Australasia had produced
its own critics, in a peculiarly strong position to make judgements about
the experiment of Labor-in-politics. Nor could Labor governments
deliver the very limited number of goods promised: 'it is pleasing to note
that the Labour Parties of Australia, when gaining a majority on the
plush cushions in the various Parliaments have displayed absolutely their
utter impotence to do anything for the workers'. The precocity of the
political labour movement in Australia, its unprecedented occupancy of
Treasury benches in parliaments throughout the country, enabled the
IWW to form conclusions and indulge in polemical abuse, based on concrete evidence about the performance of Labor representatives:
'Workers of Australia, you have raised up unto yourselves gods, in the
shape of Labor politicians, and behold events have proved that their feet
are but of clay.'[15]

The IWW was also scathing about the Labor Party's vision of socialism,
inasmuch as it was deemed to have such a vision. A striking feature of
labour conferences, it noted, was the simplicity with which most delegates were convinced that state control of industry was socialism, even
though Australian workers had had it for years and were no better off
than those who worked for private profiteers. In Queensland, where the
Ryan Labor government established State enterprises, the local Wobblies
were unimpressed. Dick Surplus maintained the Brisbane Local considered the State butchery 'a bit of a racket by the trade unions' because
union leaders would shop there and obtain two to three times more
meat than they paid for and they suspected similar rackets in other State-
run businesses. Such enterprises, Surplus pointed out, were not supported by the rank and file to any great extent. *Direct Action* emphasised
the harsh working conditions in the State enterprises established by the
New South Wales Labor government:

> The State makes a hell for every worker employed under it by placing its time-
> servers and toadies in the most desirable positions of authority, by systems of
> pimping and espionage, while superannuation schemes and sliding wage-
> scales are used to sap and demoralise whatever militant spirit there may be
> among the men.

It asserted that the Sydney tramway system, owned by the State, was the worst in Australia in respect of working conditions. And the State bakery always employed exclusively non-union labour. In fostering hopes in the benefits of state-managed capitalism, the Labor Party was leading the workers away from an understanding of their real class interests: 'the State is our worst foe and the ones who are advocating State ownership and control of industry are traitors to the labor movement'.[16]

Writing at a time when governments were acquiring rather than disposing of public property, A.A. MacInnes noted that it was the tendency in all modernised countries, even without Labor parties in command, for governments to control the chief industries. This 'State-managed Capitalism' was not a step towards socialism, for capitalism could not be 'bought out'; only confiscation to redistribute ownership could make the proletariat economically and industrially free.[17] Indeed, public ownership often constituted a 'bailing out' of individual capitalists in distress. Tom Barker argued:

> The capitalist class are aware that old forms of production are being superseded, and therefore they look round for possible purchasers so as to protect themselves against loss . . . They find salvation in Labour parties, State socialists, and other people who believe in nationalisation and municipalisation schemes . . . this is good business for Mr Capitalist, for he has palmed his unprofitable and useless industry on to the State; his interest comes in regularly year by year, and he is saved the worry of managing the industry and trying to calm the troubled waters of industrial discontent . . . It is no consolation for the worker to know that the State exploits him now, in the place of his former capitalist employer . . . there is no hope for the working-class in State ownership . . . Let us organise to control society by organising to control the job . . . 'They who would be free themselves must strike the blow.'[18]

The labour movement's enthusiasm for state ownership, this 'new incarnation of Authority', this 'new idol', was simply a tool in the hands of property-owning classes to keep the propertyless people propertyless. Contrary to labour movement mythology, state ownership would not be 'a sort of wet nurse to the oppressed' but would serve as an ally to private enterprise and 'establish a sort of socialism for the few built up on the exploitation of the many'. In municipal and state enterprises and in the system of compulsory arbitration, the IWW noted the 'strenuous endeavours of Capitalism to render itself, at the expense of the worker, more stable'.[19]

The Labor Party obscured the reality of the class struggle, and preached class-collaboration. Nowhere was this more evident than in the way Labor governments adhered to arbitration, 'the very essence of capitalism', enforcing its awards with injunctions, fines and the jailing of strikers.

Direct Action explained that, despite the support for it since its inception of craft union leaders and Labor MPs, the arbitration court was 'the off-spring of modern day capitalism, which fears the dangers of working class discontent gaining cohesion and intelligence. It . . . has been purposely established to prevent working class organisation "making laws" on its own account to supersede the economic and legal code of the exploiting class.'[20] Wobblies were fond of denouncing the 'Go Slow' policy, the cumbersome and protracted procedures, of the industrial courts. Because the state effectively sponsored union organisation and growth via the arbitration system, union bureaucrats were unlikely to oppose the state; and arbitration increased the power within each union of these bureaucrats involved in preparing court cases, serving to frustrate attempts at rank-and-file control of union affairs, to which the IWW was dedicated.

Arbitration, Glynn argued, was a 'masters' scheme', a ruling-class mechanism that not only prevented workers bettering their conditions but placed strikers in the position of criminals; it sanctioned the unlimited right of employers to exploit and remain dominant over the working class; it deprived the workers of the rights to protection except through the medium of courts and judges sworn to perpetuate the system that robbed workers. The pernicious effect of arbitration was material and ideological: 'The Arbitration Court has bled the pockets and befogged the minds of the Australian workers, and it has filled the pockets of the parasitical gang of legal luminaries . . .' Arbitration and arbitration awards had accomplished nothing for workers: 'They never can and never will; never were so intended.'[21]

The Wobbly critique of industrial arbitration was timely. Invented in Australia and New Zealand in the aftermath of the great strikes of the early 1890s, introduced in piecemeal fashion by Labor and non-Labor governments during the first decade of the new century, arbitration did not establish the 'new province for law and order' that H.B. Higgins (a butt of the Wobbly song 'Bump Me Into Parliament') described when he looked back on his fourteen years as president of the Commonwealth arbitration court. Some of its shortfalls were all too apparent to him. Employers had challenged the jurisdiction of his court, governments had interfered and workers had defied its awards.

For a time the new method of conducting industrial relations had seemed to hold out the promise of modest sufficiency for workers. In their weakened condition following the strikes and depression of the 1890s, court recognition and an industrial award enabled unions to form or re-form in order to establish minimal entitlements. The Harvester judgement of 1907 established the right of a worker to live 'as a human being in a civilized community'. But for more than a decade only a minority of wage-earners were covered by this basic wage, and those who were covered by the State systems of arbitration found that these were riddled with deficiencies. The strains on the Australian system of industrial arbitration became most apparent as the economy prospered in the years leading to the First World War, as workers sought wage rises and employers resisted them. The ineffectiveness of arbitration was demonstrated in a series of major confrontations, several involving police and punitive legislation. The tendency of Labor politicians and moderate trade union officials to blame Wobblies for these industrial stoppages merely attested to the cogency of their message. Then the economic disruption of the war, which threw many workers into unemployment while the wage determinations of arbitration tribunals lagged far behind price increases, made the Wobbly critique of the state even more compelling.

In 1912 the IWW Clubs claimed that workers had woken up to arbitration and that employers, rather than workers, were the system's most ardent admirers.[22] By 1915 even craft unions, according to the IWW, were becoming uneasy about the effects of arbitration. From the dock in Perth in 1916, Alexander Horrocks explained that the reason he had joined the IWW was because the award covering the miners on the goldfields did not make provision for higher wages to meet the increased cost of living.[23] Military intelligence noted that the aim of the IWW activists within the Queensland Railways Union was to remove the union from the control of the arbitration court. That there was substantial support for the IWW position is borne out in the voting at a QRU meeting early in 1919 on a Warwick branch motion 'that as organizer Eastcrabb has continually advocated I.W.W.sm, and the abolition of arbitration, it . . . be recommended . . . to take steps to remove him from the position of organizer': it was 7 for and 27 against.[24]

The IWW argued that employers would always ignore or subvert the verdicts of the arbitration court when it suited them. For instance, in December 1912 the Adelaide tramway men went on strike to better their conditions and Justice Higgins had found in their favour; but when the men returned to the tram sheds, they were informed by the Adelaide Municipal Tramway Trust that, if they were not prepared to go back under the old conditions, they would not be employed. If the workers desired other examples where awards and arbitration courts had demonstrated their futility, *Direct Action* announced it had a gross of them on file. Instances of the absurdities of arbitration could be given in volumes, but the paper could not afford the space. The new unionism of the IWW 'refuses to meddle in conciliation and arbitration, signs no agreements with the master, thereby dividing our forces . . .'[25]

In any case, arbitration court awards were but the reflex of the economic power wielded by the workers concerned.[26] In stark contrast to those within the labour movement who advised workers to leave the work of reform to their representatives, the IWW counselled always the necessity for direct action: 'the worst use you can make of a member of your own class is to place him in parliament; you, yourselves, must be your own legislators; the place to do it is in the Industrial Union of your class'. Reforms initiated by parliaments were gained invariably because of extra-parliamentary pressure, through direct industrial action; they were 'a sop . . . to keep back the wolves of Socialism, Syndicalism and Anarchy'.[27]

The pathetic creature of Craft Unionism is here beseeching Labor Premier Holman for More Wages, Better Conditions. In the background, the strong figure of Direct Action is taking More Wages, Better Conditions, and banishing the Holman figure from the picture. (*Direct Action*, 8 January 1916)

Just as the IWW believed that the attainment of reforms was in the hands of workers themselves, organising where they worked, so also did they maintain, vehemently, that the ultimate salvation of the workers was in their own hands; their failure to achieve the abolition of capitalism was their fault alone. 'The continued existence of the Wage System is a standing reflection on the working Class. Get wise, and Organise for your own emancipation.' Action was in itself better than inaction, wherever the battle was fought: 'It is action, not argument, that settles problems . . . An ounce of action is worth a ton of philosophy . . .' The *Direct Action* logo regularly appeared with slogans expressing this direct action persuasion: 'The Emancipation of the Workers Must be Achieved by the Working Class Itself'; 'All forms of Direct Action are Labour's Best Tactics. GET BUSY!'[28]

Direct action, essentially, was the opposite of parliamentary action: it entailed active strikes, passive strikes (staying on the job and working slowly) and sabotage. 'Direct action is the great WAR METHOD of the workers in the class struggle.' The place for action, Norman Rancie argued, was not in parliament but 'in the industries where we work – at the point of production – on the job . . .'[29] The Sydney Local's 1911 recruiting leaflet warned workers that

> The Capitalist Class and their political agents – many who are called friends of the workers – plan to keep you under the yoke of tyranny by offering you what they are pleased to call working class legislation, such as Arbitration Courts, Wages Boards, Labor Exchanges, National Insurance and Workers' Compensation, etc., on condition that you smother your discontent, and have nothing in common with those who desire you to act for yourselves.

However, it insisted that 'In the history of the world, right down the stairway of time, no tyranny has been overthrown, no tyrant vanquished, except in consequence of the action of those who have been tyrannised.' The 'victims of tyranny to-day' could only become free men and women by taking action on their own behalf, by becoming organised in the IWW.[30]

Direct action, 'Ajax' claimed, 'was ever the governing factor in every social change'; it was direct action that overthrew serfdom and feudalism. 'Historically everything of any value has been forced from below by direct action . . .' Though politicians informed people they must wait for 'Evolution', A.A. MacInnes insisted workers should ignore this advice: 'without Revolutions there'd be no evolution or at any rate no advance, for evolution appears to me but a period of apparent stagnation interspersed by violent upheavals'. Some useful reforms had fallen to the workers through the quarrels that raged between capitalists and landlords about a century ago, but since that time, the IWW insisted, 'concessions have been wrung from the employers only by a display of working-class solidarity and determination'.[31]

Accordingly, the IWW aimed for much greater unity than that provided by existing trade unionism; it aimed to combat all capitalist and craft union notions and habits that divided the workforce ideologically and segmented it in practice, which weakened its resistance to the encroach-ments of capital. The IWW charged craft unionism with encouraging notions of class collaboration and neglecting 'class education', with fos-tering and promoting 'ideas which prevent the development of class consciousness on the part of the workers'. The division of the workforce achieved in practice by craft union methods was symbolised in demarca-tion disputes; the IWW was contemptuous of the way craft unionism encouraged these pointless squabbles.[32]

Existing trade unions were hopelessly incompetent, too, at fighting worthwhile battles. During the 1914 Sydney bakers' strike, the IWW was appalled to find the bread-carters discussing their attitude to the strike, as though there could be any doubt about their response; the bakers in nearby Newcastle not only remained at work but sent a wire condemning their fellow workers for taking action to better their conditions; and the 'higher lights' at the Trades Hall were all unanimous in joining the cap-italist press in a chorus of disapproval of the bakers' action. However, the most remarkable feature of this strike was the manner in which all con-cerned – master bakers and unionists, strikers and non-strikers – were concerned that there should be no shortage of bread.[33] When 3000 coalminers in the Maitland district went on strike, the IWW noted that the union leaders were 'alarmed' lest there be any extension of the strike to other areas. It was amused that a deputation of these miners to the minister, requesting parliamentary interference, was informed that it was simply a question of whether the miners themselves were strong enough to enforce their demands. The IWW would have organised the strike very differently.

> If the coal miners of Australia were so educated as to recognise that this is a fight of their class against the organised forces of capitalism, that every ounce of coal produced is making victory for their fellow-miners more remote; if coal-lumpers tied up every port in Australia by refusing to place scab coal in the bunkers of steamers; if firemen and engine-drivers paralysed the railway arteries of the country . . . the bosses, the press, and the politicians would take a different view of the afternoon shift.[34]

Direct Action considered that a review of the previous ten years' strikes should convince the unbiassed reader that trade unionism had out-grown its usefulness and existed only upon the traditions of the past and the conservatism of its members. Despite the hard and bitter fights they had put up, despite the suffering which always resulted from badly organised strikes, the militant workers were more and more meeting with defeat. The only way to defeat a trust was by creating a stronger one. The 1338 trade unions, each acting independently, each fighting its own battles and being beaten by other unionists, should be replaced by the One Big Union as advocated by the IWW.[35]

The net result, it claimed, of three-quarters of a century of trade union effort in Australia was a great collection of disjointed federations, rickety affiliations, and disconnected craft unions, united only in their officials coming together to bleed the workers for their own paltry personal advancement. 'A ridiculously inefficient hotch potch; incapable, incoherent, and serving only the interests of the employers by keeping the workers industrially divided . . .' It could show nothing but the same eight-and-three-quarter-hour day workers had twenty years ago and an average real wage fully 30 per cent lower than at that time. The boss, the IWW claimed, believed in this kind of trade unionism; therefore, it was 'no use to the working class'. Dick Surplus joined the IWW because he was 'dissatisfied with the trade union movement': as a canecutter in north Queensland he found it 'impossible to get anything done through the AWU'; as a building worker in Brisbane he discovered the building trades were 'hopelessly disorganised' and, with other Wobblies, he helped form the building trades group as a preliminary step towards one industry in the union.[36]

Though the IWW achieved very little on its own account, its revolutionary propaganda aided and abetted the impulses within the labour movement towards rationalisation and modernisation, albeit of a reformist kind achieved primarily by amalgamations of existing unions.[37] By insisting upon the necessity for revolutionary industrial unionism, it persuaded many unionists that the existing unions should at least be reorganised along industrial rather than craft lines. IWW ideas seeped osmotically through into the wider labour movement, strengthening the degree of irritation felt at this time with craft unionism and the concomitant enthusiasm for industrial unionism, if not of the revolutionary kind.

Wobbly invective against craft unionism was aimed more at its officials than its members, 'trade secretaries, who live on the backs of the slaves'. Union officials, according to Reeve, were 'troglodytes from the slimy caverns of the Trades Hall'. Melbourne Wobblies referred to the Trades Hall as 'The Morgue'; for Sydney Wobblies this institution was 'the deadhouse'. And the reciprocal hostility towards the IWW on the part of craft unionists was expressed much more forcibly by its officials than by its rank-and-file members. The secretary of the Broken Hill Local reported in June 1914 that the IWW was 'meeting with the usual opposition from Craft Union officials and would-be politicians'.[38]

The distrust evinced by the IWW towards union leaders, towards union bureaucracy in general, was distinctive and remarkable for the time. Most militant workers were inclined to look with varying degrees of disfavour upon individual trade union leaders for their timidity and conservatism; but the IWW, in a new departure, identified the entire layer of officialdom as necessarily a problem for workers in struggle with their employers. Unlike the Communist Party, the IWW never endeavoured to win elected positions in the trade union hierarchies; always its efforts within unions were at the lowest levels, fomenting militancy on the job, making trouble, often for the officials as well as for the bosses. Communists, by contrast, aspired to become union officials, and Communist union officials were influential within the Communist movement.

The Wobblies were not interested: 'A serious bar to effective union organisation is highly paid union officials. Once an individual is financially raised above the working class, he ceases to think as a worker, he seeks a different environment, and lives a different life to the toiler . . .' Very often, Norman Rancie alleged, the trade union secretaries were greater autocrats than the boss on the job: 'So long as we have highly paid union officials, and poorly paid slaves, the boss will be happy. It is difficult to tell sometimes which is our greatest enemy – the trade union secretary or the boss . . .'[39]

The contempt of the IWW for union officialdom in general earned it support from rank-and-file militants whose experiences with individual union officials inclined them to a similar viewpoint, to the conclusion that the individual trade union official who betrayed a struggle was not an aberration but an example of a general tendency. Ernest Scott, in his official history of the home front during the First World War, states that 'there was no strike during the war years which the union officials did not strive to prevent, and, when the flames spread beyond their powers of extinction, to bring to a conclusion'. In 1916, 1.7 million working days were lost in strike action. Try as they certainly did, the trade union leaders were unable to restrain the rank and file, who turned increasingly to the IWW, whose direct action philosophy gave expression both to their immediate needs and their discontent with their official leaders.[40] The Wobblies exploited the discontent of many workers during these years, not simply with their wages and conditions, but with those they had elected to lead their industrial battles.

The Wobblies boasted that their own paid organisers, who were very few and always short-term, received no more than the average wage existing in the place they were working, so it was 'impossible for them to rise superior to the rank and file'; and, though allowed to speak, they had no vote in the conducting of industrial disputes, which was to be determined by the organisation as a whole.[41] Thus the IWW believed that financial parity with the workers they represented was not sufficient to prevent organisers selling out; also necessary were structural restraints on their power to deal with the boss or other unions or whomever. IWW organisers were distinguished from ordinary trade union officials by their working-class standard of remuneration; their subjection to the discipline of the rank and file; and the very limited nature of their tenure, usually no longer than the few weeks' or months' duration of a strike or propaganda tour.

The IWW seemed sensitive to the problem, within working-class organisations, of leadership and personal power. In the place of the craft-union leader with his 'autocratic' powers and his constituency of indifferent followers, the industrial union hoped to provide organisers 'who have been and are living the life of the working class; who "embody the tendency of the movement"; who respect the constitution and are amenable to the discipline of the organization and who possess the ability to administer its affairs in accordance with its purposes . . .'[42] The IWW aimed and claimed to be 'a rank and file organization', which, in contradistinction to traditional trade unionism, would serve as a training ground and headquarters for activists on the job who were also bent upon more grandiose plans, the formation of One Big Union:

> Within the I.W.W. the workers find a common ground to meet upon – the building up of their respective unions. Here they meet and discuss the problems confronting them as workers and organisers, for it has oft been said that every member of the I.W.W. is an organizer for the One Big Union.
>
> The principal function of these workers is educational in nature, and for that reason the members meet en masse to lay plans for educating the workers of the various industries as the opportunity presents itself, the members of all industries assisting each other in this work, selecting the industry that presents the greatest opportunities.[43]

In pursuing the formation of the One Big Union, the IWW argued it was necessary to start anew, to build the new structure from outside of the existing union network, not to attempt to transform the old. Norman Rancie asserted:

> BORING FROM WITHIN IS OUT OF HARMONY WITH PROGRESS. It is a retrogressive step. So soon as an organisation has fulfilled its purposes, it is time for it to die. It is useless trying to transform an obsolete institution . . . A palace cannot be built out of tenements; a healthy child cannot be reared in the slums; fighters cannot be made out of dead matter. Nor can the I.W.W. be organised at the Trades Hall . . . The I.W.W. is made up of the advanced and militant section of the working class who are finished with fighting shadows, and trying to kick into life a worn-out and dying organistion.[44]

'Boring from within' was doomed to failure, because craft trade unionism was out of date, dividing workers on the basis of tools used, in an era
where machines had made such a distinction and hierarchy redundant.
Direct Action maintained that, to attempt to fight the boss through the
craft unions when the IWW was at hand, was like wanting to wade
through a quagmire when a solid metal road was provided. It stressed
the need to 'smash from without' instead of sinuously 'boring from
within', to organise thoroughly and imbue workers with the feeling of
solidarity, to 'cast aside those accursed distinctions . . . which now blind
the craft unionists'.[45]

Although the IWW aspired to create a new union structure, initially in
competition with and ultimately replacing existing unions, in practice it
had little choice but to bore from within. While it loudly proclaimed
against this very tactic and espoused noisily the principle of 'dual unionism', it saw the opportunity, indeed necessity, to spread its ideas by working within the existing trade unions. Many Wobblies were members, also,
of established trade unions. According to Roly Farrell, the terms 'bonehead' and 'scab' were never, as craft-union officials alleged, applied to
craft unionists, only to un-unionised, anti-union workers. Detective
Moore noted on the basis of private IWW correspondence seized by
police that Wobblies advised each other not to antagonise craft
unionists.[46] Tom Barker expressly warned the miners establishing the
Tottenham Local in 1915 not to 'antagonise the crafties', for 'they are
the material we have to work upon, and therefore every care should be
taken to keep their good will'. The *Barrier Daily Truth* observed in
December 1916 that many IWW men were joining craft unions 'so that
the principles of their organisation may be more widely known'.[47] A security file on the IWW noted that

> there has been a growing movement on the part of the I.W.W. men to join
> Unions so that the principles of their organisation might be more widely pro-
> mulgated. They conducted an active propaganda amongst the members of
> Craft Unions and succeeded in converting a great number of them.[48]

In 'boring from within', reluctantly infiltrating existing unions, the IWW
never contemplated transforming these unions, for that was impossible;
instead, it aimed at making recruits amongst, and building links between,
rank-and-file militants within the existing union movement.

This departure from American IWW practice was in reaction to
Australian circumstances. In the United States the Wobblies had persisted with the practice of dual unionism, for the IWW there was stronger
and the official labour movement weaker; but the Australian IWW, relatively underdeveloped, was operating in an environment where the

labour movement was well-organised by international standards, with considerable coverage in many areas.[49] An American Wobbly, writing to the *Industrial Worker* from Australia, contrasted American labour organisation and working-class wages and conditions unfavourably with the situation he had encountered in Australia.[50] The Australian IWW was not, like the American, aiming to organise workers completely neglected by trade unionism; it was hoping, rather, to change the basis on which all workers were organised.

Dual unionism remained a long-term aspiration, but not an immediate tactic; still in the stage of forming propagandist Locals, the IWW proceeded to 'bore from within' with its propaganda about the need for building from without: 'The I.W.W. in Australia is the Recruiting Force and concentration camp for Industrial Unionists until there is a unit of their industry fully organized in their localities in which to place them . . .' *Direct Action* admitted that, while it was impossible that craft unions, with a few alterations, could function successfully as industrial unions, excellent propaganda work could nevertheless be done within these unions. However, 'while the principle of "boring from within" the craft unions may possibly show good results when put into practice, "building from without" is absolutely essential too, for precept and example are the best methods by which principles can be illustrated and explained'.[51] In theory, then, the IWW embarked on elaborate industrial organisation, 'dual unionism', the formation of One Big Union, which aimed both at marshalling the forces of the revolution and at improving wages and conditions under capitalism; in practice, it bored from within the existing trade unions.

Inasmuch as the IWW was successful in its circumscribed sphere of paid, predominantly male, labour, it was as borers from within. The closest it ever came to dual unionism was only by negotiation with the existing union. The AMA at Broken Hill agreed to recognise the IWW pence card as an alternative union ticket, and IWW members worked alongside regular unionists in the mines; the Broken Hill Local had established a Mining Industrial Union, whose membership was much the same as that of the Local. The IWW was never ready, as Tom Barker admits, to organise Australian workers into the One Big Union, not even to launch a single department. Important in the meantime, however, was fanning the flames of discontent in workplaces the length and breadth of the continent, showing workers 'the power they possess, if only properly organised'.[52] How the Wobblies fared in directing industrial action from below, in confrontation with employers, is the subject of the next chapter.

CHAPTER 11

'An Injury to One An Injury to All': Direct Industrial Action

In 'boring from within' the existing trade union movement, Australian Wobblies did not experience the same degree of concerted employer resistance encountered by their fellow workers across the Pacific in forming an embryonic dual union structure. The notorious brutalities inflicted on the American Wobblies were not mirrored in the experience of the IWW in Australia, where industrial relations were conducted with a comparative gentleness, disdaining use of the Gatling gun and savage lynchings, resorting merely to frequent dismissals, systematic blacklisting, regular brawls, police interference with strikes and the occasional arrest. Australian employers could not easily isolate and physically intimidate Wobblies because they worked under the cover of an established and comparatively strong trade union movement that had even secured the added respectability of sponsoring one of the main parties of government. Thus, where American Wobblies were defeated ultimately by the employers and their thugs, the Australian Wobblies were restrained and contained industrially by the trade union movement itself, especially by the bureaucracy.

Many union officials shared employers' anxiety about increasing IWW influence within the existing unions, its success in boring from within. In addition to its members and supporters, Wobbly language, attitudes and methods were also permeating sections of the working class who had little or no contact with the IWW. With wartime profiteering, high food prices, long working hours, the refusal of the arbitration court in most cases to increase wages to catch up with price rises, and the increasing use of speed-up methods in production, discontent was widespread; and the IWW was effectively exploiting the failure of Laborism, arbitration and union officialdom to assuage the workers' grievances. The IWW recognised the community of interest between employers and union

officials, boasting that its power was 'feared by the parasite class, including their lieutenants, the labor politician and trades union fakir'.[1] P.H.
Hickey, organiser of the Victorian Railways Union, wrote to the AWU in
August 1916 that he believed the IWW was going to develop into 'a very
serious menace'. Its adherents, with their 'astonishing enthusiasm' and
an ever increasing literature distribution, were 'penetrating everywhere',
endeavouring to 'destroy the prestige of officials'. He asked whether, if
he wrote a propaganda pamphlet to 'counteract the sinister campaign
of the I.W.W.', the AWU would publish it. It did.[2]

The lines of conflict were most clearly marked in the AWU. Pastoralists
and AWU officials were both aghast at the number of IWW followers
amongst the rank and file, especially in the Queensland and western
New South Wales branches. A member of the House of Representatives
and the Council of the Pastoralists' Union assured the House in July
1917 that the Pastoralists' Union was 'doing its best to retain in office
the present officials of the Australian Workers' Union, because the
Industrial Workers of the World section of it has been getting completely
out of hand'.[3] Military intelligence commended the officials of the AWU,
who displayed 'a very commendable spirit' in their attempts to prevent
IWW intrusion into AWU affairs. During a canecutters' strike at Innisfail
in August 1918, the local police assured their commissioner that the
AWU would 'oust the IWW element which is accountable for the continuation of the strike'; when the strike finished, military intelligence
noted 'the chorus of I.W.W. discontent when the A.W.U. saved the industry from ruination'.[4]

Military intelligence invariably echoed the mutual concerns of
employers and union officials. It regretted that IWW theories had 'struck
deep into the militant unions', especially the AMIEU, the QRU and the
Painters Union, as well as the AWU. It compiled dossiers containing
details of the private lives of those considered the most dangerous of the
IWW activists: William Jackson, 'a swindling I.W.W. agitator' in northern
Queensland, and Gordon Brown, insurance salesman and stump orator
who 'always associated with the worst revolutionary elements in Brisbane';
Percy Mandeno, Harry Barcan and Archie McNeill in the AMIEU; Archie
Eastcrabb, Jim Quinton, Geo. W. Rymer, W.E. Sampson, E. Phillips and
E. Radford in the QRU; John Christie and Ted Stewart amongst the sugar
industry workers; W.J. Eccles amongst the shearers; and P. Stalker, 'the
ringleader of I.W.W.ism . . . in Ipswich'. These dedicated spies were convinced that 'The taint of I.W.W.ism' is disaffecting unionism throughout
Queensland. There is no question of its growing influence in Brisbane
while Northern districts, Cairns, Cloncurry, Townsville – are riddled with
it.'[5] In a long memorandum on IWW activities, the deputy chief censor
wrote to the chief of the general staff in September 1918 that a personal

visit to Queensland was necessary 'to realise the State of disloyalty into which a very large section of the population has sunk'. A large number of unionists 'are now identified as a body with the revolutionary section and

In some country districts the polling has been postponed for a week owing to heavy floods.— (News item, 1/11/16.)

Wobbly:—''I s'pose I'll get the blame for this.

The IWW was blamed for the defeat of the conscription referenda, most industrial disturbances and more besides. This Wobbly expects that he will be blamed for the flood. (*Direct Action*, 11 November 1916)

have, in most cases, allowed that section to take full control of their organisation'.[6]

Estimating the real influence of the IWW in the industrial disputes of the time is difficult, not only because the IWW was subject to hysterical accusations about the extent of its support and the Wobblies themselves were no less prone to exaggeration than employers and spies, but because Wobbly support subsisted in unstructured, informal and ground-level networks of militancy. Detective Moore referred to the 'insidious nature' of the IWW's industrial activity and complained that, while the 'open propaganda' of the IWW was an 'easy matter' to deal with, its propaganda within trade unions was 'a much more difficult matter to solve'.[7] The IWW's following was rather less than it or its opponents claimed but considerably more than most trade union officials could tolerate. A well placed and acute contemporary observer, Childe, concedes that the IWW had immense influence: 'On the union movement it left an indelible mark.' And, as Churchward notes, there are 'many echoes of I.W.W. phraseology in trade union pamphlets of the period . . .' Jimmy Seamer, an active unionist in the mining industry in Wonthaggi, Broken Hill and the southern and northern mining belts in New South Wales, maintained that: 'You met Wobblies wherever you went . . . All militants followed the Wobblies . . . They had a foot in everywhere.'[8]

Barker describes the way IWW ideas were spreading amongst rank-and-file workers, from the bottom and outwards:

> All kinds of movements and strikes were going on outside. There were troubles in Broken Hill; there was a great build-up of IWW sentiment in North Queenland, from Cairns and Townsville to Cloncurry. The engines and box cars on the railways were carrying our slogans. The same thing applied in Sydney Harbour, where we had a big following amongst the ship repairers and painters. When they were painting the side of a ship they would first draw 'IWW' in very big letters on it, and then would start on the outside and work gradually towards this, so that during the whole of the time anybody coming into the Harbour or passing would see these enormous letters on the side of the ship, waiting to be painted in. One night at Central Station I saw an engine come in from the shops groomed ready for going out on the road, and the way it had been done reflected light on the side so that you could distinctly see the letters 'IWW' shining on the engine. We used all kinds of methods like that in order to make the organisation well known through the country.[9]

Jim Courtaul refers to visits of IWW transients to his mine in North Queensland: they would stay a short time, 'stir-up militancy' and then move on. Thanks to military intelligence, we have a complementary picture of IWW activities. One exasperated censor noted that in Queensland it had become 'quite the regular thing' for an IWW 'to drop down in some community in which industrial peace reigns, and in a short while to set that community by the ears and precipitate industrial chaos'.[10] Wobblies could not help it. They were incorrigible militants, remorselessly ingenious, immensely irritating to bosses and union leaders alike.

Wobbly influence amongst rank-and-file militants frequently expressed itself in support (against the opposition of union officials) for classic IWW practices such as sabotage and the go-slow. For example, a general meeting of the Tramway Employees Association early in 1915 had seriously discussed the 'scientific strike' and a large number of rank-and-file members, in opposition to the union executive, viewed sabotage favourably. Turner maintains that IWW concepts, particularly the 'go-slow' and working-class solidarity, were winning a growing number of adherents among railway and tramway workers, especially in the workshops, the rank and file running ahead of their officials. An AWU pamphleteer regretted in 1918 that the 'strange school' of the IWW, with its message of sabotage and its plan of direct action, had been particularly active in North Queensland of late, especially within the ranks of the AWU and AMIEU.[11]

Instances of sabotage and slow down are less amenable to measurement than strike action, and Wobblies usually resorted to the former practices in the first instance, preferring 'to strike on the job, and use any and all tactics while there, to cause the greatest amount of loss and injury to the employer'.[12] Dick Surplus recalled the response of some fellow Wobblies engaged in fruit-picking in Victoria: when the farmers refused to improve the poor pay-rates, they placed notices on the trees offering advice to disgruntled pickers: 'Please do not drive copper nails into the fruit trees as it will destroy them.' The farmers conceded the extra pay. Fred Coombe's initiation into IWW circles occurred before the war when, as a 14-year-old hand at a shearing shed on the Darling River, he was prevailed upon by a Wobbly rouseabout to crawl under the door of the shed late at night and to remove a vital piece of the engine that operated the shearing machines, which the rouseabout promptly threw into the river, disrupting shearing for three days while a replacement part was procured in Mildura. In 1935 a member of the Graziers' Association of New South Wales recalled that between 1914 and 1917 there was a gang of IWW men operating along the Flinders River and adjacent north-western districts in Queensland who introduced the limitation of tallies to bring about the 44-hour week: 'Durkin, Bellamy, Victor Prince, Spencer Bardon, Mick Kelly and other I.W.W. men . . . kept up the sabotaging of the sheds . . .' He expressed relief that current-day workers, agitating for a 40-hour week in 1935, knew nothing of the history of this sabotage movement in support of shorter hours.[13]

Employers and managers were alarmed about these coded examples of Wobbly influence amongst workers. Meredith Atkinson received many concerned letters on the subject, a 'clear indication of the widespread interest displayed by the public in the pressing problem of sabotage' as advocated in the 'dreadful publication' called *Direct Action*. Allegations of sabotage were rife; invariably the IWW was to blame. For example, the untimely firing of canecrops was laid at the door of the IWW at this time, though it was a long-standing tactic of disgruntled canecutters.[14]

The go-slow was rather more readily adopted by militant unionists; its use, too, was invariably taken as evidence of IWW machinations, often with good reason. During 1916, for instance, the New South Wales railway workshops were afflicted with an IWW-induced bout of indolence. The assistant railway commissioner complained that the go-slow doctrines of the IWW 'imported pests, bred in other lands, where freedom as understood by Australians was unknown', had penetrated his workforce, that IWW propaganda stickers, messages of 'diseased minds', were being placed around railway workplaces: 'Fast workers die young; live a long life'; 'Don't be a pace-maker; someone has to be slowest; let it be you' and 'Don't be a boss's man by trying to do more work than other men.' The deputy chief commissioner alleged that over the past eighteen months production had dropped in the railway workshops: 'there are some sections undoubtedly where there is a tendency to reduce output'. Around the same time, Defence Minister Pearce personally investigated allegations that workers were 'going slow' in the Commonwealth Clothing Factory where army uniforms were manufactured. He reported that the machinists and cutters 'had adopted the I.W.W. tactics by slowing down and reducing output'. In November 1916 the president of the Employers' Federation bewailed the decreasing production rate throughout industry as evidence of IWW influence.[15]

Whether the IWW was responsible for all the alleged instances of the go-slow is uncertain, but it was certainly believed by employers and government that it was. Ironically, employers' fearmongering helped spread IWW ideas. Mat Hade observed that, when Barker was prosecuted, the go-slow policy was unheard of outside the IWW but from then on the capitalist press took the matter up and spread the doctrine unconsciously all over Australia. The *Bulletin* announced that 'THE GO-SLOW LUNACY' was caused by the boot of IWW 'sabotage' being sunk into the distressed bride, 'PRODUCTION'. According to an *Argus* report of 22 June 1917, a group of 'AGGRESSIVE NEWSBOYS' had informed employers that 'they had joined the I.W.W. and intended in future to do as little as possible'.[16] The right to be lazy was, after all, an intrinsically appealing philosophical position that only needed a bad press in order to catch on.

In general, the direct actionist convictions of the IWW, its commitment to permanent struggle at the point of production, attracted many of the most militant workers of this time, annoyed as they were with the slow progress made in securing reforms through parliament:

> The I.W.W. is organizing the working class for more aggressive action within the present society, so that with every advance gained, the workers will increase their appetite for more and more, until finally they will demand the full product of their labour, and will find a way to get it.[17]

It was through victories that the One Big Union would ultimately be built; industrial defeats, on the other hand, encouraged demoralisation. Where syndicalists viewed strikes as an end in themselves as a demonstration in proletarian self-activity, the IWW was concerned above all with the actual outcome of any industrial action. Wobblies aimed to show workers, through demonstrating the practical benefits of militancy on the job, that they could achieve even greater benefits through forming One Big Union.

Saposs has argued that the chief accomplishment of the American IWW was the provision of expert strike leadership to unorganised workers.[18] In Australia, the IWW was busy amongst organised workers; its chief accomplishment was in securing a greater degree of job control in many workplaces than would otherwise have occurred under the prevailing union leadership. Yet, as Peter Sheldon has argued, the IWW never showed any likelihood of making the transition from job control to mass mobilisation. And its success in boring from within was limited by existing structures. Navvies' Union militants saw their best prospects for spreading IWW ideas in supporting, rather than opposing, amalgamation with the AWU.[19] Moreover, in its tendency to define 'work' as that performed by male, manual workers, the IWW restricted the areas in which it could bore from within.

The IWW always had the problem of relating its rather abstract and necessarily centralising strategy, the formation of One Big Union, to its everyday audience engaged in concrete and decentralised struggles. IWW strength in practice was at job level and its successes, such as they were, the achievement of job control alone; in theory it aimed at an elaborate unity unimaginable, probably not of pressing interest, to workers in immediate conflict with their employers. In examining a few of the workplaces where it attempted, sometimes successfully and sometimes not, to encourage what it termed 'Industrial Control', it is apparent that its successes remained merely temporary victories for workers in specific struggles. These did not add up to mass mobilisation or even greatly augment the growth of the IWW as an organisation.

IWW involvement in the 1916 shearers' strike in Queensland and New South Wales aided the shearers' cause and earned the IWW the enduring wrath of the AWU. The award under which the shearers, shed hands and pressers were working had been handed down in October 1911. The AWU Convention of 1916 had resolved to apply to the arbitration court for a new award, but by March the men in Queensland, where the shearing started, were out, refusing to work under the old award, unprepared to await the court's deliberations, and determined not to return to work until increased rates were introduced. The strikers appealed to the AWU for funds to sustain the strike, which request was ignominiously refused. Accordingly, the strike committee, chaired by Fellow-Worker H.L. Fish, appealed to the IWW in Sydney for help: 'There is a big agitation for an I.W.W. organizer out here. The men are disgusted with the A.W.U.'[20] Tom Barker recalls:

> They didn't have any money, naturally enough, coming back to start the season; they were all dead broke. They camped on the banks of a river near a road bridge and got in touch with us in Sydney. We took collections on the following Sunday in the Sydney Domain and we sent dozens and dozens of pounds to them so these fellows could buy themselves flour and keep alive until the squatters came to time. They won, through us finding the money on the Sydney Domain to keep them on strike.[21]

Direct Action also appealed to all its country members and all Locals to send in donations for forwarding to the strikers.[22]

As the AWU organs, the *Australian Worker* and the Brisbane-based *Worker,* disowned or ignored the strike, it was *Direct Action* that provided the medium by which the strikers' view of events was circulated to other shearers, warning them not to seek work in Queensland shearing sheds and keeping them informed of the AWU's attempts to subvert the strike action, for which it received many letters of thanks from strikers. AWU officials had toured the various sheds denouncing both the IWW and the strike and attempting, unsuccessfully, to get the men to vote in secret ballots for a return to work. Eventually, the pastoralists submitted to the demands of the men, who had stood firm, thanks to what *Direct Action* called the leavening influence of IWW rebels amongst slaves in the north: one shed after another started up at the higher rates.[23]

The strike spread to New South Wales as the shearing season there commenced. Many Wobblies were on the strike committees set up in centres such as Moree, Bourke and Walgett. In response to the plea for an IWW organiser, J.B. King was despatched to Moree where, with the assistance of some local IWW men, he 'piloted the shearers to victory', in the words of Bill Beattie. Again, the IWW raised money for the strikers through appeals to its Locals and through collections in the Domain, and this help was gratefully acknowledged in letters to *Direct Action* from the strikers. Again, too, *Direct Action* was the paper in which the strikers kept each other and other working-class militants informed of the progress of the strike and of the attempts of the AWU to curb it. The strikers' treasurer installed himself at the Sussex Street Hall, where the Sydney strike committee also held its meetings. And the Sydney Local printed thousands of stickers for the strikers: 'Don't scab on the Shearers – Let the Blowflies win the Strike' and 'Give the warm weather and the blowflies a chance.' The secretary of the Pastoralists' Union expressed his confidence to the *Daily Telegraph* that the AWU would not support 'such outrageous and despicable instructions'. The *Argus* congratulated the AWU for working on 'pacific lines', unlike the IWW agents who preached 'the gospel of industrial disruption'.[24]

The pastoralists, fearful of losing the entire season's clip, began to agree to the men's demands, and conceded an extra 1/6d. per hundred so shearing could proceed. By September most of the sheds were shearing at the new rates.[25] F.B.S. Falkiner of the Pastoralists' Union complained to the House of Representatives that the IWW had tied up shearing operations to such an extent in 1916 that the sheep were dying in thousands from fly-blow, and that pastoralists had been obliged, reluctantly, to allow IWWs to shear their sheep.[26] Michael Karabogias's research on the IWW's role concludes: 'Their organisational ability, uniting tactics, slogans and money gave the strikers strength and a sense of direction; *Direct Action* kept the issues alive and the working class informed; Wobbly rebels offered support and confidence. These factors were instrumental in the eventual victory . . .' The manager of the Australian Mercantile Land & Finance Co. wrote to the managing director in London on 19 February 1917 that 'the I.W.W. type appears now to be dominating the Union . . . The shearing troubles towards the end of last year, when demands were made regardless of the Court's Award, were due to the revolutionary element I refer to.'[28]

The agreement that had ended the 1909 Broken Hill lockout expired on 30 June 1915. The AMA informed the companies it wanted to negotiate a new award with an increase in wages and a cut in working hours. In a cunning move, which divided the workers' ranks, the companies offered an extra shilling per shift but no reduction in working hours: this was acceptable to the Port Pirie smelter workers and the surface men at Broken Hill, but the underground miners at Broken Hill, a number of IWW members among them, were determined upon a reduction of hours from 48 to 44 hours. Accordingly, they walked off the job in the middle of every Saturday. The AMA told them to go back to work but the underground men held a meeting on 3 October 1916 at which, under the influence of Wobblies, they 'told the A.M.A. to go to Hell, thanked the executive for their advice to go scabbing, and elected a president and secretary to carry on the fight'.[29]

The arbitration court offered to hear the men's claim, but only if they returned to work on Saturday afternoons. The AMA officials accepted the offer on behalf of the men; but the miners continued to treat Saturday afternoon as a holiday. On 10 January 1916 the companies sacked the men who had not worked the previous Saturday; in sympathy, the other miners refused to work. The strike was on. The miners were solid, but the Pirie smelter workers did not support the strike, nor did the FEDFA on the Barrier, which resented the involvement in the strike of the IWW. The FEDFA general secretary confessed to the *Australian Worker* of 27 January that the FEDFA regarded the IWW as a threat. Other trade unions supported the strike, but formally rather than enthusiastically. The only organisation fully behind the strikers was the IWW, which expended considerable effort in raising money. At one large Domain meeting, Barker, King and Grant spoke about the strike and the importance of supporting it, and a collection was taken. The meeting was held under a huge banner: 'CLASS WAR. BROKEN HILL WORKERS STRIKING FOR 44 HOUR WEEK. WHAT ARE YOU DOING ABOUT IT?' Throughout the dispute the miners wore buttons with the direct action slogan: 'If You Want a 44-Hour Week, Take It!' The Wobblies had long been calling for a shorter working day and pointing out that it could not be obtained through arbitration or reliance on union officials. When circumstances bore out their analysis, the recourse to Wobbly ideas and slogans, which had been circulating on the Barrier for several years, was natural. During the dispute, a miner claimed that the action was the outcome of IWW propaganda.[30]

As in many of the disputes in which the IWW was prominent, the obstructionism of moderate labour leaders turned the strike into a question of the IWW versus the Labor Party, union officials and arbitration. When the Sydney Labor Council twice refused to endorse the dispute, the IWW organised demonstrations from the public gallery of the Council. And, as often happened, IWW militancy and the solidarity it promoted so assiduously stood the strikers in good stead. By February the arbitration court, seeing that the men were still united and determined to win, granted the men a 44-hour week as well as a guaranteed minimum wage for contract miners. Admittedly, economic circumstances were favourable, as metals were needed for munitions and overseas markets were improving; but such circumstances also encouraged employers to insist on the longer working week. It was undoubtedly the determination of the men, under Wobbly influence, to bypass arbitration, to take what they wanted by direct action, that ensured they got what they wanted – from arbitration. The Port Pirie men, who had refused to strike, were not awarded the 44-hour week.[31]

The coalminers' strike later in 1916 also revealed the extent to which IWW ideas were accepted by workers. For many years the coalminers had been demanding a working day of eight hours 'bank to bank' rather than eight hours at the coal face. The militants in the lodges, influenced by IWW propaganda, wanted direct action to secure their demand; their officials wanted the matter to go to arbitration. Under increasing pressure from the rank and file, the central council of the Miners' Federation decided that if their claims were not met by 28 October, the day of the first conscription referendum, they would resort to direct action. On 1 November 1916 New South Wales miners went on strike, followed shortly by miners in Queensland, Victoria and Tasmania; 11 500 men were involved in a strike which lasted two months.[32]

Tom Barker hailed the strike itself and its rationale:

> After many years of celebrating annually the Eight Hours, the coal miners . . . have gone out on strike to gain it. New conditions and propaganda have begotten a solidarity that possesses great potentialities for the future. . . . The miners . . . have come to the conclusion that militant and aggressive tactics alone will get results . . . This fight shows the growth of the idea of 'Industrial Control,' the new philosophy of the new labor movement.

He hoped that it would be the 'precursor of a six-hour movement'.[33] As factories were forced to close, as ships lay idle and transport services became restricted, Sydney newspapers intimated that the trouble, which would soon see Sydney in darkness, was caused by the IWW, German spies and lawlessness. The *Sydney Morning Herald* of 7 November claimed that 'the story of slowing down and actual destruction of property, as a result of I.W.W. propaganda has been full of a sinister significance'. Labor Attorney-General, D.R. Hall, declared there was no hope of industrial peace 'until the spirit of syndicalism is overthrown in this State', until the socialists within the labour movement, with their respect for law, triumphed over the syndicalists.[34] Private individuals clearly believed the press. Amongst the letters written to men at the front was one that reported 'bad times' in New South Wales: 'we'll soon be in the dark and have nothing to cook [for] our dinner with coal strikers – and I.W.W.s and non-conscriptionists trying to turn the world upside down'. An anonymous Wobbly boasted to American fellow workers: 'Thousands of tons of shipping idle, no lift to carry the Fat man to his flat, no power, curtailed time-tables on the Labor government's trams and trains. Not a mine working . . . The Press is howling, the bosses are squealing, and arbitration court horse-haired fossils are in a hell of a state.'[35]

The miners had struck at an advantageous moment as coal stocks were vital for the war effort and the federal government was weakened politically by the defeat of the conscription referendum. Prime Minister

Hughes called a compulsory conference at which he secured an agreement from the Federation leaders to recommend a return to work, to await the deliberations of a special tribunal. However, the men boycotted the return-to-work ballot. Despite this, or because of it, Hughes called on the tribunal to resolve the dispute anyway; within three days a pay increase as well as the reduction in hours were conceded and the mines reopened. *Direct Action* claimed that the success of the strike in tying up the mining industry throughout the continent had been made possible because 'an appreciable advance has been made in the psychological "make-up" of the coal workers'. It was a victory for industrial strength, for 'intelligent Direct Action', over the '"go-slow" methods of the Arbitration Court'. Hughes had almost certainly instructed the tribunal under Justice Edmunds to grant the men's claims; Higgins, initially asked to hear the case, admitted later that Hughes had demanded this action of him.[36] It had been a Wobbly strike, both in the opportune timing of the dispute and in its conduct, and the success of this strike was encouraging to militants in other unions.

Working-class militancy in the Cloncurry district copper mines of northwest Queensland, employing 5000 men, received a fillip with the visit of IWW propagandists – Brown, Jackson and Shannessey from the south and Denny Foley from Cairns – between June and August 1917. Impressed by the enthusiastic response to their meetings and the number of rebels already on the job, Jackson was confident of the IWW's future in the area. The Russians who flocked to the Cloncurry mines at this time, many of them émigrés from the 1905 revolution, were among the most prominent IWW supporters in North Queensland; the general manager of the Mt Elliott mines and smelters noted that the IWW 'made every use of the Russians to advance their cause'. Circumstances favoured IWW-style militancy amongst these itinerant workers: like the meatworkers of north Queensland, the miners were a large and isolated workforce subjected to onerous labour in desolate living conditions; and, like the meat industry, the mining industry was enjoying boom conditions in these war years, encouraging employees to seek a better deal, especially as inflation was eroding the real value of their wages.[37]

A right-wing pamphleteer complained towards the end of the war that at the outbreak of the war the Cloncurry copper-field miners had given handsomely to the patriotic funds, 'but when the I.W.W. germ infected the veins of the industrial body, they desisted – and to-day not a penny can be got from them'.[38] Doug Hunt's research shows that many miners sympathised with the 'crude ideology' and anti-capitalist slogans of the IWW; and even those who did not appreciated the entertainment provided by the Wobbly stump orators and sing-songs in this area where social diversions were few. However, Hunt believes that in this situation the IWW organisers often misconstrued their bumper meetings as an indication of support for their philosophy. Jackson, he suggests, attached too much significance to the fact that the camp at Selwyn resounded with the strains of IWW songs, that all the musical instruments in the boarding houses and pubs were going day and night, hammering away at Wobbly refrains.[39]

In this district, as elsewhere, the lines of conflict did not run neatly between employer and employees, but also between the AWU officials and their own rank and file, influenced at least in part by the IWW and manifested in the go-slow strikes and lightning stoppages that were frequent on the Cloncurry mineral fields by August 1917. The unsatisfactory working of the arbitration system and the ease with which the mining companies evaded clauses of the award strengthened the appeal of the IWW. An AWU representative complained to the *Worker* on 16 August 1917:

> We get an award, and there is no-one to see that the award is carried out. If it is not carried out the men have to use direct action to get what they are legally entitled to, and that is what is giving the IWW such a strong hold in this and other districts.[40]

As in the pastoral industry, the AWU officials endeavoured to quell IWW influence in the mining industry.

A Wobbly at the Mt Cuthbert mine wrote to Jackson early in 1918 that some militants had been sacked; when the workers had resolved to go on strike, 'the usual bonehead AWU slave demanded a secret ballot'. But, he added, 'we won hands down'. After the meeting, over 100 assembled in front of the hall and sang IWW songs till after midnight; there were concerts and dances every day and 'real good meetings'; every night the choir of about eighty led the songs and amused the crowd. The censor agreed with this assessment: 'The condition of industrial affairs is deplorable. I.W.W. have control of the district.' After the IWW, with 110 supporters, had allegedly taken charge of union meetings at Mt Cuthbert, the AWU district secretary visited the area, declared two IWW ring-leaders 'non-union' and, with the connivance of the manager, ensured they were denied work. The IWW members and supporters, and Russians, left work in sympathy, leaving the orthodox AWU in control at Mt Cuthbert. Dick Surplus explained that, strong though the IWW was generally in north Queensland, it could not take over that part of the State because of 'the hold of the AWU'.[41]

This resumption of AWU authority did not, however, stem the tide of industrial militancy on the mineral fields. Until the end of the war, economic conditions meant that the workers were in a strong bargaining position. However, the end of the war led to a fall in demand for metal and a sudden drop in prices. Thousands were thrown out of work as the mines closed. By the end of 1920 mining on a large scale was virtually finished in the Cloncurry area, until revived by a subsequent world war. Many people blamed the IWW for the demise of the mineral field. Notwithstanding the obvious cause of the depressed copper market, there exists an intelligence report for May 1919 on 'The closing of the Cloncurry Copper Fields due to the tactics employed by the I.W.W. Section.'[42]

The IWW did not fare well in its industrial agitation in Western Australia in the war years. Naomi Segal contends that the union movement in Western Australia comfortably contained the IWW's influence: 'although the I.W.W. had scored temporary successes, and though it was considerably stronger in membership than police and military records indicate, in the final analysis, it clearly failed in Western Australia, and did so earlier and more readily than in Eastern Australia'.[43]

Employment was precarious in the West during the war years. Apart from the effects of war, drought and recession, the goldfields had been in decline for some time. Wholesale layoffs were occurring on these fields, and known Wobblies were often the first to be sacked. In a one-industry town, in an isolated area, fear of dismissal was felt seriously. The Boulder Local's secretary, Fred Lunn, complained late in 1915 that fellow workers there were fired with such rapidity there were hardly any left, 'and those that are, run when they see me, for fear I would speak to them and a crawler may see our recognition and then they would be fired also'. The Westralian IWW was powerless to protect its members from victimisation; the most it could do was to act as a clearing house for information that would help find them employment elsewhere, saving them much futile tramping.[44]

This IWW network directed Wobblies to the job opportunities and better working conditions of the small Corinthian Mine in the Yilgarn goldfields. By October 1915 Wobblies constituted 40 per cent of the workforce on this site, many of them Italians encouraged to go there by Alex Boggio, an Italian IWW organiser with experience in the United States. Corinthian meetings were spirited and well attended; the Italians, according to Pat Daly, were 'as good rebels as any seen at Broken Hill'. IWW strength at the Corinthian Mine was sufficient to force other unions into co-operation to maintain a closed shop of sorts, and to support financially a new member injured shortly after abandoning his union for the IWW. In an open display of strength one evening, the IWW seized the Workers' Club, which it considered the craft union was not running in the workers' interest, ejected the manager and proceeded to pour the beer for the 'thirsty and admiring crowd'.[45]

Far less impressive was the IWW's role, or lack of role, in the Boulder woodcutters' struggle for a new agreement. The firewood companies refused cutters an increase of threepence per ton and, for the men loading the trucks, a halfpenny per ton. The woodcutters went on strike in the first week of January 1916; by the middle of the month the mines had shut down and over 5000 men were out of work. The Boulder fields were short of IWW soapboxers in this dispute, for the Corinthian rebels had either drifted back to Broken Hill or preferred to stay quiet in their camp at Corinthian, because, as Daly wrote to Lunn, 'we know there are very few of its kind left for us, the militant wanderers'. Lunn wired Reeve in Fremantle, who ignored the appeal, having advised earlier that a fight on the goldfields was out of place until the boys were organised enough to win it. Sawtell in Bruce Rock expressed his reluctance to go on a 'wild goose chase' to Boulder and advised Lunn that the IWW should be careful not to associate the IWW too closely with the strike, which was likely to be unsuccessful.[46]

In fact, the woodcutters won the strike, to the discomfort of the Wobblies. Segal notes that: 'Disappointment and embarrassment about I.W.W. inaction ran deep in I.W.W. ranks.' Lunn resigned as secretary of the Boulder Local in March 1916 and the Local ceased its activities in May due to lack of support. Its members had resolved on a policy of 'boring from within' exclusively, and had subsequently rejoined the Miners' Union. Sawtell, now in the Fremantle Local, disapproved of the Boulder Local's dissolution; he likened 'boring from within' to joining the Catholic Church in order to make rationalists of its members.[47]

The Wobblies had long warned workers of the dangers of the craze for efficiency on the part of employers: 'Hand in hand with the increase in the intensity of labor goes unemployment, with the starvation and misery which follows in its train.' Tom Glynn's *Industrial Efficiency and its Antidote* was written in 1915 in response to the developing vogue for 'scientific management', for 'every wail for industrial efficiency on the part of the master class and their satellites is at bottom but a cry for more profits, and should sound a note of warning to the workers if an increased proportion of their numbers is not to be dumped on the human scrap-heap'. He reminded workers that deterioration in material conditions must as surely follow apathy as improvement follow intelligent agitation and action. 'Scientific Management' must be met by 'Scientific Sabotage'. The antidote to the 'Industrial Efficiency' cry was 'an immediate agitation for a shorter work-day, combined with the intelligent adoption of . . . sabotage on the job'.[48]

As early as December 1914 *Direct Action* reported of its propaganda meetings at the Randwick workshops of the New South Wales Railways and Tramways Department that they were 'well attended, and the exposition of Fellow-worker King on labor-saving machinery and its effects are listened to with the keenest attention and interest'. Over the next few years, King held regular meal-break meetings at these workshops, attended by a couple of hundred employees, resulting in 'scores of subscriptions' to *Direct Action* and 'many new members'.[49] When a strike broke out in these workshops in March 1916 the rail authorities and the press were quick to blame the IWW for the rank-and-file unrest.[50] This was not difficult, considering that IWW posters had appeared in these workshops for some time. In the wake of this strike, Bill Teen, a Randwick branch delegate to the Council of the ARTSA and later one of the Twelve, was dismissed from the railways; according to ARTSA Minutes of 31 March and 17 July 1916, he had nonetheless managed to persuade the ARTSA to investigate the possibility of using sabotage. After the police raided IWW headquarters in September 1916 and obtained membership lists, a number of other IWW men were sacked from the service. The Assistant Railway Commissioner regretted that there were employees 'who seriously and deliberately debated how they could best bring about a condition of chaos under the name of a scientific strike, which was really sabotage, thinly disguised'. Late in 1916 and early in 1917, the heads of both the New South Wales and Victorian railway departments warned of the spread of the 'go-slow disease' among their employees.[51]

On 2 August 1917, 5780 repair and maintenance men in the Randwick workshops left work in protest against the introduction of an information system which was intended to record on cards the exact time taken by each workman over each particular job. They felt this 'card system' was calculated to enforce 'speeding up', and without any extra reward. An IWW leaflet, 'What is the Card System', which outlined the history of the Taylor System in the United States, described it as 'a systematic form of intensified slavery . . . an expert system of wringing the last ounce of energy out of the human frame. It will mean unemployed on the one hand and overworked and physically exhausted beings on the other.'[52] The strike spread quickly to other employees in the tram and railway service, then into private industries, particularly in fuel, food and transport companies. About 97 507 workers went on strike throughout Australia during the eighty-two days of the strike, until 22 October. The number of working days lost was roughly 2 570 000; wage losses were about £1 780 000. The strike was concentrated in New South Wales – in Sydney, Newcastle, Broken Hill, Wollongong, Lithgow, Bathurst and Goulburn. Of those who went on strike, 76 000 were in New South Wales, representing one-third of union members.[53]

Childe writes that the IWW 'partly inspired' both the great coal strike of 1916 and the general strike of 1917.[54] To the extent that IWW ideology had penetrated significant sections of the workforce, including that involved in the initial walk-out, this is true, but it was not a Wobbly strike. Apart from the fact that by this stage, as we shall see, the Wobblies were suffering severe state repression and had too little energy left for masterminding an intrigue such as a general strike, the conduct of the strike shows no stamp of IWW influence. The circumstances of the 1917 strike were precisely those in which the Wobblies would counsel, at least in the first instance, a passive strike rather than an active one: staying on the job but slowing down concertedly and collectively, while systematically but furtively destroying the employers' machinery until the card system was revoked. Instead, the workers had walked out in a grand gesture of defiance to face defeat and victimisation. The strike resembled more closely an eruption of syndicalist spontaneism than the 'scientific' and carefully constructed battle plan recommended by the IWW. Of course, once out, the IWW supported the strike as a matter of principle and applauded the fact that the strike action was done 'by the workers themselves, in **opposition** to the union officials . . . and without the sanction of the strike committee'. It regretted that 'high salaried officials' were in charge of the strike; these officials, it noted, 'seem to be hanging back, and the strike committee seem to be afraid to move'.[55]

Though the nature and timing of the dispute was not a result of IWW intrigue, it suited the government and employers, during this period of suppression of the IWW, to maintain otherwise. They were out for Wobbly blood. Acting-Premier Fuller declared that the objection to the card system was 'but a flimsy pretext' and that the strike was caused by 'the influence of the I.W.W. and the Direct Action party . . . and this influence must and will be broken'. Dan Coward confirms that the confrontation represented an opportunity to cure industrial inefficiency among workmen who, it was generally believed, had been corrupted by IWW ideology.[56] The government issued a statement on 11 August:

> The Enemies of Britain and her Allies have succeeded in plunging Australia into a General Strike . . . AT THE BACK OF THIS STRIKE LURK THE I.W.W. AND THE EXPONENTS OF DIRECT ACTION . . . Every striker is singing from day to day the hymns of the I.W.W. and marching to their music . . .[57]

During September, Fuller issued a government circular, reprinted in the loyalist press, which, in Fuller's words, set forth the 'obvious association of the strikers and the IWW'. He assured Holman overseas on 13 September that 'We are taking strong steps with the I.W.W.'.[58]

So virulent were the attacks on the strikers for their supposed IWW credentials that many involved in the strike were anxious to dissassociate themselves openly, to distance themselves publicly, from IWW influence. Lucy Taksa records that, during the strikers' protest marches, some workers carried banners declaring: 'Not one of the I.W.W. is on this Committee.' On another occasion, marchers refused someone carrying an IWW banner permission to join the procession. At the same time, IWW slogans did appear occasionally in the processions, as did some of their songs, particularly 'Casey Jones' and 'Solidarity Forever'.[59]

Clearly, there was an IWW influence of some sort amongst a minority of workers involved in this strike, for the strike was a protest against the scientific management that the IWW had opposed more vociferously than any other organisation. But, as Tony Birch argues, that workers chose to strike against the indignity of scientific management rather than deploy IWW methods against it proved to be an unwise tactic, for the government and employers used everything in their power to smash the strike. Far more difficult to deal with, from the employer viewpoint, would have been scientific sabotage.[60]

Relatively easy to effect, on the other hand, was the utter humiliation of the strikers and their subsequent victimisation. This was achieved with the help of the strikers' supposed leaders in the strike defence committee, which included representativess of the unions involved. This committee accepted the government's terms for the workers' surrender on 10 September: a return to work in exchange for the promise of a Royal Commission into the speed-up system. Though denounced by the workers at stormy mass meetings, the official surrender broke the ranks of the strikers, who began returning to work, often to find their re-employment was conditional upon accepting reduced pay and status. At the BHP Newcastle steelworks, returning strikers were forced to sign forms giving personal details of age, height, colouring, marks, marital status, number of dependants – an identification system designed to discriminate against the IWW. Shipowners instituted a new system of hiring waterside workers, who were now required to have no association with the IWW.[61]

The failure of the strike was being used not only to humiliate the strikers generally but to drive out all remaining vestiges of Wobbly influence. The IWW was being victimised for a strike it did not engineer but whose collapse also disgusted it. H.L. Denford expressed his anger and bitterness at the defence committee's acceptance of the government's terms:

> If one took an English Dictionary, cut out each word separately, placed them in a basket and then asked a passer by to draw out about 500 and place them in rows of six you would have something just as understandable and to the point as the agreement between the Defence Committee and Government.

There was fury at this union meeting which, at Denford's instigation, rejected the committee's action 4000 to 10 votes. The failure of the strike was not the failure of the philosophy of the IWW, as Communist writer Edgar Ross would have it.[62] More accurately, the collapse showed the difficulty that unions, tuned to arbitration, have in adapting their methods and outlooks to strikes. E.J. Kavanagh, who was involved in the strike until his arrest, argued that the outcome of the strike proved 'the failure of direct action of unions organised on arbitration lines'.[63]

IWW influence was substantial among the North Queensland meatworkers, organised in the AMIEU, who by 1916 had decided to abandon arbitration in favour of direct negotiation. Doug Hunt concedes that the anarcho-syndicalist tendency of many of these itinerant meatworkers, long evident in their scorn for work discipline, arbitration, and union head office authority, was reinforced by IWW propaganda around this time. Terrence Cutler insists that by 1916 the IWW was gaining a 'strong foothold' in the Queensland meatworks; in Townsville there were a 'considerable number' of active members amongst the meatworkers, and it is clear that 'the rest responded sympathetically to the emotional gospel of industrial liberation'.[64]

William Jackson made the first of a number of visits to Townsville in May 1915, where he found many meatworkers attracted to IWW ideas about working-class emancipation through direct action. He and other Wobbly organisers such as Edward Shannessey and Gordon Brown reported that meatworkers provided much of their strength and support in the North. A considerable number of AMIEU members bought *Direct Action* and other Wobbly publications. Bill Davis, an Alligator Creek meatworker, stated in the July 1943 issue of the *Meat Industry Journal of Queensland* that in 1916 'Revolutionary Industrial Unionism' became the keynote of the northern AMIEU militants. The IWW claimed credit for the strike at the Alligator Creek meatworks in June 1916.[65]

The northern meatworks continued to be disturbed by industrial disputes, to the distress of both the companies and the Queensland Labor government. When the Alligator Creek workers boycotted John Gilday, State president of the AMIEU and MLA for Ithaca, resolving to 'have nothing to do with politicians and to rely on "Direct Action"', Jackson reported on 18 August 1917 that the 1000 workers at Alligator Creek were 'scientific in the application of the conscious withdrawal of industrial efficiency' and over 900 of these men were 'with the I.W.W.'.[66] Certainly, IWW-style militancy had forced employers to make significant and speedy concessions. By 1918, however, there was a decline in the supply of stock available for slaughtering, and the meat companies seized this opportune moment to file a claim for an arbitration award that would give them greater control over their labour force. The scene was set for the confrontation of 1919.[67]

The underlying issue in the meatworkers' strike in the middle of 1919 was the attempt by the companies to curb the northern AMIEU's control over the selection of meatworks labour. This system, they complained to the Industrial Court, forced them to accept 'malcontents, professional loafers, revolutionaries, disloyalists, irreconcilables and I.W.W. sympathisers'. However, the meatworkers' award of 12 March 1918 ignored the employers' request that union preference be abolished and raised wage rates by 5 per cent. Though this award appeared to favour the employees it represented a tactical victory for the employers, for it manoeuvred the union back into the arbitration system it had flouted for several years. The award was made conditional upon 'responsible' behaviour by the workers and the elimination of sectional militancy. The northern meatworkers, who felt confident they could gain even more from direct negotiation, rejected it on 27 March. Hunt states that, to many northern meatworkers, arbitration was merely an instrument of working-class oppression fostered by a compromised Labor Party; they preferred the IWW credo of aggressive direct action and industrial unionism.[68]

From May to September 1918 the Townsville meatworks were continually held up by 'go-slow' and 'lightning' strikes, as employees pursued better conditions, higher wages and shorter hours. At Alligator Creek the output of 500 cattle per day was brought down to 50 cattle. One spook noted at a meeting at Alligator Creek that employees addressed each other as 'Wobbelies'. Red Cross women collecting money at Alligator Creek were rebuffed with the suggestion that, if they gave 10 shillings for the IWW prisoners' relief fund, the workers would give 5 shillings to the Red Cross.[69] Wobbly activists wrote glowing reports to fellow workers down south about the successful application of IWW tactics, and how the IWW was 'a nightmare to the company'. Military intelligence monitored the progresss of these activists. Edward Shannessey, for instance, was 'a notorious I.W.W. agitator in the Townsville district', who 'worked persistently amongst his fellow employees', collecting subscriptions and distributing IWW literature. By August 1918 the meatworks were deemed 'a hotbed of I.W.W.ism'.[70]

In September the companies were forced to grant a general wage increase of 7 per cent. The perishable nature of the product and the imperative of meeting overseas contracts made the meat export industry vulnerable to direct action by a strong, belligerent union. In November strikes broke out again at Alligator Creek and Ross River. The superintendent at Alligator Creek wrote to the company in Brisbane: 'We feel sure that not only the Meat Companies but every business and industry in the North and also the State Government must unite to fight and ultimately eliminate the I.W.W. Doctrine from Queensland.' The companies became determined to see the deletion of the union preference clause of the meat industry award granted early in 1919 by Justice McCawley, who argued that employers should not be compelled to give preference to men 'whose intention was to promote industrial turmoil and who disregarded the law'.[71]

Following the court's decision, the meatworkers went on strike and declared the northern meatworks black. While many unionists honoured the ban, many others, conforming to the arbitration court's decision, did not. These internal divisions not only weakened the strike movement, but caused deep and bitter repercussions in the northern labour movement. The strike was called off on 19 March 1919. With non-union labour firmly entrenched at Ross River and Alligator Creek, many known militants were refused re-employment. The left of the labour movement, now organised in the WIIU or the WIUA, resolved on ridding the meatworks of scabs and regaining union preference. As the companies refused the demand, another strike commenced at both plants on 23 June 1919, leading to militant protest marches and the infamous events of 'Bloody Sunday', 29 June, in which police and unionists exchanged gunfire in the streets of Townsville. The day before, 300 militant rank-and-file unionists had raided the railway cattle yards at Stuart, torn down the gates and released 500 head of cattle owned by the Queensland Meat Export Company.[72]

The government sent police reinforcements to Townsville, which greatly increased militant workers' hostility towards the Labor Party. Still rejecting arbitration, the northern district council of the AMIEU sought a private conference with the meat companies to settle the strike, but the local company managers refused. McCawley called a compulsory conference, but both sides were intransigent, the union refusing to give an undertaking there would be no more strikes if preference was restored. By the middle of August many union members had drifted back to work. The strike was officially declared off on 7 September 1919.[73]

Rank-and-file militants opposed the decision to call off the strike, declaring that 'the officials had scabbed on their fellow unionists'. Militants had all along questioned the outlook of the strike committee; many on this committee were strong opponents of IWW militancy, which, Cutler argues, was seen as a threat to the established hierarchy in the labour movement. The northern AMIEU had lost both its union preference and an envied measure of job control. The labour movement itself was riven, not simply between the Labor government and the unions but within the unions. Henceforward, the division between unionists who maintained a strong commitment to direct action and those who accepted arbitration became more clear-cut.[74]

In an article on 'How the Boss Fights', Norman Rancie claimed in January 1917 that, ever since the advent of the IWW in Australia, 'craft union officials, politicians, and the master-class in general, have never ceased to hurl maledictions at the head of that fighting organisation'. The 'furious hate and spiteful anger which the master-class have given vent to of late only goes to prove their impotency in trying to stop the industrial propaganda and silence the voice of the labor agitator'.[75] Rancie's bravado was ill-timed; the executive committee of this master-class was preparing, in the conducive war-induced climate of popular hysteria and increased state power, its fatal assault on these agitators.

CHAPTER 12

'Let Those Who Own Australia do the Fighting': Opposing the War

In Europe, the outbreak of the First World War on 4 August 1914 halted abruptly the growth of internationalist socialist consciousness, which had been a marked feature of working-class development in the preceding decades. The wave of syndicalist revolt that had battered liberal England in the immediate pre-war years receded as surely as did the storm of suffragettes. In Australia, on the other hand, the war prompted a stark polarisation of attitudes within the labour movement. Though imperial patriots among the workers were undoubtedly many, sceptics and opponents also abounded: apart from the pacifists and anti-militarists, the Irish Catholics within the movement were ever wary of British imperialism and to others the war seemed simply too remote to concern Australian workers. This opposition mounted as the horror of warfare manifested itself, as the material situation of the workers deteriorated with rising unemployment and the freezing of wages at their pre-war level, and as the Labor government placed social reform well below the war effort in its list of priorities.[1] Already divided over the issue of the war and Australia's involvement in it, the labour movement ultimately tore itself apart over the question of conscription. The role of the IWW in encouraging this fragmentation of the labour movement, its regroupment into left/anti-conscription and right/pro-conscription forces, was crucial.

No organisation in Australia at the time opposed the outbreak of the Great War as promptly and determinedly as did the IWW; its internationalist, anti-militarist and anti-imperialist precepts enabled it to respond quickly. The front page of *Direct Action* for 10 August 1914 declared:

WAR! WHAT FOR? FOR THE WORKERS AND THEIR DEPENDENTS: DEATH, STARVATION, POVERTY AND UNTOLD MISERY. FOR THE

CAPITALIST CLASS: GOLD, STAINED WITH THE BLOOD OF MIL-
LIONS, RIOTOUS LUXURY, BANQUETS OF JUBILATION OVER THE
GRAVES OF THEIR DUPES AND SLAVES. WAR IS HELL! SEND THE CAP-
ITALISTS TO HELL AND WARS ARE IMPOSSIBLE.

In the editorial, Tom Glynn deplored the way in which: 'Hangers-on of
the system, the whole host of rulers and statesmen, pillars of church and

The IWW immediately condemned the war and urged workers not to enlist.
(*Direct Action*, 10 August 1914)

state, politicians of every hue, are all endeavouring to infest the workers with the microbe of patriotism, in the name of which half the crimes of history have been committed.' Glynn noted how differences of language and geographical boundaries, 'which separate the workers in imagination, but not in the reality of their common interests', were being used as pretexts by 'this blood-thirsty tribe' to shatter the bonds of the ever increasing international fraternity and solidarity of the working class, 'that their own interests may remain free from proletarian aggression for some further period'.

On 7 August, the Saturday night following the outbreak of war, the IWW speakers in Bathurst Street were heckled by 'patriotic interrupters', and much argument ensued. The following day, the IWW organised an anti-war demonstration in the Domain at which its most eloquent orators denounced the war in forcible terms under an IWW banner bearing the 'WAR! WHAT FOR?' motto. A week later, the Sunday Domain meeting drew an exceptional crowd, 'ringing cheers' were given against the war and 800 copies of *Direct Action* were sold. Detective Nicholas Moore visited IWW headquarters and asked J.B. King for an undertaking that the Wobblies would stop criticising the war; no such promise could be extracted.[2]

On 22 August, Tom Barker urged: 'LET THOSE WHO OWN AUS-TRALIA DO THE FIGHTING. Put the wealthiest in the front ranks; the middle class next; follow these with politicians, lawyers, sky pilots and judges. Answer the declaration of war with the call for a GENERAL STRIKE.' He cautioned the workers not to be fooled by jingoism: 'The workers have no quarrel with Austria, Germany or Japan. The workers in those countries are as ruthlessly robbed and exploited as the workers of Australia.' In the same issue, 'Pessim' noted that the capitalists had taken great care to instil into workers the spirit of patriotism, so that when occasion arose 'it may overshadow our minds, clothe our reason, and brutalise our actions'.[3]

The IWW had long been contemptuous of British imperialism: the Empire was an aggregation of countries from which the original possessors of the soil had been either driven off, exterminated by war, decimated by famine and disease, or enslaved for purposes of exploitation, as in Australia with its 'dying aboriginal race'. It stressed that to wage slaves there was no advantage in an Empire 'upon which the sun never sets and the sun of Freedom never rises'.[4] In response to Labor Prime Minister Fisher's promise to fight for this Empire to the last man and the last shilling, *Direct Action* of 1 October 1914 implored:

Workers, you have nothing to gain by volunteering to fight the battles of your masters. Dismiss from your minds, all geographical boundaries; tear down once and for all those rags of flags that have long helped to keep the workers of the world divided . . . Make class before country your motto . . . you have interests in common with workers of all nations. Organise to fight the war promoters!

Workers of the World! Unite! You have no country to defend. You have a common enemy to fight! . . . you have nothing to lose and a world to gain so join the One Big Union.[5]

The Australian Administration was more loyal to the internationalist principles of the IWW than was the American organisation. Although opposed to the war, many in the American IWW thought that because this view was not shared by the overwhelming number of wage workers, their policy towards the war must be tempered. Moreover, after the USA joined the Allies in April 1917, they feared that anti-war activity would hasten the forcible suppression of the organisation. To other American Wobblies the war was a gigantic capitalist plot which had to be opposed. This conflict was never resolved: no policy decision was ever taken, though anti-war pamphlets were withdrawn. During its suppression, Haywood denied the American IWW was officially opposed to the war and many individual defendants testified they had never advised opposition to the war. Dubofsky concludes: 'The IWW did nothing directly to interfere with the American war effort.'[6]

The Australian organisation, though aware of the danger of becoming an anti-war machine, sidetracked from its primary purpose of organising at the point of production, threw itself wholeheartedly into the anti-war movement. In so doing, it increased its opportunities to organise at the point of production, because its anti-war activity won it many supporters amongst workers inclined to be critical of the senseless slaughter. Carnage on such a massive scale gave credence to Wobbly arguments about the nature of the capitalist system. As time went on and as casualties mounted still higher, the most extreme allegations of the IWW seemed more plausible; here was imperialist capitalism at its ugliest, with a seemingly ruthless disregard for the lives of those it enrolled in its defence. As Fred Coombe recalls of this time, people were sickened by the war: 'the thoughts in people's minds they couldn't articulate, but the old Wobblies could'.[7]

During 1915 the IWW meetings in the Sydney Domain attracted larger and larger crowds, bigger collections and many new members; the circulation of *Direct Action* grew and covered a wide area of the country.[8] The IWW had a team of speakers – Donald Grant, Tom Barker, Tom Glynn, J.B. King, Charlie Reeve, Peter Larkin and Jock Wilson – who, according to Norman Jeffery, were 'unrivalled in their agitational vigour', as they alerted people to facts about the war obscured or repressed by the authorities. In the West, too, from the onset of war,

Monty Miller, Mick Sawtell and other Wobblies 'exhibited courage and steadfastness with their anti-militarist views and critical attitude to the War'. Ted Moyle claims that the IWW in Adelaide 'faced up to the hostility of the soldiers and the "patriots" practically on its own' as it 'gave to its audiences what it considered to be the plain unvarnished Truth of having been wage-slaves they were now to become cannon-fodder in the interests of the same master class'. In Queensland, IWW agitators regaled the crowds with anti-war propaganda; and when Prime Minister Hughes addressed a lunch-time meeting from the post office steps in Brisbane, Wobblies decided to 'count the bastard out' and, by the time they reached ten, the crowd had joined in so loudly Hughes could not continue to speak. By November 1916 Prime Minister Hughes was complaining that the IWW was 'largely responsible for the present attitude of organised labour, industrially and politically, towards the war'.[9]

Just as the IWW was established in the patriotic public mind as the source of disloyalist infection, so also was it confirmed in the radical working-class mind as the centre of anti-militarist resistance. The explicit and developed basis of IWW anti-patriotism, inherent in the principles and tactics of revolutionary industrial unionism, enabled it to use this favourable moment to grow in size and influence. Workers in their thousands were now interested in hearing the senseless slaughter denounced by those whose understanding of the phenomenon seemed so clear and systematic.

This opportunity was made all the greater by the collapse and disintegration of the Second International when most of its affiliated socialist parties supported their respective national war efforts. Parliamentary socialism was discredited by the inability of its major European protagonists to resist the siren entreaties of their governments to encourage working-class support for the war. *Direct Action* was scathing about the performance of the Second International: the potential solidarity of the European working classes and their ability to prevent the war by organising a general strike had been thwarted by the leaders of the major socialist parties. The politicians had betrayed the class they claimed to represent by acting as bell-wethers in amassing working-class fodder for the guns of the ruling class; the intellectuals had become recruiting sergeants for soul-devouring war.[10]

Although the ASP and the SLP also denounced the war and most members of the VSP were sympathetic to the anti-war agitation, these parties were nonetheless damned by default because of their association with the aims and methods of the Second International: the pursuit of socialism by parliamentary means. The failure of the International to avert war, which had proven the shortcomings of 'political Socialism', gave the IWW the opportunity to argue that the aims and methods of the International generally were flawed, that the attempt 'to transform the capitalist State into an instrument of working-class deliverance' was always 'a hopeless task'. The socialist parties of Europe, placing their faith in a collection of ballot papers rather than industrial organisation, was a 'howling farce'; it had failed the workers and been foremost in plunging the world into the present holocaust: 'The State socialistic "Internationale" has fallen to pieces, but that was quite a natural consequence of the State socialistic ideal, the State principle in Socialism had to lead the Socialist parties to the defence of the national state . . .' In an article on German socialism *Direct Action* maintained the top-heavy structure of the movement, typical of parliamentary socialist parties, prevented rank-and-file workers from pursuing their class interests: 'It is despotism and leader domination which is the characteristic of German Socialism, and which has made it possible for a few unscrupulous German generals to deliver the workers of Europe to capitalistic murder.'[11]

The hope of the future lay in industrial organisation. Militarism, like the state, would only collapse before the organised solidarity of labour; an industrial International would in its very nature overleap the narrow parochial spirit upon which patriotism was built, evoking a new internationalist spirit in the working class. Barker argued that the only way to avert war was for the international working class to pick up the broken threads of their organisation when the war was over, trusting only their force as a concrete organisation throughout the modern world: 'The working class alone can abolish war. No one else will, no one else can.'[12] The overcoming of racial and national prejudice was to be both a method and an aim of the new order.

> It is from the working class that the final word will come that will settle war for all time . . . we shall stop war, and shall put by racial hatred and prejudice for the International Solidarity of Labor. We shall in the future society be all workers, working for the common good, and war shall be relegated to the dark ages of barbarism.[13]

The present war, the IWW claimed, was being prolonged because workers did not understand their class interests. The Wobblies could not conceal their contempt for the 'mugs' and 'patriotic boneheads' who allowed their opinions to be manufactured for them by priests, parsons, politicians, newspapers, schools, and so on: 'Reflecting on this scientific course of stultification, we are not surprised that droves of gulled workers can be found willing to don the uniform of slavery and wholesale murder, and when the big war drum beats rush to the aid of a master class to slaughter their foreign class-brothers.'[14] Mr Simple, the cartoon character lampooned in *Direct Action*, was the type to go to war, devoid of class-consciousness, lacking the insights into the nature of capitalism and imperialism attained by those schooled in revolutionary industrial unionist ideas.

Wobbly invective against the stupidity of patriotic workers reached fever pitch when some groups of workers refused to work alongside workers of German, Austrian and Turkish origin:

> Now then, you boneheads, rub the rust off your thinking apparatus and ask yourselves a few questions, and don't always depend upon the boss and his hirelings to think for you . . . a thousand times is it better to be a traitor to your country than a traitor to your class.

Direct Action mused how the boss must smile to himself when he witnessed his slaves snarling at each other like wild beasts. *Direct Action* explained that it was 'simply because you are so stupid and ignorant and do not understand your position in society'. As 'the wise ones', the IWW offered to

> help you, with all your faults, to think this matter out, and organise you on a solid basis on the lines of the class struggle, where the workers will not fight in sections, but as a class. . . . it is up to you, 'Mr Blocks,' to get rid of your stone age ideas and come along and join in the fight for freedom.'[15]

However, many recruits were not patriotic boneheads but desperate, workless men, 'recruited from the social depths to fight for the continuance of the system that put them there'.[16] To such as these the IWW extended understanding and sympathy. A poem, 'The Recruit', described him in his tattered garments, homeless and friendless, destitute and forlorn:

> In all the world not one small spot on earth
> To call his own. The land that gave him birth
> Had naught to heap upon him but abuse
> For such as he HIS country had no use. . . .

Until the war, when he 'turned to help her in her hour of need'.

> And then, at last, a place for him was found –
> A little spot on earth – BENEATH A MOUND
> OF TURF. There he did his best
> In safety lies, and takes his well-earned REST.[17]

In an article on 'Conscription by starvation' in December 1915, *Direct Action* noted that it was an open secret that governments and other large employers of labour were preparing to refuse employment to men of military age who had not answered the recruiting committee's questions satisfactorily: 'Instead of the Iron Heel we are to have the cold whip of want.' Who would blame the worker if, stranded and penniless, he decided 'to face the bayonets instead of the infinitely more cruel weapon of starvation?' A scheme such as this, which drove 'the common herd' into the firing line and left the sons of the wealthy to show their patriotism by growing fat on gilt-edged securities was, from the ruling-class viewpoint, superior to compulsion.[18]

A recurring theme in Wobbly propaganda was the discrepancy between the lives offered up by the working class and the profits secured by many capitalists in the course of the war. Jock Wilson's deportation resulted from an anti-conscription speech in the Domain in which he declared: 'I am not going to the war to have Broken Hill lead pumped into me by the Germans.'[19] When the campaign to coerce single men to the front commenced, *Direct Action* noted the 'incessant howl' from pulpit, press and platform for more men for murder: 'Of course this is directed solely against the poor. Society snob and aristocratic shirkers, with few exceptions, take no notice of the country's need. This opprobrium and abuse is levelled at the worker, not at the real shirker.'[20] Those who bade the worker die for his country, 'the whole horde of capitalist flunkeys', would sacrifice the last man and the last shilling, 'so long as he was not the last man and the shilling was not his own'. When a Manly councillor in Sydney rose 'from his patriotic brain-box' to denounce the IWW speakers in the Domain who had, he averred, prevented many would-be recruits from performing their patriotic duty, a *Direct Action* editorial promised that, if any Manly councillor could not pass the medical test and did not have his fare to the front, it would take up a collection to get him to where the bullets were flying: 'Let these cowardly wind-bags stop bleating and howling for blood.'[21]

Direct Action's commentary was remorseless in its exposure of the hypocrisy of the warmongers, the class-based inequality of the sacrifices demanded and the privations imposed. It leapt to the attack when the *Sydney Morning Herald*, at the onset of war, lectured workers on the need to become accustomed to a lower standard of living. As prices rose and trade unionists were enjoined to discard their rules, it deplored the 'spectacle of our wealthy classes cynically increasing their private wealth and economic status while calling upon the poor to sacrifice both'. The state, it noted, met the complaints of labour with the pleas of the profiteers about the sanctity of the law of supply and demand: 'The State, too, has appealed to the patriotism of Labour, not only to man the trenches, but to starve and surrender their rights at home, while their employers battened.'[22]

Bosses, the IWW pointed out, used the increasing unemployment in the early years of the war to attack wage levels and working conditions, to make workers work harder for less money. Landlords evicted the wives and children of men who had joined the army, even of those killed at the front. It was wage-workers who lost their jobs as government finance was directed towards the war effort. Employers profiteered in providing the Australian government with goods for the army that were grossly under-weight or woefully inadequate. Tom Glynn perused the weekly trade reports of the Merchants and Traders' Association of Australasia, and regaled *Direct Action* readers with details of the pleasure expressed by 'these industrial and commercial Huns' at the business opportunities offered during and after the war, especially in the provision of a labour force willing to work long hours for low wages. The IWW argued that, apart from the obvious opportunities for making vast profits, the war was useful to the capitalist class as a means of dividing workers and checking their rising aspirations.[23]

The upheaval was a war for trade and class domination, yet the churches on each side appealed to God for victory: 'It is sheer clerical hypocrisy to pretend that we are fighting for the ideal of Christianity.' Religion had never practised anything compatible with the 'Brotherhood of Man'; it had made a show of denouncing social evils but had never stood up to the devil of industrialism or the social anti-Christ of trade. 'Rather in effect has it been the religion of war, persecution and all unrighteousness. Thus we find the ministers of him, who preached peace on earth and goodwill to all men, on recruiting platforms.' To those who prayed for an Allied victory, Mick Sawtell responded: 'War cannot be abolished by prayer, but by work, by working to destroy Capitalism, by means of international revolutionary industrial unionism.'[24]

Direct Action indicted 'the humbug Australian Press' for its role in herding young men to the front. The 'unscrupulous press' had con-tributed to the promotion of war fever, fostering and promoting 'the mil-itarist spirit so vital to the interests of the ruling class'.[25] Wobbly antipathy towards the press was reciprocated, with the newspapers sooling the vio-lently patriotic onto the peacable Wobblies as they proclaimed their anti-militarist viewpoint from public platforms. A Melbourne socialist, F.J. Riley, complained in a letter to the press in December 1915 that the majority of writers for the 'capitalistic sheets' never missed an opportu-nity to sneer at the IWW.[26] In identifying the IWW as the principal source of ideas that challenged the heroism and worth of their calling, the press encouraged soldiers in particular in their assaults on IWW anti-war meet-ings, attacks which became more concerted in the later years of the war as the issue of conscription was contested. The IWW, in the patriotic world vision of its fiercest opponents, was not simply a revolutionary body contemptuous of militarism but the enemy within, undoubtedly aiding the enemy without. Much was made of foreign members' names, all reputedly German or Austrian; the organisation was allegedly funded from Berlin to weaken the Allied war effort and all its members were cowards and traitors.[27]

It was the prosecution of Tom Barker for anti-war activity that launched the IWW in the public mind as the quintessential anti-war organisation and also marked the beginning of a state terrorist campaign against the IWW. The Sydney police had been paying 'special attention' to the IWW since August 1914,[28] but concerted harassment began with the prosecution of Barker. The 'recruiting poster' that started appearing on Sydney buildings in July 1915 was the ultimate Wobbly commentary on the hypocrisy of the war-mongers:

> TO ARMS!!
> Capitalists, Parsons, Politicians,
> Landlords, Newspaper Editors, and
> Other Stay-at-home Patriots.
> YOUR COUNTRY NEEDS YOU IN
> THE TRENCHES!
> WORKERS
> FOLLOW YOUR MASTERS!![29]

The police were sent to remove these offensive bulletins. As they scraped each one off, Wobblies were ready and waiting around the corner with more to paste up the moment the police had moved on.[30]

On 14 September 1915 Barker appeared at the Central Police Court charged under the War Precautions Act, introduced in October 1914, with publishing a poster prejudicial to recruiting. After arguing, with typical Wobbly panache, that the poster was a serious attempt at raising recruitment levels, Barker was fined £50 and given a £200 bond or six months imprisonment with hard labour if he failed to comply with the Act in the future. The Barker Defence Committee called upon fraternal organisations to register a protest against 'sending a working man to rot in gaol for the crime of telling the boss to go to the front'. Broken Hill miners responded by refusing to hear Labor Premier Holman on his propaganda tour; he was obliged to stay on his train and return to Adelaide.[31]

Although Barker's case was not the first under the Act, the penalty was easily the most severe yet imposed. For good measure, he was also fined £20, in default three months imprisonment, for the production of some anti-war stickers which failed to bear the printer's imprint. Barker appealed successfully on a technicality, as the New South Wales government was deemed not to have the necessary power to have prosecuted him under a federal Act. 'It was just an accident', Barker recalled of this triumph.[32]

(The Commonwealth Government is floating a further £10,000,000 for the War Chest. The prospectus calls upon investors to "show a patriotic spirit . . . . especially as no sacrifice is entailed . . . . the rate of interest being far higher than in normal times.")

FAT (intoxicated with "patriotism"): "LONG LIVE THE WAR! HIP, HIP, 'OORAY! FILL 'EM UP AGAIN!"

Syd Nicholls' cartoon which led to the jailing of Tom Barker. (*Direct Action*, 4 December 1915)

In March 1916 Barker was again convicted of offences against this Act, for publishing the previous December a cartoon by Syd Nicholls, the talented young cartoonist for *Direct Action*, which depicted vividly the shocking contrast in wartime experience between that of the worker who died at the front and the war profiteer who prospered at home. Barker was fined £100, in default twelve months hard labour; his appeal failed in May 1916, he refused to pay his fine and he was sent to jail on 4 May.[33] Around the same time, Louis Klausen of the Sydney IWW Club was prosecuted for making statements in the Domain likely to prejudice recruiting; he was fined £100, or three months imprisonment in default, and was obliged to take the latter.

All manner of socialist and peace organisations, trade unions and labour councils protested at the sentences on Barker and Klausen.[34] Leaflets circulating in Melbourne announced:

> Workers wake up . . . The Australian Labor Govt., under its War Precautions' Act, is jailing Working-Class Agitators for daring to expose the Sham Patriotism of the Food Ring Pirates and other Commercial Thieves. Demand the Immediate Release of TOM BARKER . . . Don't let your leaders rot in jail for your cause.[35]

By Christmas 1915 the Barker Defence Fund stood at more than £160.[36] Mat Hade considers the Barker incident the breakthrough for the IWW: 'the prosecution of Barker made known to everyone that the organisation was in existence. And from then on, it received a tremendous advertisement, and went ahead enormously.' The IWW launched a 'Set Barker Free' campaign, supported by kindred groups; 'there was a tremendous noise about me', Barker recalls, and he was released on 3 August after serving only three months of his sentence. Barker believes this concession was part of a dastardly plot on the part of the authorities: 'They released me to take the steam out of things for a little while, but all the time they were concocting the biggest scheme which they had in mind.'[37] The story of this scheme is told in the next chapter.

The threat of conscription gave the IWW its greatest opportunity to have its voice heard. Ted Moyle considers that this issue was 'food to the I.W.W.', giving it 'life and movement' and 'elbowroom to agitate', because it was 'in the front line of a great & popular mass struggle'. According to police reports and military intelligence, the IWW expanded rapidly in this period; the IWW in Sydney, for instance, was admitting eight to twelve new members every week. Through the anti-conscription campaign, whose meetings drew crowds of up to 100 000 in Melbourne and Sydney, Wobbly ideology was widely disseminated. Jim

Scott's diary records how effectively Alf Wilson in Melbourne used the platform of the No Conscription Fellowship to publicise IWW ideas.[38] The Wobbly-baiting tactic pursued by the pro-conscriptionists, the attempt to damn the entire anti-conscriptionist cause by dint of its association with the IWW, failed to limit the appeal of the IWW: it greatly increased its following as a result of its outspoken part in the campaign.

At the same time, the absurd allegations made about the 'pro-German IWW' and the publicity thereby given the 'disloyalist' outlook of the IWW played into the hands of the less extreme proponents of the anti-conscription cause. Bill Beattie believes the extremity of the propaganda war against the IWW and the physical attacks on it by pro-conscriptionists, helped turn public opinion against conscription. Norman Jeffery was convinced that the attack on the IWW, plus the crushing of the 1917 strike, were factors aiding the anti-conscription victory.[39] By comparison with the extremists of both camps – the seriously disloyal Wobblies and the virulent pro-conscription patriots – the moderate sections of the anti-conscription movement must have appeared to many waverers as the voice of reason. In both referenda, on 28 October 1916 and 20 December 1917, a narrow but decisive majority rejected the conscription proposals, with an increased majority in the second poll.[40]

IWW anti-conscription propaganda did not confine itself to the issue of conscription, but condemned the war itself. Arguably, the IWW did more to aid the anti-conscription cause than those who merely opposed conscription or simply concentrated their propaganda against it. Concerned with class struggle rather than mere civil liberties, the IWW insisted that wars between nations were never justifiable, and it favoured an abrupt halt to the present carnage by the workers of the belligerent countries refusing to fight or to work. Most of the other organisations within the constellation of forces that comprised the anti-conscription movement were either opposed simply to the use of compulsion to fight a war that might or might not be justifiable or in favour of securing a negotiated peace between the warring nations 'by means of international arbitration'. Groups such as the Women's Peace Army and the Australian Peace Alliance subordinated anti-war activity to the fight against conscription.[41] The IWW was careful to distinguish its extreme anti-war position from the more muted philosophy of most of those with whom it cooperated in the anti-conscription movement, the 'pure and simple antis', who were 'unscientific and illogical since they uphold the capitalistic system'. The IWW 'not only opposes conscription, but it attacks militarism in all its forms'.[42]

The ASP shared the IWW's anti-war position, but the IWW made considerably more noise about it than the ASP. Bertha Walker concedes that the IWW was the only party uncompromisingly against the war itself.

Ernie Lane recalls that the IWW played a prominent and uncompromising part in the anti-conscription campaign: 'Unlike the official Labour movement, the I.W.W. with rare courage and reckless of all consequences denounced and exposed the true causes of the war as a deadly clash of interests of conflicting imperial capitalist groups.' On the twentieth anniversary of the first referendum, the Communist Party acknowledged that 'The I.W.W. was in the forefront of the struggle, and not only against compulsory service, but against the war itself.'[43]

It was not simply that IWW propaganda, in its denunciation of the war, was more extreme than the anti-conscription rhetoric generally; so also were the means by which it hoped to contest any introduction of conscription. As early as 1 October 1915 it urged workers to answer the threat of conscription with a general strike: 'A Conscription Act should be the signal for industrial revolt and insurrection.' Be prepared, it advised workers, 'to stop every industry and every wheel in Australia, and tell these unscrupulous vampires that if they want blood a little may be shed at home'. Childe notes how effectively it produced the impression that it was a formidable and desperate body that would resist to the utmost any attempt to impose compulsory service.[44]

This was the IWW's finest hour. In contrast to so many other sections of the international working-class movement, which capitulated to the war fever, the Wobblies remained resolute. The Second International, which before 1914 had declared its opposition to war, proved utterly ineffective once hostilities were formally declared. Indeed, the shock of war was crucial to the transformation of the post-war left. Lenin, Trotsky and Luxemburg, the most innovative minds of revolutionary socialism, were not confounded by the retreat of the Second International – they had expected nothing more from revisionists. Rather, it was the mobilisation of popular support for the war, and the extent of the bellicose enthusiasm revealed after 1914, that called into question the received ideas that class came before nation, and that war was simply a product of capitalist imperialism.

Hitherto these theorists had regarded patriotism, militarism and xenophobia as devices foisted on the working class by their exploiters. It was the shock of the First World War that stimulated the Bolsheviks and the Spartacists, and after them such creative Marxist intellectuals as Lukàcs and Gramsci to go beyond this understanding. All of them had to find some way of proceeding beyond the axioms of working-class gullibility and passivity; they had to find ways of explaining how these sentiments and attachments were generated from within working-class culture. To this extent they were wrestling with problems of class-consciousness that were denied by the older reductionist orthodoxies of which the Wobblies were such eloquent expositors.

The comparison is unfair. How could these beleauguered and isolated anti-war Australian activists have been expected to explore their doctrinal assumptions? It was enough that they kept the flag flying and gathered others around it in the depths of the war when others, even Lenin, seemed close to despair. The comparison is only useful if it sheds light on the limited repertoire of Wobbly anti-war arguments. According to these arguments, it was a bosses' war, all evidence of working-class participation notwithstanding, and the workers who donned uniform were gulled by the parsons and politicians. Denunciation and defiance were the devices that would break this spell, defeat conscription and release the volunteers from their false consciousness.

To this end the IWW directed its anti-war propaganda. By February 1917 the IWW in Sydney alone had held 120 Sunday afternoon Domain meetings, 240 hall lectures and over 300 outdoor street meetings, and sold over 1000 copies of *War, What For?*, in addition to its sales of *Direct Action* and other revolutionary literature. This unrelenting campaign 'not alone against conscription, but also against the war',[45] probably helped to shift the spectrum of public opinion towards a more circumspect approach to the war effort. Though the IWW presence in the anti-conscription movement was used by the pro-conscriptionists in their attempts to discredit the entire anti-conscription cause, the ploy did not work. Though very few could accept the IWW's intransigent hostility to the war, the majority of the population agreed with the moderate anti-conscriptionists' opposition to the means by which the Hughes government wanted to fight the war. The IWW provided the ultra-left viewpoint that most people rejected; but in rejecting this anti-war position, perhaps many were persuaded to adopt a more critical, anti-conscription outlook.

May Brodney discounts as counter-productive to the cause the extent to which the Wobblies campaigned against war in general and the evils that cause it, rather than concentrating on the specific issue of conscription. She scorns the extent to which the anti-conscription victories have been laid at the door of the IWW by contemporary activists and subsequent scholars alike, insisting that the IWW was 'more of an embarrassment than a help to the Anti-Conscriptionists'.[46] Of course it embarrassed the May Brodneys of the movement: to discompose was its important and decisive role.

In expounding the 'myth' that May Brodney scorns, Ted Moyle contends that 'most of the credit' for the success of the anti-conscription movement must go to the IWW: its 'early propaganda of direct struggle against the War, however little appeal it may have had in the beginning, undoubtedly prepared the ground for the easier setting up of the platform of the Anti-Conscriptions'; given the small 'No' majority, 'without this early start . . . the Referendum would have gone the other way'. Tom

Barker, too, stresses the amount of leg-work the IWW put into the anti-conscription movement:

> I am sure that the work we did made all the difference to the Australian work-ers and the Australian people generally when the question of conscription came up in 1916 and 1917. There is no doubt at all in my mind, if it hadn't been for the presence of our organisation and what we did in those days, the history of Australia might have been vastly different as far as the war itself was concerned.[47]

Quantifying the Wobbly contribution to the anti-conscription movement is not the most significant consideration; crucial to the success of the position the IWW did not endorse, that of the pure and simple anti-con-scriptionists, was the quality rather than the quantity of the IWW's con-tribution, its uncompromising rejection of all wars other than the class war and the energy with which it propounded its ideas.

This is not to argue, however, that the IWW did not also make an orig-inal contribution to the arguments specifically against conscription. It made two distinctive and important points: that conscription would be used to discipline the workforce; and that, in opposing conscription, it was an important matter of principle that there be no pandering to racial fears about the import of coloured labour to replace the white labour at the front.

When conscription was first mooted late in 1915, the IWW warned that attempts were being made to render capitalism stable by the intro-duction of compulsory labour: the 'principle of compulsion must be applied to labor in mine, workshop and factory, even if it has to be done at the point of the bayonet'. Conscription was 'a mighty weapon in the hands of the master-class', hence, it had to be faced, grappled with, and fought. 'Conscriptionists are really after industrial conscription . . . to conserve their class interests after the war.' In July 1916, urging a gen-eral strike against conscripton, *Direct Action* reported that Senator Pearce, Minister for Defence, had said no more men could be sent away than at present; and conscription was not envisaged for the manufacture of munitions as the British government had just stated it did not require any munitions from Australia: 'So it must be plain that the real reason why they want conscription is to more effectually carry on their indus-tries.' The week before the first referendum, *Direct Action* listed as the first of the reasons for conscription 'the subjugation of labour'.[48]

The other distinctive contribution made by the IWW was its disavowal of the racist arguments deployed in the anti-conscription campaign. The arrival in Fremantle of a boatload of Maltese immigrants on the eve of the first poll was used by Labor anti-conscriptionists to encourage fears that coloured workers would be imported to replace the labour of conscripts. The IWW line was that, if it could be proven these men were indentured labour, the unionists were right to be angry, but it feared there was a good deal of racial hatred at the bottom of the cry against the Maltese; the 'only logical solution' was to accept the Maltese as fellow labourers. It was careful to emphasise that its objections were to the indenturing, not the colour, of this labour.[49] On the day of the first referendum, it stressed that the danger of conscription lay, not in the possibility that coloured labour would be imported to carry on the industries of the nation, but that, under a conscription regime, the organisation of these men would not be permitted:

> The I.W.W. does not object to colored labour, simply because it is colored labour, nor does it oppose conscription merely because the introduction of cheap labor is the motive, but we attack it because it will deprive us of the right to educate and organise our class-brothers, be they black, white or brown, for the overthrow of the Capitalist system.

This position, it stressed, differentiated the IWW from the 'pure and simple anti-conscriptionists' who wanted to rely on voluntary recruiting to win the war for the master class, because they wished to keep Australia white. After the campaign was over, *Direct Action* regretted the introduction into an otherwise great campaign of the ancient bogey of race hatred, for 'race hatred keeps the workers separated, and . . . has for ages blighted the brains of the workers'.[50]

The extremity and distinctiveness of the IWW position apart, it made also an important contribution to the anti-conscription movement in terms of sheer organisational effort, and promptly. Back in 1911 the IWW Clubs had been quick to denounce the introduction of compulsory military training for teenage boys, an agitation kept running by the Chicago IWW. It suited the prejudices of the IWW that Labor had been complicit in the conscription of voteless, working-class lads and it referred to the Compulsory Training Act as the Compulsory Traitor Act, because it bade these lads betray their class. Well before the outbreak of war, *Direct Action*'s 15-year-old writer on the subject announced: 'Conscription is an audacious attempt on the part of the master-class to enslave the sons of the workers, and to use them as their tools and cats-paws. Working men, you must oppose this! It endangers your interests, and, therefore, it is your enemy.'[51] Although the first referendum was not announced until 30 August 1916 the IWW had long been preparing for the possibility, denouncing the curse of conscription in the pages of *Direct Action*, with posters and stickers, and in propaganda meetings organised by its Locals for at least a year before this announcement.

On 20 July 1915 at a meeting at the IWW hall in Sydney, the Anti-Conscription League was launched by the IWW, socialists and other 'advanced thinkers'. The address of this League was the same as that of the IWW. In Melbourne, likewise, the Local formed an Anti-Conscription and Anti-Militarist League in July 1915; and when Bob Ross, a month later, formed the VSP-dominated No Conscription Fellowship, the IWW, along with the IWW-dominated Anti-Conscription and Anti-Militarist League, combined with Ross's Fellowship and other organisations, such as the Australian Peace Alliance, in holding anti-conscription meetings.[52] In 1918 a censor's note on two Queensland Wobblies, Jim Quinton and Harry Barcan of Toowoomba, recalled they had been closely associated with the Queensland Anti-Conscription League, which, the censor insisted, was really an IWW organisation.[53]

The IWW played an active part in the special Trade Union Congress in September 1916 that called a stop-work meeting on 4 October to protest against the idea of conscription: the Barrier mines were shut down; 70 000 workers took part in Melbourne of whom 50 000 came to the Yarra Bank to hear anti-conscription speakers, including Jock Wilson and Alf Wilson of the IWW; direct actionists were prominent among the 3000 strikers who met in the Sydney Town Hall.[54] IWW anti-conscription agitation within the union movement confirmed its prejudices against union officials, for it was the rank and file rather than their officials who most clearly provided the union movement's contribution to the anti-conscription cause. Wobbly Ted Moyle, one of the central figures in the anti-conscription movement in South Australia, found that union officials were more likely than unionists to favour conscription; unionists, on the other hand, were overwhelmingly against conscription.[55]

Otherwise, Wobbly involvement was unsectarian in relation to other anti-conscription organisations. The IWW, according to Dick Surplus, 'worked with anyone who was opposed to conscription'. Joint activity and combined propaganda meetings with parliamentary socialists, the left of the Labor Party, craft unions and even the De Leonite IWW was considered justifiable and necessary, this open-minded approach extending even to the hierarchy of the Catholic Church. Of Archbishop Mannix, Tom Barker recalled of the IWW mood at the time: 'We might not have followed him to heaven, but we certainly weren't going to deny him his right as a partner in the battle.'[56]

Some partners in the battle attempted to infer inconsistency on the part of the IWW from its professed hostility to parliamentary activity while throwing so much effort into the 'No' campaign. The ASP commented: 'The ballot-box smasher will be up against it, so to speak, when the coming referendum is taken. The temptation to vote against conscription will be almost unbearable.'[57] This alleged contradiction was more apparent than real as the situations were quite different to the IWW mind: the election of governments in capitalist society was futile

tinkering with the political superstructure without alteration to the economic base; a referendum, though it could be ignored by the government, as the IWW suspected possible, was an opportunity for the
working class to express its opinion on a specific issue and one of vital
importance to it. In any case, the potential for propaganda during the
referenda was too good for an organisation like the IWW to pass up, concerned as it was with educating the working class.

'Great crowds used to come to our anti-conscription meetings', Tom
Barker recalls, 'up to a sixth of the population of Sydney gathering
around and trying to hear the speakers.' Where there were no Locals,
visiting Wobblies were often an important asset to anti-conscription
forces. For instance, Alf Wilson attended the Waterside Workers
Conference in Hobart in 1916 and used the opportunity to conduct a
series of successful public meetings in the Hobart City Hall and in the
streets of Hobart and country towns throughout Tasmania. For the second referendum in December 1917 Wilson was invited by the Adelaide
Anti-Conscription League to be its paid speaker for the duration of the
fight, addressing meetings at lunch hour and every night 'in some street
or another drawing hundreds and hundreds'.[58]

IWW speakers were regularly assaulted by soldiers, police and other
enraged patriots. The most infamous incident was on the night of 8
October 1916 when several dozen soldiers attacked the IWW hall, throwing bricks and tearing down palings, an action defended as understand-
able 'impatience' by Professor Macintyre of the New South Wales
Recruiting Committee.[59] Obliged to disperse the soldiers, the police officer in charge regretted that the 'ill advised' action of the soldiers had
forced the police to 'appear as if they were supporting people with
whom they have nothing in common'. An old-time activist, George Bliss,
was told by older comrades that the soldiers at Liverpool Military Camp
were supplied with free beer if they would break up IWW meetings. But,
as Bliss points out, when men that can fight and have been drinking
come up against men who can fight and have not been drinking, they
have no chance. On one occasion, according to Bliss's source, 'Soldiers
were laying everywhere, the Police came to their aid, they sent for more
Police . . .'[60]

Wobblies defended themselves physically from intimidation. Norman
Jeffery, who was hit full in the mouth with a big bunch of wet grass
hurled at him by a group of soldiers while speaking from an IWW platform in Melbourne, recalls that many such meetings were 'rugged
affairs' and that he only escaped serious assault thanks to 'adequate protection' by fellow Wobblies. *Direct Action* pointed out that the patriotic
rowdies were most obnoxious when the police were present in large
numbers and could protect them from Wobbly retaliation.[61]

At their Domain meeting on 13 August 1916, attended by 80–100 000 people, the police went even further. After soldiers attempted to rush the platform at least a dozen times but were repulsed on each occasion by Wobblies taking direct action against the intruders, the police stopped the meeting and two constables smashed the platform into matchwood. Chief Secretary George Black, the man who had promised in 1890 that the Labor Party would make and unmake social conditions, had instructed the Inspector General of Police to 'stop any speaker who made any disloyal statement'. The following week the IWW decided to protect its Domain speakers by forming a circle around them, 'and do all in their power to protect them from molestation'. This defensive move was successful; *Direct Action* declared the day 'a triumph for the I.W.W. and the principle of free speech'.[62]

Precisely because the Australian contribution to the war effort was dependent still upon volunteers, the anti-German propaganda had to be such as to move people emotionally, to persuade enough men to ignore their instincts of self-preservation. By the same token, those who queried the war effort had to be discredited, and vehemently so. Hughes led the attack on the IWW on behalf of the forces of conservatism and imperial patriotism, while attempting also to recreate the labour movement in his own image through exorcising IWW influence within it.

That Hughes resorted to referenda rather than legislation to introduce conscription indicated that he was rather more confident of the conscriptionist leanings of the nation at large than of his own political party, infected as he saw it with the IWW germ. The Labor mind of 1916 was very different from that of 1914, which had been ready to give its last man and last shilling. Three-quarters of the Caucus indicated they would refuse to pass a Conscription Act. For this transformation he blamed the IWWs, who had 'nothing in common with Labor or Unionism' but were 'foul parasites', who had 'attached themselves to the vitals of labour'.[63]

In his pronouncements on the IWW, Hughes was as much concerned to cleanse the labour movement and regain control of it as to frighten the populace into voting for conscription by telling them that the IWW opposed it: 'These men know no country, nationality, religion, or principle, and in the name of unionism and labourism I pass them out like devils out of swine.' At a January 1916 meeting of trade union leaders, he stated of the IWW, and ominously for it: 'there is only one thing they understand, and that is force'.[64] The IWW must, therefore, be attacked 'with the ferocity of a Bengal tiger'. After the arrest of the Twelve in September–October 1916 he stressed their anti-conscriptionist credentials. Shortly before the first poll he declared that the IWW was the enemy of society: 'Its ideals are German, and its only weapon is force.' He appealed to 'organised labour' to cast out from its midst those who dominated the anti-conscription wing of the movement: 'Extremists – I.W.W. men, Revolutionary socialists, Syndicalists, "red-raggers" . . . who seek to use labour for their own purposes.' Around the same time, Premier Holman blamed the drift into the anti-conscription camp on 'the secret but steadily growing influence of the Industrial Workers of the World over union organisations'.[65]

After the first referendum defeat, Hughes walked out of the Caucus meeting that was debating his removal as Party leader, followed by twenty-four pro-conscriptionists. He formed a minority 'National Labor' government on 14 November 1916, discarding anti-conscriptionists and taking on pro-conscriptionists, and governing with the support of the Liberal opposition. Two months later, on 17 February 1917, the Liberals entered into coalition with National Labor, and a Nationalist Coalition government was formed that was easily returned at the general election of 5 May.[66]

The equation made by the pro-conscriptionists between anti-conscription and the IWW in fact galvanised the militant labour movement's determination to stop conscription. When the Brisbane *Telegraph* argued shortly before the first poll that a 'Yes' victory would be 'the deadliest blow ever dealt to Industrial Unionism', and all conservative papers made similar arguments, it was reasonable for concerned trade unionists to infer that it was in the interests of the trade union movement that the 'No' vote win. Many unionists and, indeed, many liberal-minded people generally, reacted adversely to Hughes' over-kill in his attempts to discredit the IWW and with it the anti-conscriptionists, to his flagrant disregard for the rules of justice in publicly condemning the Twelve before they were tried, in the absurd allegations made about the IWW being a German plot or financed by German gold.[67]

Of course the Wobbly-baiting tactic worked to some extent. The most moderate sections of the anti-conscription labour movement were at pains to dissociate themselves from the IWW, to insist that they were respectable. They even formed new anti-conscription organisations, such as the No Conscription Council in New South Wales, to proclaim their independence from the IWW. In assuming such a position, they weakened the labour movement by attempting to pander to the prejudices of those whom the rest of the labour movement opposed.

Far from discrediting the labour movement, the IWW, on the other hand, helped to rehabilitate it, to become the anti-conscription party that could later claim credit for its opposition to the Prussianism that Australia was allegedly fighting against. As Judah Waten's George Feathers explained: 'I reckon half of those anti-conscription Labour politicians would have ratted like Hughes but for the way we stirred the wage plugs up against conscription.'[68] Childe notes: 'Before "No

Conscription" became a popular watchword, while the Labour Party was still toying with militarism, the I.W.W. steadily and unflinchingly denounced the curse and prepared the field where the Labour Party afterwards reaped.' The IWW, he argued, 'can claim the credit for the defeat of conscription'; its members and sympathisers within the Leagues and unions prompted the emphatic decisions against conscription by the AWU Convention and the New South Wales and Victorian Labor Parties; it prepared the way for the ALP peace proposals of 1917, the Labor Council's resolutions against recruiting and the Perth Conference decisions in 1918.[69] Childe's claim might be exaggerated, but the IWW's uncompromising and outspoken opposition to the war certainly made it a lodestar on the left at this time. It was Hughes' desire to beat back all IWW influence from within the labour movement that prompted the response of his governments to this presumptuous movement that threatened, truly, to make and unmake social conditions.

CHAPTER 13

'With the Ferocity of a Bengal Tiger': the State Responds

The Australian IWW did not endure to the same extent the privatised retribution inflicted upon their American fellow workers: the beatings, the lynchings, the intimidation and torturings by individual loyalists. However, the state-sponsored suppression of the IWW here, which occurred well in advance of the criminal syndicalism legislation to suppress the IWW in the United States,[1] was sufficiently draconian to achieve the eradication of the IWW as a viable organisation. On 29 June 1919 the Sydney *Truth* regretted that, with the help of a miscarriage of justice, the IWW had been more effectively repressed in Australia than in the USA.[2]

This suppression was achieved primarily by Labor administrations, in New South Wales and the Commonwealth. It was the outcome of the hard work and dedication to duty of the police, the censors, military intelligence, and the Counter Espionage Bureau established late in 1915, acting on instructions from governments, the most enthusiastic in hunting down the Wobblies undoubtedly being those in New South Wales and the Commonwealth. The Labor-controlled Commonwealth legislature furnished the executive with sweeping powers, under a War Precautions Act, to make most forms of resistance to the war illegal. It was Labor Premier Holman who, late in 1914, first urged Prime Minister Fisher and military intelligence to take seriously the threat posed by the IWW and instructed police to report on the organisation.[3] After Hughes, a long-time opponent of IWW influence within the labour movement, became Prime Minister the forces at the disposal of the federal government worked closely with the New South Wales authorities to meet the challenge laid down by the IWW.

Engineered in the main by the right wing of the Labor Party, the suppression of the IWW was prompted more by a desire to retain control of the labour movement than by a need to preserve society at large. For the

IWW was far better placed to destroy the labour movement of Hughes and Holman's pragmatic imagination than to wreak havoc upon existing social relations. Moreover, a strong-armed approach to the IWW was useful to this faction, intent on achieving respectability, for improving the credentials of their Labor governments in the eyes of employers. So that the threat to the right's control of the labour movement posed by the IWW could be contained, and so these governments could satisfy the class of people they now sought to serve, the Hughes/Holman wing of the movement chose wilfully to misrepresent the IWW as pro-German, rendering its forcible suppression easy in the wartime climate of patriotic hysteria.

Though other left-wing groups also suffered from state interference in various forms, attention paid to them was motivated more by the desire to extract information about the IWW than to investigate these organisations on their own demerits. R.S. Ross reported to a VSP Executive Meeting in August 1915 that a Detective Burvett had called upon him 'regarding the publications of the non-political I.W.W.'. In October 1916 the head of the Commonwealth Counter Espionage Bureau, Major Steward, organised raids on the Melbourne left. Instructions for the assault on Ross' left-wing publishing house were to search for material 'indicating the source from which the IWW may be receiving funds'. Of greatest interest to the raiders of the VSP's headquarters and Ross' home were letters from Tom Barker, which were seized and sent to the Sydney CIB. F.J. Riley wrote to the Brisbane *Standard* on 20 October about these raids on Melbourne radicals: 'Many private individuals have had their houses ransacked and searched by police officers with the view of finding, if possible, letters, documents, posters, etc., to connect them with the I.W.W.' Kevin Fewster's study of wartime repression and censorship concludes: 'The IWW was the one group against which a systematic repressive assault was instigated.'[4] However, in a liberal democracy, with its emphasis on the importance of public opinion, manufactured panic would have to precede such persecution. The press was to prove obliging in this respect.

Early Surveillance

While Tom Barker was in prison between May and August 1916, the IWW threw much of its energy into the campaign to release him, hinting in Wobbly jargon in *Direct Action* of the need for rough play: 'Boys of the Wooden Shoe Brigade should not let their soles rot for want of use. Barker is still in gaol.' All this was duly taken down and later used in evidence against the IWW, for, by the time Barker was imprisoned, Sydney police were preparing weekly reports of Wobbly meetings in the

Domain and military censors were paying particular attention to IWW correspondence.[5]

In June 1916 the Commonwealth Inspector General of Police called for information on the IWW from his various police districts. A report by Detective Nicholas Moore, a 'subversion expert' in the Sydney police and one of the detectives assigned to liaise with military intelligence, lamented that the police could not obtain exact data about the IWW and stressed that 'some such power should be given the Police, which would enable them to gauge the extent of their operations, and be in a position to cope with any of their actions which might lead up to industrial crimes'.[6]

On a warrant issued by the military commandant of the 2nd District, Detective Moore searched the IWW headquarters on 15 July 1916. In August 1916 confiscation of imported IWW literature, especially the booklet on sabotage, was stepped up significantly. On 11 September censors were instructed to read all IWW correspondence then reseal letters so the correspondents would remain oblivious to the surveillance. Fewster notes these Commonwealth government actions were taken after consultation with New South Wales police, who were preparing their own assault on the Sydney IWW.[7]

The Counterfeiters

A small number of Wobblies played into the hands of their enemies at this stage. On 17 August 1916 several men were arrested for printing and distributing about £25 000 worth of forged £5 notes. Amongst them were Wobblies, J.B. King, John Ferguson and Fred Morgan. Morgan and Ferguson were linotype operators who did the typesetting for *Direct Action*. Also arrested was my grandfather's first cousin, Henry Bradbury, the process engraver who made the plates for the forged notes. The press described the Wobblies involved as agents of Germany and informed readers that 'Hun money was used to get the plant going for the express purpose of dislocating the currency of the Commonwealth.' Morgan skipped bail and never re-emerged. Ferguson, Bradbury and King were found guilty and sentenced to ten years, two years and three years respectively, on 23 October 1916. The sentence on King was unusually long as he had been less involved than the others, but his prominence in the IWW condemned him. On appeal his sentence was reduced to two years.[8]

Whether the forgeries were intended to debase the currency to the detriment of the capitalist order or simply to finance Wobbly propaganda, it is apparent that some Wobblies considered the activity justifiable. There was, after all, no threat to human life involved. Wobblies were involved in distributing the fivers, usually on racecourses where they would put a pound on a horse and receive four good notes back from the bookie, and several received jail sentences for the offence. Roly Farrall tried passing the notes in a pub in Perth. When the hotelkeeper said 'Is this a bodgey?', Roly and his drunken mates abused him, so the hotelkeeper rang the police and Roly was arrested then jailed. Other Wobblies who came into contact with the forgeries were appalled: in the comparatively respectable Melbourne Local, members buried or attempted to burn the notes. Tom Barker is adamant that the forgery business 'wasn't an I.W.W. thing', that the IWW had plenty of other things on its plate without being interested in breaking up the social order through forgeries.[9] Certainly, it was not organised or sanctioned by the organisation; however, Wobblies as individuals were undoubtedly involved in the scheme, and this real involvement assisted those who would frame up Wobblies on a much more serious charge.

Suppression Begins

Increasingly careful attention was being paid by this time to IWW speeches in the Domain.[10] In September 1916 the Sydney police became especially diligent in prosecuting Wobblies under the War Precautions Act for uttering inflammatory and seditious words and advocating sabotage. For example, Charlie Reeve was charged for alleging, in words extreme even by the standards of Domain oratory, that 'Billy Hughes and Senator Pearce are the scabbiest, lousiest pair of crawlers that ever crept into Parliament on the backs of Labor'.[11] The press provided invaluable backing to this campaign of suppression, alerting the public in various ways to the danger of the IWW, emphasising how strong and influential in working-class circles the IWW was becoming. Invariably, press discussion of the IWW practice of industrial sabotage made it appear synonymous with violence against people, though the IWW formally repudiated such violence as unscientific, antiquated and dangerous. As in the United States, the newspaper was the greatest influence in weeding out the most defiant labour elements and upholding the most conciliatory.[12]

Thus, the public had become well aware of the alleged treachery of the IWW by 23 September 1916 when police raided the IWW hall. While the thirty or so men on the premises were detained and questioned for three hours, other police removed three vanloads of IWW property, including all money, £400 worth of literature, private letters, bankbooks, the charter and the big red banner. They forcibly broke open locks, though keys were offered them. From evidence obtained during this raid police compiled a list of members and another list of people believed to be members, which they forwarded to military intelligence.[13]

Around the same time, police without warrants were breaking into members' houses, searching them and confiscating all documents and literature. Raids had become a way of life for the Wobblies. Tom Barker recalls: 'They had the habit of coming in, seizing the place and throwing you out for two or three days.' He regrets that, in the course of one raid, the Sydney Local's share of Joe Hill's ashes, which they were intending to scatter ceremonially in the Domain, were confiscated and ended up being thrown on the back of the fire at Darlinghurst police station. During raids, Jock Wilson remembers 'everything . . . being done to humiliate and intimidate'. He was convinced that those who were engaged in the raids and searches mentioned were 'specially selected men whose mentality was such that they took a delight in the dirty work they were called upon to do'. Otherwise, he adds, 'the frame up of the twelve men . . . would have been impossible'.[14]

The Arrest of the Twelve

Within a fortnight, in late September and early October on the eve of the first conscription referendum, the police arrested Charles Reeve, Tom Glynn, Peter Larkin, Jack Hamilton, Donald Grant, J.B. King, William Beatty, Morris Fagin, Bernard Bob Besant, William Teen, Donald McPherson and Thomas Moore. Apart from Moore, these Wobblies were prominent within the movement. They were refused bail and denied the right to see or communicate with anyone. The 'Twelve', as they became known, were charged, on the alleged evidence of police informers, with treason–felony under the New South Wales Crimes Act of 1900, which carried a maximum penalty of life imprisonment: that they did 'feloniously and wickedly compass, imagine, invent, devise or intend to levy war against the King within the State of New South Wales'.[15] The alleged means by which the IWW was to levy such a war was by incendiarism on Sydney business premises. Thus, the instructions sent to the Broken Hill police about the arrest of Donald Grant stressed that 'every care should be taken to take possession of anything found on the IWW premises in the nature of or likely to be of use in evidence such as cotton waste or phosphorous'.[16]

Yet, in the straitened circumstances of the time, an outbreak of fires could be explained by the interests of those whose premises were fired. One company that had a fire had bought the business premises shortly before for £7500 but insured it for over £13 000.[17] A press report of the time noted that two brothers in Sydney were charged with having maliciously attempted to set fire to Ayrshire House in King Street, Sydney, after being found in the cellar with several tins of kerosene. One brother stated he had persuaded his brother to do it, as his father's stock and machinery were there, and his father was not doing well in business, but was insured: 'He told his brother that the I.W.W. would probably be blamed.'[18] Bill Beattie (William Beatty of the Twelve) argues the fires were a 'double-barrelled bonanza, for they presented a political as well as a business opportunity'. The government saw in them a means to break up the IWW; they were also a way out for firms in difficulty. To the question: 'What caused these fires?', the reply was tailormade: the IWW. 'So generally accepted was this solution, that Insurance Companies had no alternative but to pay up', although the suspicions of one insurance inspector led him to suggest that the fires were 'inside jobs', prompted by a business slump. May Brodney, no fan of the IWW, believes that the depression in business circles in the early years of the war undoubtedly caused the outbreak of fires, which were then conveniently blamed on the IWW, 'when the authorities saw fit to smash the organisation'.[19] Ted Moyle is convinced that, if the small fires allegedly started by Wobblies were not simply part of the record number of fires at this time, they were 'at the instigation of someone desirous of trapping the I.W.W.'.

After the Twelve were arrested, Grant's landlady of four years called on Henry Boote, editor of the *Worker*, weeping and declaring Grant was everything that was good. Boote's diary noted: 'Shameful that the I.W.W. men have been arrested on a treason charge – just to get them out of the way.' He described the cases as 'a frame-up by the police' and 'a political dodge to identify anti-conscriptionists with the I.W.W. The police chosen can supply evidence for any case.' Norman Jeffery, too, insists that it was 'an outrageous police and Government frame-up'. Norman Rancie, writing in 1957 to the author of a newspaper article alleging the Wobblies were out to burn down Sydney, was furious:

> It is putrid and a mass of lies, and could only have been written by a bigoted, sensation-loving irresponsible . . . you have gladly lapped up the statements by pimps, agents provocateurs, and paid informers who were in subsequent trials found to be 'liars and forgers'. . . . what good could have been established by wanting to burn down Sydney? That could only be the act of madmen, and the I.W.W. members were not mad.

Far from starting the fires, Rancie pointed out that one Wobbly at the time was a member of the fire brigade at Castlereagh Street station and was engaged in fighting the fires.[20]

A few days after the arrests, the Inspector General of Police ordered that a guard be placed on Darling Harbour railyards every Wednesday when explosives were delivered, because the IWW was supposedly planning to fire the powder wagons in retaliation for the conscription of single men. Melbourne Wobblies were also omnipresent or at least highly manoeuvrable. On 2 October 1916 Major Steward visited the

Russell Street Watch House at 8.10 p.m., announced that 'an attempt might be made to blow up the Federal Government House by the IWW' and despatched armed constables to protect the building until a military guard could be established.[21]

The Murders

The campaign of suppression was facilitated by the murder on 26 September 1916 of a police constable at Tottenham, a small mining town in western New South Wales. Three Wobblies, Roland and Herbert Kennedy and Frank Franz, were arrested and charged with the murder, instigated by the constable's preparation of a warrant for the arrest of Roland Kennedy on a charge of insulting language. The raid on IWW headquarters had unearthed a letter from Roland in which he assured Sydney Local that he and his brother were 'doing all that is possible for Barker's release – a wooden shoe'. At the trial in October it was easy for the prosecution to connect the murder with the IWW, though *Direct Action* insisted: 'It is a sad, and a mad, and a bad thing for a man, or men, to murder anyone – even a policeman.' Herbert Kennedy was discharged but Franz and Roland Kennedy were hanged for the crime a few days before Christmas 1916, the first hanging at Bathurst jail since 1894.[22]

The remnants of the IWW responded to the uses to which this 'private feud' between two members of the IWW and a country policeman had been put: 'The thing was made to appear as an I.W.W. affair . . . Because one or two members of the I.W.W. commit a crime, the whole organisation is to be termed criminal.' On the same reasoning, the IWW argued that the police force was a criminal organisation because a member of that force recently shot his wife and sister-in-law in Sydney.[23]

To make matters worse for the embattled Wobblies, another Wobbly was arrested late in 1916 and charged with the murder the previous April of George Pappageorgi, a cafe proprietor, after raiding his till for money. James 'Paddy' Wilson, an Irish sailor and a Wobbly in jail for passing some of the forged notes, confessed to the murder and blamed the bad influence on him of the IWW, which was played up by the press.[24] *Direct Action* responded with a clear statement on individual violence and 'crime as protest':

> The IWW has never taught anything but industrial revolution . . . Those workers whose brains are so deranged by the system as not to know the difference between social war and individual spite, between social restitution and individual garotting, are respectfully requested to first earn a stretch in gaol on their own responsibility, and on release to become agents for the police after the manner of their kind. The IWW needs their room for reasonable men.[25]

Tom Barker insists that, on the night in question, Wilson was 'fast asleep, dead drunk' on top of a pile of paper in the corner of the IWW head-quarters and could not possibly have committed the murder. Barker sus-pects that his time in jail for the forgeries made him suddenly 'hate the whole thing' and so, 'like a nut, gave himself up for this murder'. Wilson was hanged on 31 May 1917.[26]

The Offensive Stepped Up

Against this backdrop it was not difficult for Hughes to press home his political message to the labour movement: that the IWW were mur-derous, violent saboteurs whose influence amongst workers should be confronted by the 'true' representatives of the labour movement. On 9 October 1916, the day before the preliminary hearing of the treason–felony cases, Hughes, clearly in contempt of court, claimed the IWW not only preached but practised sabotage, 'the wilful destruction of fac-tories, machinery and plant'. 'These men have perverted industrial and political unionism to their own base purposes. I hope the workers will arise while there is yet time and put these men out.' Around the same time, New South Wales Attorney-General Hall announced that the IWW membership list procured in the recent raid showed fifty names 'clearly of German origin'. These associates of the anti-conscription party, 'the men who honeycombed the trades unions', would rejoice with their countrymen in Germany if Australia turned from the path of honour and duty.[27]

In the meantime, Major Steward was conspiring to stage a series of simultaneous pre-dawn raids on the homes and premises of prominent radicals and anti-conscriptionists across Australia on 17 October 1916. These raids failed to uncover evidence of any dastardly activities on the part of the IWW, but Steward was not a man easily deterred. He now attempted to link the IWW with alleged sabotage at Sydney's Cockatoo Island naval dockyards in October–November 1916. Hughes intimated in the House that the IWW had damaged the *Brisbane*'s electric plant and shot one of the agents of the government: 'Here then is Murder, Arson, Forgery, aiding and abetting sabotage in its attack upon the life of the nation.' A report by the manager of the Cockatoo Island dockyards cred-ited the IWW with establishing go-slow tactics and dominating the dock-yard trade unions. The Governor-General, as the official conduit between British and Australian security, forwarded this report to the Secretary of State for the Colonies and informed him that 'conditions of things there is notorious'.[28]

On 1 November Major Steward wrote to Defence Minister Pearce that the time had come to take unified action Australia-wide against the 'sedition, treason and sabotage in its most vicious forms' used by the IWW, and that to this purpose, New South Wales police should meet with a federal officer to plan 'well-defined and concerted action'. Two days later, Brigadier-General Ramaciotti, Commandant, Second Military District, advised the Department of Defence that police should intern any IWW members of enemy origin and that legislation should declare the IWW an illegal organisation and membership of it a felony. His rationale was that the IWW was being used by 'pro-enemy persons to handicap the government in the present crisis and thus materially assist the enemy although the absolute proof of this has not so far been obtained'. As Fewster points out, the fact that 'absolute proof' of the connection between the IWW and the enemy could not be found was seen as confirming the incredible cunning of the German.[29]

The membership list compiled by police after the raid of 23 September 1916 was set at the disposal of employers wishing to victimise Wobblies. At one railway workshop several Wobblies were summoned to see the boss who, with detectives beside him, showed them their IWW application forms and told them they were no longer wanted. By December 1916 *Direct Action* was commenting upon the number of Wobblies who were losing their jobs in both government and private industry.[30]

While the Twelve were detained and under trial, more police informers were strategically placed within the movement and mail surveillance intensified. Pearce took an unhealthy interest in the operation, reading many of the censors' reports and appending his own apoplectic comments. Customs officers were asked to send all imported IWW publications to the local censor and many of these were placed on the prohibited list. Though the case was sub-judice, the integrity of the accused was regularly impugned by politicians and the press. Norman Jeffery recalls the 'frenzied incitement and provocation' to which the IWW, particularly the Twelve, were subjected: 'Slanderous references to traitors, seditionists, fire bugs, in pay of the Germans, and saboteurs, etc., were bandied about and widely publicised.'[31]

The Western Australian Wobblies

Shortly before the first conscription referendum, Western Australian police, with the aid of military intelligence, started rounding up prominent Westralian Wobblies, whom they had been observing for some time. The police gave the impression they acted independently, but the decision to prosecute these Wobblies was made by the federal Labor government. The Military Commandant in Perth was advised by telegram from Commonwealth military authorities on 17 October that the police had been requested to take such action; and the prosecuting counsel were briefed with the approval of the federal government, which footed the bill.[32]

On 9 November eleven Wobblies were committed for trial on a charge of seditious conspiracy, in attempting 'to raise discontent and dissatisfaction amongst the subjects of our Lord the King, to promote feelings of ill-will and enmity between different [classes of the] subjects of our said Lord the King . . .'; participating in the class struggle was an indictable offence. The Crown case stated that the IWW was an organisation that advocated sedition, sabotage, and other 'lawless acts': Crown witnesses were therefore called to establish the link between the accused and the IWW. Witnesses for the prosecution, mainly plain-clothes police officers, gave evidence of IWW meetings they had attended which had advised workers to be as unproductive as possible.[33]

Clem Macintyre has argued that the IWW was seen as such a danger that mere membership implied guilt; the prosecutor had stated that 'membership of the organisation would form portion of the evidence against the accused – or even association without membership'. The magistrate found there was a prima facie case against eight of the men: Mick Sawtell, Monty Miller, Alexander Auwert, Alexander Horrocks, William Johnston, Frederick Hugh Lunn, John Goller and George Hanscombe. Along with a newly arrested Wobbly, Christopher Parkinson, they were committed for trial in the Criminal Court on the seditious conspiracy charge. The trial in December 1916 followed the same pattern as the committal proceedings. The same prosecutor, Pilkington KC, argued that, if the Crown established the fact that the accused men had actively participated in the dissemination of IWW doctrine, the charge against the men in the dock would be proved; membership of the IWW was in itself a crime, unless a person could prove he was ignorant of the objects of the organisation.[34]

Johnston declared he was a member of the IWW and proud of it: 'Had I used what little intelligence I possess in decrying the working class and calling them loafers, I would not be in the criminal dock.' Miller and Sawtell, who defended themselves in impassioned speeches, insisted that, as there were undoubted inequalities in the world, who could blame the IWW for seeking to redress the balance and it was only through class struggle that workers could improve their conditions; and IWW sabotage was not aimed at human life, whereas 'master class sabotage' was 'anti social and aims at the worker's life'. Miller's examination of Sawtell, seemingly impromptu, but in fact rehearsed between them in the prison cells, was a superb set-piece of elegance and erudition. His address to the jury lasted over three hours; even the *West Australian* conceded that he spoke 'with a wealth of gesture and a wonderful flow of language'.[35]

After three and a half hours the jury found all nine guilty, after Judge Burnside had opined that the IWW was out of place in Australia, as there was no class conflict. However, Burnside was surprisingly lenient in passing sentence. They were each sentenced to two years' imprisonment, suspended on entering into two recognisances of £25 for good behaviour during the term of the sentence. The *West Australian* objected to the mercy shown the defendants because the IWW was a dangerous organisation intent on destroying society.[36]

Only Sawtell received a prison sentence – for an additional charge laid against him, of threatening the property of Senator Lynch. Miller suffered the possibly crueller fate of having his old-age pension cut off. Aged 85 but badly in need of remuneration, Miller accepted an invitation from the Broken Hill Local to visit as an organising lecturer, on miners' pay of £4/4/- a week. After some months there, he visited Adelaide, then Melbourne, as lecturer and propaganda speaker for Local no.8. He reached Sydney in time to assist the agitation on behalf of the general strike, for which he was duly arrested and charged under the provisions of the Unlawful Associations Act. As he refused the magistrate's offer of clemency in return for a promise to 'withdraw altogether from this striking business', he was sentenced to six months hard labour.[37]

The Trial of the Twelve

After the first referendum, the charge against the Twelve was changed to seditious conspiracy, conspiracy to commit arson and conspiracy to secure the release of Barker by unlawful means. The original more spectacular charge of treason–felony had probably been a pre-referendum stunt; the less serious charges laid in November 1916 made conviction by a jury, and therefore punishment, more likely. The conspiracy charges, apart from being difficult to disprove, also allowed the Crown to cast its net very wide and with a greater certainty of a catch.[38]

The Twelve protested their innocence. Glynn maintained: 'I am no criminal, and no verdict of the jury, and no sentence that your Honour may impose . . . can make me a criminal.' Besant insisted the only conspiracy that had taken place was the one on the part of the police. This possibility was ignored by the trial, despite the admission by one policeman that he had seen Detective Robson place the 'fire dope', the spontaneously combustible material allegedly used to start the fires, in Fagin's bag.[39]

Without going into the details of the case, exhaustively related by Ian Turner in *Sydney's Burning*, suffice it to say that, in the words of Bill Beattie, it 'stank to high heaven'. Counsel for the Twelve provided evidence that: police promised £2000 to the informer Scully to procure sufficient evidence to secure a conviction; Detectives Pauling and Turbet asked other witnesses to place fire-dope in the pockets of the IWW men arrested; police supplied fire-dope for the purposes of making evidence; police put cotton waste into the pocket of Bill Teen; police prepared the statements of evidence given by Scully; Detective Leary suggested Scully should manufacture evidence against Grant; police arranged for Scully to be deported to prevent his divulging the circumstances of the case; and the whole case was in great part made up of fictitious evidence concocted with the knowledge of the police. (On 28 August 1921 Scully was kicked to death by police who were afraid he was about to squeal.) Grant wrote later that when he heard men swear that he was guilty of the most heinous conspiracy, 'and heard them the while knowing that they knew I was innocent', he realised he had not learnt all that life could teach him.[40]

By 1 December 1916 justice had taken its course. On the evidence only of police informers and witnesses who had turned King's evidence in order to avoid prosecution themselves, and corroborated only by the police whose evidence contained many inconsistencies, the jury, one of whom was an employer who had sacked Donald Grant a year earlier, found the Twelve guilty. Kevin Seggie's research concludes that informers, motivated by self-preservation, were 'vital in securing convictions against the I.W.W. Twelve'.[41]

Before sentence was passed, the Wobblies were allowed their say. Reeve declared: 'I have always had a great ideal to fight for – the complete freedom and happiness of all humanity. And that is not to be attained by any such foul work as arson . . . before God, I had nothing to do with it.' King declared: 'I am not the cause of class strife; I am a product of it . . .'; and Larkin commented: 'Have I anything to say against a Star Chamber? . . .' Justice Pring, generally regarded in labour circles as a 'hanging judge',[42] then informed the prisoners:

> You are members of an association which I do not hesitate to state, after the revelations in this case, is an association of criminals of the very worst type, and a hotbed of crime. I hope that now very strong and drastic steps will be taken to uproot that association . . .[43]

Glynn, Hamilton, McPherson, Teen, Beatty, Fagin and Grant were found guilty on all three counts and sentenced to fifteen years' imprisonment; Reeve, Larkin, Besant and Moore were found guilty of conspiracy to commit arson and seditious conspiracy and sentenced to ten years; and King was found guilty of seditious conspiracy alone and sentenced to five years. All sentences were with hard labour. In the words of Henry Boote, Grant received 'Fifteen Years For Fifteen Words', a reference to his Domain speech made much of by the prosecution: 'For every day Barker is in jail it will cost the capitalist ten thousand pounds.' When Grant's mother in Scotland heard of his sentence, she collapsed and never recovered.[44]

In March 1917 the government paid gratuities ranging from £12 to £50 each to the police officers involved in bringing the Wobblies to trial, 'for exceptional zeal and assiduity . . . in bringing to justice offenders charged with serious crime'. The attempt by Sydney businessmen to open a fund to show their gratitude to the police had not been necessary. Constable William McKay was promoted to Sergeant for his part in securing the convictions of the Twelve.[45]

The Unlawful Associations Act

In introducing this Bill in December 1916, Hughes referred unequivocally to its principal object, the IWW: 'I say deliberately that this organization holds a dagger at the heart of society, and we should be recreant to the social order if we did not accept the challenge it holds out to us. As it seeks to destroy us, we must in self defence destroy it.' In supporting the Bill, Joseph Cook for the Liberals deplored the way that: 'The doctrine of "go-slow," and the other vicious ideas of the Industrial Workers of the World, are creeping into the unions.' For the Opposition Labor Party, Senator Gardiner repudiated any connection with the IWW and claimed the Bill was part of 'the unscrupulous attempt made . . . by Mr Hughes and others to associate the party with the methods and the members of the I.W.W.'. National Labor Senator De Largie deplored the difficulty in keeping IWW members out of the trade unions, noting that a man who regularly advocated IWW doctrines in public was responsible for driving the Prime Minister out of the union he had practically built up. He was relieved that 'certain precautions may be taken to keep the Labour movement clean'.[46]

Under this Act, passed on 19 December, any member of the IWW who advocated any action calculated to hinder the war effort was to be imprisoned for six months with no provision for a lesser sentence. Still the forces of law and order did not desist. The relentless Detective Moore decided the Sydney Wobblies must be arming themselves and set out on an exhaustive tour of the local gunsmiths. Though failing to discover any increase in the sale of firearms, he was unwilling to abandon his theory, so put it on record that IWW purchases of firearms were probably being made from pawn-shops and second-hand dealers, which were too numerous to inspect. Nor did Major Steward relax his vigilance. He assumed, as did the Navy, that the sinking of the SS *Cumberland* off Gabo Island on 6 July 1917, caused by an explosion in the hold, was the result of IWW sabotage.[47]

When not interfering with allied shipping, the response of the IWW to the Unlawful Associations Act was to carry on business as usual. Hughes admitted within a few months that the IWW had not been effectively muzzled and sought to amend the Unlawful Associations Act so as to destroy the IWW once and for all. He based his arguments for this final solution on the self-encouraging comments that Wobblies wrote to each other and which were reported to Hughes by the censor. An exasperated Hughes explained to the House: 'This organisation is going on now, it is flourishing. It boasts openly that its organ has wide circulation and that money is coming in freely.' At a raid of the IWW hall on 22 July 1917, about thirty detectives and a large body of police interrupted a meeting attended by about 600 men and women, a number of whom had children in their arms, with an overflow meeting being held in the street outside. All were searched and 'everything appertaining to the I.W.W. organisation was seized'.[48]

Under the new Act, passed in July 1917, any association could be banned by proclamation of the Governor-General, which overcame the problem of having to pass new legislation if the IWW renamed itself. Moreover, membership of an unlawful association carried automatic liability to six months' imprisonment and the onus of proof of non-membership was on the defendant. Members were to be barred from any form of Commonwealth employment. No publications of unlawful associations could be transmitted through the post. Any property of such organisations could be seized by the authorities.[49]

The artful Wobblies attempted to circumvent the order that *Direct Action* no longer be allowed transmission through the post. Tom Barker recalls:

> on nights when the paper was ready, we had to seal and stamp every one separately, then the men would go out all over the place and put them through the post boxes. As a matter of fact, it's said that the paper was better delivered in the time when it was illegal than it was before, because people took a pride in getting it and a pride in posting it, and the postmen were largely on our side. A good deal of our stuff went to places like Goulburn by train or by boat to Western Australia, so it didn't come into the postal system. We just made them up into rail parcels to go that way . . . The paper kept alive.[50]

This bravado notwithstanding, the new draconian legislation seriously hampered the spread of IWW ideas, either verbally or in print. As Detective Moore reported with satisfaction, the amendment 'struck at the root of the whole organization, by preventing its propaganda work without which it cannot exist, and must sooner or later become extinct'.[51]

The Opposition Labor Party opposed neither the original Unlawful Associations Bill in December 1916 nor its strengthened version in July

1917. Frank Tudor, as leader, boasted during the May 1917 election campaign that his party had 'refused to be trapped' into opposing the original Bill, which was an 'electioneering dodge' to trap the Party into appearing to support the IWW. 'We gave them the Bill', he commented with satisfaction. In debating the amendments to the Act in 1917, Tudor flaunted his Party's concurrence with the repressive legislation as proof of its lack of connection with the IWW. All he asked was that 'bona fide trade unions' be free from being declared unlawful associations, for, as he acknowledged, there could be no appeal from any decision given under the Act. If his plea were granted by the Ministry, 'they can have the Bill with very little debate from this side'. Another Labor member, explaining his support for the legislation, 'so far as it purports to be an attempt to deal with the Industrial Workers of the World', averred: 'There is no need for any such institution to exist in Australia. Its members are strong opponents of the principle of arbitration . . . are opposed to constitutional action.' The Governor-General noted in his despatch to the Secretary of State for the Colonies that the Bill was passed at a sitting, the Opposition leaders having disclaimed any connection with the IWW.[52]

The Tiger Unleashed

After this new Bill was enacted on 27 July 1917 the IWW hall was raided for the last time, the most recent issue of *Direct Action* (18 August) confiscated, all present arrested and the hall sealed. Against the background of the general strike, a much more thorough round-up of Wobblies now took place. In the next few months, 103 were imprisoned, usually for terms of six months with hard labour, and many more were sacked from their jobs. On the one day, 1 September, thirty-five were captured in Broken Hill as sixty unmarried Wobblies mounted the stump in turn to declare their allegiance to the IWW. Of these thirty-five Broken Hill Wobblies, twenty-five were Australian-born. According to Shor, this tally suggests the recent immigrant members stayed out of jails while the IWW members with some history in Australia went to jail, implying 'a commitment to a ritual of manhood and mateship that helps define the virile syndicalism of the Australian IWW'.[53] A more likely explanation is that immigrant members who courted arrest faced deportation; in any case, ten of the thirty-five were immigrants and prepared to face this outcome.

The temper of the average Wobbly was ill-suited to the indignities of prison life: they could not help but stand up for themselves and the other prisoners. Of Mick Sawtell's term in Parramatta jail, Betsy Matthias wrote to Kathleen Hotson in January 1918: 'He is very rebellious and having a very difficult time . . . has already incurred the displeasure of

the Controller of Prisons.' Ted Moyle from Adelaide, transferred to
Long Bay jail, recalls: 'The discipline of the gaol was severe, the warders,
on occasions, acting like brutes, but we prisoners were a bit of a conun-
drum.' He tells how he and the other Wobblies under threat of deportation, including Barker, prevented the solitary confinement of fellow
Wobbly Frank Ward by refusing to come out of their cells until he was
reprieved.[54]

    They were all made to suffer. According to John Randolph's sister, he
'Looked thin, worn and 10 years older than a year ago . . . He sleeps on
a concrete floor – no mattress – food very bad . . .' A labourer, who
served a sentence in company with nine of the Twelve, wrote a pamphlet
in which he refuted the belief of many workers that the Twelve received
special consideration as political prisoners. He alleged that the Twelve
were actually treated worse than ordinary prisoners, being 'specially singled out amid the horrible conditions . . . for still worse treatment'.[55]
Donald Grant's *Through Six Gaols* gives a detailed account of his suffering
at the hands of vindictive prison authorities. A letter from Reeve to his
mother explained how he kept up his spirits:

> I have sung our songs softly to myself, a million times, they give me courage;
> one must not make any noise here, so I have too softly, oh so softly hum
> over, the old old songs, I often think of Joe Hill, & the others, & my heart
> goes out to them, I . . . try to penetrate the walls & send hope, love & cour-
> age to the dauntless ones, Brave Men & Women, fighting for a Splendid
> Ideal.[56]

Twelve foreign-born Wobblies were deported; at the same time,
United States authorities were shipping some of their convicted
Wobblies to Australia. Those removed from Australia were not necessarily despatched to their country of origin but to anywhere convenient
without immigration restrictions. Eight, including Barker, ended up in
Chile. Alex Rosenthal described the ordeal: 'We were forcibly taken
aboard and in spite of threats we consistently refused during the whole
voyage to sign ships articles and so acquiesce in our deportation . . . We
were dumped in Valparaiso, Chile, against our will.' Jock and May Wilson
were subjected to a terrifying two and a half month trip by sea to
Liverpool, via Panama, narrowly avoiding German submarines.[57]

    There was no trial or appeal against deportation. For instance, from
Melbourne, 'Whiskers' Hill was shanghaied aboard a ship at midnight;
no one would even have known about it except a baker who attended
Yarra Bank meetings was delivering bread to the ship and saw him
brought on board. Paul Freeman, regarded by the authorities as the
leader of the IWW in the Dobbyn area of north-west Queensland, was
roused from sleep in his lonely prospector's tent by police, escorted to

Donald Grant, who received 'Fifteen Years for Fifteen Words'. (Donald Grant, *Through Six Gaols*)

Townsville, conveyed to Brisbane, and on to a ship bound for the United States, which refused to receive him, condemning him for a while to a life as a human shuttlecock, struck back and forth across the Pacific by

Australian and US authorities. He had not been charged with any offence and had received no semblance of a trial. Almost certainly, his removal was at the behest of an associate of Hughes, W.H. Corbould, the Australian general manager of the London-based Mt Elliott Mining Co., who blamed Freeman for helping the spread of direct action tactics amongst his employees.[58]

Like the criminal syndicalism legislation in the United States, the Unlawful Associations Act in both its versions did not simply cover the actual commission of acts of violence against life, property and government, and conspiracy thereto, but made criminal the advocacy of *doctrines* of arguably violent change to the existing economic and political order. The ideas of the IWW were on trial; it was judged, not for what its members had done but for what the IWW had said or written. Thus, the conservative opposition turned economic and social problems into an IWW problem; the attack on the IWW centred on its philosophies and ignored the social and economic injustices which prompted the IWW's existence. As Donald Grant declared from the dock: 'You are putting us in jail to prove there is no class war. But there is, and it is not of our making.'[59]

Despite expressions of bravado on the part of the Wobblies, confident statements that the Law of Evolution was on their side, that repression would beget retaliation, that persecution would breed solidarity and ultimate triumph, and despite the fact that the jailings and repression increased the number of sympathisers with the IWW,[60] the prognosis of the state proved essentially correct: the IWW could not in itself survive concerted suppression. Though local units reacted differently, all went under.

Melbourne Wobblies responded in a way that protected them, as individuals, from punishment, but only by ceasing to be Wobblies. They decided, three days before the Act became law on 27 August 1917, to disband the Local, and the authorities were duly notified that the IWW in Melbourne no longer existed. They disposed of the furniture and gave the money to the fund for the wives and children of the Twelve, and used packing cases as seats for the remaining few days. The day before the law came into force, Alf Wilson assured listeners on the Yarra Bank:

> I suppose you think that this is our last appearance on Yarra Bank, but we will be here the same as ever. We stand for the One Big Union, and neither Hughes nor any other Prime Minister will prevent us. I for one will be on Yarra Bank next Sunday even if I have to wear a frock coat and carry a bible in my pocket . . . I shall find scripture warrant for what I desire to say.

The Melbourne Wobblies then departed for their gloomily furnished hall, for the last meeting as the IWW. In 1969 Bill Genery recalled the disbanding of the Melbourne Local: 'That was the end of us. We never met anymore.' Hughes, he added, was 'a clever bastard'.[61]

On the following Wednesday, Wilson spoke at a demonstration of striking unionists at the Yarra Bank. The police, considering that he was representing the IWW, arrested him and charged him under the Act; they informed him that the prosecution was ordered from the Prime Minister's Department. As he was able to prove he was not a member of an illegal organisation, the case was dismissed. Wilson boasted in his memoirs: 'Sunday by Sunday I went down and talked about Socialism and Industrial Unionism.'[62] But he did not talk about being a member of the IWW. Melbourne Wobblies had chosen to deny the very basis of IWW existence: openness.

A special meeting of the Broken Hill Local on 28 July 1917 resolved 31 to 24 'to fight the Authorities to the last ditch and that all single members . . . volunteer their services to defend our principles as soon as the Authorities Attack and retaliate by Filling the Gaols . . .'. In an additional gesture of defiance it decided to post the names of members on the windows of the IWW hall 'as a Challenge'. For as long as any Broken Hill Wobblies remained at liberty, the Local there continued to hold meetings at the corner of Argent and Chloride Streets, even after the mass arrest of 1 September and the subsequent raid of the Local's rooms, in which all its property was removed. In Adelaide, amidst raids on members' homes, the IWW continued until early September to hold open-air meetings in Victoria Square at which speakers openly professed membership of the IWW and made no secret of the location of IWW headquarters at a little shop in Pitt Street, the front of which was covered with IWW placards.[63]

The Sydney Local also chose to stand on principle and suffered accordingly. Two days before the Unlawful Associations Act first became law, Detective Sergeant McKay visited the Sydney IWW and pleaded with them formally to disband, so no charge could be laid against them. They told him it was impossible, they intended to stick to the IWW to the end, that 'it was against all principle to disown the I.W.W.'[64] On the night of Sunday 2 September, about 400 men and women marched through the city, singing Wobbly songs. Halting outside the old Sussex Street hall, they were addressed by two men from the top of the building after they had given cheers for those in jail. A few days later, about 1500 Wobblies and their sympathisers rallied and sang songs in opposition to a recruiting meeting in Bathurst Street. About 100 police surrounded the crowd: 'Every time an I.W.W. member was seen he was arrested.'[65] Ultimately, the Sydney Wobblies were frightened out of business as surely as the Melbourne Wobblies liquidated themselves. A letter from a long-standing Sydney Wobbly in September 1918 bemoaned the dearth of speakers and commented: 'An awful lot of my fellow workers of the late

I.W.W. seem to of got scared to death and now do not function but meet in back lanes . . .'[66] It seems that Wobbly audacity could work up to a certain level, by attracting support and sympathy, but beyond that level – especially in extreme circumstances such as the war – audacity then became self-destructive.

The Sydney and Broken Hill tactic of clogging the jails 'didn't have any appeal' to the Brisbane Local because, according to Dick Surplus, an unusually large number of the members were married; its timid, or sensible, response was to change its name immediately to the One Big Union Propaganda League. The Brisbane Local, according to Ray Evans, had always been the weakest, ideologically and numerically, and this faint-heartedness distinguished them from their more impetuous counterparts in Sydney and Broken Hill.[67]

In the West, according to Naomi Segal, the 1916 trial 'ended the active challenge which the I.W.W. in Western Australia sought to present to State and capital'. In subsequent mopping-up operations the Westralian Wobblies, who adopted the defiant attitude of the New South Wales Locals, were arrested under the Unlawful Associations Act and for offences such as 'interrupting Senator De Largie and pelting him with small apricots'. Late in October 1917 the police raided simultaneously IWW premises on the goldfields and in Perth, informing the press that the result of these raids could not be disclosed but was 'important'.[68] Norman Jeffery's teenage sister was intimidated by detectives who called on her seventeenth birthday and removed copies of *Direct Action*, pamphlets and photos of Monty Miller; Mrs Jeffery informed Norman that Dorothy was still unemployed, victimised at every turn.[69] After another stint in jail, Monty Miller became the object of special restrictions early in 1918, denied the right of speech in the open or in any hall; he was dependent on speaker's fees for his livelihood. After Mick Sawtell returned to the West after six months imprisonment in Parramatta jail under the Act in 1917, followed by another lengthy sentence for a riot offence in Broken Hill, the Employers' Federation debarred him on the wharf. By March 1919 he was desperate for work and felt there was no chance of getting any, owing to 'a systematic boycott'. He had secured work at the State Mills, which lasted only four days before 'word came to sack him'.[70]

It was in Queensland that the IWW continued longest to function. Ray Evans has shown that IWW activity in Queensland up to 1919 upsets the unstated assumption in the writings of Childe, Turner, Rushton and others that, with the parent body suppressed in New South Wales, other Locals withered away. Even in Brisbane, where the IWW had been least dynamic, 'a pattern of radical survival rather than resignation may be traced'. Certainly, as we have seen in chapter 11, there is considerable evidence of continuing activity in workplaces throughout Queensland, especially in the north. Partly, these eruptions were the achievement of southern Wobblies seeking sanctuary north of the border. Military intelligence noted the 'big influx of Southern I.W.W. into Queensland' for the cane harvesting in the second half of 1918, and many sugar centres subsequently became nurseries for IWW propaganda. Another censor, rejoicing that the 'scientific slave' was now missing from Sydney, regretted this was not so in the Townsville meatworks, 'where the arts of I.W.W.ism have reached their maximum of development'.[71]

The Commonwealth authorities held that the Labor government of T.J. Ryan, representing the left rather than the right of the Party, was to blame for offering Wobblies a relatively safe haven by the standards of the rest of the country. A Queensland Labor propagandist of the time accused the Wobblies of being 'cowards who rush to Queensland to get under the wings of a Labor government . . .' It was not that the Queensland government did not deal with Wobblies with the customary severity when they were actually engaged in fomenting industrial strife; yet it is true that the Ryan government chose not to incarcerate Wobblies merely for publicising their ideas. In this it differed markedly from the ex-Labor governments of Hughes in the Commonwealth and Holman in New South Wales. Indeed, to a large extent its apparent indulgence of the IWW was occasioned not by any love for Wobblies, whose doctrines it regarded as 'malignant and poisonous', but by hatred of the Labor rats, epitomised in Hughes and Holman, who had split the Party in 1917.[72]

Hughes had attempted unsuccessfully to alarm the Queensland government into suppressing the IWW. He wrote to Ryan in September 1917: 'I have information I.W.W. fomenting serious industrial trouble with shearers at Winton and Hughenden and also with miners at Mt.Cuthbert and elsewhere.' Ryan responded by telegram that his police had reported there was nothing to justify alarm or uneasiness. Undeterred, Hughes wrote again to Ryan that members of the IWW were 'flocking to Queensland' because it was the only State in which police were not enforcing the Unlawful Associations Act. These men, he warned Ryan, were 'openly spreading the dangerous propaganda of the Association to the great danger of industrial peace and in defiance of the Act. I earnestly urge that instruction be given for strict enforcement of Act.'[73] The Commonwealth Attorney-General reiterated these warnings, alerting the Queensland government to IWW activity: the sale of their literature in the Trades Hall; their activities in Townsville, Cloncurry, Cairns, Innisfail and other northern towns where handbills and stickers 'freely circulated'; and the activity of Brown and Jackson and other well-known IWWs. 'It is most emphatically the time', he considered, 'for vigorous administration of the law to prevent Queensland being refuge and rallying around for this destructive organisation.' The Counter Espionage Bureau, renamed the Special Intelligence Bureau in January 1917, devoted additional attention to Queensland during 1918.[74]

Regarding the IWW menace in Queensland, it was 'utterly impossible', the Commonwealth military authorities complained in September 1918, to depend on the Queensland police for any assistance in prosecuting offenders because they generally replied that they had no instructions to take action or that the matter was not worth bothering about.[75] As late as October 1918, one censor reported of the Queensland scene:

> IWWism would hardly survive a hard knock such as a stiff sentence of impris-
> onment on ten or twenty of them. They are curs – at present they are making
> a bold showing. Imprisonment of the ring leaders would scare the seasoned
> rascals as well as the young man just out of his teens. The latter class has to be
> reached, and the effective way is to compel men to respect the law by instilling
> fear into them. This will not come from Queensland authorities – it is looked
> for from Federal administration . . .[76]

Indeed, distrust of the Ryan government ran deep amongst the Commonwealth intelligence services. A 'Summary of Ryan's Disloyal Associations', which detailed his occasional connections with IWW members, was compiled as a secret Defence Department document late in 1918. Early in January 1919 the censor made a report on Deputy-Premier Theodore's alleged 'inactivity in dealing with the I.W.W.'.[77]

The remaining IWW activists in Queensland were nonetheless hemmed in with restrictions enforced by local officials and zealous citizens. According to Evans, the police circumscribed the IWW's public meetings in several centres. And loyalists performed the duties police could not. Archie Eastcrabb in Hughenden informed the QRU Secretary in Brisbane that he was attacked by a dozen returned soldiers in the main street of the town, 'knocked down, kicked about the head and body', and that several men had suffered similar treatment. Early in 1919 the censor noted of an IWW public meeting at the North Quay in Brisbane that soldiers rudely interrupted, threw the platform into the river and chased the IWW with the intention of sending them after the structure.[78]

Moreover, without its strong Sydney headquarters, without the production of *Direct Action*, the Wobblies in Queensland could not continue as effectively as in the past. Mick Sawtell wrote to the Chicago-based *One Big Union Monthly* in June 1920 that, officially, the IWW no longer existed in Australia. The frame-up against the IWW was 'cunningly and well stage-managed'; the jailing of the Twelve and declaring the organisation illegal was 'a great set-back for us'. Fred Coombe maintains the frame-up 'wrecked them absolutely'; he considered, too, that the 'hysterical conservative reaction' against the IWW was much greater than any subsequent response to the Communist Party. Donald Grant wrote that 'the evidence which was used to gain my conviction proved to me that those who desired my imprisonment and obtained the verdict they wanted were prepared to do anything to gain their ends'.[79]

What was it about the IWW that, by comparison with other radical contenders in the field, caused it to be singled out for special attention by the authorities? Part of the answer is that the IWW, as Hughes pointed out, held a dagger at the heart of society; it was considerably more threatening to the capitalist order than the socialist parties who busied themselves theorising about the nature of the exploitation the Wobblies were actually contesting.

The Wobblies themselves believed they were suppressed because of the direct challenge they laid down to capitalism. Dick Surplus maintained the IWW was eliminated because it was 'a danger to the employers'. Tom Barker insisted that 'many times the governments, both the Federal government and the government of New South Wales, were really very worried about whether we might not have sufficient power to turn them out or to break them up and even, in a sense, to become masters in our turn'.[80] A Wobbly writing to American fellow workers at the time argued the 'iron heel' was with the IWW, because the Australian boss was worried 'and he has ample reasons for his worry':

> Politics and arbitration, trade unions and wage boards are back numbers, outgrown, useless and worse. A new spirit is abroad and growing. The philosophy of the One Big Union grows everywhere.
> The workers of Australia are also slowing down. Very much so . . . Shortening of the hours, and reduction of the output are weapons that speak more loudly of increasing working class power than all the elections and ballots have done in twenty years.[81]

Mat Hade wrote of the hysterical press and arbitration court commentaries about the spreading of the go-slow disease:

> From this it can be seen that the I.W.W. was becoming formidable in the eyes of the capitalist class . . . Consequently as the I.W.W. was becoming a menace to the capitalists it had to be put out of action. Prosecutions were tried over and over again . . . But still the organisation steadily grew . . . It was not till the great conscription conspiracy was hatched that it occurred to the conspirators, in their desperate efforts to enslave the Australian people, that it might help their nefarious purpose to represent the I.W.W. as a sort of Black Hand Gang, and connect it up with the Labor Movement . . . From that moment the men who are in gaol HAD NO CHANCE.[82]

In this analysis, it was the industrial practices of the IWW, its encouragement of permanent militancy at the point of production, and the rate at which its tactics appeared to be spreading amongst workers generally, that prompted the violent retaliation of the state; and, in propounding all along that it was action not words, agitation not theory, which mattered, the IWW proved itself correct by its own annihilation.

The Wobbly version of events is exaggerated but contains a kernel of truth. Employers were inclined to agree with the *Argus* that, whatever the strength or otherwise of the IWW, 'the best thing to do with sedition-mongers is to put them in gaol, for it does rid society of their presence'.[83] The right-wing Labor governments of Hughes and Holman were happy to demonstrate to employer interests whose side they were on by a firm response to these sedition-mongers. In New South Wales and the Commonwealth, the state in various aspects – the executive, the legislature, the police and the judiciary – worked harmoniously with employers and the press to frustrate the long-term plans of the IWW to organise the workers of Australia into One Big Union.

The Wobblies were outmatched in their capacity for overstatement by these governments. Most Wobbly 'crimes', political or otherwise, were the products of a fevered official imagination that sought to convince itself and the public of the need for suppression. For the classical freedoms of liberal democracy – of person, of expression, of association and assembly – made necessary a certain degree of public outrage about Wobbly intentions. Perhaps McCarthyism and its prototypes are the appropriate inventions of liberal democratic state forms, which can thus be seen to be responding to popular demands for action more typical of authoritarian styles of government. So that the IWW's potential power could never be realised, the authorities chose to exaggerate its actual power. This is not to belittle the achievements of the IWW. Indeed, the rate at which its ideas were spreading amongst workers partly explains the state backlash, but the IWW was not then, as its own accounts suggest, in any position to bring about a revolutionary change in Australian society.

The dagger held by the IWW was pointed far more clearly at the fragile construction of the organised labour movement, always a site of struggle between left and right, than at the capitalist order, disturbed though employers undoubtedly were by the Wobbly menace. The IWW was persuading many unionists that revolutionary industrial unionism offered workers a better prospect than the increasingly discredited tactics of Labor parliamentarians and trade union bureaucrats. Some contemporaries observed of Hughes: 'He had felt the I.W.W. influence creeping into his party . . . He was enraged at it.'[84] In October 1916 Holman regretted that:

> For the last five years, there has been a continuous process of infiltration or peaceful penetration into influential positions in the world of unionism on the part of I.W.W. men. The members of that organisation have succeeded in gaining a good many important posts in the Labour world, and they have had a controlling effect quite out of proportion to their numbers on the guidance of union policy . . . I know that to many decent members of my own party the

measure of alliance with the I.W.W. which our movement has reached has
come as something of a shock. We knew that we were working with the union
movement, but few of us realised how largely that movement had fallen under
I.W.W. control.[85]

It was this process that the Hughes and Holman governments wished to
prevent – the formation of revolutionary industrial unions that would
seize control of the labour movement, if not of the means of production.
After November 1916 the battle for hearts and minds within the labour
movement expressed itself in even more savage form in the split between
National Labor and Opposition Labor.

Although its anti-war stance was a major irritant in itself, the IWW was
not suppressed because it hindered the war effort. Rather, the fact that
it hindered the war effort was used by officialdom as one of the reasons
for its suppression and as a hoped-for means of discrediting the IWW in
the eyes of those sections of the working class that were still patriotic. As
we have seen in chapter 12, the Hughes and Holman Labor governments utilised the paraphernalia of patriotism, casting the IWW as an
enemy agent, to contest the radical economic and social ideas espoused
by the IWW that were becoming increasingly influential within the
labour movement. The IWW was persecuted not because it opposed the
war, nor because it constituted a serious threat to the established order,
but because it provided a focal point of opposition within the labour
movement, and an expanding one, to the right-wing of that movement,
seriously challenging the personal power bases of Hughes and Holman
in particular.

The comparative ease with which governments suppressed the IWW
can be explained by the fact that the IWW was what it was: it could only
respond incompetently to suppression, since its practice was singularly
ill-suited for guaranteeing its own organisational survival. It was a rank-
and-file bottom-up movement, hostile to bureaucratic and hierarchical
organisational forms, and aggressively democratic. Central to its philosophy and practice were open defiance and public forms of agitation.
Operating first and foremost in the semi-public arena of the workplace,
its One Big Unionising activities were necessarily exposed. Though sabotage may have been practised individually and quietly, the doctrine of
sabotage and its justifications were brazenly stated. To have survived, to
have retreated into secretive, underground activity, the Wobblies would
have to have ceased being Wobblies; furtive manoeuvre was simply not
their political style.

They had no plans, even of the most rudimentary kind, for survival in
the event of suppression. As Tom Barker noted: 'We didn't go into hid-
ing. I don't think we ever thought much about what we should do if we
were declared illegal. We expected it to come and we just waited until it

did come and then carried on despite it.'[86] Except in the circumspect
Melbourne Local that abolished itself and the cautious Brisbane Local
that kept quiet, the Wobblies continued in open forms of agitation and
propaganda. Even when the penalty for membership was six months'
jail, they continued to declare their membership openly in the streets.
For an overnight stay in the cells, such a gesture of defiance was good
publicity; in the new circumstances, it was organisational suicide.

Tom Glynn, during his very brief spell in the Communist Party,
deemed this 'ultra-revolutionary spirit' to be 'misplaced bravado'.
Turner notes that the movement which had declared politics impotent
and the state a fraud was crushed by politics and the state, and that their
sacrifice underlined a central weakness of their theory and organisation:
they had set themselves to defy the law and the state, but they had made
no effective preparation for illegal organisation when the state moved
against them. Other Communist writers argued that, when confronted
with the organised political power of the ruling class, the anarcho-syndicalism represented by the IWW 'revealed its futility', that its rejection of
all political action, both reformist and revolutionary, was 'incorrect' and
'self-defeating'.[87]

Yet the characteristics that rendered its suppression possible were those
that were fundamental to its contemporary appeal and its continuing
value and significance. Twenty-three years after the Wobblies were suppressed, another revolutionary organisation was declared illegal for its
opposition to Australian participation in a second world war. By operating underground, the Communist Party survived the period of illegality to
re-emerge and achieve unprecedented support; and it abandoned its
opposition to war after the Soviet Union entered the conflict and prospered because of the success of the Red Army. It is impossible to imagine
the Wobblies staging such a come-back. Like the ideal-type Communists
of Marx's imagination, and unlike the Leninists of later years, the IWW
disdained to conceal its views and aims. Norman Rancie recalls:

> We used to boast that we had nothing to hide and our hall, office, and all our
> meetings were open for any one to attend . . . We believed that the best way to
> achieve our ends for a better, and brighter world for the working class was by
> working legally and in the open . . . Never at any time was the I.W.W. a secret
> society . . . [we never] held a secret meeting.

By its very nature, the IWW was not and could not become a Bolshevik-
type organisation, centralised and disciplined; it lacked, therefore, its
defence mechanisms, its ability to preserve itself in the face of state persecution. But, in being what it was, there was never any danger that the
IWW would inflict upon Australian society the sort of tyranny with which
the Stalinised Bolsheviks eventually replaced Czarism.

CHAPTER 14

'Set the Twelve Men Free':
the Release Campaign

In less than a week after the Twelve were convicted stickers demanding their release, many of which advocated 'Go Slow' and 'Sabotage', were pasted all over Sydney to the annoyance of Hughes, who expressed his irritation in a letter to Holman on 15 December 1916.[1] Organisations in the major centres known variously as the Labor Agitators Defence and Release Committee or the Workers' Defence and Release Committee raised funds for an appeal and pledged themselves to stir up 'an agitation for their release'.[2] These committees stressed the extent to which prejudice and hysteria had denied the Twelve a fair trial. The Defence and Release Committee in Sydney issued *A Challenge to the People who Malign the Industrial Workers of the World*, which pointed out that the IWW's opponents did not besmirch other organised bodies in the same way: 'They don't announce "Member of the Millions Club Arrested for Wife Beating"; or "Liberal Pickpocket Caught Red-Handed"; or "Methodist Communicant Convicted of Murder"; or "Conscriptionist Gets Five Years for Larceny".' In fifteen weeks, from early December 1916, the committees raised over £1000, distributed 160 000 leaflets and 10 000 pamphlets and organised hundreds of meetings. Over the next few years, these committees and other organisations continued to collect funds to support the Glynn, Larkin and Teen families, who received £2 per week each; and held public meetings and sold huge quantities of release campaign literature, not only in the major capital cities but in smaller towns throughout the continent.[3]

Military intelligence expressed its irritation at the extent of the movement. That Commonwealth authorities felt uneasy was indicated around July 1917 when James Larkin was refused entry to Australia; it was feared that his visit was designed to aggravate the agitation on behalf of his brother and fellow prisoners. Delia Larkin, their sister, organised a large

Direct Action's sombre comment on the imprisonment of the Twelve.
(*Direct Action*, 20 January 1917)

gathering in Dublin, to hear Jock Wilson speak on the fate of the Twelve. Tom Barker, from London, was especially active in organising expressions of international concern. The New South Wales Nationalist government received wires from the Norwegian and British Labour Parties urging the release of the Twelve, and hundreds of letters from trade union, Labour branches and socialist groups in Britain, including one from the National Union of Police and Prison Officers.[4]

The appeal was heard in March 1917. Apart from quashing the convictions of Glynn and McPherson on the charge of conspiring to secure the release of Barker by unlawful means, it confirmed their other convictions and all those of the others. *Direct Action* commented: 'APPEAL FAILS. JUDGES REFUSE TO SCAB. MEN SENT BACK TO DURANCE VILE.' The Twelve were unanimously of the opinion that further action through the courts was useless; they preferred 'to leave their destiny in the hands of the class to which they belong'.[5] In the main, this class responded: not the boneheads derided by the IWW but the organised labour movement came to play a crucial role in the campaign to secure justice for the Twelve.

The movement spread outward from the Wobblies themselves to embrace all manner of labour organisations: trade unions; labour and trades hall councils and regional industrial councils; left-wing parties such as the VSP, the SLP and the Social Democratic League; and even sections of the Labor Party. The labour press published all relevant disclosures bearing on the case, pages on pages outlining the perfidy of the detectives and the Crown witnesses, the arguments of defence counsel at the various Commissions. Unions the length and breadth of the country passed indignant motions at the jailing of the Twelve and collected money in aid of the defendants and their dependants.[6] These labour organisations believed that, in the words of the Newcastle Industrial Council, the Twelve were the 'victims of one of the foulest conspiracies and frames-up known in history'. As Fred Coombe recalls of the mood, 'anybody with any working-class understanding realised it was a frame-up'.[7]

Although some union officials and Labor activists responded unfavourably,[8] most lent a hand: the moderate sections of the movement demanded a new and fairer trial; the more militant, left-wing section insisted upon unconditional release of the Twelve. Mick Sawtell explained in a letter to Chicago in 1920: 'The old conservative labor politicians are standing for a new and "fair" trial, but the new aspirants in the big industrial centers, sensing the workers' discontent, are advocating an unconditional release.' These divisions were contained within the Defence and Release Committees, as the ambivalent name implied.[9] Although these committees were a shelter for former Wobblies, they also comprised many concerned citizens, mainly labour movement activists, who were not and never had been Wobblies. In addition, labour bodies conducted their own independent agitation on behalf of the Twelve.[10] Why did so many of those who had been abused by the IWW as 'fakirs' spring to its defence in its hour of greatest need? Different sections of the labour movement had different motives in espousing the IWW cause in the manner appropriate to them.

The right of the campaign, represented in the main by Labor politicians and the Labor Party machines, was determined to dissociate Labor from the IWW, deploring the fact that conservative forces and the capitalist press had attempted to discredit Labor by accusing it of supporting the IWW. The central executive of the New South Wales Labor Party, in calling for a new and fairer trial, stressed its abhorrence of IWW aims and methods: 'The fact that Labor demands a fair trial for the I.W.W. men does not mean that it supports the propaganda and methods of this body, which is anti-A.L.P.'[11]

Why not, then, go along with Nationalists' hue and cry against the IWW? The Labor Party was constrained here by greater considerations than its hatred of the IWW. Hughes and Holman, the rats who had split the Party over the conscription issue and turned Labor out of office, had effected their dire deeds against Labor by misrepresentations of the IWW extreme even by the standards of the right-wing remaining within the Party, seeking to substantiate these wild allegations by a frame-up and a trial that defied the usual rules of the British legal system, and by alleging that the anti-conscription majority of the Party were hand in glove with these dastardly criminals. The Victorian PLC and Trades Hall combined circular to unions and Labor Party branches appealing for funds for a retrial stated: 'the I.W.W. is in no way officially connected with the Labour movement but as men they have not been fairly treated, their case being hopelessly prejudiced and a fair trial made impossible by the wild utterances of men who have proved recreant to the Labour movement . . .' Henry Boote, editor of the AWU's paper, the *Worker*, insisted that 'the real object of the Prosecution was not to get these men in jail, but through them to DEFAME AND DAMAGE THE LABOR MOVEMENT, and secure in office a pack of political crooks utterly devoid of scruples or any sense of public honor'.[12]

If the IWW could be exonerated, if the trial could be shown to be a frame-up, the Nationalists' political credibility would be shaken, which would not only restore the Labor Party's electoral fortunes but vindicate the stance of those remaining within the Party against those who had deserted it. In these circumstances, it made sense for the moderates to close ranks in defence of the IWW, to espouse the minimum position of the demand for a retrial or inquiry. Labor Opposition Leader John Storey called in July 1918 for a 'fair and impartial investigation into all the circumstances surrounding the trial and conviction of the twelve I.W.W. imprisoned men'. The Wobblies were somewhat bemused by their accomplices, one observing: 'there are several of those despicable limelighters who condemned those men twelve months ago just as severely as did the capitalist – have now for some reason proclaimed the men martyrs, heroes, etc . . .'[13]

Moreover, in making the limited demand for a new trial or inquiry, the moderates sought to appease the growing agitation for an unconditional release of the men, waged by those more militant, in concert with Wobbly remainders. One PLL organiser reported early in 1918 that there was 'a growing feeling that the present Labor Party is too weak and "not working class in truth" since they are dumb towards the fate of the twelve men . . .' The PLL was thus forced to declare its attitude. Mick Sawtell believed that: 'The Labor party would do nothing for the twelve unless the workers in the industries pushed the issue.'[14]

This section of the movement in New South Wales, forced into the minimum position by the clamour for the maximum position of unconditional release, attempted to turn the IWW issue into political capital for themselves by arguing that the best hope for the Twelve lay in the return of a Labor government in New South Wales, pledged to give the IWW men a new and fair trial. It insisted that those who demanded an unconditional release, 'the methods of Percy Brookfield and other disruptionists', were jeopardising Labor's chances, and hence those of the Twelve, since electors might interpret this as signifying that Labor was opposed to law, order and justice; any well-supported IWW agitation, which gave the Nationalists the opportunity to spread misrepresentation, would hinder the prospects of Labor being placed in power. 'The one hope of an impartial inquiry into the trial depends on the return of a Labor Government to power.'[15]

A new trial would also prove that the system was not as corrupt as the IWW claimed it to be, that where injustices occurred they could be redressed. The mainstream of the labour movement was attempting to justify its own commitment to the system, its belief that reform was possible, that revolution was unnecessary, that Laborism was right and the IWW wrong. This moderate position, epitomised in the writings of Henry Boote, was genuinely committed to the principles of toleration and justice for all.

Boote was 'entirely opposed to the doctrines of the I.W.W.', but he had 'formed the opinion, after an extensive analysis of the evidence, that the men had not had a fair trial, that some of them at least were innocent, and that a great injustice had been done'. Boote's articles in the *Worker* and his three pamphlets – *The Case of Grant, Fifteen Years for Fifteen Words; Guilty or Not Guilty?* and *Set the 12 Men Free* – exposed the inconsistencies, contradictions and absurdities in the Crown case, and the way the accused were convicted solely on the evidence of 'men either in the power or the pay of the police', men who were 'shameless liars and slanderers'. There was 'an intimate relation between Grant's career as an agitator against Capitalism and the fact that he has now been put where he can agitate no more'.[16] The labour movement had accordingly to respond:

> As members of a Movement that is founded on JUSTICE, that has no meaning unless it DEMANDS justice for every man who wrongfully suffers, it is our bounden duty to do what in us lies, either to have the guilt of the twelve men demonstrated, and wash our hands of them, or – as I believe, from my study of the depositions, we can – prove their innocence of the foul crimes charged against them, release them from the grave that is called prison, and restore them to the living world and those they love, and to that liberty which is the most cherished of all the possessions of mankind.[17]

He hoped for such an agitation 'as will force the Government to the tardy acknowledgment of a great judicial crime . . . Every day they are kept in jail is a day of reproach for us'.[18]

The equivalent to the liberal outrage manifested in the United States at the treatment of the IWW was here conducted by the labour movement, anxious as it was that society should live up to its own ideals. One of the petitions circulating announced that the undersigned believed that the Twelve 'were not given a fair trial, within the true meaning of British Justice'. As 'Citizens of Australia', they asked the Governor-General to reopen the case of the twelve men 'and give us British fair play . . . When we get fair play, Britain will then indeed be a Democracy – and never until then'. The Sydney Defence and Release Committee implored 'the liberty loving people of Australia to give their hearty support to the movement'. In Brisbane, the committee declared of the Twelve: 'They are the Victims of a Gigantic Conspiracy, which aims at the Subjugation of Working-class Liberties and the Establishing of the Iron Heel.'[19]

The left of the campaign demanded the unconditional release of the Twelve. Harry Kelly, secretary of the IWW Sympathisers Committee in Broken Hill, explained:

> This committee is not in favor of a new trial or any Commission being appointed to inquire into the conviction of the twelve men, as any new trial will only be another frame-up . . . We cannot get justice from a Government that already has proved corrupt, and we therefore demand the release of the twelve men.[20]

Rather than entrust the Twelve once more to the courts, many unions and labour bodies preferred to stand in judgement on the matter themselves. For example, the annual delegates meeting of the Queensland branch of the AWU resolved on 10 January 1917 that the meeting 'emphatically protests against the grossly unfair trial and savage sentences accorded to the twelve I.W.W. members recently sentenced . . . and demands their immediate release from jail . . .'[21]

In April 1917 the Coledale miners at Broken Hill demanded the immediate release of the Twelve and appealed to all unions for a general stoppage if they were not released. Accordingly, on 20 August 1917 the Broken Hill miners came out on strike. On 13 December 1917, their patience exhausted, miners raided the mines, gaining possession of some of them and putting them out of action. Ted Moyle records that the raid, 'the outcome of the Coledale miners resolution in respect to the twelve I.W.W. prisoners', was 'a very vicious affair' and South Australian police reinforced the local police during the ensuing 'street fighting'. Seventeen men were charged, including Mick Sawtell.[22]

The Barrier AMA published a pamphlet by George Kerr, *Solidarity Sentenced; the Conscription Aftermath: Labour Agitators get 150 Years*, which declared:

> If the advocates of One Big Union for the working-class are to be cast into the dungeons for their propaganda, how long will it be before all unionism is crushed in the dust under the iron heel of capitalism? For it is only a matter of degree after all . . . the men who advocate the greater unity represent the greater menace. But those who advocate a unity slightly less comprehensive are the next in the danger zone. And they will be the next into the stone cells unless they are prepared to act now and in no half-hearted manner.[23]

George Dale, a Broken Hill union activist, considered that, if half the energy expended in official enquiries had been transferred to the industrial field, 'the jail gates would have opened'. He was incensed that those in Broken Hill who favoured a new trial claimed that the release in June 1918 of the Broken Hill men imprisoned during the recent strike was due to purely political action, although 'a live agitation' had been waged by industrial militants since they were sentenced in April: 'These men have been liberated as the direct result of protests emphatically made by their industrial mates, yet an attempt is being made to gull you into the belief that the political machine was responsible for the men being set free.'[24]

This militant section of the release movement believed that the IWW, while perhaps foolish and outlandish in many of its postures and methods, was essentially correct in its analysis of capitalist society; a new trial was therefore pointless. Rather, the workers of Australia had to be persuaded to engage in concerted industrial agitation to force the authorities into releasing the Twelve. Former Wobblies were associated with this wing of the campaign. Monty Miller was adamant that commissions and enquiries were useless, as it would be performed by 'the same master class owned and controlled machinery of law'. Mick Sawtell insisted that industrial job action was the only way; his own release, he claimed, was due to continual agitation kept up by the workers outside.[25]

Rather than concluding that political action was necessary to neutralise the state apparatus, many Wobblies were confirmed in their convictions that such activity was pointless. Some of these formed the Industrial Labour Party (ILP) in Sydney in November 1917. Despite its name, it was even more vehemently opposed to political action: 'Labor politicians, who threw, by their acquiescence, Labor agitators into prisons, in Australia, are to our minds criminals and traitors . . .' It regretted that 'A lot of would-be Industrialists like scared rats have run in under the political machine to bore within; but we realise like the late I.W.W., that we must stand outside and ostracise the wonderful Labor buffoonery of politics.'[26] The ILP explained its relationship to the IWW in no uncertain terms:

> The I.W.W. in Australia was a non-political organization. The Industrial Labor Party is an anti-political organization. An aggressive fight is necessary against all misleading Labor fakirs whose aim is to smash the industrial movement . . . Out of the misfortunes of the I.W.W. in Australia and the tragic experience resulting and the new needs dictated by new conditions, the I.L.P. proceeds on more scientific lines in construction and propaganda.

According to police reports up to 300 people attended ILP meetings, including a significant number who had served their term of imprisonment under the UAA.[27] The ILP issued a fortnightly paper, *Solidarity*, between 24 November 1917 and 26 April 1919, edited and published by Betsy Matthias, whose Wobbly husband, Rudolph, was imprisoned for six months under the UAA.

Solidarity was regarded, by the authorities and former Wobblies alike, as an avenue for the suppressed IWW. Monty Miller noted of *Solidarity* that 'a new bird of organization Phoenix like has risen from the flames and ashes of the I.W.W.'[28] Military intelligence deemed *Solidarity* 'too dangerous to ignore'; Betsy Matthias, who was 'of more than average ability and viciousness', was 'flooding the country with propaganda'.[29] Plain-clothes detectives mingled with the crowds at ILP meetings in the Domain, attempting to secure evidence that the ILP was really the IWW. Federal authorities sent detectives to interview Betsy Matthias, confronting her at the printer's, at her home and at a public meeting, pressuring her to admit that she had got in touch with the IWW men in jail and conspired with them to launch *Solidarity* and that the ILP was really the IWW. Matthias insisted she had never communicated with the Twelve and that the ILP was not the IWW.[30] And it was not. It was merely the first of the two successor organisations, neither of which could claim, or indeed tried to claim, that it was the true heir of the old IWW. With the UAA still in force there was no rush to be in any sort of apostolic succession when it came to the old IWW.

The ILP maintained a hard-line opposition to any 'pandering to Parliamentary action'. The ILP deemed the Sydney Release and Defence Committee guilty of such, so Harry Meatheringham of the ILP resigned as president of the committee in June 1918 and *Solidarity* sundered its connections with it. The ILP, it explained, was not in favour of a new trial or a Royal Commission, 'believing it to be futile'. Its preferred course of action was 'a vigorous campaign by the workers of Australia on an industrial basis, demanding their unconditional release'; it would not 'compromise with any Parliamentary machinery in our demands for the liberation of the prisoners'. It had severed its links with the committee, because its secretary had stated it must be 'respectable' and 'get under the PLL for safety'.[31] Under the headlines 'WE WILL FIGHT ON INDUSTRIAL LINES WHILE FAKIRS SPOUT HOT AIR', Matthias declared: 'We have ever contended that if the 12 are to come out the prison doors must swing open as the result of class conscious industrial action, and not from any cringing appeal to the job-conscious "bump me into parliament Brigade".'[32]

Because of its definitive rejection of political methods, the ILP rather than the committees became the more popular avenue for former Wobblies and sympathisers to express their support for the imprisoned men. Doug Sinclair, an ex-IWW political prisoner, and Jim Duncan wrote *Justice Outraged. The Case for the Twelve*, which was published by the ILP executive. By September 1918 the intelligence service noted that *Solidarity* had increased its circulation in Queensland sixfold in six months, because it was recognised as the IWW organ and published in the interests of the imprisoned men; and its appeal for funds was 'not unheeded'.[33]

Matthias's trojan efforts notwithstanding, her forceful personality antagonised many of the former Wobblies working with her. Thus another successor organisation was formed on 1 February 1919: the International Industrial Workers. This breakaway group prompted the collapse of the ILP. It produced eight issues of the *Proletariat* during February and March 1919, which devoted most of its column inches to the imprisoned men and the need for their unconditional release. Every Sunday it took its place in the Sydney Domain, demanding the release of the Twelve 'class-war prisoners' and selling copies of the *Proletariat*.[34] A former meatworks militant, Denis Foley, wrote to Pearce Carney at the AMIEU in Townsville: 'We have made an effort in Sydney to revive the "Wobs". An organisation has been formed called the I.I.W., the International Industrial Workers. It is identical in structure and policy with the "Wobs".' The censor was delighted to obtain this 'further evidence that the I.W.W. – the illegal association is still alive under the style of I.I.W.' George Washington's letter to Tom Barker in Chile on 5 March 1919, giving Barker details of the IIW organisation, was also seized upon gleefully by the censor as 'useful evidence to declare the IIW an unlawful association'.[35]

The IIW, like the ILP, was convinced that direct action, not court action, was essential: 'How can the I.W.W. get justice in the Courts of Law as they menace the very foundation upon which these courts exist? . . . The twelve men deserve a fight being put up for them.' A.E. Brown insisted: 'Action is needed to release the I.W.W. men . . . Politicians will do nothing – their job depends on their servility to the class which controls industry. Organize in the I.I.W. for the immediate release of all class-war prisoners and the final overthrow of capitalism.' When the *Australian Worker* suggested 28 October be declared a public holiday to 'celebrate the grandest victory ever achieved by organised labour, a Royal Commission to inquire into the arrests, trial and conviction of the 12 members of the I.W.W.', *Proletariat* was offended because the men were still in jail. The Royal Commission, it contended, was established to stop the agitation for the release of the men and to gain the Labor Party a few more votes from the workers.[36]

The IIW intended to use the 'old form of organisation', accepting only wage-workers and debarring any person connected with a political party.[37] Its statement of principles bore the same relationship to the IWW Preamble as the revised standard version of the Bible to the King James, saying the same thing as the Preamble but in balder, less rhythmically evocative language. Its politics and its prejudices were indistinguishable from those of the IWW. Unemployment was due to over-production: in order to make more jobs, workers must reduce their hours. Arbitration merely fixed wages at a subsistence level and distracted workers from industrial agitation. Parliament did not govern but merely answered to the voice of the master class. 'The battle-ground is on the economic field – not in Parliament.' The labour movement had institutions existing 'on the back of labour', full of future politicians, unsuccessful candidates for parliament and ambitious young men. Labour parties have betrayed the workers; socialist parties will betray them in the future. Orthodox Marxian socialist movements were too dogmatic to cater for the needs of the advancing proletariat. Industrial unionism was the 'height of proletarian organisation' prior to the revolutionary change from capitalism to socialism.[38]

The Sydney IIW was hounded out of existence by repression and disease. Early in April 1919 police and military intelligence ransacked the IIW hall, confiscating books, papers and notebooks, and subjecting the fellow workers to body searches, overlooking nothing. By May the restrictions imposed by the influenza epidemic were seriously curtailing IIW operations.[39] After the *Proletariat* ceased publication in Sydney, the IIW re-emerged in Melbourne a few months later. Under the editorship of Guido Baracchi, it produced seven issues of *Industrial Solidarity* between 14 June 1919 and 7 February 1920.

Industrial Solidarity recalled that to many a wage-slave depressed by the pettinesses of the craft unions and the tragic futilities of Labor politics, the IWW came as the harbinger of a new hope; to the master class, who had found the Hugheses and Holmans and the trade union officials eminently reasonable, the IWW came as a shock. 'But that men of the working-class should preach direct action to their fellows, and that they and their fellows should act accordingly on the job: this was the class war in earnest.' And so, with production of profits down, the master class resolved to eliminate the IWW. Framed up, then rendered unlawful with the help of Labor, the IWW, 'the hope and admiration of the militant proletariat', was down and out. Since the death of the IWW its former members and sympathisers have been left like souls without a body: 'The I.I.W. is accordingly an attempt to provide those souls formerly interested in the I.W.W. with a new body.'[40]

The Melbourne IIW was mindful of its difficult position in relation to the Labor Party. If the New South Wales Labor government released the Twelve, the advocate of political action would turn to the class-conscious industrialist and say:

'There! you see what can be done by political action . . .' And the class-conscious industrialist will never be able to make the political actionist realise that it is precisely because the worker refuses to exercise his power upon the industrial field that we have to turn in despair to the "Labor" Party and the professional politician.

Here, then, *Industrial Solidarity* conceded, was a chance for the Labor Party to justify its existence as a party of reform.[41]

As the IIW petered out in Melbourne early in 1920, it bobbed up in Adelaide. Mick Sawtell had been hired by the South Australian Socialist Party as its organiser; he succeeded in organising its members to become instead the Adelaide Local of the IIW.[42] This Adelaide IIW reported: 'Persistent and intelligent propaganda is being carried on for job control and the release of the twelve.' It produced its own *Industrial Solidarity* for nine issues between February and December 1920, edited by Harry Clark-Nikola, who looked forward to the building of 'a New World in the shell of the old . . . a world of hope and gladness, a world of peace and plenty, a world of art, science, and beauty . . .'[43] Mick Sawtell reiterated that the 'higher and nobler form of civilisation' could only be made possible by an industrially organised working class, that the IIW was not concerned with parliament or politics:

> The smooth running of the capitalist state is not our function. We are out to destroy the capitalist state. The taking of delegates from the ranks of the working-class and putting them into Parliament with the master class cannot help our ideal or plan of organisation.[44]

However, the release of the Twelve constituted a litmus test for Labor in New South Wales, 'the supreme chance of it demonstrating itself as a decent humanitarian body'. Since it professed to represent the working class, 'it is their obvious duty to at once justify that claim by wiping out the stain put upon Australia's fair name by the capitalist-ridden, so-called Nationalist Government'.[45]

The pressure on the new Labor government elected in New South Wales early in 1920 was mounting, its credibility amongst its own supporters threatened. The British Labour Party, too, was anxious that this government release the Twelve, in order to show that a Labor Party could free political prisoners 'and do things for the workers generally'.[46] The discontent at home grew stronger, informed by the efforts of Henry Boote as a propagandist and the revelations of E.E. Judd, a leading member of the SLP, as an amateur detective.[47] Boote's *Guilty or Not Guilty?* sold 100 000 copies and thousands attended the meetings he addressed. The censor regretted that Boote was 'probably one of the most influential publicists in Sydney at the present time'. While the AWU was allowing Boote to defend its arch rivals in the industrial sphere, the SLP, sponsors of the 'political' IWW, threw its resources behind Judd. The *People* published long articles on the case and made a 'scoop' out of Judd's sleuthwork in relation to the Crown witnesses.[48]

Early in 1918 the New South Wales Labor Council had appointed its own Release Committee, headed by Jock Garden and Doug Sinclair, which appointed Judd as its investigator and subsequently published *I.W.W. Cases. Sensational Disclosures. Sudden Disappearance of Important Crown Witnesses.*[49] Judd procured written statements from two of the four Crown witnesses, Scully and Davis Goldstein, to the effect that they had given false evidence, that vital sections of the police evidence were concocted, and that, to their knowledge, nine of the Twelve were entirely innocent. In July Brookfield confronted the government with this in the Legislative Assembly and demanded an inquiry, which was finally conceded in the form of a Royal Commission under Justice Street, to investigate allegations of police misconduct and to report on any fresh evidence which could cause any doubt as to the guilt of the prisoners.[50]

After a sitting extending over ten weeks and which excited intense public interest throughout, the findings of the Street Commission were presented in over 700 pages of closely printed report late in 1918.[51] Despite discrediting of Crown witnesses and some startling revelations about the police conduct in relation to the case, Street found there was no case against the police and no new evidence that would warrant a re-trial. The report was welcomed enthusiastically by the government and rejected outright by the release movement. Boote made detailed criti-cisms of the report and concluded that it was impossible to accept the Commission as an honest attempt to get to the truth of the matter; the country, he insisted, could not be satisfied to keep prisoners incarcer-ated on the evidence of convicted liars and perjurers. Moyle noted that, although Scully had received large sums of money from the police and the Goldstein brothers some army contracts for military clothing, Street had failed to take cognizance of the fact that they were 'birds to pluck'. Barker referred to the inquiry as a 'whitewashing of the police', because the Nationalist politicians were in the hands of the police, who knew too much for their masters to get rid of them.[52]

Nonetheless, the revelations of the Street Commission added sub-stance to the release campaign's arguments; more sections within the campaign came to demand the release rather than yet another trial or inquiry. The agitation was redoubled. Stickers and leaflets proliferated about the inconsistencies of the Crown witnesses revealed in the Street Commission and the unreliability of the police evidence.[53] The Release and Defence Committee issued for free distribution *The I.W.W. Inquiry. Mr. Windeyer's Great Indictment*, a summary of the defence counsel's argu-ments. Its frontispiece announced: 'We demand the immediate release of the 12 I.W.W. men, victims of a vile capitalist conspiracy.' The Labor Council's Release Committee inundated Sydney with leaflets and stickers on behalf of the Twelve. One sticker announced: 'SHOULD THE TWELVE I.W.W. PRISONERS BE KEPT IN JAIL on the evidence of wit-nesses described by Mr. Justice Street as UTTERLY UNSCRUPULOUS MEN, who only told the truth when it suited them, and are capable of wicked concoctions and deliberate perjury?'[54] One of its leaflets declared: '12 men had their liberty stolen on evidence of crooks and per-jurers and are now waiting for honest men and women to take a hand in the matter.' Jock Garden alleged in March 1920 that the police were harassing speakers who advocated the release of the Twelve, referring to 'an organised attempt by the police to hinder the full facts of the case regarding the IWW men now languishing in gaol being placed before the public'.[55]

While many ex-Wobblies saw the report as further proof of the futility of political action, other campaigners concluded the only hope lay in a

change of government to secure the men's release. Storey promised support for another inquiry, even the AWU supporting this, in his policy for
the 1920 election; the Labor Council went further and asked all candidates to pledge themselves personally to the unconditional release of the
Twelve. Only Brookfield and P.J. Minahan responded, for which they
were expelled from the Party. However, no Labor candidate nominated
against them.[56] Storey became Premier on 20 March, but only just. As
the *Sydney Morning Herald* explained, Labor's slender claim to office
depended on the support of two Independents: Brookfield, 'who had
been cast out of the party for his extremism, and who blazoned his advocacy of the cause of the IWW men to the world'; and Minahan, 'whose
promise to urge the immediate release of the prisoners, should Labor
succeed to power, had earned him an ostentatious ejection from the
party'. Thus, the Storey government's reopening of the IWW cases was
'the price which had to be paid for the very chance of the party to get
onto the Treasury benches'.[57]

In exchange for a large consignment of cement, the Tasmanian government agreed to make the services of Justice Ewing available to the
Storey government.[58] The counsel for the defence argued that whoever
started the conspiracy, it was not the IWW men, that there was no evidence of sufficient weight to establish that they deliberately set out on a
crusade to burn down Sydney to secure the release of a man who was
already free. During the inquiry, a 'Monster Protest Meeting' against the
continued imprisonment of the Twelve was staged in the Domain under
the auspices of the Labor Council.[59]

Justice Ewing's official report in August 1920 found that in the cases of
Hamilton, Besant, Moore, McPherson, Teen and Fagin, it was 'not just
and right' that they should have been convicted at all; that Glynn,
Larkin, Beatty and Grant were wrongly convicted on all but the charge of
seditious conspiracy and had been sufficiently punished for this; that
Reeve was rightly convicted of conspiracy to commit arson and seditious
conspiracy, because his letter written from Western Australia suggested
he was conspiring with Morgan and others and advising the destruction
of property by fire for the purpose of inflicting injury on certain individuals and classes of society, so his ten-year sentence was not excessive in
the case of such a terrible crime; that King was rightly convicted of seditious conspiracy but the sentence of five years cumulative upon his three-
year sentence for forgery was greatly in excess of the offence. Ewing
concluded that the principal Crown witnesses were 'persons of such a
character that they may justly be described as liars and perjurers' and
that the full infamy of these witnesses had not been known either to the
trial judge and jury or to Justice Street. As Turner observes, the implication was a conspiracy among the police to concoct the case, but this was

scarcely a finding that Ewing could make, since it would have involved a direct conflict with the Street report.[60]

Storey released all but Reeve and King on 3 August 1920, within a few days of publication of the Ewing report. In reply to Opposition criticism, he explained:

> The extremists wanted the unconditional release of the prisoners, guilty or not guilty. This demand was emphatically, and without hesitation on my part, refused. Constitutional methods were adopted, and we have got a constitutional result . . . I never at any time said, as suggested by Sir George Fuller, that the Labor Party, if returned, would get the men out. What I did say was that, if returned, the Government would give them a chance to prove their innocence before a judicial tribunal with full powers of inquiry.[61]

The extremist position so emphatically rejected had rendered comparatively respectable and reasonable the demands for a new trial or inquiry. *Labor News* expressed its satisfaction that Storey did not lose his sense of proportion but kept calm, disregarding the 'inane demands' for unconditional release: 'The ten liberated men owe their freedom to the fact that the ALP was in power . . . It was not through the efforts of J.S. Garden that the men were released (or others who demanded their unconditional release) but through the efforts of the Labor Party.'[62]

The ten were greeted as returning heroes by large and enthusiastic audiences across the country. The appalling poems written in their honour expressed the sense of restored faith in the system resulting from the inquiry, one ending on an especially reformist downbeat: 'May Judge Ewing live for many years/In happiness and peace.' An ALP propaganda committee meeting carried a motion that the committee congratulate the Labor government; an amendment urging a further inquiry into the action of the police so that justice could be done to King and Reeve and the guilty detectives removed from the force was lost. Storey's Cabinet decided compensation would not be paid to the six men exonerated completely by the Ewing Commission.[63]

This decision against compensation was made despite the urgings of labour councils, unions and left-wing parties. The anger of the far left of the release campaign had not abated; it was convinced that the Two were being retained to deflect accusations of police conspiracy. At the Townsville School of Arts 2000 people voted unanimously:

> That this meeting of citizens of Townsville views the prolonged imprisonment of Charles Reeve and J.B. King as being for the purpose of whitewashing the corruption of the New South Wales detective force and the late New South Wales Government. We view Reeve and King as standard bearers in the working-class movement and we demand their immediate release.

With Doug Sinclair and Donald Grant touring Queensland in the spring
of 1920, many similar meetings were held in other Queensland centres
and committees formed to coordinate workplace-based agitation for
their release.[64] Across New South Wales the words 'FRAME-UP' appeared
on fences and telegraph poles, and more leaflets and stickers appeared
on behalf of the Two. The Newcastle Industrial Council's paper, the
Toiler, declared:

> The capitalist class, in keeping Reeve and King in jail are challenging the
> working-class. Is there no spirit of revolt in us? Are we weaklings and mean-
> spirited slaves to see our working-class brothers still remaining in jail? No! We
> have still the hearts of oak of the English, we have still in our blood the rebel
> spirit of the Irish: we have still in our souls the dauntless courage of the
> Scotch.[65]

The Adelaide IIW commented: 'A.L.P. enthusiasts sometimes wonder
why they are criticised by advanced workers. It is actions of this weak-
kneed type that are the cause . . . spineless compromise with the class
who in their hearts despise and hate them is ever the path they follow.'[66]

Jock Garden, for the Sydney Trades Hall Reds and the Communist
Party, expressed his opinion in March 1921 that the Labor government
would do absolutely nothing on the men's behalf until the organised
unions demanded their release in no uncertain terms. On May Day 1921
Grant appealed to the masses in the Domain to agitate for the release of
Reeve and King; every hand in the crowd was held up in favour of the
two men's release. Glynn, representing the CPA, moved a resolution for
the immediate release of the men, which was carried. The meeting
closed with cheers for the IWW men in jail and for May Day. In the
evening, a meeting was organised at the Sydney Town Hall; the speakers
stressed that the workers demanded the freedom of the Two.[67]

Under pressure from the campaign forces, the Storey government
sought a private arrangement that the Two would be released on condition that they left the country, which became public when the federal
government refused to issue the necessary passports.[68] The *Age* commented that 'the continued presence of men whom some regard as
political prisoners – and therefore martyrs – in a State governed by a
Labor Ministry is embarrassing . . .' King was released on 21 September
1921 but Reeve remained, in the words of J.J. O'Reilly, secretary of the
Barrier District WIUA, 'imprisoned as a result of a vile and hideous
frame-up by a capitalist government, desirous of venting its spleen on
working-class fighters . . .' Reeve was released by Storey's successor,
Dooley, on 27 November 1921.[69]

Turner states that the Twelve had from three to eleven years of their
lives for which to thank the members of the New South Wales Labor

Party and the Labor Council supporters of political action. He considers it unlikely that, as they walked out of Long Bay, they were humming 'Polly, we can't use you, dear . . .'[70] Yet the outcome did not repudiate the IWW argument that political action was useless for emancipating the working class, 'to lead us into clover'; it showed that industrial and political action on the part of the working class could on occasion be necessary merely to ensure that society conformed in the meantime to its declared juridical principles.

Moreover, as the IWW had always argued, it is unlikely that the politicians would, of their own accord, have instigated a new inquiry; it was only because of the strength of the movement on the ground, especially in urging the release of the men, that the politicians felt obliged to respond at least to the demand for an inquiry. As the Newcastle Industrial Council newspaper argued in August 1920, the government was compelled to take notice when the working class became so insistent in their demands for the release of the Twelve. Or, as Charlie Reeve wrote from Long Bay jail in May 1920: 'I know the situation too well, to be deluded with any idea that The Vulture releases its Prey untill forced to.'[71]

CHAPTER 15

What Happened to the Wobblies?

Part of the mythology surrounding the early days of the Communist Party is that large numbers of Wobblies realised the error of their syndicalist ways and joined.[1] In fact, very few Wobblies joined the Communist Party in the 1920s: if they had joined in larger numbers the Party would not have been the derisory size it was in this formative decade. Moreover, very few of the early members of the Party had been Wobblies, formed as it was largely by a merger of two groups always remote from, and often hostile to, the IWW: the ASP and the union bureaucrats in Sydney known as the 'Trades Hall Reds'.

Most Wobblies, as Tom Glynn commented, found 'urgent business in other parts of Australia'. They scattered, to find employment in places where imprisonment, deportation or victimisation were a little less likely.[2] They did not hang around in Sydney, prey to spies and police, plotting with their erstwhile sparring partners on the left to found an organisation whose strategy and tactics were contrary to those of the IWW. Jim Scott records that a 'Terrible lot of IWW elements didn't join the CP . . . for those who did it was a "Terrible task for them to advocate political action at all." The others remaining aloof said: "This is it" – shop control – industrial organisation. Still didn't see any political action needed.'[3]

Two weeks before the founding conference of the Communist Party, Bill Beatty departed in a fishing boat for a trip to Port Stephens in the hope of curing his indigestion. Making no mention of the moves to form the Party, he wrote to a mate: 'The present condition of the labour movement is painful to Wobblies. The O.B.U. is about the most hopeful thing . . . and is doing good work among city navvies and labourers.' The proper work for the IWW, he felt, whose 'philosophy still holds good', was to stick to purely industrial propaganda work, to try to force the OBU to build up an organisation before the impending revolutionary crisis and 'hold I.W.W. aims and forms in front of them to lead them on'. Betsy Matthias did not join the Party, she explained to Miriam Dixson in 1963, because its leaders did not 'go forward' as 'militants in the proper manner'. Katharine Susannah Prichard concedes that, despite the triumph of the Russian revolutionaries, members of the IWW in Western Australia at that time were not prepared to change their tactics.[4]

The mythology served Communist ends admirably. In claiming the Wobblies, reformed, as their own, the Communist Party was aiming to consign the IWW to the dustbin of revolutionary history while, at the same time, endeavouring to capture its undoubted following and use it for Communist purposes. As Peter Morrison's study of the early Party points out, its very foundation in the wake of the Bolshevik Revolution was meant to imply that 'older doctrines, like I.W.W.'ism, were relegated to the "unscientific" past'. Mary Wright, who joined the Party in 1929, recalls 'a certain amount of condescension towards the IWW' on the part of her comrades, a feeling that the Party was an advance upon this earlier group.[5]

The Communist movement throughout the world was anxious that Wobblies renounce their revolutionary industrial unionist past and join the Communist Parties; it urged them to do this in January 1920 in *The Communist Internationale to the I.W.W. An Appeal of the Executive Committee of the Third Internationale at Moscow*. Trotsky was delighted when he was informed by the Australian delegation to the 1922 congress that some IWW members had joined the CPA: 'That is good because the I.W.W. are the real proletariat and real fighters . . .' W.P. Earsman in this delegation was struck by Trotsky's 'weakness' for the IWW: 'He has a great regard for them and those who come through that school to Communism . . .'[6]

For a while Tom Glynn went with the Communist current. On 15 September 1920, in the lead-up to the Party's founding conference on 30 October, which he attended, an Australian edition of the International's *Appeal* to the IWW was published with a foreword by Glynn. He conceded that 'the experience of Russia would indicate the necessity of something more than the industrial weapon . . . during the transition period towards a Communist social order', but insisted that 'the view that the Industrial Union shall ultimately be the unit of administration in the Communist State remains unchallenged'. He assured his fellow workers that the Communist International emphasised the 'absolute necessity' of the industrial union movement.[7]

The Australian Party made elaborate overtures to Wobbly remnants, while the *Australian Communist* charted the closer movement of the American IWW towards the Communist International. In his final months, Monty Miller was wooed by those organising the formation of the Party in the West, notably Katharine Susannah Prichard, anxious to receive the old man's blessing. Miller died on 17 November 1920, a few weeks after its formation; though he allegedly endorsed the new Party and conceded that the Bolsheviks' political action was distinct from the political action denounced by the IWW, Prichard admits that Miller was adamant that the political machine within the Soviet Republic ought quickly to destroy itself: 'The less government we have the better . . .'[8] The new Party made extensive use of those Wobblies who did join, especially Glynn and Larkin, to popularise it amongst their associates. Alf Wilson considered the Party was 'trading on the martyrdom of Glynn and Larkin'. It campaigned for the release of Reeve and King, though Reeve insisted he would rather do his time than owe his release to the 'mysterious workings' of Glynn's 'outfit'. He referred darkly to the 'Vultures & Boodle seekers, in the Party that T.G. belongs to', who were involved in 'intriguing and smooging from the Trades Hall, to Pollies'.[9]

The making of the myth was facilitated by the fact that many Wobblies reacted with enthusiasm, initially, to the October Revolution, believing that it heralded not the rule of a Party but of the working class.[10] It was easy in the early days of the Russian Revolution for Wobblies to imagine that the Bolsheviks, as direct actionists of a sort, with their rhetoric about giving power to the soviets, were interested in establishing a regime based on workers' control of industry. However, doubters amongst the Wobblies became considerably more numerous as Bolshevism consolidated itself after victory. The enthusiasm of most Wobblies for the Russian Revolution did not entail any subsequent devotion to the new regime or its instigators. Mick Sawtell, for instance, wrote in March 1919 of his 'great hopes of the Russian Revolution' but insisted there was 'something wrong in a socialist State having an army for I hold violence is a wrong under any circumstances'. In mid-1921 he debated the matter with Guido Baracchi, who had become a founding member of the Communist Party. Against Baracchi's contention that only force would overthrow capitalism, Sawtell maintained that an enlightened working class had great power and an appeal should be made to reason. Russia, Sawtell concluded, was not a socialist country, as compromise had been made.[11]

Many of the small number of Wobblies who joined the Party did not stay members for long. Coming from an elaborately democratic and open organisation, they were astounded by their reception within the Party as it began implementing the authoritarian and hierarchical forms of organisation for which it became renowned. When the Party split into its original parts in December 1920, the Wobbly Communists stayed with the Trades Hall Reds, because of their apparent commitment to industrial organisation. This group called itself the Communist Party but was commonly termed the Sussex Street Party; its rivals in the ASP were referred to as the Liverpool Street Party. The ex-Wobblies in Sussex Street were expected to toe the line or shut up, to cease being Wobblies. Earsman accused them of having 'joined the C.P. of A. with the object of capturing it to make it an I.W.W. turn out'. Where Wobblies saw industrial unionism as the most important aim of the Communist movement, this movement saw dangers in too much attachment to industrial unionism, which might threaten the Communist Party's attempts to constitute itself as a revolutionary vanguard.[12]

The continuing adherence of Glynn and other former Wobblies to industrial unionism caused dissension within the Sussex Street Party and their existence within this Party was deemed by Liverpool Street to be a serious obstacle in the way of unity. Alf Wilson, who had defected to the ASP and was expressing its prejudices, observed that 'the old IWW element' in Sussex Street constituted 'the greatest menace that a revolutionary body could have about it'.[13] Inevitably, tensions developed between the Party and those Wobblies within it, notably Glynn, who remained loyal to IWW principles.

Glynn became the first editor of the *Australian Communist* and used this position to define the role, as he saw it, of Party members in industrial life. One of the aims of the Party was to replace existing craft unions with more efficient industrial unions; therefore its members should work within craft unions to this end, disseminating propaganda about the importance of industrial unionism. The industrial union would play an important role in the new social order, 'the communist reconstruction of society'. If revolutionary activities were systematically maintained amongst the rank and file, trade unionism could be transformed into a most potent weapon for revolutionary aims: 'The more the influence of Communist propaganda is felt . . . the less need is there to worry about the capture of executive positions within the unions.' The Communist wage-worker could more effectively serve the Communist movement 'by being in constant touch with his fellow-slaves on the job, sharing in their struggles, their defeats and their successes, and ever guiding them towards the revolutionary goal'. By such means would the bureaucracy of craft-union officialdom be smashed.[14] As an organisation whose influence within the labour movement was to depend in future decades on its success in winning positions in trade unions, by fair means or foul, the fledgling Communist Party was not likely to take Glynn's observations to heart.

In March 1921, Glynn resigned from the central executive and as editor. On 12 October 1921, a two-page leaflet signed by Glynn and entitled 'Industrial Union Propaganda League' (IUPL) appeared with the warning: 'Look out for Direct Action appearing shortly.' The leaflet argued the need for a movement 'which shall exclusively devote its attention to the infusing of a new spirit of aggressiveness and militancy into the existing organisations' as well as actively participating in the work of transforming these unions into industrial unions.[15] Associated with Glynn in the formation of the IUPL were other ex-Wobblies within the Communist Party, notably J.B. King, George Washington and Norman Rancie.[16] In November 1921 a debate was held at the Newcastle Trades Hall: 'That the principles and policy of the Australian Communist Party is sufficient to achieve the emancipation of the working class.' Those opposing the motion complained that industrial unionism was being neglected by the Party; they contended that thorough industrial unionism was the only way in which the workers might accomplish their freedom for, if Communists were elected to parliament, they would only betray the workers as all other politicians had done.[17] IUPL organisations appeared in Perth, Adelaide and Melbourne, undoubtedly contributing to the weakness of the Communist Party in its earliest days in Perth and Adelaide. On Reeve's release from prison on 27 November 1921, he went to Perth as an organiser for the IUPL; in the meantime, Grant was promoting the IUPL in Adelaide, where it had been established by Harry Clarke, Ted Moyle and other ex-Wobblies.[18]

The Communists in both parties were disturbed, their internal correspondence making many agitated references to the Glynn manifesto.[19] At a time when Moscow was instructing the two warring parts of the Australian communist movement to achieve unity, the IUPL was an embarrassment in Sussex Street and a cause for concern in Liverpool Street. Sussex Street responded by declaring the IUPL 'bogus', expelling them on charges of syndicalism and forbidding any member to join the IUPL. Expulsion notwithstanding, Liverpool Street felt the old Wobblies should have been dealt with even more severely by Sussex Street, referring to 'their failure to clear up their party in this respect', for 'the Glynn–King expulsion' should have been followed up by 'a general revision of the membership'.[20]

The IUPL proceeded, as threatened, to resurrect *Direct Action*. The first issue on 1 December 1921 continued the argument with the Communists. The dictatorship of the proletariat meant the rule of the working class organised as the ruling class: 'Then by organising the workers in Industrial Unions we are organising the future "Dictatorship of the Proletariat". Industrial Unions will largely constitute the "Soviets" of Australia.' Instead of waiting for a coup, it was necessary to organise the structure of the new society, the One Big Union of all workers:

> We are far from denying the necessity of a powerful Communist Party acting as the general staff of the working class movement. But we are insisting that the immediate struggle against the reactionary influences in Trade Unionism

must be carried on by an organisation wide enough to embrace all industrial rebel elements. . . . This cannot be done by manifesting a spirit of petty sectarianism to other industrial rebels, but in co-operating with them in the fight and endeavoring to secure the leadership by displaying the capacity for that leadership.

In enjoining workers to return to industrial organisation, the IUPL commented pointedly: 'We must make up for the lost time that the working class of this country has been cheering the revolutions of other countries and not putting its own house in order.' [21]

On 30 January 1922 a meeting between the Party and the IUPL resulted in 'a working agreement for propaganda purposes between the two organisations', which envisaged the two sides sharing Domain platforms and indoor facilities. The Party stipulated that the IUPL must endorse the programme of action of the Red International of Labour Unions (RILU); the IUPL remarked this was easily done, since RILU principles had been advocated by the 'industrial element' since the formation of the IWW. *Direct Action* officially declared its adherence to the programme of action in its March 1922 issue. The IUPL also agreed to become a Group (IUPG) instead of a League and the Communist Party executive motion expelling King and Glynn was rescinded.[22]

The deal foundered a few weeks later when the powerful Communist Party members on the Labor Council, with Party approval, encouraged and supported a Council motion calling on workers to support the Labor Party at the forthcoming election.[23] *Direct Action* was outraged:

And these Trades Hall communists have the hide to call themselves revolutionary Marxians! . . . If the toilers allow themselves to be doped by labor politicians, and lulled to sleep by the Trades' Hall communists, then look out for trouble in the future. . . . Bitter and grim experience has taught the fighting toilers, that they must cast aside all parties who dabble in politics, as they are only smoke-screens for the guns of the bourgeoisie.

The revolutionary movement in Australia had been 'pested by a species of spurious intellectual', who strut and parade themselves, announcing that they are the only people capable of leading a revolution: 'They appeared on the horizon following the Russian Revolution, and all those having the hardihood to criticise them, are described as traitors to the Russian proletariat.' But now, 'The Communist Party has at last appeared in its true colours. At last their inherent weakness for politicians and parliamentarians has mastered their theories.' By inducing the Labor Council to endorse the Labor Party, the Communists had corrupted an industrial organisation 'which showed promise of becoming of some revolutionary value'. Communists would combat Revolutionary Direct Action wherever it was attempted, inventing a subtle justification:

> The Communist Party reactionary will justify anything under the Sun, provided you allow him to govern your process of reasoning. In contradistinction to Marxism, the Communist reactionary first decides upon his 'tactic' and then proceeds to justify it afterwards, a method adopted by metaphysicians and social quacks of every variety.[24]

The IUPG informed the Communist Party that the working agreement was arranged on the tacit understanding that the Communist Party would continue revolutionary propaganda, including condemnation of all capitalist organisations and parties, such as the ALP, 'one of the greatest bulwarks of capitalism'; the IUPG considered itself absolved from observing the terms of agreement with the Party.[25]

The battle lines had been redrawn. To the Wobbly mind the Communist Party was now like the Labor Party, the concern for political processes representing an obstacle in the way of militant direct action and the formation of revolutionary industrial unions. Lecturing for the IUPG, King criticised the Communist tactic of 'capturing the machinery' of the unions. When Jack Howie, Communist president of the Labor Council, asked: 'then how can we expect to capture the more powerful machine of the capitalist state?', King replied: 'One doesn't want to capture a mad dog before shooting it'. *Direct Action* considered Howie's question expressed the psychology of parliamentarism that had recently become endemical at the Trades Hall.[26]

By the time the Sussex Street Party received the blessing of Moscow and became the Communist Party of Australia in August 1922, and some members of the ASP reluctantly came across, very few of the small number of Wobblies had survived as members; and for those remaining, life became even tougher. According to Jim Scott, IWW-type militants within the Party were discouraged, their major opponents being those who came in from the ASP.[27] Most of those who remained were not seeking in a new organisation a continuation of Wobbly principles and practices but making a break with their Wobbly past. By remaining in the Party, these Wobblies changed themselves. Norman Jeffery, for instance, recreated himself in the image of Communism and became accepted by his fellow Communists. He claimed in 1960 that the Russian Revolution left many of his colleagues in the IWW 'floundering'.[28] The mythology about Wobblies joining the Party probably owes much to Jeffery.

If the hopes placed by a small number of Wobblies in the Communist movement of the early 1920s were cruelly dashed, the enthusiasm of a far greater number of Wobblies for the One Big Union movement ended likewise in bitter disappointment. For Wobblies still politically active, these were the two rather stark alternatives – the Communist Party or the OBU – that presented themselves in the immediate aftermath of the First World War. Support for the OBU movement amongst former Wobblies was both more widespread and longer lasting; disillusion when it came was accordingly all the more bitter.

The OBU scheme proposed by the Sydney Labor Council, the Workers' Industrial Union of Australia (WIUA), was formally embraced by a congress representing more than 150 New South Wales unions in Sydney in August 1918 and by a similar gathering of Queensland unions in Brisbane the same month. It was subsequently approved by a larger conference representing unions from all States in Melbourne in January 1919. Stylistic changes apart, the Preamble to the constitution of this OBU was the Detroit IWW Preamble; and the WIUA's declared first step was the 'scientific' organisation of the working class into a confederation of six great industrial unions, resembling the six departments outlined in the IWW blueprint.[29] OBU militants saw the scheme as a means to control politicians more effectively. Hughes and Holman had played traitor, they argued, because the movement allowed them the freedom to do so: 'The One Big Union will limit the scope of those who would follow their example.'[30]

Despite the Detroit Preamble, former Wobblies were prominent amongst those militants on the ground who campaigned for the OBU in its early days. The very idea of One Big Union was widely acknowledged as an IWW idea.[31] In Sydney and Melbourne the movement was controlled by left union officials such as Jock Garden and Ben Mulvogue, but former Wobblies were important as OBU activists in Western Australia, South Australia and Queensland.[32] The frenetic activities of erstwhile Wobblies on behalf of the OBU gave credence to the attacks of those within the labour movement who branded the OBU scheme an IWW plot and alluded frequently to the similarity in the two Preambles.[33]

In the West, the OBU movement was, as Segal remarks, inspired directly by the IWW.[34] As early as July 1918, before the initial OBU conference, Monty Miller wrote from Perth that he was 'busy . . . organizing the OBU League'. By September 1918 he had formed a 'One Big Union league' at Fremantle. In the previous month he had been to Kalgoorlie on a propaganda campaign amongst the miners and the men on the woodlines, his lectures and speeches, though ostensibly for the ALF, being 'all for the One Big Union'. He described those he visited on the woodlines 90 miles out in the desert from Kalgoorlie as '500 stalwarts of labour . . . all tired of the futility of politics and the politicians and in a state of mental perception fitting them for the new idea of the O.B.U.'. Returning to the coast, he busied himself with OBU propaganda in Perth and Fremantle,

A Broom That is Urgently Needed.

The organ of the Newcastle Industrial Council portrays the One Big Union as an effective way of dealing with renegade politicians. (*Industrialist,* 17 November 1921)

especially amongst the lumpers, a section of whom, he reported, were in the OBU. Mick Sawtell wrote to Betsy Matthias on 21 October 1918 that the OBU was 'still keeping the flame alive'. To Beth Pole in Perth he reported 'great work' done for the OBU.[35]

As Organiser of the OBU in Perth, Sawtell wrote to Ben Mulvogue on 19 April 1919 describing the formation of the OBU League. As he was boycotted on every job and in every industry in Western Australia, he was putting all his energy in to the OBU. To Don Cameron, he reported that OBU sentiment was growing in Western Australia. There were 'great sales' of OBU literature.[36]

Sawtell continued his efforts for the OBU after moving to Adelaide later in 1919. By February 1920 Alf Wilson was making disparaging remarks about how the 'bummery element' in Adelaide had 'formed up in a propaganda League of the O.B.U.'. This became, as we have seen, the Adelaide IIW. Late in 1920 the Adelaide IIW declared that, with the approval of the ten IWW men already released, the IIW was to become 'the educational and agitational factor' in the WIUA. The IIW would be of very great assistance to the OBU rank and file as instructors, on-the-job agitators and educational experts. It would aim to make 'EVERY MEMBER AN INTELLIGENT, WELL-READ FIGHTING AGITATOR'. In December 1920 *Industrial Solidarity*, the IIW newspaper, became the official organ also of the OBU in South Australia.[37]

The OBU movement in Queensland was based on former Wobbly strongholds in the north.[38] The deputy chief censor in Melbourne regretted in September 1918 that:

> The idea of the One Big Union has commended itself to the Majority of working men in the North, and I often heard the remark made that the O.B.U. had taken the place of the I.W.W. and that there was no need to advertise its methods of gaining control of industries . . . there is absolutely no doubt that the goal aimed at by [this movement] is the control of industries by means of the methods originated, preached and practised by the organisation known as the Industrial Workers of the World.[39]

According to military intelligence, the inaugural meeting of the One Big Union Propaganda League (OBUPL), formed by Brown, Quinton, Jackson, Burke 'and other I.W.W.', was held in Brisbane on 10 September 1918. The OBU scheme 'contains the worst of bad elements of I.W.W.ism in its constitution – and it is safe in that it has not been declared an unlawful association'. One spook who attended OBUPL meetings complained that 'The O.B.U. meetings are more virulent than ever the I.W.W. meetings were.' The spies also counted heads; about 400 people attended the OBUPL meeting on 5 December 1918 at the North

Quay, at which Gordon Brown and William Jackson spoke.[40] Active amongst the militant OBU proponents in Brisbane were members of the Brisbane IWW Local: Claude Anlezark, T. and J. Dwyer, Percy Mandeno, Gordon Brown, A.E. Williams, George Bright, W.K. Sydes and Gordon Major. The censor noted in February 1919 that the IWW now 'style themselves' the OBUPL. Brisbane police refused the OBUPL permission to sell its literature or to speak outdoors; at least one employer, the Darra Cement Works, sacked militant workers associated with the OBUPL.[41] Donald Grant and Doug Sinclair toured north Queensland late in 1920, visiting all the chief centres around Cairns and Townsville, speaking on job-sites and distributing large quantities of OBU literature. In the Queensland AWU ballot on arbitration in December 1920, 33 per cent opposed arbitration; in the northern district the vote was 46 per cent against. Craft-union officials claimed the unions had been taken over by extremists and members of the IWW. The evidence, according to Armstrong's research, supports the craft-union officials' claims.[42]

The distinctive ex-Wobbly contribution to the OBU movement was an emphasis on job control and 'bottom-up' methods of organisation. As Sawtell explained: 'As the O.B.U. Movement increases, so must the rank and file realise and undertake their own responsibilities of self organisation and self discipline.' The Adelaide IIW argued: 'Nothing is more important at present than the job committee.' Workers organised on the job retained the initiative in their own hands and were not dependent on union officials. From the 'Job Control Acorn' would grow the 'Industrial Control Oak'.[43]

In contradistinction to the enthusiasm of old Wobblies, the support for the OBU from trade union leaders was no uncomplicated yearning for a movement that would place control of the means of production, distribution and exchange in the hands of rank-and-file workers. As Miriam Roberts points out, the right wing within the union movement wanted the OBU to bring centralised control by officials over the rank and file to prevent strikes; many of the left-wing officials, too, disliked strikes and hoped that reorganisation would mean fewer and smaller strikes. Ben Mulvogue maintained that, with One Big Union formed, 'we could march triumphant to the Arbitration Court'. Generally, the left officials aimed to constitute the existing craft unions as sections of the OBU, with the officials keeping their jobs, at least initially.[44]

The formation of the Workers International Industrial Union (WIIU), which also operated on the Detroit Preamble, added to the confusion within the OBU movement. In September 1915 the IWW Clubs had become the WIIU to disassociate themselves from the IWW. During 1916 another WIIU Local was formed in Sydney by members of the ASP, who somehow induced the American WIIU, formerly the De Leonite IWW, to grant them a charter to form an Australian Administration of the WIIU. The Melbourne WIIU, also formed by members of the ASP, became the Australian Administration of the WIIU after the Sydney WIIU collapsed in January 1921.[45]

The WIIU emphasised the shop committee approach. Its stickers proclaimed: 'The Dinkum O.B.U. is not built in the Trades Hall But ON the JOB!' and 'Without Job Control Boards There Can be NO One Big Union.' Its first leaflet announced: 'We can and we will own the workshops . . . The workers take part directly in the production of wealth. They should not shrink from taking part in the management of that production . . .'[46] The aim of the WIIU was to organise for 'Industrial Self Government', building from the bottom up, and not from the top down, beginning with workshop committees. In an 'Appeal to the rank and file of the trade unions', the WIIU explained it was a democratic, or rank-and-file organisation: workers on each job would form the unit of the OBU by electing a job control board to deal with the boss directly on matters pertaining to the job and to replace 'bossdom' with workers' control the moment political power was gained by the working class.[47]

Though formed by a strange conglomeration of IWW Club and ASP members, some former Wobblies, such as Alf Wilson and Harry Clarke in Adelaide, became involved with the WIIU, which remained committed to the shop-committee approach as the WIUA became increasingly less amenable to rank-and-file activity.[48] In contradistinction to the WIUA, which became known as the official OBU, the WIIU was deemed the unofficial OBU. The WIIU criticised the constitution of the WIUA for providing for a Grand Council of twelve to be paid £600 a year each. Its *How One Big Union Works* noted that the WIUA scheme 'seems to have the dangerous weakness of being organised from the top downward'. An 'unwieldy conglomeration of crafts and semi-industrial unions', it was not a genuine democratic rank-and-file OBU but one by and for officialdom, a bureaucratic abortion; it preferred to encourage, not working-class self-reliance but only reliance upon a bureaucracy; instead of reducing the number of officials it would increase the army. It excluded Chinese, Japanese etc., 'evidently preferring their competition rather than their unity and co-operation'. It adopted the revolutionary Preamble purely so as to retain a following.[49]

It was in Victoria that the WIIU fared best, with a membership of about 500 workers, about 150 of whom were Wonthaggi miners in Local no.3.[50] Other areas of strength were among the workers building Eildon Weir, among saw-mill hands in the Powelltown and Warburton districts, and in the Geelong freezing works. According to one of its organisers, J.B. Scott, the WIIU emphasised 'job control, job committees, conditions of work, meals served, huts provided, transport, wages etc. . . . .' The

Melbourne Local began producing the *One Big Union Herald* in October 1918, edited by Jim Dawson, a labourer from Collingwood. Melbourne sales exceeded 6000; Adelaide sales, mainly in the Botanic Park, were about 1200; Sydney's were less. By 1919 the Trades Hall, which formerly took a few dozen copies of the *OBU Herald*, stopped handling copies.[51] The mainstream unions were moving against the WIIU.

The WIIU, unlike the old IWW, put its dual unionist principles into practice. In August 1919 more than 300 men employed on the construction of the Eildon Dam left the AWU and joined the WIIU. Consequently they were sacked, the engineer saying he had no alternative since the AWU organiser would not give AWU men permission to work with members of another union. According to Wilson the AWU officials intimidated the boarding-house keepers to evict WIIU men and induced the local store-keeper, a shareholder in mines in the ranges worked by AWU labour, not to supply WIIU men with provisions.[52]

In the West, too, the AWU conspired with employers to dispense with the WIIU, which had strong support amongst the woodcutters, many of them Italians, of the Kurrawang and Lakeside woodlines that supplied the goldmines of Kalgoorlie and Coolgardie with fuel: a ballot on Kurrawang went WIIU 153 and AWU 2; and there was a similar ballot on the Lakeside line. The employers became strong supporters of the AWU and refused to recognise the WIIU, so the WIIU men went on strike in December 1920, disabling the mines. With Labor MPs denouncing the strike and with the ALF actively intervening in support of the AWU, the strike failed to secure recognition of the WIIU and the employers set up a job control board of previous AWU executive members to police work at an award 5 shillings a day less than the navvies on the nearby government railway. Although the WIIU organisers were driven off the goldfields by 'paid hoodlums', about 100 cutters at Kurrawang were still in the WIIU in June 1921 and became the object of a successful 'cleaning up' operation on the part of the AWU.[53]

By 1925 the surviving WIIU Locals in Melbourne and Adelaide had followed the American and English suit and were absorbed into the SLP.[54] WIIU fortunes had waned with the re-establishment in Melbourne of a CPA branch in 1924, notwithstanding the *OBU Herald*'s warning in 1923:

> The WIIU is opposed to the Communist Party's concept of socialism in that it is not democratic. The C.P. relies upon the few leading the mass – a dictatorship by the Communists through a political State (how not specified). This must result in a dictatorship in industry and result in a bureaucratic State – not socialism.[55]

Apart from Wilson, now in the SLP, the ex-Wobblies in the various wings of the OBU movement had mostly stood aside from the internal wrangling, preferring to expend their efforts on workplace agitation, arguing for the importance of building the movement from the bottom up and opposing the strategy of top-down amalgamations of craft unions. Mick Sawtell argued that the diversity in the OBU movement was good, providing all the OBU organisations advocated shop committees: 'the more rival organizations, the less chance there is for reactionary union executives and opportunists to live on or sell the working class'.[56]

As the form of the official OBU, to be achieved merely by top-down amalgamations of unions in different branches of the same industry, became more apparent, the IWW successor organisations were as strong in their criticism as the WIIU. The March 1921 OBU conference approved the old revolutionary Preamble but the name of the OBU was to be the Australasian Workers' Union: it maintained a colour bar; there was no mention of job control; the annual convention would be constituted from the departments on the basis of one delegate per 5000 members and between conventions the governing body was to be the General Council. Rank-and-file control over industrial action was abandoned in favour of control by the 'supreme governing body'. The IUPL argued that the adoption of the OBU Preamble was 'merely an attempt to throw dust in the eyes of the militant element in the industrial movement by appearing to subscribe to revolutionary principles'. The incorporation of the old AWU colour bar must, Glynn insisted, 'come in for the severest condemnation from all class-conscious workers'; the unorganised worker was a menace to unionism and doubly so when racial prejudices were raised as a barrier to admission to a union. This OBU secured the control of union officials and these, Glynn maintained, were ever reluctant to encourage rank-and-file militancy.[57]

The Wobblies could recognise the danger signs for militant workers in the final outcome of the OBU movement, but they and their like had not succeeded in providing an alternative, some way of combining rank-and-file control and revolutionary initiative with large-scale and effective trade union organisation. Bedford argues that the IWW demand for workers' control of industry could not survive intact at a time when working-class standards of living were rising: 'What the I.W.W. wished to assert . . . was contrary to appearances, once conditions threatened to improve.' The OBU failed to survive because it could not attract a following sufficiently resolute to do something about what it stood for. And yet, Bedford adds, if the emphasis on workers' control gave way before the opportunism of the leaders, this should not put paid to the emphasis itself, and subsequent left-wing organisations would be better deserving of respect if, instead of identifying the desirable end with Soviet Russia, they had kept the IWW emphasis in mind.[58]

Monty Miller had expressed his fears back in 1918 that a real OBU would never be countenanced. That trade union officials went along with the scheme at all was to dampen rank-and-file ardour for a more thorough-going OBU scheme. Workers were getting tired of slow union leadership, he noted; 'to keep them quiet some old fake OBU is being made the cry of salvation'. It was 'the plum exploited from the I.W.W. cake to keep down discontent among the dupes . . .'[59] The IIW condemned the WIUA as a useless half-way measure designed by trade union officials to defuse rank-and-file discontent with craft unionism, 'to put a spoke in the wheel of "dinkum" industrial unionism'. Miriam Roberts notes that AWU officials were indeed feeling the threat to their power from below, in the motions to give officials the same pay as union members, in the discontent with the conditions negotiated for the 1920–21 season. Thus, some time after the middle of 1920 the AWU leaders sought to lessen their burden by a superficial rapprochement with the OBU, to alleviate rank-and-file discontent and stop the OBU activists from encouraging dissatisfaction.[60]

Analyses of the sorry fate of the OBU movement tend to blame one of the extremes: either the conservative AWU for sabotaging the movement;[61] or the much too radical Wobblies for blunting with 'bludgeoning' methods the enthusiasm for industrial unionism and closer unity.[62] However, the role of the middle ground, the left trade union officials, should not be overlooked. Frank Bongiorno notes that Jock Garden was making 'conciliatory gestures towards the AWU' early in 1921 and the Trades Hall Reds generally supported the Australasian Workers' Union scheme.[63] Crucial in the process by which the 'fake OBU' came to be was the Communisation of the previously syndicalist-inclined left-wing trade union leaders.

Miriam Roberts notes that, from the vantage point of their control of Labor Council, the left-wing officials could have sponsored shop-committee based campaigns, giving a lead to the rank and file in the struggles to improve working conditions; by such means the OBU could have been built more surely from below than by waiting for craft-union officials to sanction its existence. However, during 1920 there developed a startling change in the left viewpoint: that the success of Russia's revolution endorsed a 'political' view of how the social revolution would be made. By late 1920 the red union officials were involved in forming the Communist Party and hence responded keenly to Comintern propositions that revolutionaries should assign less importance to industrial unionism than syndicalists, and should cooperate with unionists still loyal to the Labor Party. Thus, by the All-Australian TUC in June 1921, the Trades Hall militants had ceased to look upon the OBU as the revolutionary weapon *par excellence*. Since the desirability of formal AWU participation in the scheme was rated higher, so accordingly was the desirability of shop committees and rank-and-file participation rated lower; they ceased to push for shop committees and local autonomy in the OBU movement, endorsing the scheme put at the congress which bore no trace of these. The left union bureaucrats, themselves mainly craft-union officials, 'formally turned their back on the shop-committee method of building the One Big Union, exchanging it for the goodwill of the Australian Workers' Union leaders'.[64]

The OBU movement was formally laid to rest with the refusal of the Commonwealth Industrial Registrar to register the Australasian Workers' Union in 1924. In 1927 the Australian Council of Trade Unions (ACTU) was imposed upon the existing craft-union structures. Mark Feinberg, a WIIU propagandist on the Yarra Bank, insists the ACTU was a compromise response on the part of unionists who had become frightened by the OBU movement.[65] The ACTU was a travesty of IWW ideals: it was formed to function within the capitalist system that the real OBU wished to abolish; it was not based, in the main, on industrial unions but on traditional craft formations; and it was a federation at merely the highest levels of the union movement, encouraging those tendencies within the trade union movement towards increasingly bureaucratic and hierarchical forms of organisation that the IWW had so often denounced. In the United States, too, the CIO, the alleged IWW legacy to American unionism, evolved into an effective means to discipline workers and integrate a whole stratum of Americans into the system.[66] The hijacking of the OBU movement, in which the Communist Party played a part, and the subsequent form assumed by the ACTU, consolidated the predominance within trade union circles of the paid officials.

While the AWU hierarchy was anxious that the remaining outposts of Wobbly resistance to conservative union leadership were simply defeated, the Communist Party was concerned that militant industrial initiatives be waged under the banner of Communism not of revolutionary industrial unionism, and harnessed to the greater project of building the Party. W.P. Earsman, CPA general secretary, advised May Francis, secretary of the original but short-lived Melbourne Branch, that care must be taken in not endorsing in any way the WIIU form of organisation. He added confidently: 'There will be no reason for the existence of the W.I.I.U. when the Melbourne branch is organised so as to enter all fields of Communist activity.' When the Melbourne CPA was re-formed in 1924, it saw the WIIU as unnecessary and undesirable competition. The Party's cavalier attitude towards the WIUA, too, can be detected in the machinations to found the Adelaide branch of the Party. Fred Wilkinson wrote to Earsman that the local sympathisers of the Third

International planned to capture the propaganda section of the WIUA, with its assets of £50, 'even if we have to employ Third International tactics – force and terror, etc. to hurry it through'. According to plan, Adelaide's Bolsheviks forcibly entered the WIUA's hall, transferred the property of the propaganda section to themselves, and established the Adelaide branch on 26 January 1921.[67]

By the early 1930s the Communist world vision had triumphed over the Wobbly ideal of a society free of leaders and politicians of all kinds, but the battle between these competing forms of revolutionary working-class politics had been protracted. Throughout the 1920s it was former Wobblies who most clearly expressed the dissatisfaction of the militants within the AWU with the union hierarchy. The formation in December 1930 of the Pastoral Workers' Industrial Union, with Norman Jeffery as assistant secretary, was a Communist Party initiative designed, almost certainly, to wrest leadership of the AWU's militant rank and file away from IWW types and place it firmly under Communist control. Similarly, the Communist Party's sponsorship of the Unemployed Workers Movement was no mere desire to help the unemployed organise. In November 1927 ex-Wobblies and others had formed the One Big Union of Unemployed, whose constitution declared a desire 'to obtain not only the O.B.U. of Unemployed, but the O.B. Industrial Union of Australia, the organisation of the workers, and Freedom of our Class'. As Nadia Wheatley points out, the choice of title, grandiloquent and optimistic for a new struggling organisation, suggests the continuing appeal of IWW ideas. The CPA executive committee declared the OBUU 'unsound' and, by 1930, the CPA had established its Unemployed Workers Movement as the recognised unemployed organisation represented on the Labor Council, absorbing the OBUU.[68]

Moreover, despite the worst intentions of the Communist Party, the IWW kept making organisational reappearances during the 1920s, the timing and location of which were affected by Charlie Reeve's parole conditions. Reeve was released on the undertaking that he did not return to Sydney before five years, and was deported in the first instance to Western Australia where, according to the Premier, he began making statements 'calculated to promote disorder'. Perth police began preparing a dossier on Reeve with the aim of persuading federal authorities to take action against him.[69] Reeve escaped this attention by departing for Adelaide where, according to Alf Wilson, he 'stormed the citadel . . . He was a new type of speaker, and half the Park gathered to hear him . . .' John Playford's research concludes that it was Reeve's arrival in December 1922 that caused the collapse in February 1923 of the Adelaide CPA branch formed there in January 1921, because he persuaded most of the militants to leave the Party. In front of crowds of thousands he would ridicule the CPA, referring to it as the 'Comical Party' and its local representatives as 'tinpot Lenins'; the CPA lacked forceful speakers to combat the 'magnetic histrionics' of Reeve.[70]

Reeve continued his way round the underbelly of Australia. By July 1924, the Unlawful Associations Act having expired, Reeve had re-formed the Melbourne IWW, which survived until 1931, holding regular propaganda meetings on the Yarra Bank and at the South Melbourne Market. 'They used to dish it out', recalls Jim Garvey. Jim Scott concedes that the IWW leftovers were conducting more propaganda work in Melbourne than the WIIU. 'Roly Farrall, Bill Coombes – they could hold a crowd.' Mark Feinberg, too, admits the IWW had a bigger following than the WIIU, and that a lot of them were also members of unions. The IWW was likewise revived in Perth during 1924. By mid-1925, the IWW was re-formed in Sydney by Noel 'Ham and Eggs' Lyons, a seaman recently deported from New Zealand for leading the 'Ham and Egg Strike' over food on the SS *Wanganella* in the Tasman Sea.[71]

Still barred from Sydney, Reeve returned to Adelaide from Melbourne where he relaunched an Adelaide IWW. It took possession of a ring in the Botanic Park; however, the Board that governed the park enforced a by-law prohibiting any person from speaking without a personal permit, and Reeve was denied one. A Labor member of the Board, Arthur McArthur, boasted while speaking from the Labor ring in 1925 that the IWW would 'never get a permit while I am on the board'. An IWW-inspired free-speech fight began in the winter of 1926. Reeve kept returning to speak, was fined and arrested several times then jailed for non-payment. Many others, such as Jack Zwolsman and Ted O'Reilly, came forward and spoke without permits. They were locked up, tried and fined; soon there were a dozen in jail. Out again, Reeve took the platform only to go through the same arrest, fine and imprisonment. Not only was it a Labor government that presided over this victimisation of the Adelaide IWW but ALP members, perturbed at losing most of their audiences at the park to the IWW speakers, gave evidence against the free-speech fighters. According to Morrison, the militants in South Australia, most of whom belonged to the IWW, suffered heavily under the successive Labor governments from 1920 to March 1927.[72]

On 31 November 1926 Reeve was released from jail, after which he returned finally to Sydney. The Adelaide Wobblies, still battling for free-speech rights throughout 1927, appealed to the Melbourne IWW for help, who sent Ted Dickinson and Jim McNeill across in November. Dickinson was a labourer, born in Grimsby in England in 1903, who had arrived in Australia as a three-year-old and had been involved with Lyons in leading the 'Ham and Egg Strike'. McNeill, a metal worker, had been born in Redfern in 1900.[73] A new generation of Wobblies was emerging.

In 1927 the Sydney IWW, operating from Box 11 at the Surry Hills Post Office, near Charlie Reeve's house in Yurong Street, reissued Trautmann's *New Industrial Methods* and distributed other old IWW publications such as *The Immediate Demands of the I.W.W. Unemployment and the Machine* and *Industrial Union Methods*. Crowds of thousands attended IWW meetings in the Domain during the late 1920s. In these days, the IWW referred to the Communists as 'the dirty unwashed', disapproving of their ill-kept appearance and the bohemian milieu they frequented.[74]

Bluey Howells, who joined the IWW in 1929, recalls his first meeting on the Domain in 1928. Attending with some trepidation, expecting to see people resembling the dangerous arsonists of public perception, he found instead that the IWW members closely gathered around the stump were

> earnest looking men of varying ages and several middle-aged and elderly women. . . . Few could be described as shabbily dressed and on the whole they presented . . . a spectacle of neatness and respectability . . . In front of the stump, laid out on the ground for inspection, was an array of literature . . . A roughly printed notice read: 'Take home some Mental Dynamite'.

The audience became quieter as Reeve, with sleek jet-black hair and sparkling black eyes, mounted the stump:

> He stood, hands on hips, lapping up the applause . . . He attacked everything: Royalty, the Roman Church, the Protestant Church, Soviet Russia, the Labor Party, the Socialists, the Communists, the Trades Unions . . . Archbishop Kelly was 'an ignorant bog-Irishman with a dirty mind, like all priests . . .' . . . Jack Lang was 'a tool of the boss class' . . . Bruce was 'a puffed up stool pigeon of British Imperialism'.[75]

When two plain-clothed policemen spoke loudly during the speech of a nervous woman speaker appealing for assistance during the 1929 timber workers' strike, Reeve abused the police, who grabbed him by the legs, smashing the back of his head on the hard boards of the platform; blood ran down the back of his neck and his shirt was in ribbons. Uniformed police then drew batons and, wielding them indiscriminately, broke up the crowd after arresting seven people. Reeve was found guilty of abusive language and fined £10, Carl Jensen of assaulting police and fined £20, at a time when the basic wage was about £4 a week.

In May 1928 the Adelaide IWW, once more the Australian Administration of the IWW, commenced another series of *Direct Action*, edited by Zwolsman and Dickinson. 'Our hands will be full', this *Direct Action* predicted, 'in exposing certain new bred craft union officials and pimp Labor politicians, who, along with the old gang have got saucy during the enforced absence of the I.W.W. from the industrial arena.'

Usually, 2000 copies were printed and it was sold on the job, at employment centres, and in the Botanic Park on Sunday afternoons. Outside of Adelaide, it was distributed by the Italian Club in Broken Hill, J. Markland in Melbourne, Annie Westbrook in Sydney, Noel Lyons in Brisbane, H.H. Wooding in Paruna (SA) and Harry and Violet Wilkins in Perth. A letter from north Queensland informed the Adelaide centre that, as a result of the reappearance of *Direct Action*, the 'old Wobbly bunch up here are stirring into increased activity', especially the 'waterfront slaves' at Lucinda, Mourilyan Harbour and Cairns.[76]

The Adelaide IWW of the late 1920s was especially active amongst the unemployed who gathered miserably in hope of a day's work at the unemployed shelter. Jim McNeill recalls:

> Our daily procedure was to go to this hall. There'd be about half a dozen speakers. Dickinson took the stump every day. He had the crowd in his hands and he'd lead them out into the streets in demonstration after demonstration. They'd go down King William Street and Rundle Street. Adelaide became familiar with the singing of Wobbly songs!

Sometimes, the IWW mob would prevent an eviction, on one occasion shaming the police into putting money into the collection for the evicted family. Unemployed demonstrations were organised by Dickinson and Zwolsman and other Wobblies such as Ted Moyle of the Carpenters' Union, who had formed the Local back in 1911, and Ted O'Reilly, an Aboriginal, who had been a capable soap-box orator for the IWW over sixteen years. The esteem in which the authorities still held the IWW was evident during an unemployed march in September 1929; the Liberal Premier refused to receive Dickinson and Zwolsman as members of the deputation of unemployed.[77]

On 1 October 1928 Dickinson had been arrested for his alleged role in leading the march of 27 September to Port Adelaide in support of the waterside workers' strike. He was charged with 'unlawfully taking part in a riot' and with seditious libel in connection with an article in the first strike edition of *Direct Action* on 30 September: 'if a bloody revolution is forced on the workers it will be so forced by the master class . . . Therefore, fellow-workers, be prepared and ready to use the weapons of the day.' Dickinson was sentenced to three months' jail for the riot offence and six for the seditious libel. After his arrest, the resurrected *Direct Action* he was then editing only survived for one more issue.[78]

In Perth, too, the re-formed IWW was active in agitation amongst the unemployed and in opposing the repressive actions of the State Labor government, the use of baton-wielding policemen against the peaceable protesters of the unemployed movement. In August 1928 this Labor government banned the sale of *Direct Action* throughout the State; the Perth Trades Hall likewise barred the two leading IWW members, Harry Wilkins and Violet Clarke Wilkins, from entering the Trades Hall, even though Harry Wilkins was a financial member of a craft union.[79]

These resurgent Locals in Sydney, Melbourne, Adelaide and Perth in the late 1920s sapped the strength of the CPA branches, especially in Adelaide. As late as August 1930, the Adelaide IWW could draw a crowd of 5000 to its meeting in denunciation of the Premier's Plan; the Labor Party speakers at the adjacent ring needed police protection from this crowd after the Wobbly speakers had ventured their opinions on wage cuts and rising unemployment. Jim McNeill, who joined the CPA after it was re-formed in Adelaide in 1929, insists the level of activities of the Adelaide IWW in the late 1920s was not matched by the Party until 1931–32 and only in Melbourne and Sydney. The Party admitted that the influx of Wobblies into the Adelaide CPA in 1931 caused an 'unprecedented stimulation of activity'. Ted Moyle attests that when these Wobblies were 'eventually won over' it greatly increased the number of speakers for Party work. In Melbourne, Jim Garvey maintains that the IWW was still important in the late 1920s, in the waterside and timber workers' strikes for instance, and that it was not until 1931 that the Communist Party assumed a role more significant. The same process occurred in other centres.[80]

In Britain, where the IWW had never been of any consequence, the Communist Party had prospered in the 1920s. In Australia, it was not until the later Depression years that the Party succeeded in laying to rest the ghost of the IWW that had haunted it in its formative era. Ironically, it achieved this primarily in its notorious 'Third Period' that signalled increasing Stalinisation, because this period was characterised also by hard-line opposition to reformist parties. The twists and turns of the CPA in relation to the Labor Party had been the subject of much scornful comment in the resurrected *Direct Action*. When the CPA's December 1929 conference made plain that the Party would confront the ALP, the IWW began to view the CPA with more sympathy. The Adelaide Local was disbanded in February 1931 and most of its members absorbed into the CPA, including Ted O'Reilly and his brother Bill, Jack Zwolsman, Ted Moyle and Jim McNeill, who later fought in Spain. Ted Dickinson had left Australia in 1930 for Britain where he helped to found the International Freedom League to fight Sir Oswald Mosley's British Union of Fascists and later lost his life fighting Spanish Fascists. This process of absorption of Wobblies into the CPA was probably repeated in Perth, the Local there seeing its demise at the same time as the one in Adelaide. However, it appears this was not the case in Sydney: a 1931–32 Legislative Assembly list of 159 known Communists includes only three names familiar as ex-Wobblies: Norman Jeffery, Joseph Shelley and Lucy Eatock; and Matthew Hade was a sympathiser.[81]

Nonetheless, in June 1931 *Workers Weekly* boasted that 'practically the whole of the leaders of the I.W.W.' had been won over to the Communist Party. The Party wanted former Wobblies to join, but only Wobblies tired and beaten, with not a glimmer of syndicalist life left in them. Mary Wright recalls that Lucy Eatock's direct actionist temper met with disapproval from Party members. Late in 1931 the visiting Comintern agent and FBI spy, Herbert Moore, made veiled threats against the 'I.W.W. element' within the Party. *Workers Weekly* warned that 'nobody must imagine that syndicalist tendencies have been definitely disposed of in Adelaide', because 'the propaganda of a dozen years cannot be broken by a mere eighteen months of Communist teachings'. As late as 1933 the central hierarchy was still accusing the Adelaide branch of being 'anarcho-syndicalist'.[82]

The CPA resented the fact that Wobbly ideas maintained a tenacious hold on the minds of many militants, making them wary about the methods, if not the aims, of the Communists. When J.B. King rejoined the Party in 1930, he was sent immediately to the Soviet Union for six years for re-education. His return in 1936 was nicely timed, just when needed to justify the new united front tactic to those still inclined to Wobbly ideas.[83]

And still the IWW refused to die out completely. Within a few years, the Perth Wobblies had left the Communist Party once more and re-formed the IWW, aggravated by the Party's united front tactics after 1935 and the performance of a State Labor government from 1933, which, they noted, presided over pathetic relief work allowances while drawing enormous salaries for themselves. When J.B. Miles visited Perth during the federal election campaign of 1937, urging a Labor vote, the Perth Wobblies confronted him. According to Violet Wilkins, they 'criticized the policy of the comics in supporting the Labor party', whereupon Mr Miles 'got very abusive' and refused to debate the subject. Writing for an American IWW publication, she warned American workers not to imagine that the election of Labor or Communist politicians would make a great improvement in the standard of living: 'The example of how "Labor" governs in Australia should help to dispel any false hopes in this direction.'[84]

The Perth IWW was holding regular meetings on the Esplanade in 1939, though its minutes suggest its membership was less than a dozen. When war broke out the Perth Wobblies advocated a boycott of the compilation of the National Register of Manpower, holding a demonstration through the main streets in the form of a funeral procession, since those revealed in the register as unemployed 'would be given a very prominent

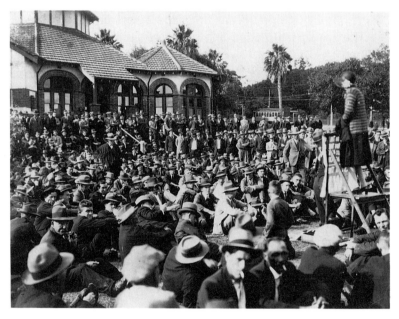

(Top) In August 1939 the Perth IWW demonstrated in Hay and Murray Streets against the National Register of Manpower and were arrested for their efforts. (Archives of Labor and Urban Affairs, Wayne State University, Detroit, Michigan, USA) (Above) Violet Wilkins addressing an IWW meeting in Perth during the Second World War. (Archives of Labor and Urban Affairs, Wayne State University, Detroit, Michigan, USA)

position in the firing line'. Several were arrested and sentenced to a few days' jail after singing 'Solidarity Forever' loudly during the court proceedings. Violet Wilkins was contemptuous of the 'Stalinites' for promoting war by the signing of the Nazi–Soviet Non-Aggression Pact in August 1939: while urging workers throughout the world to defend democracy against fascism, 'Russia jumped in behind the Fascist countries thus culminating in one huge betrayal her long series of treacheries to the workers of the world'.[85]

After the end of the Second World War the IWW pamphlet, *One Big Union of All Workers*, was reissued in Melbourne, sponsored possibly by the former editor of the *OBU Herald*, Jim Dawson. His journal, *Southern Socialist Review*, reprinted the Preamble in 1946 and announced: 'The IWW is still the salt of the labor movement that needs to be rubbed into the wounds of the workers in their fight with the employing class.' Norman Rancie contacted Dawson, expressing his pleasure at Dawson's suggestion that workers should organise along IWW lines: 'Parliamentary Socialism only fools and misleads the masses . . . How that name politician stinks – everywhere – in all lands!'[86]

Rancie and others in Sydney re-formed a Sydney IWW for a time in 1946–47, which denounced the 'comrats' for their Stalinism and 'super-patriotism', then faded away. It was revived yet again in 1948 by the remorseless Violet Wilkins, now in Sydney, who reported to Chicago in January: 'I have 5 new members and they are a decent type of fellows so now we will build a branch in Sydney, and then I will go on to Melbourne, and do likewise also South Australia then back to Perth . . .' The new Sydney IWW was launched on 8 February 1948 with about eight members.[87] Fellow-Worker George McFarlane wrote to Chicago: '

> The Wilkins are doing a good job in organising a branch here . . . The I.W.W. was very strong here in World War 1. Many old hands would like to see it revived. The Communist Party is very strong and practically all the militants are roped in. They are past masters at organising. We hope to take some of their members.[88]

The Sydney IWW maintained links with 'Fellow-Worker Dawson' in Melbourne, whose journal was now called the *Southern Advocate for Workers' Councils*.[89]

In a remarkable feat of personal political continuity, Annie Westbrook, nearly 80 years old, was involved in this Sydney group: 'I have been an Industrial Unionist for 35 years; never fell for the Como line . . .' While acknowledging that the 'IWW has been killed thru apathy & warring Political Parties', she noted that great upheavals may come when least expected. There was an awakening the world over as to the futility of political parties: 'No one expected the great upheaval of the Russian

Peasant in 1917, tho it has landed that country into the Totalitarian State the war was fought to save us from.'[90]

Though the 1920s generation of Wobblies, especially in Adelaide and Perth, had largely disappeared into the Communist Party, most of the original Wobblies, like Westbrook, remained averse to 'the Como line' or quickly became so after short spells within the Communist Party; and their antipathy was reciprocated. Before he left Australia in May 1922 Peter Larkin had left the Communist Party because, like Tom Glynn, he reckoned they would 'never get Industrial Unionism through the Party'. Back in Ireland he fell out with his Communist brother James because of his continuing affection for dual unionism. While James was in Moscow in mid-1924 Peter encouraged the militants to break away from the Irish Transport and General Workers Union, launching the Workers' Union of Ireland. While Tom Glynn was slowly dying from the illness that origrinated from his time in Long Bay jail, the Communist Party was lambasting him for remaining an 'Anarcho-Syndicalist', for failing to understand the Marxist–Leninist position in regard to the state, the dictatorship of the proletariat, and the mechanism of the revolution. He died in December 1934 and was buried in Botany Cemetery, near Long Bay jail.[91]

Lesbia Harford died of pneumonia in 1927 at the age of thirty-six. In editing and introducing her verse for *The Poems of Lesbia Harford* in 1941, Nettie Palmer, whose brother and daughter were Communists, presented her poems as concerned more with nationalism than class and made no mention of her IWW membership. In 1964 Guido Baracchi suggested that Lesbia would never have joined the CPA, that she could never have accepted its hierarchies and authoritarianism. Drusilla Modjeska suggests that, although neither the IWW nor the CPA challenged old patterns of sexual power, the IWW's looser structure left more room for the reconciliation of class and sexual politics, perhaps offering working women the promise of direct action and control over their situation in a way a hierarchical party could not.[92]

J.B. King's reprogramming at the hand of Soviet authorities was only briefly effective. The *Sydney Morning Herald* had been delighted that an IWW man, who had advocated go-slow methods, had become 'a Fast Worker in Russia', a hero of the Five Year Plan for producing twice as much as expected while superintendent of a Russian coal mine. He had wanted the workers to produce 'in less than Johannesburg time', but the antiquated machinery had broken down in the attempt. After his return to Australia in 1936 he eulogised the Soviet experiment in a speech on 8 November in the Friends of the Soviet Union Hall in Sydney. However, King soon became disillusioned with the CPA, explaining in 'an unpleasant letter' to Percy Laidler that he did not believe in it any more. He moved to Queensland and drifted out of political activity.[93]

Together with the other Wobblies deported to Chile, Tom Barker was dumped over the border into Argentina, where they found work on the wharves of Buenos Aires and became active in the Marine Transport Workers' Union. In 1920 Barker represented the Argentine Labour Federation at the conference of transport unions in Oslo. After this meeting, he attended a Syndicalist Conference in Berlin which rejected the principle of the dictatorship of the proletariat on the ground that the state was inherently bad. In the middle of 1921 he visited Moscow as an Argentine delegate to the RILU conference. He wrote enthusiastically to Glynn that politicians 'will have no place in Russia', that Lenin had denounced them. He became involved with Big Bill Haywood in working on the Autonomous Industrial Colony Kuzbas, which aimed to utilise foreign expertise in establishing heavy industry in Siberia. With his new wife, Berta Isaakovna, Barker was sent to New York where he worked until 1926 on recruiting American technicians and engineers for the Kuzbas project. He never joined the Communist Party, informing Soviet authorities that his IWW ideas, to which he remained loyal, did not agree with some of the Communist ideas. The matter was taken to Lenin who approved Barker's stand; like Trotsky, he was more tolerant of Wobblies than their Australian emulators. After returning to Siberia in 1926 Barker was less impressed by the Soviet achievement: 'Things were changing and a new generation had arisen.'[94]

Ultimately, Barker worked as a clerk with the London Electricity Board, became a Labour member of the St Pancras Council in 1949 and mayor in 1958–59, at a time when the council was resisting the Tory government's determination that council tenants' rents be increased, refusing to operate civil defence arrangements, insisting on a closed shop for council employees and flying the Red Flag each May Day. As a Camden councillor until the late 1960s, he was remembered with great affection by the locals as a socialist who helped the ordinary people of the borough towards a better life and a better home. He died in April 1970 at the age of 83, having looked after his blind wife for more than twenty years. In 1973 a documentary play about his life was produced and performed by the Unity Theatre at the Camden Festival.[95]

Donald Grant left the Communist Party in February 1922 and informed the Brisbane branch that it could think of him as they wished. By 1923 he had decided there was no chance of 'successful action' outside of the ALP. Lloyd Ross believes Grant was 'insincere in his support for the Labor Party', that he was 'a bit of a political lair'. Probably he saw the ALP as his best opportunity for a political career, a way to continue a life of public speaking; in time, he became a Labor man. A City Council alderman from 1931 to 1944 and a member of the Legislative Council from 1931 to 1940, he entered the Senate on the Labor ticket in 1943. In 1945 he was photographed in evening dress beside the Duke and Duchess of Gloucester; the socialist press was scornful. During the 1949 coal strike he incurred the wrath of industrial militants for his support for the jailing of the union leaders. According to Mick Sawtell in 1967 he was regarded by old Wobblies as a traitor. He was dropped from the Labor Senate ticket in 1959, after which he lived in obscurity in Double Bay, suffering from emphysema, which had been aggravated by a lifetime of public speaking, until his death in June 1970.[96]

Alf Wilson joined the SLP when the WIIU collapsed. Returning to Melbourne, he worked as Depression labour on the rockery and water-falls in the land around the Shrine, while conducting classes for the SLP and speaking for them on the Yarra Bank on Sundays. Rejecting the pretensions of the CPA, he insisted in his memoirs that the SLP was 'the one and only party that has adhered strictly to the Marxian position'. Subsequently, it expelled him for failing to produce proper statements of accounts and balance sheets. He died suddenly of a heart attack while working on the sewerage scheme at Benalla on 19 August 1937.[97]

Mick Sawtell, who settled in Sydney and opened a small health food shop in the Victoria Arcade, became so dismayed by the emergence in the 1930s of Stalinist standards of socialist correctness that he abandoned his faith in socialism, while remaining of an interventionist disposition. He was arrested in December 1934 for his part in a demonstration against war and fascism, convicted of assaulting police and inciting the crowd to violence. Denying the charges, he explained the police action: 'They of course know me . . .' In 1940 he was appointed a member of the Aborigines Welfare Board. He became a popular lecturer at the House of Culture above the Hasty Tasty Cafe at 86 Darlinghurst Rd, the head-quarters of the Australian Cultural Society, formed in 1942 by Friends of the Soviet Union members who had either been expelled or left in dis-gust. A champion writer of letters to newspapers, a poet, a vegetarian and an exponent of yoga with a fondness for standing on his head, his last great cause was a campaign to divert the water running to waste down the coastal rivers of Queensland into central Australia, to turn the desert into a lush paradise, hosting a community of self-supporting towns. He died in Kings Cross on 1 October 1971.[98]

After their removal from Australia, Jock and May Wilson joined the Communist Party of Great Britain: Jock was made an organiser for the Party in south Wales, its candidate in Caerphilly and a member of its national executive, attending the Third Congress in Moscow; in 1928 May was a member of the first British women's delegation to the USSR. However, by the 1930s the Wilsons had come to disagree with the 'foolish branding of people as social fascists' and 'administrative bureau-cracy'. Jock was accordingly removed from leadership positions. They returned to Australia, where, in retirement on the New South Wales south coast, they became active in the anti-Vietnam War movement and May in the Nebo mine women's auxiliary. Still professing themselves ardent socialists, they did not join the CPA, being critical of the Soviet Union and the witch-hunting within the Party: 'It's happened so often; people who make honest criticism find themselves accused of being ene-mies of the working class, traitors to the revolution, slanderers of the Soviet Union and all the other stock-in-trade names. It's verbal vomit.'[99]

Charlie Reeve opened a small radical bookshop in Broadway, where Tooths Brewery is now located, which flourished in the 1930s as a drop-in centre for all kinds of radicals from American IWW merchant seamen to university students on their way to and from lectures. Charlie would make tea and invite debate from all quarters. He maintained his belief that bloody revolution was not the way to a socialist society, that educa-tion and the organisation of the masses into a cohesive, intelligent majority was necessary before any such goal could be achieved; revolu-tion by an ignorant herd, no matter how intelligent its leaders, could only end in bureaucratic dictatorship. He regarded J.B. King as 'a mis-guided fool' for rejoining the CPA; Donald Grant was 'a traitor to the working class' for joining the Labor Party.[100]

Charlie hurt his head badly in a fall, then contracted pneumonia. He died in June 1942 in the arms of a lover, not a working-class Wobbly, but a middle-class bohemian 'queen', Ernest Guthrie. He was buried with full revolutionary honours, his coffin shrouded in the Red Flag, the ser-vice being conducted, unfortunately, by Norman Jeffery, who had emerged as a hatchet-man of the CPA, a man to whom the Party word was law and critics anathema.[101]

From Long Bay jail in September 1919, Reeve had written to his mother that it was 'useless waiting for heaven born leaders, saints or prophets, in our hands, lies the remedy'. He was confident that 'that great goal, liberty' would be attained:

> There will come a time, when we, the workers, will put our arms around the world, & make it a playground for all humanity, when each will give his best, & all the evils that now exist, will be swept away; with the light of gladness in our eyes, with the song of freedom, singing in our hearts we will march to the haven of reality, of life, see our children happy, our wives, equal mates, and love, sunshine, flowers, songs, ours, all ours, because we have striven . . . we have a world to win, a hell to lose.[102]

However, by January 1921 his mood had changed. He wrote to those 'still interested in the Working Class Movement' that:

Not many years ago, it seemed, that for the first time in the history of union-ism, (at least, as far as this country was concerned) that the Workers were on the right road to emancipation, Per medium of Revolutionary Industrial Unionism. But, it seems that they are slipping back further than ever, by being fooled & strangled, by such outfits as Communists Parties, Political Claused One Big Unions, etc.

Since both movements encouraged office seekers and parliamentarism, both were doomed to failure: 'I cannot understand why the workers are fooling with all kinds of fake outfits'.[103]

The IWW still exists today as an exceedingly pale reflection of its former self, appearing in its new guise around the time that the very last rem-nants of the old IWW petered out. In Sydney in 1967 Bert Armstrong was speaking and selling American IWW literature in the Domain, living in dire poverty but scrupulously forwarding all monies from paper sales to Chicago. Around the same time, a new-style Melbourne IWW branch appeared, producing an occasional broadsheet called the *Wobbly*, bear-ing the IWW badge and the running head: 'If voting could change things, it would be against the law.' About 1977 in Sydney, Wobblies emerged from Jura Books, Michael Matteson amongst them. In the early 1980s this Sydney IWW group began producing a newspaper, *Rebel Worker*, 'Paper of the Australian IWW', with contact addresses also in Fremantle and Brisbane. With the eastern bloc countries in mind, it argued that no socialist society could be built by the capturing of power by a vanguardist party: 'This kind of Socialism is but a window-dressing for exploitation, strong state centralism, totalitarianism and bureau-cratisation of human activities. It survives thanks to state terrorism: secret police, prisons, gallows and labour camps.'[104] Collapsing into the anarchist and anarcho-syndicalist movements with which the original IWW had little sympathy, *Rebel Worker* became within a few years the paper of the Anarcho-Syndicalist Federation.

Currently, there exists a Melbourne IWW, operating from a post office box at the GPO and advertising itself in the Anarcho-Syndicalist Federation's new newspaper, *Burning Issue*. Its banner has appeared at the demonstrations of enraged parents rallying in protest at the Kennett government's closures of State schools. The *Industrial Worker*, newspaper of the modern-day American IWW based in San Francisco, lists the Melbourne group in its directory and a Sydney area group on the cor-ner of Dittons Lane and the Old Illawarra Highway in Sutton Forest.[105]

The IWW, once capable of mobilising workers in their thousands, can meet now in the proverbial phone-box. And yet, the fact of these modern-day re-enactments attests to the durability of the IWW legend. With the discrediting of the Bolshevik tradition, the alternative form of

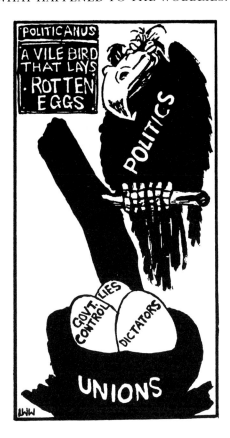

POLITICANUS

A VILE BIRD THAT LAYS ROTTEN EGGS

POLITICS

GOVT. CONTROL

LIES

DICTATORS

UNIONS

The IWW in Melbourne in the 1970s had more in common with anarchist groups than the original IWW. This cartoon appeared on a poster advertising a fund-raising entertainment. (F.J. Riley Ephemera Collection, State Library of Victoria)

revolutionary working-class politics espoused by the IWW before 1917 deserves renewed consideration. With the advantage of hindsight we can now view the Communist Parties of the world, and the historians who glorified them, with the critical gaze they once turned upon the IWW. It is worth bearing in mind, too, that it was the Wobbly tradition to which Communists often appealed in moments of doubt, to express their misgivings about the Communist project that had supplanted the grander aims of revolutionary industrial unionism.

Other scholars, too, have tended to interpret the IWW from a spurious vantage point, the knowledge of the IWW's failure; in the light of the demise of Communism and the acknowledged shortcomings of the social democratic project, the lost cause of the IWW is worth rescuing from the dustbin of history, if only to examine its critique of the labour movement ideologies and practices, of Communism and Laborism, that triumphed over it.

Or, if the IWW cannot serve as a model for emancipation in this supposedly postmodern era, if chains are now too lightly worn, it can offer at the very least an example of more effective oppositional politics whether within the labour movement or in the wider society. The activist temper of the Wobblies had clearly remained with those interviewed in their declining years. Bill Ivey was busy organising protests to force a local council to preserve a children's playground; Jimmy Seamer had co-ordinated protests in his nursing home about the standard of catering; Fred Coombe had persuaded his colleagues in the Malvern Senior Citizens Club not to stand for the National Anthem on the grounds that it was patriotic rubbish and, in any case, old folk should not be required to stand. The emancipatory project of the IWW may have become as incomprehensible to those conditioned by postmodern prejudices and consumerist practices as any other great mission, cause or vision. Yet there remain many aspects of Wobbly political practice still relevant to contemporary existence, of enduring use to people determined upon enlarging the realm of freedom and restricting that of necessity.

Notes

Chapter 1
'Flowers to the Rebels Failed'

1 For example, Tom Rogers in *Bensons Valley*, who fights evictions; 'The stranger in the camp' in *The Man from Inkapella and Other Stories*; and McDougall in 'How Sandy Mitchell won the lottery' is based on McDermott, a Wobbly friend of his father. Hardy interview (with Adams, 12/9/90).
2 Hardy interview (with Adams, 16/9/89).
3 Hardy, *Power Without Glory*, p.373.
4 Hardy, *Power Without Glory*, pp.255–8. See IWW, *Rebel Songs*, p.16.
5 Hardy interview.
6 Hardy interview; Hardy interview (with Adams, 12/9/90).
7 Mackie, *Mount Isa*, p.13.
8 Mackie interview; Pat Mackie, Sydney, 13/2/89, to author.
9 Riedlinger, 'The red north recalled', p.9.
10 Mackie, *Mount Isa*, p.115.
11 Riedlinger, 'The red north recalled', p.11.
12 LT10772/10.
13 Matteson interview.
14 Quoted in M. Burgmann, 'A new concept of unionism', p.405.
15 Mundey interview.
16 M. Burgmann, 'A new concept of unionism', pp.398–411.
17 Rushton, 'Revolutionary ideology', p.446.
18 Below, *The Vedgymight History of Australia*, p.53.
19 American literature that pays tribute to the IWW includes: John Dos Passos, *1919* and *The 42nd Parallel*; James Jones, *From Here to Eternity*; Wallace Stegner, *The Preacher and the Slave*; Barrie Stavis, *The Man Who Would Not Die*; and Eugene O'Neill, *Hairy Ape*. In the early 1970s the Swedish filmmaker, Bo Wilderberg, produced a film on Joe Hill. In 1979 Stewart Bird and Deborah Shaffer in the United States produced *The Wobblies*, based on a play of the same name by Bird and Peter Robilotta.
20 Lindsay, *Life Rarely Tells*, pp.133, 160, 139, 189.
21 Sendy, 'The founders', p.6.
22 Waten interview.

23   Alan Marshall, 17/10/80, to Tom Payne, in possession of author.
24   p.39.
25   Robert Corcoran, Melbourne, 21/5/93, to author.
26   Coombe interview.
27   Hardy interview.
28   Audley interview (with Gowland and Saffin); May Brodney, 'Histortions', LT10882/10/31; Bertha Walker, 20/2/64, to Roly, LT10772/3.
29   Bedford, 'The IWW', p.46.
30   For instance, P.R. Stephenson, 'The bunyip critic', *The Publicist*, no.3, Sept. 1936, p.7.
31   Howells interview.
32   Nairn, review of Turner's *Sydney's Burning* in *Historical Studies*, 13, Oct. 1967, p.131.
33   Hayden, 'The Wobblies at War', esp. pp.5, 8.
34   Renshaw, *The Wobblies*, pp.258–9.
35   Ross interview.
36   Mansell, 'The yeast is red'; McQueen, *A New Britannia*, p.191; 'Laborism and socialism', pp.61–2; May Day file, Riley Collection, LT.
37   Zieger, 'Workers and scholars', p.256.
38   Bedford, 'The IWW', p.46.
39   Reeves, 'Yours 'til the war of classes is ended', p.24.
40   Karabogias, 'Fanning the flames', p.87.
41   Preston, 'Shall this be all?', p.437.
42   Saville, 'The radical left expects the past to do its duty', p.273.
43   Childe, *How Labour Governs*, p.150.
44   Principally in the work of Philip Foner and William Z. Foster (Buhle, 'The Wobblies in perspective', p.45; Dubofsky, 'Dissent', p.179).
45   Campbell, *History of the Australian Labour Movement*, p.38; Sharkey, *An Outline History of the Australian Communist Party*, pp.12–15; E. Ross, *The Russian Revolution*, pp.27–8.
46   Turner, *Industrial Labour*, p.64.
47   Gollan, 'Has the Australian labour movement ever been radical?', pp.43–4.

Chapter 2
'On the Industrial as well as on the Political Field': the IWW Clubs, 1905–1910

1   IWW, *How Capital has Hypnotised Society*, p.16.
2   *The Founding Convention of the IWW*, pp.247–8.
3   Renshaw, *The Wobblies*, pp.268–9, 50; Conlin, *Bread and Roses*, p.3; Brissenden, *Launching of the IWW*, p.40; Dubofsky, *We Shall Be All*, p.159. See also Cornford, *Workers and Dissent*.
4   Quoted in Kiek, 'South Australian labour unions', p.78.
5   ASL Minutes, 3/10/05, 3/4/06, ML2042/2/73, 84–5; P, 18/11/05.
6   SLP, *The Unity Question*, pp.4–5, 11.
7   *ISR*, 22/6/07, pp.3–4.
8   *Edinburgh Socialist*, May 1909, ABLN57/246.
9   *Flame*, July 1907, p.2.
10   H.J. Hawkins, Broken Hill, 25/6/07, to 'Dear Comrade', NL3516.
11   SLP, *The Unity Question*, pp.4–5, 11.
12   A.K. Wallace, Sec. Barrier Socialist Group, 1/10/07, to F. Hyett, Melbourne, NL3516.

13 De Leon, *Socialism Versus Anarchism*, p.5; SLP, *The Unity Question*, p.5; *P*, 26/1/01, 5/4/02, 13/12/02.
14 McKee, 'Daniel De Leon', pp.273–4.
15 De Leon, *Socialist Reconstruction*.
16 IWW Club, *An Open Letter*.
17 IWW Club, *The Two Wars*, pp.1, 8, 26, 28, 30.
18 Rushton, 'The IWW in Sydney', p.53.
19 SLP, *Report to International Congress*, 1910.
20 IWW Club, *Constitution*, Sydney, 1909, pp.5, 7, 12–13.
21 Letters from Holland and Scott Bennett, 23/9/08, both to Sec. Sydney IWW Club, NL3516.
22 IWW Club, Sydney, no.2 Minute Book, 28/7/09, 12/8/08, 9/9/08, 7/4/09, ABL N57/131; Edward Jancke, 1/9/10, to A.J. Edwards, Hon. Sec. IWW Club, ML262/1.
23 IWW Club, Sydney, no.2 Minute Book, 30/12/08, ABL N57/131.
24 SLP, *The Unity Question*, p.11; W. North, Kurri Kurri, 4/5/08, to Moroney, NL2576/8; IWW Club Correspondence, 1907–21, ML262/1; J.W. Ring, Nat. Sec. IWW Clubs, Sydney, 24/12/12, to fellow workers, NL2576/3.
25 M. O'Dowd, 15/3/08, to J.F. Neill, ML A1333; VSP Minute Books, 11/5/08, also 13/4/08, 26/10/08, 10/11/08, NL564/1/1.
26 IWW Club, Sydney, no.1 Minute Book, 15/1/08, ABL N57/131; *Socialist*, 8/2/08, p.3; Hewitt, 'VSP', p.68; Merrifield, 'IWW', *Recorder*, 47, pp.10–11; ibid., *Recorder*, 48, pp.1–2.
27 Merrifield, 'IWW', *Recorder*, 47, p.11.
28 Fitzpatrick, *British Empire*, p.322; Rushton, 'The IWW in Sydney', pp.56–7.
29 IWW Club, *The Two Wars*, pp.26, 31.
30 Fitzhardinge, *Hughes*, I, p.224.
31 15/3/08, to J.F. Neill, ML A1333.
32 R. Wright, 17/11/09, to J.F. Neill, ML262/1.
33 Childe, *How Labour Governs*, p.105.
34 Gollan, *Coalminers*, p.124; Bedford, 'The IWW', p.44.
35 Churchward, 'American influence', p.275.
36 Fitzpatrick, *British Empire*, p.322.
37 Gollan, *Coalminers*, pp.122–4.
38 *Truth*, 1/12/07.
39 O'Farrell, *Harry Holland*, p.28; Gollan, *Coalminers*, p.124.
40 O'Farrell, *Harry Holland*, p.28.
41 *Socialist*, 20/3/08, quoted in Merrifield, 'IWW', *Recorder*, 47, p.12.
42 *Worker*, 9/2/08, quoted in Childe, *How Labour Governs*, pp.107; Child, *Unionism*, p.118.
43 Childe, *How Labour Governs*, pp.106–7; Child, *Unionism*, p.118; Coates, 'Note on the IWW', p.25.
44 *ISR*, 2 May 1908.
45 E. Ross, *These Things Shall Be*, pp.81, 83.
46 Quoted in Holland, *Labor Sledgehammered*.
47 *Industrial Worker*, 8/1/10, p.3.
48 IWW Club, *An Open Letter*.
49 NL3516, esp. J.E. Dodd, Sec. Goldfields Federated Miners' Union of WA, Kalgoorlie and Boulder branch, 1/8/11, to H.J. Hawkins, Sec. IWW Club, Sydney.
50 Child, *Unionism*, p.118.
51 O'Farrell, *Harry Holland*, pp.31–2.

52 Considine, *The Strike-Breakers*. See also Holland, *The Tramway Spy*.
53 Coates, 'Note on the IWW', p.25.
54 O'Farrell, *Harry Holland*, p.27.
55 Rushton, 'The IWW in Sydney', p.54.
56 *Railway and Tramway Review*, 7/9/08, quoted in *P*, 19/9/08, p.3.
57 Rushton, 'The IWW in Sydney', p.55; *SMH*, 4/11/08, quoted in Evatt, *Labour Leader*, p.231.
58 *Worker*, 3/9/08, p.5.
59 Sec. Sydney Labor Council, 7/9/08, to J.F. Neill, Sec. IWW, Sydney, NL3516.
60 *Worker*, 3/12/08, p.29.
61 Quoted in Hewitt, 'VSP', p.108; Merrifield, 'IWW', *Recorder*, 47, pp.10–11; ibid, *Recorder*, 48, pp.1–2.
62 Churchward, 'American influence', p.275.
63 Barrier Socialist Group Minutes, 2/2/08, 16/2/08, NL3939/50; Howard, 'Industrial relations in Broken Hill', p.38; E. Ross, *These Things Shall Be*, p.52.
64 Osborne, 'Town and company', p.37.
65 Osborne, 'Town and company', p.33.
66 Quoted in Kennedy, *Silver*, p.110.
67 *Industrial Worker*, 9/9/09.
68 *Socialist*, 25/6/09, p.1; 23/7/09, p.2.
69 Chas. H. Green, Broken Hill, 5/8/11, to *People*, NL2576/7.
70 Torr, *Tom Mann*, p.36; Brown, 'Introduction' to *The Industrial Syndicalist*, p.7; CPGB, *Tom Mann in Australasia*; Mann, *Tom Mann's Memoirs*, pp.185–96.
71 Unidentified clipping re Tom Mann speech at Beaconsfield Town Hall, 31/3/10, Tom Mann Collection, CPGB.
72 Tom Mann Speech at Fargwell, 19/2/09, notes by Dona Torr; Tom Mann, 26/6/36, in reply to letters on his 80th birthday; Tom Mann, *Industrialism and Parliamentary Action*, c.1910, 4 pp., all in Tom Mann Collection, CPGB.
73 Tom Mann, 26/6/36, in reply to letters on his 80th birthday, Tom Mann Collection, CPGB.
74 *Socialist*, 26/2/09, 23/4/09, 24/12/09.
75 Mann, *The Way to Win*.
76 Tom Mann, Sidcup, 19/3/36, to Dona Torr, Tom Mann Collection, CPGB; W. McCartney, *Syndicalism. What is it?*, Anti-Socialist Union of Great Britain, Westminster, 1912, in Jack Tanner Papers, Box 5/2, Nuffield College.
77 Osborne, 'Tom Mann', p.153.
78 Osborne, 'Tom Mann', pp.117, 152–3.
79 O'Farrell, *Harry Holland*, p.30.
80 Minutes, 12/4/08, 26/6/08, 19/7/08, 2/8/08, 29/11/08, Barrier Socialist Group Minute Book, NL3939/50; William Rosser, Broken Hill, 26/6/08, to J.O. Moroney, Gen. Sec. SLP, NL2576/7.
81 R.S. Ross, Broken Hill, 13/8/08, to Tom Mann, Melbourne, NL3222/1/6.
82 William Rosser, Broken Hill, 26/6/08, to J.O. Moroney, Gen. Sec. SLP, NL2576/7.
83 For instance, Holland, *Labor Leg-Ironed*, p.19; Holland, *Labor Sledgehammered*; Considine, *The Strike-Breakers*.
84 *Westralian Worker*, 22/7/10; Minutes, 9/4/10, Minute Book of International Socialist Club of Broken Hill, NL3939/50; Hewitt, 'VSP', pp.113, 79, 81–2, 108; *Industrial Worker*, 11/5/11, p.3; Walker, *Solidarity Forever*, pp.96–101.

85 IWW Club, *An Open Letter*; IWW Club, Circular to fellow workers, Sydney, 1/9/11, ABL N57/347; J.W. Ring, Nat. Sec. IWW Clubs, Sydney, 24/12/12, to fellow workers, NL2576/3.
86 Chas. H. Green, Broken Hill, 5/8/11, to *People*, NL2576/7.

Chapter 3
'Wild Men from Yankeeland': the Arrival of the Chicago IWW, 1910–1914

1   Hector, 'Carnival', p.1117; Merrifield, 'IWW', *Recorder*, 47, p.12.
2   Childe, *How Labour Governs*, pp.131, 135.
3   *Socialist Standard*, Jan. 1911, p.39; Barker, 'Self-portrait', p.20.
4   Renshaw, *The Wobblies*, p.73.
5   Barnes, 'The ideology of the IWW', p.93.
6   J.R. Wilson, Hon. Sec. International Socialist Party, Sydney, 6/4/11, to Sec. IWW Club, NL2576/3.
7   Turner, *Industrial Labour*, p.38.
8   Hagan and Turner, *A History of the Labor Party*, p.100.
9   Quoted in *Industrial Worker*, 30/5/12, p.2.
10 Lane, *Dawn to Dusk*, p.225.
11 H.J. Hawkins, Gen. Sec. IWW Clubs, 11/4/11, to A. Shawcross, Sec. Lithgow branch SFA, NL2576/3.
12 Dale, *Industrial History*, p.147.
13 Coombe interview.
14 P. Murphy, Melbourne IWW Club, n.d. [c. Aug. 1910], to Sec. Sydney IWW Club, ML262/1; Rushton, 'The IWW in Sydney', p.58; *IS*, 10/9/10; P. Christensen, 25/4/11, 18/5/11, 21/7/11, to H.J. Hawkins, ML A1333; Turner, *Industrial Labour*, p.64.
15 IWW Club, *Industrial Unionism*.
16 Coates, 'Note on the IWW', pp.26–7.
17 *IS*, 17/12/10.
18 *IS*, 31/10/10, 4/2/11.
19 Taylor, 'Worker's vanguard', p.34; ABL N57/131.
20 P. Christensen, 5/10/10, to Sec. IWW Club; Moss, *Sound of Trumpets*, p.220; P. Christensen, 18/5/11, to H.J. Hawkins, ML A1333.
21 H.J. Hawkins, 29/4/11, to P. Christensen; P. Christensen, 18/5/11, to H.J. Hawkins, ML A1333.
22 P. Christensen, 18/5/11, 7/6/11, to H.J. Hawkins, ML A1333.
23 Adelaide Local, organised May 1911, ML772/20/11.
24 E. Moyle, 23/6/11, to G.G. Reeve; D. Mallon, 23/7/11, to G.G. Reeve, ML A1334.
25 E.A. Giffney, 20/9/11, to fellow workers, ML2184/8.
26 1/11/11, ML2184/8.
27 Minutes, Sydney Local, 13/10/11, 25/11/11, 26/11/11, ML A1333; E. Moyle, 13/10/11, to J. Dwyer, ML2184/8; Minutes, Sydney branch IWW, 19/11/11, 23/11/11, ML2184/8; List of names of members IWW Sydney Local from first meeting, supplied by G.G. Reeve to Fred Hancock, ML772/20/13–15; List of names of members IWW Sydney Local (Chicago) 1908 Preamble organised 27/12/11, ML772/20/3–5; E. Moyle, 18/4/12, to G. Reeve, ML A1334.
28 E. Moyle, n.d. [Nov. 1911], to J. Dwyer, ML2184/8.

29 *IS*, 9/8/13; Rushton, 'The IWW in Sydney', p.62.
30 Minutes, Sydney Local, IWW, 10/6/12, ML A1334.
31 *IS*, 22/7/11; Minutes, Sydney Local, IWW, 3/6/12, ML A1334.
32 *IS*, 28/9/12.
33 J.M. Ring, Nat. Sec. IWW, to fellow workers, 24 Dec. 1912, NL2576/3; SLP, *The Unity Question*, pp.7, 12, 19.
34 *IS*, 16/12/11, 13/1/12; SLP, *The Unity Question*, p.7; *IS*, 1/6/12.
35 Rushton, 'The IWW in Sydney', pp.62–3.
36 AA1979/199 Item WA1024A vol.1, p.3; Correspondence between Glynn and others, various dates, NL2576/5, 2576/2; Rushton, 'The IWW in Sydney', pp.86–7.
37 E. Moyle, 31/1/13, to J.A. Keefe, ML A1334.
38 *IS*, 9/8/13, 6/9/13, 13/9/13; Geo. Reeve, 9/12/16, to Hugh Wright, ML A1334.
39 E. Moyle, 4/6/13, to G. Reeve, ML A1334.
40 Rushton, 'The IWW in Sydney', p.79.
41 Farrell, 'Donald Grant', p.75; McNamara, 'Donald Grant', p.63.
42 *Sol*, 4/5/18, p.3.
43 Farrell interview.
44 Boote, *The Case of Grant*, p.7.
45 Quoted in Rushton, 'The IWW in Sydney', p.86.
46 AA1979/199 Item WA1024A vol.1, p.4; Rushton, 'The IWW in Sydney', pp.87–8; Olssen, *The Red Feds*, p.128.
47 AA ACT CRS A3932 Item SC292 pt.3; AA1979/199 Item WA1024A vol.1, p.4; Rushton, 'The IWW in Sydney', p.89; McGillick, *Comrade No More*, p.36.
48 *Socialist*, 21/3/13, quoted in Rushton, 'The IWW in Sydney', pp.122–3.
49 *IS*, 12/7/13, 19/7/13 (L), 26/7/13, 27/9/13, 29/11/13; SLP, *The Unity Question*, pp.7, 9, 12.
50 See *IS*, 20/12/13.
51 R. Mackenzie, IWW, Detroit, 14/3/14 to L. Klausen, Sec. Sydney IWW Club, NL2576/3.
52 *IS*, 6/9/13.

Chapter 4
'Education, Organisation, Emancipation': the Revolutionary Project

1   Spargo, *Syndicalism*, pp.13–15. Recently Salvatore Salerno in *Red November* has traced the influence of the French syndicalists and anarchists upon the American IWW's home-grown industrial unionism.
2   *DA*, 13/5/16, p.4; 15/12/14, p.4; 15/5/15, p.2.
3   Genery interview.
4   Garvey interview.
5   Norman Rancie, Sydney, 21/5/57, to Hugh Buggy, NL6206/62/5.
6   Genery interview.
7   Groupe D'Etudes Scientifiques, *Manifesto-Protest*.
8   Dubofsky, *We Shall Be All*, pp.79, 56.
9   Bedford, 'The IWW', p.40; *DA*, 14/10/16, p.3; IWW, *The Immediate Demands*, p.14.
10 Guido Baracchi, 18/2/68, to Bob and May Brodney, LT10882/5/13.
11 Wilson, *All for the Cause*, pp.58, 137; *DA*, 1/5/14, L, p.2.
12 Glynn, *Industrial Efficiency*, section III; see, for example, *DA*, 31/3/14, p.4; 31/3/14, p.2; 1/5/14, p.4; *DA*, 26/5/17, p.3.
13 *DA*, 15/5/15, pp.1, 4.

14 IWW, *How Capital has Hypnotised Society*, pp.4, 20–2, 24, 29.
15 *DA*, 7/7/17, p.3.
16 *DA*, 15/6/15, p.4; 13/5/16, p.4; 17/2/17, p.3.
17 *DA*, 11/12/15, p.2.
18 *DA*, 6/5/16, p.2.
19 *DA*, 12/5/17, p.3.
20 Marx argued that the proletariat was a class *in itself* by virtue of its common situation and common interests against capital, but that this mass did not constitute a class *for itself* until it became united in struggle and realised that the interests it was defending were class interests (Bottomore and Rubel, *Karl Marx*, p.195).
21 *Communist Manifesto*, in Marx and Engels, *Selected Works*, p.46.
22 See McKee, 'Daniel De Leon', p.270.
23 See Hyman, *Marxism*, pp.4–11; *DA*, May Day 1915, L, p.3; 1/6/15, p.1; IWW, *Direct Action*, p.7.
24 *DA*, 24/6/16, p.1.
25 *DA*, 14/4/17, p.2.
26 Quoted in *DA*, 14/4/15, p.2.
27 *La voix du peuple*, May 1901, quoted in Conlin, *Bread and Roses*, p.27.
28 IWW, *The Immediate Demands*, p.11.
29 *DA*, 1/5/14, p.4; 15/9/15, p.1.
30 Stearns, *Revolutionary Syndicalism*, pp.3, 11–12; Conlin, *Bread and Roses*, p.17.
31 *DA*, 12/5/17, p.2.
32 *DA*, 12/5/17, p.2.
33 *DA*, 1/5/14, L, p.2; 31/3/14, p.2; 20/5/16, p.1.
34 *DA*, 1/6/15, p.1; 15/9/15, p.4.
35 Derfler, *Socialism since Marx*, pp.21, 77. Stearns qualifies this explanation in *Revolutionary Syndicalism*, p.20.
36 Ridley, *Revolutionary Syndicalism*, pp.168, 119, 127.
37 *La voix du peuple*, May 1901, quoted in Conlin, *Bread and Roses*, p.27.
38 Childe, *How Labour Governs*, pp.142–3.
39 *DA*, 31/3/14, p.1; 12/5/17, p.2.
40 Brissenden, *The Launching of the IWW*, p.41; Renshaw, *The Wobblies*, p.21.
41 *DA*, 15/6/15, p.3; 15/7/14, p.4; 28/7/17, p.3; 10/6/16, p.3.
42 *DA*, 15/6/15, p.3.
43 *DA*, 14/4/17, p.2; 15/7/14, p.4.
44 *DA*, 19/5/17, p.4.
45 *DA*, 28/2/14, p.1.
46 IWW, *The Immediate Demands*, p.4; *DA*, 15/7/15, p.3.
47 *DA*, 1/10/14, p.1; 15/6/15, p.3; 15/12/14, p.4; 3/2/17, p.2.
48 *DA*, 3/2/17, p.2.
49 For instance, *DA*, 15/5/14, p.1.
50 *DA*, 15/7/15, p.3.
51 *DA*, 14/7/17, p.4.
52 Nilsson, *Political Socialism*.
53 IWW, *Direct Action*, pp.5, 11.
54 *DA*, 11/12/15, p.2.
55 *DA*, 19/5/17, p.3; 25/12/15, p.4.
56 IWW, *The Immediate Demands*, p.3.
57 IWW, *The Immediate Demands*, pp.7–9.
58 *DA*, 25/12/15, p.4; 9/10/15, p.4; 16/10/15, p.4.
59 IWW Stickers, NL3222/6.

60 IWW, *The Immediate Demands*, p.12.
61 Luxemburg, *The Mass Strike*, pp.153–218.
62 IWW, *The Immediate Demands*, pp.11–12.
63 Preamble. In every issue of *DA*.
64 *DA*, 15/12/14, p.4; 12/5/17, p.2.
65 IWW, *Direct Action*, p.9.
66 Conlin, *Bread and Roses*, pp.24–5.
67 IWW, *Direct Action*, p.8.
68 Rushton, 'Revolutionary ideology', p.443.
69 Williams, *Eleven Blind Leaders*, Introduction.
70 *DA*, 2/10/15, p.2.
71 *DA*, 15/9/15, p.3.
72 *DA*, 23/12/16, p.2.
73 *DA*, 27/5/16, p.3.
74 Anon., 'The iron heel', p.475.
75 *DA*, 15/7/14, p.4.
76 Lehning (ed.), *Michael Bakunin*, p.132.
77 IWW, *Speeches from the Dock*, p.12; Williams (ed.), *Eureka and Beyond*, p.71; Mick Sawtell, 1/2/19, to Beth Pole, Item 1/2/1919, A6286, 5th Military Dt, 3/1/18–30/8/19.
78 *DA*, 12/5/17, L, p.2.
79 *DA*, 15/7/14, p.4.
80 IWW, *The Immediate Demands*, pp.10–11.

Chapter 5
'We, the Hoboes': who were the Wobblies?

1 Renshaw, *The Wobblies*, pp.21–2.
2 *DA*, 15/12/14, L, p.2.
3 St John, *The I.W.W., History, Structure and Methods*, 1917, pp.23–4, quoted in Brissenden, *IWW*, p.341. Against the grain, Conlin's research has shown that, according to American West Coast police records, the membership of the IWW was much like a cross-section of the region's population (Conlin, *Bread and Roses*, p.69).
4 Preston, 'Shall this be all?', pp.441–2.
5 Perlman, *History of Trade Unionism*, p.305, quoted in Zieger, 'Workers and scholars', p.255.
6 Parker, 'The I.W.W.', p.106.
7 Dubofsky, 'Dissent', pp.192–3. See also 'The I.W.W. – an exchange of views', p.371.
8 Walter Galenson, *Labor in Norway*, Harvard, 1949, p.61, quoted in Renshaw, *The Wobblies*, p.291.
9 Olssen, *The Red Feds*, pp.17, 38, 86, 108.
10 Beattie, 'Memoirs', p.35.
11 Fry (ed.), *Tom Barker*, pp.20, 34.
12 Childe, *How Labour Governs*, p.136.
13 Childe, *How Labour Governs*, pp.132–3.
14 Churchward, 'American influence', p.274.
15 Items 17/4/18, 15/5/18, A6286, 1st Military Dt, 26/12/17–29/6/18.
16 Rushton, 'The IWW in Sydney', pp.269–71.
17 *DA*, 15/7/14, p.1.
18 Wilson, *All for the Cause*, p.72.
19 Audley interview (with Gowland and Saffin).

20 Garvey interview.
21 Baracchi, paper read to Fellowship of Australian Writers, 1941, p.2.
22 *DA*, 9/12/16, p.4.
23 Seamer interview.
24 *DA*, 2/12/16, L, p.2.
25 *DA*, 5/2/16, p.2.
26 Item 22/1/18, A6286, 1st Military Dt, 26/12/17–29/6/18.
27 F. Ellis, Innisfail, 7/8/18, to A. Shepard, Ayr, Item 24/8/18, A6286, 1st Military Dt, 3/7/18–30/10/18; Mary Jeffery, 6/3/19, to Norman, Item 26/3/19, A6286, 1st Military Dt, 1/3/19–7/6/19.
28 For instance, on Norman Jeffery, see Sendy, 'The founders', pp.1–3; report on a meeting on the Domain, Brisbane, Item 19/2/19, A6286, 1st Military Dt, 2/11/18–26/2/19. On Alf Wilson, see Wilson, *All for the Cause*, Preface by T. Gilmore. On Mick Sawtell, see *Daily Mirror*, 15/11/71, p.26.
29 Draft of May Brodney's autobiography, LT10882/8/23; handwritten notes, LT10772/3; Bertha Walker, 20/2/64, to Roly Farrall, LT10772/3. See also Walker, *Solidarity Forever*, pp.128, 131.
30 Quoted in Cutler, 'Sunday, Bloody Sunday', pp.83–4.
31 Minutes, Broken Hill Local, 29/4/17, SANSW7/5588.
32 Shor, 'Masculine power', p.97–8.
33 List of names of members attending first meeting IWW Sydney Local who signed list going to Ed. Moyle, Gen. Sec.-Treas., ML772/20/13–15.
34 List no.1, AA ACT CRS CP404/1.
35 *DA*, 14/7/17, p.2.
36 Coombe interview.
37 List of names of members attending first meeting IWW Sydney Local who signed list going to Ed. Moyle, Gen. Sec.-Treas., ML772/20/13–15.
38 List of names of members IWW Sydney Local (Chicago) 1908 Preamble organised 27/12/11, ML772/20/3.
39 List no.1, AA ACT CRS CP404/1.
40 C. Reeve, State Penitentiary, 4/6/21, to Dear Little Mother, p.2, ML5653.
41 Tom Barker, St Pancras Town Hall, 23/10/59, to John Playford, ABLN57/213; AA1979/199 Item WA 1024A vol.1, p.2; Taylor, 'Worker's vanguard', p.34; Barker, 'Self-portrait', p.19.
42 *Argus*, 11/10/16, p.8; AA1979/199 Item WA 1024A vol.1; Minutes, Broken Hill Local, 10/9/16, 15/10/16, 20/5/17, SANSW7/5588; Cain, *The Wobblies at War*, p.259; Churchward, 'American influence', p.276; Rushton, 'The IWW in Sydney', pp.211–12; Shor, 'Masculine power', p.98.
43 From police records quoted in Hunt, 'Labour movement in north Queensland', p.296.
44 List of names of members IWW Sydney Local (Chicago) 1908 Preamble organised 27/12/11, ML772/20/3; List no.1, AA ACT CRS CP404/1, Bundle 1.
45 Winters, *The Soul of the Wobblies*; *Argus*, 11/10/16, p.8; Cain, *The Wobblies at War*, p.242.
46 Coombe interview; McGillick, *Comrade No More*, p.36.
47 Childe, *How Labour Governs*, p.140.
48 *DA*, 15/5/14, p.2.
49 *DA*, 27/5/16, p.3.
50 Minutes, Broken Hill Local, 25/3/17, SANSW7/5588; Ted Moyle, notebook no.2, Moyle Collection.
51 *DA*, 31/3/17, p.2.

52 O'Farrell, 'Trial of the Sydney Twelve', p.54; Coombe interview; Howells, *Against the Stream*, pp.18–22; Wilson, *All for the Cause*, esp. pp.136–7; Payne interview.
53 *DA*, 8/1/16, p.2; 15/1/16, pp.3–4; 19/2/16, p.3.
54 *DA*, 31/1/14, p.4; 1/7/14, p.3; 15/8/15, p.4; 7/7/17, p.4.
55 *DA*, 15/4/15, p.4.
56 Peterson, 'The intellectual world of the IWW', p.160.
57 Beattie, 'Memoirs', pp.35–6.
58 Rushton, 'Revolutionary ideology', pp.426–7.
59 *Daily Mirror*, 15/11/71, p.26; 16/5/86, p.24.
60 Rushton, 'Revolutionary ideology', p.433.
61 ML772/21.
62 *DA*, 18/12/15, p.3; 7/7/17, p.1; 28/2/14, p.2.
63 *DA*, 7/7/17, p.1.
64 Rushton, 'Revolutionary ideology', p.434.
65 'The I.W.W.', *Atlantic Monthly*, 120, Nov. 1917, pp.651–62, cited in Rushton, 'The IWW in Sydney', p.28.
66 Rushton, 'Revolutionary ideology', p.433.
67 Rushton, 'The IWW in Sydney', p.148.
68 Childe, *How Labour Governs*, pp.135–6.
69 Rushton, 'Revolutionary ideology', p.431.
70 Alf Wilson, Adelaide, 8/2/21, to G. Reeve, ML772/11/471–3; Wilson, *All for the Cause*, p.89.
71 Payne interview; *Bulletin*, reprinted in *Sol*, 24/11/17, p.1; *Argus*, 16/12/16, p.18; Farrall interview.
72 Brooks, *American Syndicalism*, pp.105, 225; Conlin, 'Introduction', p.13.
73 Draft of May Brodney's autobiography, LT10882/8/23; May Brodney, 'Historions', LT10882/10/31.
74 Rushton, 'Revolutionary ideology', p.429.

Chapter 6
'No Barriers of Race': the Challenge to Working-class Racism

1 *The Founding Convention of the IWW*, p.1.
2 Brissenden, *The I.W.W.*, pp.84, 208; Conlin, *Bread and Roses*, pp.4–6; Woodruff, *The Advancing Proletariat*, pp.27–9.
3 See Spence, *Australia's Awakening*, p.263; Yarwood, 'The "white Australia" policy', pp.247, 260.
4 Burgmann, 'Racism', pp.39–54.
5 *P*, 28/1/11.
6 *P*, 11/5/12.
7 *P*, 18/3/11.
8 *P*, 30/8/13.
9 IWW Club, *The Two Wars*, p.30.
10 *P*, 9/9/11. These claims were justified. See *P*, 9/9/11, 6/5/11, 2/9/11, 28/10/11, 4/11/11, 17/8/12, 26/4/13, 10/5/13; Letter from Minister for External Affairs, 26 Oct. 1911, to Geo. Waite, Corr. Sec. Sydney IWW Club, NL3516.
11 *P*, 23/2/01, 30/3/01. See also *People and Collectivist*, 20/8/98, 3/12/98; *P*, 26/4/02, 31/1/03, 28/2/03, 3/5/02, 27/6/03, 23/7/04, 19/11/04, 23/12/05, 5/1/01, 26/1/01, 28/12/01, 11/1/02, 25/1/02, 22/3/02.
12 SLP, *The Unity Question*, pp.4, 11.

13 *P*, 13/7/07.
14 *P*, 19/10/07.
15 *P*, 26/6/09.
16 *P*, 30/5/08, 4/9/09, 24/5/11, 13/4/07, 22/2/08, 27/11/09, 12/3/10, 17/9/10, 8/3/11, 12/8/11, 30/8/13, 12/11/14 L; SLP, *Sydney Labor Council and the War*.
17 *Flame*, May 1906, Nov. 1906, May 1907, July 1907, 13/3/09, 27/3/09, 10/4/09, 17/4/09.
18 For examples, see *ISR*, 6/4/07, 27/4/07, 18/5/07, 25/5/07.
19 *ISR*, 6/4/07, 23/5/08, 17/10/08.
20 *IS*, 9/4/10. See also 23/7/10, 17/12/10, 4/2/11, 19/8/11, 30/9/11, 16/3/12, 2/11/12.
21 *IS*, 8/7/11, 30/3/12, 6/7/12, 18/11/16.
22 *BDT*, quoted in *IS*, 21/6/13.
23 *IS*, 4/10/13; Burgmann, 'Racism', p.52.
24 *IS*, 22/2/13; Burgmann, 'Racism', pp.51–2.
25 IWW, *The Immediate Demands of the I.W.W.*, p.14; *DA*, 9/10/15, p.2.
26 *DA*, 25/12/15, p.3.
27 James E. Minehan, Richmond, NSW, 9 July 1984, to author.
28 *DA*, 27/5/16, p.3.
29 Leaflets, NL3222/6; Fox, *Jim Larkin*, p.160; Peter Larkin, Parramatta Jail, 2/5/18, to Thos. Byrne, Item 6/5/18, A6286, 2nd Military Dt, 23/10/17–29/7/18.
30 IWW, *Direct Action*, p.7.
31 IWW, *Preamble and Constitution* (1910 Chicago), p.23.
32 *DA*, 1/5/14, p.2; 15/6/14, p.4.
33 *DA*, May Day 1917, p.2; 1/7/16, p.1.
34 *DA*, 15/5/14, p.2.
35 See chapter 9.
36 *DA*, 23/10/15, p.2; 1/7/16, p.1; 13/11/15, p.2.
37 *DA*, 15/6/14, p.4; 1/10/15, p.4; 1/7/15, p.2; 15/9/14, p.2.
38 Shor, 'Masculine power', p.98.
39 Minutes, Broken Hill Local, 10/9/16, 15/10/16, 19/11/16, 15/4/17, 20/5/17, SANSW7/5588.
40 Rushton, 'The IWW in Sydney', pp.211–12.
41 *DA*, 11/3/16, p.3.
42 *DA*, 1/9/15, L, p.2; 11/3/16, p.1.
43 George, *Why the A.W.U.*, pp.9, 12.
44 *DA*, 1/4/15, p.2. Also 15/7/15, p.1.
45 *Northern Territory Times*, 2/9/15.
46 *DA*, 1/3/15, p.1; 1/4/15, p.2; ML772/20/297.
47 Farrell, *International Socialism*, p.84.
48 Rushton, 'The IWW in Sydney', pp.198, 268–71.

Chapter 7
It's Great to Fight for Freedom with a Rebel Girl': the Answer to the Woman Question

1 Woodruff, *The Advancing Proletariat*, p.27. See also Dubofsky, *We Shall Be All*, p.272; Brissenden, *The I.W.W.*, p.160.
2 Schofield, 'Rebel girls', pp.347–8.
3 IWW Club, *An Open Letter*, p.4; IWW, *The Immediate Demands*, p.14; IWW, Sydney, *Songs*, Preface, p.5; *DA*, 14/10/16, p.3; 1/11/14, p.1.

4 Minutes, Sydney Local, 10/6/12, ML A1334; Surplus interview.
5 List of names of members IWW Sydney Local organised 27/12/11, ML772/20/3; List no.1, AA ACT CRS CP404/1. Joy Damousi counts 25 women from the same list (*Women Come Rally*, p.44).
6 Coombe interview; Fry (ed.), *Tom Barker*, pp.19–21.
7 P. Christensen, 21/7/11, to H. Hawkins, ML A1333; Ted Moyle, 10/8/45, to Alan Finger, Moyle Collection; Police Department Special Bundles, SANSW 7/5588–98; Cain, *The Wobblies at War*, p.242.
8 Lake, 'The politics of respectability', pp.116–31.
9 Damousi, *Women Come Rally*, pp.42–3; Metcalfe, 'Sex and solidarity'.
10 Shor, 'Masculine power', pp.83–99; *DA*, 1/4/15, p.2; 6/11/15, p.1; Glynn, *Industrial Efficiency*.
11 *DA*, 11/3/16, p.4; 15/6/14, p.4.
12 Charles Reeve, State Penitentiary, 20/9/19, to Dear Little Mother, p.3, ML5653.
13 See Jauncey, *Conscription*, p.137.
14 *DA*, 1/7/15, p.1.
15 IWW, Sydney, *Songs*, p.21.
16 *DA*, 16/9/16, p.1.
17 Bertha Walker, 20/2/64, to Roly Farrall, LT10772/3.
18 Stearns, *Be a Man!*, pp.73–4; Olssen, *The Red Feds*, p.49.
19 Kelly interview; Rushton, 'Revolutionary ideology', p.436.
20 *DA*, 16/9/16, p.1; 9/10/15, p.4; 12/2/16, p.4; 10/2/17, p.3; 3/3/17, p.3; 23/9/16, p.1.
21 NL3222/6.
22 *DA*, 9/9/16, p.1.
23 *DA*, 12/2/16, p.4.
24 IWW, Sydney, *Songs*, p.43.
25 Garvey interview.
26 *DA*, 10/2/17, p.3.
27 Burgmann, *'In Our Time'*, pp.2–3, 194; Damousi, 'Socialist women', esp. pp.574–80; Damousi, *Women Come Rally*, p.35.
28 Walker, *Solidarity Forever*, p.129; Wilson, *All for the Cause*, pp.89–90; SLP Central Branch Minutes, 1914–1915, NL3544.
29 *DA*, 1/10/14, p.3; May Day 1915, p.5; 6/11/15, p.1; *Sydney Sun*, 23/7/17, NL6265/3/F5; *DA*, 9/12/16, p.2.
30 *DA*, 14/10/16, p.2; Damousi, 'Socialist women', p.506.
31 *Sydney Sun*, 10/10/17; *Sydney Truth*, 14/10/17, NL6265/3/F5; Ted Moyle, notebook no.2, Moyle Collection; Thomas, 'Two veterans', p.7; notes made by J.R. Wilson, Wilson Papers.
32 Modjeska and Pizer (eds), *Lesbia Harford*, p.77.
33 Baracchi, paper read to Fellowship of Australian Writers, p.1; Brodney, review of 'The Poems of Lesbia Harford', pp.1–2, LT10882/11; Modjeska, 'Introduction', pp.20, 23.
34 Modjeska, 'Introduction', pp.33–4; Baracchi, paper read to Fellowship of Australian Writers, p.1; Marjorie Pizer, 'Lesbia Harford – forgotten poet', *Mabel*, 4, 1976, p.12, quoted in Cuthbert, 'Lesbia Harford', p.42; Lesbia Harford, 5/336 Crown St, n.d., to May Brodney, LT10882/11.
35 *DA*, 13/1/17, p.1; Burgmann, 'Betsy Matthias', p.449; Betsy Matthias, 3/5/18, to C. Pla, Selwyn, Qld, A6286, 1st Military Dt, 26/12/17–29/6/18; *Sol*, 18/5/18, p.1.
36 *Sydney Sun*, 20/9/17, NL6265/3/F5.
37 *Sol*, 24/11/17, p.2.

38 *Argus*, 19/8/20, p.9.
39 Greer, *The Social Evil*, pp.3–8, 28.
40 *DA*, May Day 1915, p.5.
41 *DA*, 13/11/15, p.3; 15/8/15, p.4.
42 *DA*, 22/1/16, p.3; 28/10/16, p.2.
43 *DA*, 30/10/15, p.4.
44 *DA*, 4/3/16, p.2.
45 Quoted in Cuthbert, 'Lesbia Harford', p.45.
46 IWW, *How Capital has Hypnotised Society*, p.18.
47 *DA*, 22/1/16, p.3; Charles Reeve, State Penitentiary, 14/6/19, to Dear Little Mother, pp.1–2, ML5653.
48 *DA*, May Day 1915, p.5; Damousi, *Women Come Rally*, p.89.
49 *DA*, 20/11/15, p.4; 27/11/15, p.4.
50 Sidelights on Two Referendums, entry for August 1916, p.49, NL2070/4/1–7.
51 Minutes, Broken Hill Local, 4/3/17, SANSW7/5588; *DA*, 1/6/14, p.3.
52 *DA*, 22/8/14, p.4; May Day 1915, p.5.
53 Charles Reeve, State Penitentiary, 3/5/19, to Dear Mum, p.2, ML5653.
54 Schofield, 'Rebel girls', pp.338–9; *DA*, 10/2/17, p.3.
55 *DA*, 31/1/14, p.1; 9/9/16, p.1; 14/10/16, p.3.
56 Damousi, 'Socialist women', pp.489–90.
57 *DA*, 3/3/17, p.3; 29/4/16, p.3.
58 *DA*, 10/3/17, p.2.
59 *DA*, 20/1/17, p.2; IWW, *How Capital has Hypnotised Society*, p.18; *DA*, 30/10/15, p.4.
60 Greer, *The Social Evil*, pp.4, 32, 36.
61 *DA*, 9/12/16, p.2; 1/8/15, p.3.
62 *DA*, 9/12/16, p.2.
63 Greer, *The Social Evil*, pp.24–5.
64 *DA*, 9/12/16, p.2; 22/1/16, p.4; 1/1/15, p.4.
65 Greer, *The Social Evil*, pp.26–7, 48.
66 *DA*, 9/12/16, p.2.
67 *DA*, 1/7/15, p.3; 12/8/16, p.4.
68 Quoted in Young, 'Social history of the British working classes', p.263.
69 Pease, *Revolution and the I.W.W.*, pp.4–6; *DA*, 15/5/14, p.3; 9/12/16, p.2; 30/12/16, p.4; 20/1/17, p.3; 30/12/16, p.4.
70 *DA*, 15/9/15, p.1; 15/9/14, p.4; 12/8/16, p.4.
71 IWW, *How Capital has Hypnotised Society*, pp.18–19.
72 *DA*, 15/7/15, pp.3–4.
73 Charles Reeve, State Penitentiary, 5/7/19, to Dear Little Mother, p.1, ML5653.

Chapter 8
'A Real Democracy': Organisation and Practice

1 Brooks, *American Syndicalism*, p.175; Rushton, 'Revolutionary ideology', pp.425, 432; Childe, *How Labour Governs*, p.143.
2 *DA*, 15/9/15, p.1.
3 *DA*, 7/7/17, p.1.
4 Sydney Local, IWW, 'Manifesto of the Industrial Workers of the World', n.d. [1911], ML A1333.
5 *DA*, 14/7/17, p.2.
6 E.A. Giffney, 4/9/11, to G. Reeve, ML A1334.

7 Fry (ed.), *Tom Barker*, p.20.
8 Rushton, 'Revolutionary ideology', pp.430–1; Genery interview.
9 Rushton, 'Revolutionary ideology', pp.430–1.
10 Groupe D'Etudes Scientifiques, *Manifesto-Protest.*
11 Bedford, 'One Big Union', p.15; Beattie, 'Memoirs', p.35; *DA*, 27/5/16, p.3.
12 Published in *Communist*, 13/5/21, p.6.
13 Surplus interview; Walker, *Solidarity Forever*, p.129; Audley interview; May Brodney, 'Histortions', LT10882/10/31; Bertha Walker, 20/2/64, to Roly, LT10772/3; Wilson, *All for the Cause*, p.79.
14 Quoted in Rushton, 'The IWW in Sydney', pp.170–1.
15 Rushton, 'The IWW in Sydney', pp.170–1; St John, *The I.W.W.*, p.18.
16 Beattie, 'Memoirs', pp.34–5; Rushton, 'The IWW in Sydney', pp.170–1.
17 Fry (ed.), *Tom Barker*, pp.21, 29.
18 *Sol*, 4/5/18, p.3.
19 Handwritten notes, LT10772/3.
20 *DA*, 8/1/16, p.2; 15/1/16, pp.3–4; 19/2/16, p.3.
21 Fry (ed.), *Tom Barker*, pp.20–1; Beattie, 'Memoirs', p.34.
22 Fry (ed.), *Tom Barker*, pp.16, 21–2.
23 *DA*, 1/5/14, p.4.
24 *DA*, 28/2/14, p.1.
25 *DA*, 15/6/14, L, p.1; Rushton, 'Revolutionary ideology', p.427; Fry (ed.), *Tom Barker*, pp.16, 21.
26 *DA*, 28/2/14, p.3; 1/2/15, p.4; 1/7/14, p.4; 22/8/14, p.4.
27 Beattie, 'Memoirs', pp.36–7; Seamer interview; Fry (ed.), *Tom Barker*, p.17; Childe, *How Labour Governs*, p.135.
28 Churchward, 'American influence', p.268; Rushton, 'Revolutionary ideology', p.427 fn.17.
29 Surplus interview; *DA*, 30/1/16, p.4.
30 *DA*, 28/2/14, p.3; 1/7/15, p.2; 1/6/14, p.3; 1/7/14, p.4; 22/8/14, p.4.
31 Seamer interview; Coombe interview; Edmonds interview.
32 Garvey interview; Sendy, 'The founders', p.4; *DA*, 19/8/16, p.3; 16/6/17, p.3; Surplus interview.
33 *DA*, 22/8/14, p.4.
34 *DA*, 1/8/14, p.4.
35 LeWarne, 'Wobbly train to Fresno', p.264.
36 *Daily Herald*, 22/6/14, quoted in Moss, *Sound of Trumpets*, p.233; *DA*, 1/7/14, p.1; Childe, *How Labour Governs*, p.136; Fry (ed.), *Tom Barker*, p.17.
37 *DA*, 1/7/14, p.1.
38 *DA*, 15/7/14, p.1.
39 Childe, *How Labour Governs*, p.136; Fry (ed.), *Tom Barker*, p.17; *DA*, 15/7/14, p.1; Karabogias, 'Fanning the flames', pp.13–14.
40 Rushton, 'The IWW in Sydney', pp.169–69a; *DA*, 15/7/14, p.1.
41 *DA*, 15/7/14, p.1.
42 *DA*, 15/7/14, p.1; 1/8/14, p.4.
43 Fry (ed.), *Tom Barker*, p.16.
44 Fry (ed.), *Tom Barker*, p.17.
45 Childe, *How Labour Governs*, p.136.
46 Fry (ed.), *Tom Barker*, p.18.
47 *DA*, 15/2/15, p.1; 1/3/15, p.2; 15/3/15, p.4; Childe, *How Labour Governs*, pp.136–7; Karabogias, 'Fanning the flames', pp.17–18; Rushton, 'The IWW in Sydney', pp.169a–70.
48 Fry (ed.), *Tom Barker*, p.18; *DA*, 1/4/15, p.4.

49 *DA*, 1/5/14, p.4; 22/8/14, p.4; 1/1/15, p.4; 15/9/15, p.3; 15/1/15, p.4; 1/2/15, p.4; 1/6/15, p.3; 8/1/16, p.2; 15/1/16, p.4; 5/2/16, p.4.
50 Segal, 'Westralian Wobblies', pt 2.
51 *DA*, 28/2/14, p.3.
52 Coombe interview.
53 *DA*, 15/1/16, p.3; 19/2/16, p.4; 30/1/16, p.4.
54 Industrial Workers of the World, Statement giving a brief outline of the activities of the above organisation in Australia, AA ACT CRS A456 Item W26/148 P.H.B.
55 Quoted in Karabogias, 'Fanning the flames', p.9.
56 *Argus*, 8/2/17, p.4; Beattie, 'Memoirs', p.39; Fry (ed.), *Tom Barker*, pp.19, 20, 26.
57 Beattie, 'Memoirs', p.39; Churchward, 'American influence', p.268.
58 Rushton, 'Revolutionary ideology', p.424 fn.1; Childe, *How Labour Governs*, p.135.
59 Garvey interview.
60 In the USA, with a population around 100 million, the paid-up membership was 60 000 at 1/1/17; 300 000 cards had been issued since 1905 (St John, *The I.W.W., History, Structure and Methods*, 1917, pp.23–4, quoted in Brissenden, *The I.W.W.*, p.341).
61 Rushton, 'The IWW in Sydney', appendix IV, pp.283–4.
62 Minutes, Broken Hill Local, 28/1/17, 16/9/16, SANSW7/5588.
63 Surplus interview.
64 Armstrong, 'Closer unity', pp.212–13; Hunt, 'Labour movement in north Queensland', pp.296–7.
65 Hunt, 'Labour movement in north Queensland', pp.296–7; Armstrong, 'Closer unity', pp.212–13.
66 Segal, 'Westralian Wobblies', pt 1.
67 Segal, 'Westralian Wobblies', pt 2.
68 *DA*, 9/6/17, p.1.
69 *DA*, 8/1/16, L, p.2.
70 Childe, *How Labour Governs*, p.135; Beattie, 'Memoirs', p.39; Surplus interview; *DA*, 17/2/17, p.3.

Chapter 9
'A Poor Day's Work for a Poor Day's Pay': Ethics and Economics

1 Quoted in Childe, *How Labour Governs*, p.144.
2 Progressive and Economic Association, *The Second Maritime Strike*, pp.10–11, 8.
3 *DA*, 1/11/14, p.1.
4 *DA*, 4/3/16, p.2; 6/1/17, p.1.
5 *DA*, 15/7/15, p.2.
6 IWW, *How Capital has Hypnotised Society*, pp.21–2, 24.
7 Lafargue, *The Right to be Lazy*, pp.21–2.
8 Lane, *Dawn to Dusk*, p.133.
9 IWW, *How Capital has Hypnotised Society*, pp.4, 20, 29; Brooks, *American Syndicalism*, pp.109–10; *DA*, 24/6/16, p.4.
10 Rushton, 'The IWW in Sydney', pp.285–6.
11 Jeffery, 'The labour movement', pp.11–12; LT10882/10/31.
12 Childe, *How Labour Governs*, p.136.
13 Fry (ed.), *Tom Barker*, p.22.

14 Quoted in E. Ross, *These Things Shall Be*, p.50.
15 *DA*, 15/4/15, p.2.
16 Tyler, *Rebels of the Woods*; Norman H. Clark, Review of *Rebels of the Woods* in *Labor History*, 10, 1, 1969, pp.137–8.
17 ML Ai8/1.
18 *DA*, 2/10/15, p.2; 15/5/14, p.2.
19 Brown, *Six-Hour Day*, pp.1–4; NL3222/6; *DA*, 15/7/16, p.2.
20 *DA*, 15/5/14, p.2; 15/6/14, p.3.
21 Glynn, *Industrial Efficiency*, section II.
22 *DA*, 23/6/17, p.2; 1/8/14, p.1; 15/6/14, p.1.
23 *DA*, 31/1/14, p.2; 1/8/14, p.1.
24 Glynn, *Industrial Efficiency*, section II.
25 *DA*, 15/5/14, p.4.
26 *DA*, 31/3/14, p.4.
27 *DA*, 10/8/14, p.3; 27/11/15, p.1.
28 *DA*, 15/7/15, p.2; 13/11/15, p.4. The Wobblies evinced a classical Marxian aversion to the small capitalists feted by the Labor Party, contradicting as they did the law of concentration of capital; protecting this class retarded the development of the conditions favouring revolution.
29 *DA*, 11/3/15, p.2; Surplus interview.
30 *DA*, 4/3/16, p.2; 15/6/14, p.1.
31 *Sunday Times*, 19/3/16, ML A1333; *DA*, 15/7/14, p.1.
32 *DA*, 15/5/15, p.2; 15/5/14, p.2.
33 *DA*, 15/7/15, p.2.
34 *DA*, 1/6/14, p.4; 15/7/14, p.1; 28/7/17, p.2; 22/4/16, p.3.
35 The word 'sabotage' became popular after striking weavers in 1834 in Lyons smashed glass and machines with their heavy footwear, their *sabots* (Brooks, *American Syndicalism*, p.140).
36 Childe, *How Labour Governs*, p.135; *DA*, 28/2/14, p.1.
37 *The Call to Arms*, 17/3/16, ML772/20/97; NL3222/6.
38 Genery interview; Surplus interview; *DA*, 29/7/16, p.3; 15/7/14, p.3.
39 Payne, 'Contribution to human progress', p.9.
40 *DA*, 11/12/15, p.4; 11/3/16, p.4.
41 *DA*, 29/7/16, p.3.
42 Smith, *Sabotage*, pp.1–2, 15.
43 *DA*, 24/2/17, p.2.
44 IWW, *Direct Action*, pp.7–8.

Chapter 10
'Bump Me into Parliament': the Critique of Laborism

1 In reply to Sir William Irvine, quoted in *Vanguard*, 12/4/17, p.2.
2 J.W. Miller, 'The I.W.W. and the political Labor movement', 8/7/16, ML Ai8/6.
3 Conlin, *Bread and Roses*, pp.29–30, 35; Reed, 'The fighting I.W.W.', p.91.
4 *DA*, 11/12/15, p.2.
5 *DA*, 3/2/17, p.2; *Vanguard*, 19/4/17, p.2.
6 *DA*, 15/5/14, p.2.
7 IWW, *Rebel Songs*, p.15; Fry (ed.), *Tom Barker*, p.3. There is a discrepancy between these two versions on the verse about the Bible. In opting for the more blasphemous version I am guided by a letter from Victoria and Guido

Baracchi to May Brodney, 1/10/67, objecting to Russel Ward's quotation of the more respectable, but inauthentic, version in his review of Ian Turner's *Sydney's Burning* (LT10882/5/13). A version with two extra verses is printed in *Sol*, 15/6/18, p.2.

8   *DA*, 1/6/15, p.1.
9   *DA*, 31/1/14, L, p.2.
10 IWW, *Songs*, 3rd Aust. edn, p.64.
11 *DA*, 1/7/14, p.3; 15/6/14, p.2.
12 Ivey interview.
13 *Sun*, 29/3/17, NL6265/3/F5.
14 *DA*, 15/6/14, p.2.
15 *DA*, 1/5/14, p.2; 16/9/16, p.1.
16 Childe, *How Labour Governs*, p.138; Surplus interview; *DA*, 15/12/14, p.1.
17 *DA*, 3/6/16, p.3; 15/8/15, p.1; 15/6/15, p.3; IWW, *Eleven Blind Leaders*, pp.17–18.
18 *DA*, 15/6/14, p.1.
19 *DA*, 15/5/15, p.3; 15/8/15, p.1.
20 *DA*, 15/5/14, p.2; 15/7/15, p.4; 11/12/15, p.3; Ted Moyle, notebook no.1, Moyle Collection.
21 *DA*, 15/6/14, p.4; 1/1/15, p.3; 15/5/14, p.4.
22 J.W. Ring, Nat. Sec. IWW Clubs, 24/12/12, to fellow workers, NL2576/3.
23 *DA*, 11/12/15, p.3; *Argus*, 16/12/16, p.18.
24 Item 24/8/18, A6286, 1st Military Dt, 3/7/18–30/10/18; Item 5/3/19, A6286, 1st Military Dt, 1/3/19–7/6/19.
25 *DA*, 15/5/14, pp.1, 4; May Day 1915, p.5.
26 *DA*, 11/12/15, p.3.
27 *DA*, 1/7/14, p.3; IWW, *The Immediate Demands*, p.16; *DA*, 15/5/15, p.3.
28 *DA*, 31/1/14, p.1; 15/5/14, p.4; 1/5/14, p.4; 15/5/14, p.1.
29 *DA*, 28/2/14, p.2; 15/7/15, p.3.
30 Sydney Local, IWW, 'Manifesto of the Industrial Workers of the World', n.d. [1911], ML A1333.
31 *DA*, 15/6/15, p.4; 20/1/17, p.2.
32 *DA*, 13/5/16, p.4; 27/11/15, p.4.
33 *DA*, 15/5/14, p.1.
34 *DA*, 15/6/14, L, p.2.
35 *DA*, 15/6/14, p.3.
36 *DA*, 5/2/16, p.4; 15/9/15, p.4; Surplus interview.
37 The number of separate unions had risen from 200 in 1900 to 430 in 1914, while membership increased from 100 000 to 500 000. After 1914 the number of separate unions declined as industrial unionism was becoming widely favoured as the basis of organisation (Child, *Unionism*, p.124). See also Childe, *How Labour Governs*, p.144; Churchward, 'American influence', p.270.
38 *DA*, 31/3/14, p.2; McGillick, *Comrade No More*, p.36; *DA*, 28/2/14, p.3; 15/6/14, p.3.
39 *DA*, 26/5/17, p.2; 15/9/15, p.4.
40 Scott, *Australia During the War*, pp.683–4; Turner, *Industrial Labour*, pp.91–3.
41 *DA*, 14/7/17, p.2.
42 Williams, *Eleven Blind Leaders*, Introduction.
43 IWW, *Direct Action*, pp.12–14.
44 *DA*, 16/6/17, p.2.

45 *DA*, 24/6/16, p.2; 14/7/17, L, p.2; 1/1/15, p.4.
46 May Brodney, 16/2/65, to E.C. Fry, LT10882/7/17; May Brodney, 28/11/66, to Sam Merrifield, LT10882/4/8; 'The Unlawful Associations Act, 1916–1917' (Detective Moore's Report re History and Proceedings of the IWW), SANSW7/5588.
47 Quoted in Cain, *The Wobblies at War*, pp.73–4; *BDT*, 5/12/16, NL6265/3/F4.
48 IWW, Statement giving a brief outline of the activities of the above organisation in Australia, AA ACT CRS A456 Item W26/148 P.H.B.
49 Bedford makes a similar point in 'The IWW', p.43.
50 *Industrial Worker*, 11/5/11, p.3.
51 IWW, *Direct Action*, p.13; *DA*, 10/6/16, p.4.
52 Minutes, Broken Hill Local, 4/3/17, SANSW7/5588; Childe, *How Labour Governs*, p.145; Bedford, 'The IWW', p.42; Rushton, 'Revolutionary ideology', pp.425, 432; Fry (ed.), *Tom Barker*, p.20; *DA*, 22/4/16, p.4.

Chapter 11
'An Injury to One An Injury to All': Direct Industrial Action

1 *DA*, 22/4/16, p.4.
2 *Argus*, 19/7/17, p.8; Hickey, *Solidarity or Sectionalism*.
3 *CPD*, LXXXII, 19/7/17, p.337.
4 Item 3/4/18, A6286, 1st Military Dt, 26/12/17–29/6/18; Item 5/3/19, A6286, 1st Military Dt, 1/3/19–7/6/19.
5 Item 12/3/19, A6286, 1st Military Dt, 1/3/19–7/6/19; AA Accession, AA1979/199, WA1024A, vol.I, Investigation Branch Reports, Summary of Communism, vol.I, Summaries 1–25, period June 1922–Dec. 1923, p.15; Items 5/6/18, 18/2/18, A6286, 1st Military Dt, 26/12/17–29/6/18.
6 Memorandum, Deputy Chief Censor, Department of Defence, Melbourne, 27/9/18, to Chief of the General Staff, Defence Department, AA (Brighton) Accession MP 367, File C512/1/618, Farrall Collection.
7 'The Unlawful Associations Act, 1916–1917' (Detective Moore's Report re History and Proceedings of the IWW), SANSW7/5588.
8 Childe, *How Labour Governs*, pp.144–5; Churchward, 'American influence', p.271; Seamer interview.
9 Fry (ed.), *Tom Barker*, p.22.
10 Jim Courtaul, unpublished ms Mitchell Library, pp.375–6, cited in Armstrong, 'Closer unity', pp.212–13; Item 11/12/18, A6286, 1st Military Dt, 2/11/18–26/2/19.
11 Turner, *Industrial Labour*, pp.142–4; Hickey, *Solidarity or Sectionalism*, pp.3–20.
12 *DA*, 22/4/16, p.4.
13 Coombe interview; Extract from letter dated 11/7/35, Graziers' Association of NSW, ABL E256/363.
14 *Sunday Times*, 19/3/16, ML A1333; Hunt, 'Labour movement in north Queensland', p.342.
15 *DA*, 4/3/16, p.4; 11/3/16, p.4; *SMH*, 29/7/16, 21/7/16, cited in Hade, *Justice Raped*, pp.3–4; *SMH*, 6/7/16, 7/7/16, 21/7/16, 17/11/16, cited in Rushton, 'The IWW in Sydney', p.215.
16 Hade, *Justice Raped*, p.5; Birch, 'The Wobblies', p.44.
17 IWW, *Direct Action*, p.10. Also p.5.
18 Saposs, *Left Wing Unionism*, p.143.
19 Sheldon, 'Failure of the IWW'; Sheldon, 'System and strategy', pp. 123–4, 131.

20 Karabogias, 'Fanning the flames', pp.21–2; *DA*, 22/4/16, p.1.
21 Fry (ed.), *Tom Barker*, p.20.
22 *DA*, 22/4/16, p.1.
23 Hunt, 'Labour movement in north Queensland', p.266; Karabogias, 'Fanning the flames', pp.23–4.
24 Beattie, 'Memoirs', p.39; Karabogias, 'Fanning the flames', pp.24–5; *Argus*, 19/2/17, p.8.
25 Childe, *How Labour Governs*, p.145.
26 *CPD*, LXXXII, 19/7/17, p.337.
27 Karabogias, 'Fanning the flames', p.26.
28 Australian Mercantile Land & Finance Co. Records, ABL162/3132.
29 Karabogias, 'Fanning the flames', pp.28–9.
30 Karabogias, 'Fanning the flames', pp.29–32.
31 Karabogias, 'Fanning the flames', pp.31–3; Turner, *Industrial Labour*, p.88.
32 Gollan, *Coalminers*, p.146; Turner, *Industrial Labour*, p.268; Karabogias, 'Fanning the flames', pp.34–5.
33 *DA*, 11/11/16, p.4.
34 *Sun*, 14/11/16; *SMH*, 7/11/16, quoted in Karabogias, 'Fanning the flames', p.36; Birch, 'The Wobblies', p.43; *NSWPD*, LXVI, 14/11/16, p.2694.
35 [?] Percival, E. Balmain, 16/11/16, to Dear Soldier, ML772/7/566–7; Anon, 'The iron heel', p.475.
36 *DA*, 11/11/16, p.4; Turner, *Industrial Labour*, p.90; Karabogias, 'Fanning the flames', pp.36–7; *DA*, 23/12/16, p.3; Gollan, *Coalminers*, p.147.
37 Hunt, 'Labour movement in north Queensland', pp.270–2.
38 'Secret Service', *Queer Queensland*, p.45.
39 Hunt, 'Labour movement in north Queensland', p.272.
40 Quoted in Hunt, 'Labour movement in north Queensland', p.271.
41 George Henry, Mount Cuthbert, 1/2/18, to W. Jackson, Townsville, Item 26/2/18, A6286, 1st Military Dt, 26/12/17–29/6/18; Hunt, 'Labour movement in north Queensland', pp.272–3; Surplus interview.
42 Hunt, 'Labour movement in north Queensland', pp.338–9.
43 Segal, 'Westralian Wobblies', pt 1.
44 Quoted in Segal, 'Westralian Wobblies', pt 2.
45 Quoted in Segal, 'Westralian Wobblies', pt 2.
46 Segal, 'Westralian Wobblies', pt 2.
47 Segal, 'Westralian Wobblies', pt 2.
48 Glynn, *Industrial Efficiency*, section IV.
49 *DA*, 1/12/14, p.4; 22/1/16, p.1.
50 *SMH*, 9/3/16, cited in Birch, 'The Wobblies', p.52.
51 Turner, *Industrial Labour*, p.143; *DA*, 2/12/16, L, p.2; 4/3/16, p.4; *SMH*, 10/1/17, 12/1/17; *Argus*, 24/11/16, cited in Birch, 'The Wobblies', pp.43–4.
52 'What is the Card System?', inserted in *DA*, 11/8/17.
53 Coward, 'Crime and punishment', pp.51–2.
54 Childe, *How Labour Governs*, p.150.
55 *DA*, 18/8/17, p.1.
56 Ted Moyle, notebook no.2, Moyle Collection; Coward, 'Crime and punishment', pp.72, 74, 78.
57 Pronouncement and Appeal by Cabinet, 6 Aug. 1917, *NSWPP*, 1917–18, II, quoted in Gollan, *Coalminers*, p.151.
58 Coward, 'Crime and punishment', pp.57, 78; Seggie, 'Role of the police', p.198.

59 Taksa, 'Defence not defiance', pp.22–3; Turner, *Industrial Labour*, p.150; Coward, 'Crime and punishment', p.62.
60 Birch, 'The Wobblies', p.47.
61 Coward, 'Crime and punishment', p.60; Turner, *Industrial Labour*, p.156.
62 H.L. Denford, 15/9/17, to F.J. Riley, NL759/6; E. Ross, *These Things Shall Be*, pp.118–19.
63 Cited in talk by Lloyd Ross, 'Industrial unrest', to the Economic Society of Victoria, 24/5/40, LT10882/14.
64 Hunt, 'Labour movement in north Queensland', pp.263–4; Cutler, 'Sunday, Bloody Sunday', p.85.
65 Hunt, 'Labour movement in north Queensland', pp.263–4.
66 List of IWW Correspondence in Queensland, AA ACT, CRS CP404/1, Item Bundle 1.
67 Hunt, 'Labour movement in north Queensland', pp.264–5.
68 Hunt, 'Labour movement in north Queensland', pp.357–60.
69 Deputy Chief Censor, Department of Defence, Melbourne, 27/9/18, to Chief of the General Staff, AA Accession MP 367, File C512/1/618; 'Secret Service', *Queer Queensland*, p.26.
70 Items 13/8/18, 31/8/18, A6286, 1st Military Dt, 3/7/18–30/10/18; Items 12/6/18, 19/5/18, A6286, 1st Military Dt, 26/12/17–29/6/18.
71 Hunt, 'Labour movement in north Queensland', pp.361; Super., 4/11/19, to Aust. Meat Export Co., Brisbane, quoted in Cutler, 'Sunday, Bloody Sunday', p.89; Report in *Pastoral Review*, 15/2/19, p.97, ABL [S640].
72 Hunt, 'Labour movement in north Queensland', pp.371–2, 381, 387.
73 Hunt, 'Labour movement in north Queensland', pp.374–401.
74 Cutler, 'Sunday, Bloody Sunday', p.93; Hunt, 'Labour movement in north Queensland', pp.402, 405.
75 *DA*, 27/1/17, p.2.

Chapter 12
'Let Those Who Own Australia do the Fighting': Opposing the War

1 By July 1915 unemployment had risen to 9.3 per cent from a pre-war level of 6.5 per cent, due to the dislocation of trade and the diversion of government finance towards the war effort; prices were soaring; and wages were frozen at their pre-war level by the Commonwealth and State arbitration courts.
2 Australian Peace Alliance file, Merrifield Collection, LT; Jauncey, *Conscription*, p.105; *DA*, 22/8/14, p.3; SANSW7/5543.
3 *DA*, 22/8/14, pp.1, 3.
4 *DA*, 25/12/15, p.3. It stressed, too, the extent to which Australian enterprises, such as CSR, were also engaged in imperialist exploits in places such as Fiji (*DA*, 14/7/17, p.4).
5 *DA*, 1/10/14, p.2.
6 Renshaw, *The Wobblies*, pp.206–7, 216; Conlin, *Bread and Roses*, p.80; Taft, 'The federal trials of the IWW', pp.59, 71–3; Dubofsky, 'Dissent', p.202.
7 *DA*, 15/2/15, p.4; 24/6/16, p.1; Coombe interview.
8 Beattie, 'Memoirs', p.36.
9 Jeffery, 'The labour movement', p.6; Ted Moyle, 10/8/45, to Alan Finger; Ted Moyle, notebook no.1, Moyle Collection; Evans, *Loyalty and Disloyalty*, p.75; Surplus interview; Jauncey, *The Story of Conscription*, p.223.
10 *DA*, 15/10/14, p.4; May Day 1915, p.3.

11 *DA*, 15/7/16, p.3; 15/9/15, p.1; 15/5/15, p.2; 1/10/15, p.3.
12 *DA*, 24/6/16, p.1; 10/2/17, p.3.
13 *DA*, 5/8/16, p.4.
14 *DA*, 15/5/15, pp.1, 3, 4. See also *DA*, May Day 1915, p.2; 1/8/15, p.2.
15 *DA*, 1/1/15, p.2; 1/6/15, p.1.
16 Beattie, 'Memoirs', p.36.
17 *DA*, 15/5/15, p.3.
18 *DA*, 18/12/15, p.2.
19 Quoted in Wilson, *All for the Cause*, p.79.
20 *DA*, 1/8/15, p.3.
21 *DA*, 15/8/15, p.1; 15/7/15, L, p.2.
22 *DA*, 10/8/14, L, p.2; 15/5/15, p.4.
23 *DA*, 15/2/15, p.2; 16/10/15, p.1; 15/4/15, p.2; 25/12/15, cartoon, p.1;
     22/8/14, p.4; 15/5/15, p.2; 15/6/15, p.1; 1/4/16, p.4.
24 *DA*, 11/12/15, p.3; 1/2/15, p.1.
25 *DA*, 15/2/15, p.4; 15/3/15, L, p.2; 1/3/15, p.2; 10/8/14, L, p.2.
26 Newspaper cuttings and unidentified letter to editor from F.J. Riley,
     11/12/15, NL759/20.
27 For instance, *The Call to Arms*, 17/3/16, ML772/20/97.
28 'Report by Detective Moore', Feb. 1918, quoted in Cain, 'Origins of politi-
     cal surveillance', p.264.
29 *DA*, 1/10/15, p.3.
30 Fry (ed.), *Tom Barker*, p.25.
31 *DA*, 1/10/15, p.3; Turner, *Sydney's Burning*, p.16; D. Grant, F.J. Morgan, N.
     Rancie, J.B. King, *Barker Defence Committee*, NL3516; Fry (ed.), *Tom Barker*,
     p.23.
32 Fewster, 'Expression and suppression', p.128; Fry (ed.), *Tom Barker*, p.25.
33 *DA*, 4/12/15, p.1; 29/7/16, p.1; Turner, *Sydney's Burning*, pp.18–19.
34 *Worker*, 20/4/16, p.5; various letters of protest from unions against the
     incarceration of Barker and Klausen, CRS A456/78/74.
35 Tom Barker file, Riley Collection, LT.
36 VSP Minutes, 29/9/15, NL564/1/5; Sec. Victorian Council Australian
     Peace Alliance, 2/5/16, to Sec. IWW, Sydney, NL759/6/52; Australian
     Peace Alliance, 26/5/16, to G.F. Pearce, Acting Prime Minister,
     NL759/6/52; Sidelights on Two Referendums, 1916–17, NL2070/4/1–7;
     Hewitt, 'The VSP', p.191; *Worker*, 18/5/16, p.5; *DA*, 15/9/15–25/12/15;
     Rushton, 'The IWW in Sydney', p.171.
37 Hade, *Justice Raped*, p.3; Fry (ed.), *Tom Barker*, p.28; *DA*, 12/8/16, p.1.
38 Ted Moyle, notebook no.1, Moyle Collection; Rushton, 'The IWW in
     Sydney', p.190, appendix III; Jim Scott's Diary, 17/9/17, Australian Peace
     Alliance file, Merrifield Collection, LT.
39 Beattie, 'Memoirs', p.37; Jeffery, 'The labour movement', pp.14–15.
40 The figures, Australia wide, were 51.61 per cent voted 'No' in 1916, and
     54.41 per cent in 1917. In the first poll, the 'No' States were NSW,
     Queensland and South Australia; in the second poll, they were NSW,
     Queensland, Victoria and South Australia.
41 See Australian Peace Alliance, *Objects*, NL759/6; Australian Peace Alliance,
     Victorian Council, 'Demand the terms of peace! An appeal to unionists',
     NL759/6; Healy, 'The Australian Peace Alliance', p.18.
42 *DA*, 28/10/16, p.3.
43 Walker, *How to Defeat Conscription*, p.15; Lane, *Dawn to Dusk*, p.174; *WW*,
     2/10/36, p.2, LT10882/8/21.

44 *DA*, 1/10/15, p.2; 6/5/16, p.1; also *DA*, 9/10/15, p.2; 1/7/16, L, p.2; Childe, *How Labour Governs*, p.146.
45 *DA*, 24/2/17, p.4.
46 May Brodney, 'Historions', LT10882/10/31. She makes similar allegations in 'Militant Propagandists of the Labor Movement', pp.15–16.
47 Ted Moyle, notebook no.1, Moyle Collection; Fry (ed.), *Tom Barker*, p.19.
48 *DA*, 15/9/15, L, p.2; 15/8/15, p.3; 15/9/15, p.2; 22/7/16, p.1; 21/10/16, p.2.
49 *DA*, 14/10/16, p.2; 20/11/15, p.4; 30/9/16, p.2; 20/5/16, p.2.
50 *DA*, 28/10/16, p.3; 16/12/16, p.4.
51 *DA*, 1/6/14, p.2.
52 *DA*, 1/8/15, p.4; VSP, Minutes, 26/7/15, NL564/1/5; Hewitt, 'The VSP', p.190; *DA*, 15/8/15, p.3.
53 Jim Quinton, 14/2/18, to Harry Barcan, Item 28/2/18, A6286, 1st Military Dt, 26/12/17–29/6/18.
54 Jim Scott's Diary, 4/10/16, Australian Peace Alliance file, Merrifield Collection, LT; Dale, *A History of Broken Hill*, p.213; Turner, *Industrial Labour*, p.109.
55 Kiek, 'South Australian labour unions', pp.137–40.
56 Surplus interview; Fry (ed.), *Tom Barker*, p.27.
57 *IS*, 23/9/16, p.1.
58 Fry (ed.), *Tom Barker*, p.27; Wilson, *All for the Cause*, pp.80–7, 98–9.
59 *DT*, 9/10/16, NL6265/3/F5.
60 Seggie, 'Role of the police', pp.191–2; George Bliss, Tweed Heads, NSW, 6/5/89, to author, p.2.
61 Jeffery, 'A stormy period in Australia', p.3; Sendy, 'The founders', p.4; *DA*, 19/8/16, p.1.
62 *DA*, 19/8/16, p.1; *NSWPD*, LXIV, p.775, cited in Birch, 'The Wobblies', p.30; *DA*, 26/8/16, p.1.
63 Quoted in *DA*, 22/1/16, p.4.
64 *Argus*, 14/1/16; *SMH*, 19/1/16, both quoted in Birch, 'The Wobblies', p.26.
65 *DA*, 30/1/16, p.1; *Argus*, 10/10/16, quoted in Birch, 'The Wobblies', pp.33, 36; *SMH*, 25/10/16, p.34; *Argus*, 12/10/16, p.8.
66 Hutchinson and Andrade, *Billy Hughes*, pp.13–14; Fitzhardinge, *Hughes*, II, pp.226–8, 249.
67 Hunt, 'Labour movement in North Queensland', p.288; Rushton, 'The IWW in Sydney', p.213.
68 Waten, *The Unbending*, p.331.
69 Childe, *How Labour Governs*, pp.136–7, 146, 150.

Chapter 13
'With the Ferocity of a Bengal Tiger': the State Responds

1 Enacted in twenty states and two territories between 1917 and 1920 (Ficken, 'The Wobbly horrors'; Sims, 'Idaho's Criminal Syndicalism Act', pp.511–12; Dowell, *Criminal Syndicalism Legislation*, p.21; Dubofsky, 'Dissent', pp.202–3; Ficken, *The Forested Land*).
2 SANSW 7/5588.
3 Rushton, 'The IWW in Sydney', pp.200–1.
4 VSP Exec., Minutes, 22/8/15, NL564/1/5; Cain, 'Origins of political surveillance', p.190; Fewster, 'Expression and suppression', p.157; F.J. Riley,

20/10/16, to Mr McDonald, 'The Standard', Brisbane, NL759/6; Fewster, 'The operation of state apparatuses', p.47.

5   *DA*, 8/7/16, p.1. See also *DA*, 6/5/16, p.1; 13/5/16, L, p.2; 27/5/16, p.3; Fewster, 'Expression and suppression', p.154; Rushton, 'The IWW in Sydney', p.215; *DA*, 1/10/15, p.1.

6   Quoted in Cain, 'Origins of political surveillance', p.267; Seggie, 'Role of the police', pp.149, 169.

7   Seggie, 'Role of the police', p.172; Fewster, 'Expression and suppression', p.156.

8   *Mirror*, 24/3/18, IWW scrapbook, ML; Beattie, 'Memoirs', p.35; Turner, *Sydney's Burning*, p.43.

9   Farrall interview; Genery interview; Audley interview; May Brodney, 'Histortions', LT10882/10/31; Bertha Walker, 20/2/64, to Roly, LT10772/3; Fry (ed.), *Tom Barker*, pp.24–5.

10   Seggie, 'Role of the police', p.174.

11   Certificates of Conviction of the respective people, quoted in Cain, 'Origins of political surveillance', pp.273–4.

12   *DA*, 12/5/17, L, p.2; Dowell, *Criminal Syndicalism Legislation*, pp.32, 37–8.

13   E.A. Giffney, Sec.-Treas., Gen. Exec. Board IWW, 26/9/16, to Sec.-Treas., Melbourne Local, reproduced in 'I.W.W. appeal to unionists and the general public', NL3222/5; Seggie, 'Role of the police', p.181.

14   E.A. Giffney, Sec.-Treas., Gen. Exec. Board IWW, 26/9/16, to Sec.-Treas., Melbourne Local, reproduced in 'I.W.W. appeal to unionists and the general public', NL3222/5; Fry (ed.), *Tom Barker*, p.22; Notes made by J.R. Wilson, p.6, Wilson Papers.

15   J.R. Wilson and N. Jeffery, 'I.W.W. appeal to unionists and the general public'; Rushton, 'The trial', p.56; Turner, *Sydney's Burning*, pp.35–6.

16   Quoted in Cain, 'Origins of political surveillance', p.275.

17   Alleged in 'The iron heel', p.474.

18   Unidentified press clipping, NL759/6.

19   Beattie, 'Memoirs', p.38; May Brodney, untitled manuscript and 'Histortions', LT10882/10/31; draft of May's autobiography, LT10882/8/23; Ted Moyle, notebook no.1, Moyle Collection.

20   Sidelights on Two Referendums, entry for September 1916, pp.54, 56, NL2070/4/1–7; Jeffery, 'A stormy period', p.1; Jeffery, 'The labour movement', p.12; Jeffery takes issue with Gollan, *Coalminers*, for attributing the fires to the IWW, in *Common Cause*, 3/8/63, 'Robin Gollan and the I.W.W.', p.2; Norman Rancie, 21/5/57, to Hugh Buggy, pp.1–2, NL6206/62/5; Norman Rancie, 17/7/57, to Jock of 'The Guardian', Jim Garvey Collection.

21   The guard on the railyards was removed on 22/12/16. See Cain, 'Origins of political surveillance', pp.277–8, 186.

22   Turner, *Sydney's Burning*, pp.26–7, 39, 41, 43, 78–9; *SMH*, 10, 19, 21/10/16, cited in Gollan, *Coalminers*, p.142; *Argus*, 15/12/16, p.9; 21/12/16, p.9.

23   Defence and Release Committee, *A Challenge to the People who Malign the Industrial Workers of the World*.

24   For example, *Argus*, 21/12/16, p.9.

25   *DA*, 6/1/17, p.2.

26   Fry (ed.), *Tom Barker*, p.24; Turner, *Sydney's Burning*, pp.21, 76–8.

27   Reported in *DA*, 21/10/16, p.4; *Argus*, 20/10/16, p.7.

28   Cain, 'Origins of political surveillance', pp.77–9, 191–2; *CPD*, LXXX, 18/12/16, p.10101; Enclosure of secret despatch from Governor-General

to Secretary of State for Colonies, 19/11/16, cited in Cain, 'Origins of political surveillance', pp.81–4, 193.

29 Fewster, 'Expression and suppression', pp.183–4.

30 Rushton, 'The IWW in Sydney', pp.241c–d; *DT*, 2/11/16, NL6265/3/F5; *DA*, 2/12/16, L, p.2.

31 Fewster, 'Expression and suppression', p.184; 16/10/16, Police Department file, 47/78.1, cited in Rushton, 'The IWW in Sydney', p.241b; Jeffery, 'The labour movement', p.12.

32 Telegram, Victoria Barracks to Military Commandant Perth, 17/10/16, copy in possession of Clem Macintyre; Turner, *Sydney's Burning*, p.44; Cain, *The Wobblies at War*, p.241.

33 Turner, *Sydney's Burning*, pp.45–7, 75–6; Fry (ed.), *Tom Barker*, p.32; *West Australian*, 10/11/16, cited in Macintyre, 'Winning a battle', p.6.

34 Macintyre, 'Winning a battle', p.7; *West Australian*, 17/11/16, 22/11/16, 7/12/16, 15/12/16, cited in Macintyre, 'Winning a battle', pp.7–8, 9, 11.

35 *Argus*, 16/12/16, p.18; *West Australian*, 9/12/16, 14/12/16, cited in Macintyre, 'Winning a battle', pp.9–10; Williams (ed.), *Eureka and Beyond*, pp.71–3; Fry, 'Australian worker', p.180.

36 *West Australian*, 16/12/16, 18/12/16, cited in Macintyre, 'Winning a battle', pp.12–14; *Argus*, 16/12/16, p.18; 18/12/16, p.6.

37 Williams (ed.), *Eureka and Beyond*, pp.75–6, 80, 84.

38 Rushton, 'The trial', pp. 53–7; Turner, *Sydney's Burning*, pp.49–50.

39 Sidelights on Two Referendums, entry for December 1916, p.62, NL2070/4/1–7; *Argus*, 4/12/16, p.7; Rushton, 'The IWW in Sydney', p.240.

40 Beattie, 'Memoirs', p.38; Seggie, 'Role of the police', pp.186–7; Genery interview; Ted Moyle, notebook no.2, Moyle Collection; J. Le Gay Brereton, 19/2/18, to Duncan Hall, NL5547; Grant, *Through Six Gaols*, p.12.

41 Seggie, 'Role of the police', p.205.

42 IWW, *Speeches from the Dock*, pp.3–5, 7–8.

43 Class warriors who had suffered from Mr Justice Pring's interpretation of the law included Tom Mann and Harry Holland in 1909, Peter Bowling in 1910, and the leaders of the Lithgow miners' strike in 1911 (Turner, *Sydney's Burning*, p.63); *Argus*, 4/12/16, p.7.

44 Turner, *Sydney's Burning*, pp.56–8; Boote, *Fifteen Years for Fifteen Words*, p.8; Tom Barker, London, 19/8/20, to H.E. Boote, NL2070/1/51–2.

45 Rushton, 'The IWW in Sydney', pp.241c–d; Seggie, 'Role of the police', p.180.

46 *CPD*, LXXX, 18/12/16, p.10100; the Unlawful Associations Act (no.41 of 1916) was assented to on 21 December 1916; *CPD*, LXXX, 18/12/16, p.10111; *CPD*, LXXX, 19/12/16, pp.10158, 10178–9.

47 Cain, 'Origins of political surveillance', pp.285, 209, 213–14.

48 *CPD*, LXXXII, 18/7/17, pp.230–1; Cain, 'Origins of political surveillance', p.288; *Argus*, 24/7/17, p.7.

49 Unlawful Associations Act 1917, no.14 of 1917, *The Acts of the Commonwealth of Australia*, 15, Melbourne, 1918, pp.22–4.

50 Fry (ed.), *Tom Barker and the IWW*, p.31.

51 'The Unlawful Associations Act, 1916–1917' (Detective Moore's Report re History and Proceedings of the IWW), SANSW7/5588, p.39.

52 *Vanguard*, 5/4/17, pp.2–3; *CPD*, LXXXII, 19/7/17, p.316; Lord Munro Ferguson, 31/7/17, to the Secretary of State for the Colonies, PRO, CO 418/158.

53 Cain, 'The IWW', pp.57–8; Ted Moyle, notebook no.2, Moyle Collection; Shor, 'Masculine power', p.98.
54 Betsy Matthias, n.d., to Kathleen Hotson, Item 30/1/18, A6286, 1st Military Dt, 26/12/17–29/6/18; Ted Moyle, notebook no.2, Moyle Collection.
55 K. Hotson, 28/3/18, to Mrs Schofield, Item 10/4/18; John Randolph, 27/2/18, to Kathleen Hotson, Item 19/3/18; John Randolph, 1/3/18, to Kathleen Hotson, Item 19/3/18 (A6286, 1st Military Dt, 26/12/17–29/6/18); IWW Prisoners Release Committee, *Breakers of Men*, pp.4–5. On the other hand, Tom Barker was not badly treated at Albury jail (Barker, 'How I did my time').
56 Charles Reeve, State Penitentiary, 30/8/19, to Dear Mum, p.2, ML5653.
57 Dan Buckley, Chicago, 25/12/17, to Peter Buckley, Sth Brisbane, Item 26/2/18, A6286, 1st Military Dt, 26/12/17–29/6/18; Cain, 'The IWW', pp.58–9; Fry (ed.), *Tom Barker*, p.34; A. Rosenthal, London, 23/5/19, to Luke Jones, Item 26/5/19, A6286, 2nd Military Dt, 5/5/19–8/9/19; Jock Wilson, Liverpool, 6/1/18, to R.S. Ross, NL3222/1/39.
58 Walker, *How to Defeat Conscription*, p.13; Evans, 'Radical departures', pp.1, 13–19; Ted Moyle, notebook no.2, Moyle Collection.
59 See Dowell, *Criminal Syndicalism Legislation*, pp.46, 144–5; Sims, 'Idaho's Criminal Syndicalism Act', p.513; Dubofsky, 'Dissent', p.203; IWW, *Speeches from the Dock*, p.7.
60 Anon., 'The iron heel', p.475; also *DA*, 2/12/16, L, p.2; 10/3/17, p.3; 14/7/17, p.2; May Francis, Footscray, to John L. Oliver, Benalla, in censors' reports, week ending 22/7/18, LT10882/11.
61 Wilson, *All for the Cause*, pp.90–1; Genery interview.
62 Wilson, *All for the Cause*, pp.91–3.
63 Minutes, Broken Hill Local, 28/7/17, SANSW7/5588; *Argus*, 3/9/17, p.3; 4/9/17, p.5; Shor, 'Masculine power', p.98; Ted Moyle, notebook no.2, Moyle Collection.
64 Norman Rancie, 21/5/57, to Hugh Buggy, pp.2–3, NL6206/62/5.
65 *Argus*, 3/9/17, p.3; 8/9/17, p.21; 10/9/17, p.6.
66 Herbert Cosby, Sydney, 26/9/18, to George Henry, Item 16/10/18, A6286, 1st Military Dt, 3/7/18–30/10/18.
67 Surplus interview; Evans, *Loyalty and Disloyalty*, p.131.
68 Segal, 'Westralian Wobblies', pt 2; *Argus*, 22/10/17, p.7; 11/12/17, p.3.
69 Dolly Jeffery and Mother, 11/4/18, to Norman Jeffery, Item 20/4/18, A6286, 3rd Military Dt, 25/10/17–28/5/18.
70 Monty Miller, Perth, 2/2/18, to Mrs A. Craig, Brisbane, Item 21/2/18; Betsy Matthias, n.d., to Kathleen Hotson, Item 30/1/18 (A6286, 1st Military Dt, 26/12/17–29/6/18); Monty Miller, 19/2/18, to W.J. Miles, Item 20/2/18, A6286, 2nd Military Dt, 23/10/17–29/7/18; Mick Sawtell, 23/10/18, to Sec. ILP, Sydney, Item 28/10/18, A6286, 2nd Military Dt, 5/8/18–28/4/19; Mick Sawtell, 11/10/18, to Beth Pole, Item 12/10/18; Mick Sawtell, 19/11/18, to Don Cameron, Item 23/11/18; Mick Sawtell, 17/3/19, to George Ricks, Item 22/3/19 (A6286, 5th Military Dt, 3/1/18–30/8/19).
71 Evans, *Loyalty and Disloyalty*, pp.130, 132; Item 17/4/18, A6286, 1st Military Dt, 26/12/17–29/6/18; Item 13/11/18, A6286, 1st Military Dt, 2/11/18–26/2/19; Item 5/3/19, A6286, 1st Military Dt, 1/3/19–7/6/19.
72 Conroy, *Political Action*, p.10; Central Political Executive of the Queensland Labor Party, *Solidarity or Disruption*, 1919, enclosed in letter from

L. McDonald, Central Political Executive, QLP, 5/3/19, to G. Lawson, Sec. Carters and Drivers Union, Brisbane, Item 12/3/19, A6286, 1st Military Dt, 1/3/19–7/6/19; for Theodore's opinions on the IWW see *Worker*, 30/1/19, quoted in Hunt, 'Labour movement in north Queensland', p.370.

73 W. Hughes, 20/9/17, to Brisbane Premier, CRS A456 W26/148/182; Telegram from Premier Ryan, 21/9/17, to W. Hughes, CRS A456 W26/148/182; W. Hughes, 22/9/17, to Premier, Brisbane, CRS A456 W26/148/182.

74 W. Shepherd, Sec. Attorney-General's Department, 28/9/17, to Premier, Brisbane, CRS A456 W26/148/182; Seggie, 'Role of the police', p.195.

75 Deputy Chief Censor, Department of Defence, Melbourne, 27/9/18, to the Chief of the General Staff, AA Accession MP 367 File C512/1/618.

76 Item 16/10/18, A6286, 1st Military Dt, 3/7/18–30/10/18.

77 AA Accession B197 File 202/1/495; Item 15/1/19, A6286, 1st Military Dt, 2/11/18–26/2/19.

78 Jim Quinton, 18/10/18, to Hon. John Huxham, Home Sec., Brisbane, Item 23/10/18, A6286, 1st Military Dt, 3/7/18–30/10/18; Evans, *Loyalty and Disloyalty*, p.136; A.E. Eastcrabb, Hughenden, 21/10/18, to Gen. Sec. QRU, Brisbane, Item 6/11/18, A6286, 1st Military Dt, 2/11/18–26/2/19; Item 9/4/19, A6286, 1st Military Dt, 1/3/19–7/6/19.

79 *One Big Union Monthly* (Chicago), June 1920, p.28; Coombe interview; Grant, *Through Six Gaols*, p.12.

80 Surplus interview; Fry (ed), *Tom Barker*, p.19.

81 Anon., 'The iron heel', p.475.

82 Hade, *Justice Raped*, p.5.

83 *Argus*, 14/9/16, p.6.

84 Hutchinson and Andrade, *Billy Hughes*, p.8.

85 *Argus*, 12/10/16, p.8.

86 Fry (ed.), *Tom Barker*, p.31.

87 *A Comm*, 11/3/21, quoted in *I Comm*, 19/3/21, ABL N57/653; Turner, *Industrial Labour*, p.135; Turner, *Sydney's Burning*, p.89; E. Ross, *The Russian Revolution*, p.27; Campbell, *History*, p.38; *WW*, 2/10/36, p.2.

88 Norman Rancie, 21/5/57, to Hugh Buggy, pp.2–3, NL6206/62/5.

Chapter 14
'Set the Twelve Men Free': the Release Campaign

1 Quoted in Rushton, 'The IWW in Sydney', p.242.

2 G. Waurn, Sec. IWW Local no.8, 27/2/17, to Dear Fellow Worker, NL3516.

3 Turner, *Industrial Labour*, pp.131–4; *Toiler*, 16/7/20, p.5; *Knowledge and Unity*, 17/7/20, p.4; Minutes, Broken Hill Local, 18/2/17, SANSW7/5588; Surplus interview.

4 CA908, Investigation Branch, Western Australia, Summary of Communism and Index, 1922–1924 'File WA1024A Summary of Communism vol.1 Comprising summaries 1 to 25, Period June to Dec 1923', AA Accession AA1979/199 Item vol.1; Delia Larkin, Ireland, 31/7/19, to Peter Larkin, Parramatta Jail, Item 4/8/19, A6286, 2nd Military Dt, 5/5/19–8/9/19; Tom Barker, 31/5/20, to fellow workers, Barker Collection, NL; *Toiler*, 9/7/20, p.3; 24/9/20, p.7; *Ind Sol* (A), July 1920, p.1.

5 Legislative Assembly, New South Wales, *Report of Royal Commission of Inquiry*, 11/8/20, p.iii; *DA*, 17/3/17, p.1.

6 Ted Moyle, notebook no.2, Moyle Collection; CRS A456 W26/148/57; Australian Boot Trade Employees Federation, Minutes, ABL T49/1/17; Hotel, Club and Restaurant Employees Union of NSW, Minutes, ABL T12/1/2; E.J. Holloway, Ass. Sec. Trades Hall Council, 16/3/18, to Gavin (Sec. Industrial Council, Brisbane), Item 10/4/18, A6286, 1st Military Dt, 26/12/17–29/6/18; *Argus*, 20/12/16, p.9; 22/12/16, p.8; 23/12/16, p.10; 30/12/16, p.11; 6/1/17, p.15; 11/1/17, p.6; 6/2/17, p.8; 22/2/17, p.8; 31/7/17, p.5; 23/4/18, p.3; 19/6/19, p.7; Militant Propagandists, Minutes, 2/12/16–9/11/18, LT10882/4/6; Arch Stewart, Sec. PLC, 13/2/17, to Dear Comrade, circular letter, NL759/6.

7 *Toiler*, 20/8/20, p.9; Coombe interview.

8 Militant Propagandists, Minutes, 2/12/16–9/11/18, LT10882/4/6; Arch Stewart, Sec. PLC, 13/2/17, to Dear Comrade, circular letter, NL759/6; May Brodney, 'Histortions', LT10882/10/31; *Argus*, 20/12/16, p.9; 21/12/16, p.9; 18/6/18, p.4.

9 *One Big Union Monthly* (Chicago), June 1920, p.28; Ben Lewis, Sec. Labor Agitators Release and Defence Committee, 2/7/18, to Dear Comrade H. Spencer Wood, ML772/18/509; *Sol*, 9/3/18, p.1.

10 LT10882/3; Ben Lewis, Sydney, n.d., to John Christie, Brisbane, Item 3/7/18; Solidarity Hall, 16/7/18, to Mrs Bingham, Item 24/7/18, A6286, 1st Military Dt, 3/7/18–30/10/18; Ted Moyle, notebook no.2, Moyle Collection.

11 *Labor News*, 28/6/19, p.11. See also statement by W. Carey, Sec. ALP, *Sydney Sun*, 12/3/20, NL6206/63/4; *Labor News*, 12/7/19, p.3.

12 *Argus*, 5/2/17, p.6; Boote, *Guilty or Not Guilty*, pp.50–1.

13 Ted Moyle, notebook no.2, Moyle Collection; T. Riley, Sydney, 9/3/18, to E. Stewart, Sth Brisbane, Item 21/3/18, A6286, 1st Military Dt, 26/12/17–29/6/18.

14 A. McInnes, Sydney, 18/3/18, to N.A. Freeberg, Brisbane, Item 27/3/18, A6286, 1st Military Dt, 26/12/17–29/6/18; *One Big Union Monthly* (Chicago), June 1920, p.28.

15 *Labor News*, 30/8/19, p.5; 6/9/19, p.7; 13/3/20, p.1.

16 *Worker*, 12/9/18, p.13; Boote, *Set the 12 Men Free*, p.53; Boote, *The Case of Grant*, p.7.

17 Boote, *Guilty or Not Guilty*, pp.50–1.

18 Boote, *Set the 12 Men Free*, p.63.

19 *Sol*, 19/1/18, p.3, also Petition for Release of IWW Men, ML772/20/89; *Sol*, 9/3/18, p.1; 'Workers of Queensland, Attention!', F. Page, Sec. Release Committee, 'Daily Standard', Brisbane, n.d. [c.1917].

20 *Sol*, 29/6/18, p.2.

21 AWU Queensland branch, Minutes of Annual Delegate Meetings, book 2, 16/1/17–25/1/20, Fourth Annual Delegate Meeting, third day, Minutes to meeting, 10/1/17, ABL M50, Reel 5. See also Labor Council of NSW, 4/2/18, to Sec. Industrial Council, Brisbane, Item 18/2/18, A6286, 1st Military Dt, 26/12/17–29/6/18; Minutes of Hotel, Club and Restaurant Employees' Union of NSW, Minutes for 15/6/20, ABL T12/1/2; Waterside Workers' Federation, General Minutes, 2/6/20, ABL M70/2; Australian Coal and Shale Employees Federation, Minutes, 14/1/19, ABL E164/4; and 1920 Annual meeting, p.133, ABL E165/2/1; Hotel, Club and Restaurant Employees' Union of NSW, Minutes for 15/6/20, ABL T12/1/2.

22   Ted Moyle, notebook no.2, Moyle Collection.
23   Kerr, *Solidarity Sentenced*, pp.2–3.
24   George Dale, Sydney, 17/8/18, to J. Cronin, Townsville, Item 4/9/18, A6286, 1st Military Dt, 3/7/18–30/10/18; *Sol*, 29/6/18, p.1.
25   Monty Miller, Perth, 31/7/18, to E.J. Holloway, Melbourne, Item 9/8/18, A6286, 3rd Military Dt, 1/6/18–26/9/18; Mick Sawtell, 16/8/19, to Don Cameron, Item 17/8/18, A6286, 5th Military Dt, 3/1/18–30/8/19.
26   *Sol*, 18/5/18, p.4.
27   *Sol*, 14/6/19, quoted in Churchward, 'American influence', pp.272–3; Rushton, 'The IWW in Sydney', pp.266–7.
28   Papa [Monty Miller], 10/3/18, to Mrs Annie Craig, Brisbane, Item 27/3/18, A6286, 1st Military Dt, 26/12/17–29/6/18; Steve Viske, 8/12/17, to Betsy, Item 3, CP 407/1, Bundle 2; Item 15/5/18, A6286, 1st Military Dt, 26/12/17–29/6/18.
29   Item 28/2/18, A6286, 1st Military Dt, 26/12/17–29/6/18; 10/12/17, AA ACT, CP 407/1, Bundle 2, 3rd Military Dt Intelligence Reports: brief summary of information disclosing enemy trading or other suspicious actions; Item 10/7/18, A6286, 1st Military Dt, 3/7/18–30/10/18.
30   *Sol*, 5/1/18, p.1; 19/1/18, p.1; 9/2/18, p.3; Betsy Matthias, n.d., to Sid Gower, Townsville, Item 30/1/18, A6286, 1st Military Dt, 26/12/17–29/6/18.
31   *Sol*, 15/6/18, pp.2, 1; Betsy, 26/7/18, to E. Maguire, AA ACT Branch CP407/1, Bundle 2, 3rd Military Dt Intelligence Reports: brief summary of information disclosing enemy trading or other suspicious actions.
32   *Sol*, 15/6/18, p.2.
33   *Sol*, 29/6/18, p.3; Betsy Matthias, n.d., to Archie Stewart, Family Hotel, Cloncurry, Item 3/7/18, A6286, 1st Military Dt, 3/7/18–30/10/18; *Sol*, 4/5/18, p.1; 15/6/18, p.4; Item 2/10/18, A6286, 1st Military Dt, 3/7/18–30/10/18.
34   Nita Freeman, 23/1/19, to D. McPherson, Goulburn Jail, Item 149 and Betsy Matthias, 8/2/19, to Rosenbloom and Litchfield, Vesteys Meat Works, Darwin, Item 156 (AA ACT CP 407/1, Bundle 2, 3rd Military Dt Intelligence Reports: brief summary of information disclosing enemy trading or other suspicious actions); Wright interview; Rushton, 'The IWW in Sydney', p.267; *Prol*, 1/3/19, p.1; 15/3/19, p.2.
35   Item 19/3/19, A6286, 1st Military Dt, 1/3/19–7/6/19; Item 10/3/19, A6286, 2nd Military Dt, 5/8/18–28/4/19.
36   *Prol*, 15/2/19, p.4; 8/3/19, p.1; 22/3/19, p.4.
37   Item 12/3/19, A6286, 1st Military Dt, 1/3/19–7/6/19.
38   *Prol*, 1/2/19, p.3; 22/2/19, p.3; 1/3/19, pp.3, 2; 1/2/19, p.1; 22/3/19, pp.3, 2; 8/3/19, p.3.
39   Item 9/4/19, A6286, 1st Military Dt, 1/2/19–7/6/19; Item 16/4/19, A6286, 3rd Military Dt, 2/4/19–10/9/19; Item 28/5/19, A6286, 1st Military Dt, 1/3/19–7/6/19; Item 23/7/19, A6286, 1st Military Dt, 11/6/19–2/9/19; *Ind Sol* (M), 7/2/20, p.4.
40   *Ind Sol* (M), 14/6/19, L, p.2.
41   *Ind Sol* (M), 7/2/20, p.2.
42   Mick Sawtell, Adelaide, 11/8/19, to Don Cameron, Melbourne, Item 13/8/19, A6286, 3rd Military Dt, 2/4/19–10/9/19; Tom Audley, 22/1/20, to George Reeve, ML772/11/343; Alf W. Wilson, Adelaide, 21/2/20, 3/1/21, 26/1/21, to G.G. Reeve, ML MS772/11/353, 465, 469; Wilson, *All for the Cause*, pp.111, 128.

43 *Ind Sol* (M), 22/11/19, p.4; *Ind Sol* (A), Feb. 1920, p.2.
44 *Ind Sol* (A), Feb. 1920, L, p.2.
45 *Ind Sol* (A), May 1920, p.4.
46 Tom Barker, 18/5/20, to Percy Brookfield, published in *Toiler*, 9/7/20, p.3.
47 Wobblies acknowledged their debt and expressed their gratitude to these two men: Tom Barker, London, 19/8/20, to Henry Boote, NL2070/1/51–2; Fry (ed.), *Tom Barker*, p.29; Monty Miller, 22/4/18, to Mrs Annie Craig [Annie Westbrook], Item 15/5/18; Roland Farrall, 19/3/18, Melbourne, to Annie Westbrook, Item 10/4/18 (A6286, 1st Military Dt, 26/12/17–29/6/18); J.R. Wilson, Port Glasgow, 29/10/18, to Jas. B. King, Goulburn Jail, Item 26/10/18, 2nd Military Dt, 5/8/18–28/4/19.
48 *Australian Worker*, 17/8/49, ML772/25; Sidelights on Two Referendums, entry for July 1917, p.71 and entry for August 1917, p.72, NL2070/4/1–7; Item 29/1/18, A6286, 2nd Military Dt, 23/10/17–29/7/18; *P*, 3/10/18, pp.1, 4.
49 OBUPL, *I.W.W. Cases*, pp.3–4.
50 Ted Moyle, notebook no.2, Moyle Collection; Turner, 'The I.W.W. treason trials, 1916', p.4.
51 Ted Moyle, notebook no.2, Moyle Collection; Release and Defence Committee, *The I.W.W. Inquiry*, p.12.
52 Childe, *How Labour Governs*, p.150; Turner, 'The I.W.W. treason trials, 1916', p.4; *Labor News*, 21/12/18, p.7; Ted Moyle, notebook no.2, Moyle Collection; Tom Barker, Australian Workers Defence Committee, London, n.d., to Dear Fellow Worker, Barker Collection, NL.
53 ML772/20/93c-d; ML772/20/39.
54 Release and Defence Committee, *The I.W.W. Inquiry*; also leaflet, n.d. [c. Oct. 1919], ML772/20/83; Sticker, J.S. Garden *et al*, NSW Labor Council Release Committee, ML772/20/93g.
55 J.S. Garden, Sec. and D.W. Sinclair, Organiser NSW Labor Council Release Committee, ML772/20/37; *Evening News*, 23/3/20, NL6206/63/4.
56 Turner, 'The I.W.W. treason trials, 1916', pp.4–5; Childe, *How Labour Governs*, p.150.
57 Ted Moyle, notebook no.2, Moyle Collection; *SMH*, 12/8/20, NL6206/63/4.
58 Lang, 'The I.W.W., the judge and cement', *Truth*, 13/6/54, p.34.
59 *Worker*, 22/7/20, p.14; *Labor News*, 3/7/20, p.5; 10/7/20, p.3.
60 Legislative Assembly, New South Wales, *Report of Royal Commission*, 11/8/20, p.1; Turner, 'The I.W.W. treason trials, 1916', p.5.
61 *DT*, 5/8/20, NL6206/63/4.
62 *Labor News*, 7/8/20, p.1.
63 Wilson, *All for the Cause*, pp.149, 193–4; IWW File, Riley Collection, LT; P.F. Collins, August 1920, ML772/20/67; *Labor News*, 14/8/20, p.2; *Toiler*, 11/6/20, L; VSP, Exec. Minutes, 13/9/20, 27/9/20, NL564/1/7; *A Comm*, 4/3/21, p.1.
64 *Toiler*, 8/10/20, p.3; 22/10/20.
65 *Toiler*, 20/8/20, p.2.
66 *Ind Sol* (A), Sept. 1920, p.1.
67 *A Comm*, 18/3/21, p.7; 6/5/21, p.2.
68 Turner, 'The I.W.W. treason trials, 1916', p.5.
69 *Age*, 8/11/21, p.6; *Common Cause*, 16/9/21, p.6; Ted Moyle, notebook no.2, Moyle Collection; Childe, *How Labour Governs*, p.150.
70 Turner, 'The I.W.W. treason trials, 1916', p.5.

71 *Toiler*, 20/8/20, p.9; C. Reeve, State Penitentiary, 22/5/20, to Fellow Worker, p.1, ML5653.

Chapter 15
What Happened to the Wobblies?

1 Sendy, 'The founders', p.9; Gibson interview; Seamer interview; Ross interview; Wright interview; May Brodney, 10/9/64, to Sam Merrifield, LT10882/7/17.
2 Glynn, *Communist Review*, 11/3/21, quoted in Rushton, 'The IWW in Sydney', pp.266–7; Hunt, 'Labour movement in north Queensland', p.418 fn.20.
3 J.B. Scott notes, NL6206/62/3.
4 W. Beatty, 14/10/20, to 'Jim', ABL P/8/5/1; Lesbia Harford to May Brodney, LT10882/11; Dixson, *Greater than Lenin*, p.50; Throssell (ed.), *Straight Left*, p.67. New Zealand Wobblies were similarly suspicious of the Communist Party there, but a mythology about IWW enthusiasm for the Party did not develop. (Taylor, 'Worker's vanguard', p.56).
5 Morrison, 'The Communist Party', p.208; Wright interview.
6 Earsman diary, entry for 24/11/22.
7 Bob Brodney, LT10882/3; AA ACT CRSAA1979/199, Item vol.1.
8 Hector, 'The carnival at the Beaufort Street temple', p.1117; Fry, 'Australian worker', p.193; Throssell (ed.), *Straight Left*, pp.66–9; Williams (ed.), *Eureka and Beyond*, p.96.
9 CPA Minutes: Conference 13/11/20; Exec. 6/12/20; Conference 11/12/20; Exec. 22/12/20 (ML772/9/7); Alf Wilson, 26/1/21, to George Reeve, ML772/11/469; Charles Reeve, State Penitentiary, 11?/3/21, to Dear Mum, p.2, ML5653.
10 CA908, Investigation, Western Australia, Summary of Communism and Index, 1922–24, 'File WA1024A Summary of Communism vol.1 June to Dec. 1923', AA Accession AS1979/199, Item vol.1; *Prol*, 15/2/19, p.3; 15/3/19, pp.1, 3; 22/3/19, p.1.
11 Sawtell, 29/3/19, to Don Cameron, Item 9/4/19, A6286, 3rd Military Dt, 2/4/19–10/9/19; *Comm*, 3/6/21, p.1.
12 Morrison, 'The Communist Party', pp.418–19; Moscow, 2/8/21, to Central Exec., CPA, ML772/9/213; *A Comm*, 14/1/21, p.3.
13 For example, *I Comm*, 19/3/21; 26/3/21; Alf Wilson, 8/2/21, to George Reeve, ML772/11/471–3.
14 *A Comm*, 31/12/20, p.1; 8/4/21, p.7.
15 CPA Exec. Minutes, 4/3/21, ML MS772/8/78; ML772/21.
16 Morrison, 'The Communist Party', pp.418–19.
17 *Industrialist*, 3/11/21, p.1. See also *Toiler*, 20/8/20, p.3.
18 To the Director, Investigation Branch, Melbourne, 22/8/22, in (CA908, Investigation, Western Australia). Summary of Communism and Index, 1922–24, 'File WA1024A Summary of Communism vol.1 June to Dec. 1923', AA Accession AS1979/199, Item vol.1; AA ACT CRS A3932, Item SC292, pt.3, compiled 1/11/22; Playford, 'Left-wing of the South Australian labor movement', p.47.
19 Various letters (for example, J.B. Miles, Brisbane, 16/11/21, to Bob Brodney), LT10882/1/1.
20 *A Comm*, 11/11/21; Morrison, 'The Communist Party', pp.418–19; A.T. Brodney Report to Kurri Kurri Branch, 18/11/21; 'Reasons for unity decision', LT10882/1/1.

21 *DA*, 1/12/21, pp.3, 4.
22 *DA*, March 1922, p.1; Minutes Unity Conference, ML772/9/89–91; D. McDonald, Sec. IUPG, 9/2/22, to Sec. CPA, ML772/9/305.
23 See Dixson, 'The first Communist "united front" in Australia', pp.20–31.
24 *DA*, April 1922, p.4.
25 *DA*, April 1922, L, p.2.
26 *DA*, April 1922, p.3.
27 J.B. Scott notes, NL6206/62/3.
28 Sendy, 'The founders', pp.4–5a; *A Comm*, 31/12/20, p.2; 21/1/21, p.6; 8/4/21; *Comm*, 27/5/21; 1st Annual Conference, 26/3/21, ML772/9/57; Minutes Exec. CPA, 1/4/21, ML772/9/69; Jeffery, 14/5/60, to Jim Garvey, p.3, Garvey Collection.
29 WIUA, *One Big Union*; *Argus*, 16/1/19, p.6; *Sun*, 17/6/23, p.7; 'One Big Union scheme', Nov. 1921, NL3222/6; Labor Council, 'Reorganisation', 6/5/18, NL3222/5; Anderson, *One Big Union for Australia*, esp. pp.16–17; Bedford, 'One Big Union', p.19; Churchward, 'American influence', pp.270–1; Turner, *Industrial Labour*, pp.182–3; Hunt, 'Labour movement in north Queensland', p.377; Judd, *The Case for the O.B.U.*, p.2; Young, 'The NSW One Big Union, 1918–1919'.
30 *Labor News*, 26/10/18, p.7, quoted in Bongiorno, 'The AWU', p.13.
31 Lane, *Dawn to Dusk*, pp.206–7; Childe, *How Labour Governs*, pp.130, 151; Churchward, 'American influence', p.275; Hagan, 'The A.C.T.U.' in Fry (ed.), *Common Cause*, pp.42–4; Hagan, *The History of the A.C.T.U.*, p.18.
32 J.S. Garden, Sec. OBUPL, Sydney, 3/2/19, to J. Quinton, GPO Brisbane, Item 19/2/19, A6286, 1st Military Dt, 2/11/18–26/2/19; Norman Jeffery, 16/12/18, to Mrs M. Jeffery, Item 21/12/18, A6286, 5th Military Dt, 3/1/18–30/8/19; Throssell (ed.), *Straight Left*, p.88; Jack Cosgrave notebook, LT10882/4/6; Wilson, *All for the Cause*, p.110.
33 For example, NSW Labor Conference Report, *Labor News*, 14/6/19, p.9; *Labor News*, 26/7/19, p.9; Cleary, *The One Big Union, Will it Emancipate the Workers?*, quoted in Wilson, *All for the Cause*, pp.20–1, 42, 48, 111; Hickey, *Solidarity or Sectionalism*, pp.3–20.
34 Segal, 'Westralian Wobblies', pt 1.
35 Miller, 24/7/18, to A.F. Gorman, Item 7/8/18, A6286, 1st Military Dt, 3/7/18–30/10/18; Miller, 17/9/18, to Mr and Mrs W. Davis, NSW, Item 26/9/18, A6286, 4th Military Dt, 6/12/17–30/8/19; Miller, 26/9/18, to Mrs A. Gray, Item 30/9/18, A6286, 2nd Military Dt, 5/8/18–28/4/19; Miller, 18/10/18, to Mrs Sarah Davis, Broken Hill, Item 16/11/18, A6286, 4th Military Dt, 6/12/17–30/8/19; Sawtell, 21/10/18, to B. Matthias, Item 21/10/18, A6286, 2nd Military Dt, 5/8/18–28/4/19; Sawtell, 17/12/18, to Beth Pole, Item 21/12/18, A6286, 5th Military Dt, 3/1/18–30/8/19.
36 Item 30/4/19, A6286, 3rd Military Dt, 2/4/19–10/9/19; 7/5/19, Item 14/5/19, A6286, 3rd Military Dt, 2/4/19–10/9/19.
37 Alf Wilson, 21/1/20, to G.G. Reeve, ML772/11/353; *Ind Sol* (A), Dec. 1920, L, p.2.
38 A. Eastcrabb, Townsville, n.d., to J. Henry, Innisfail, Item 11/9/18, A6286, 1st Military Dt, 3/7/18–30/10/18; Geo. Rymer, Dist. Sec. QRU, Townsville, 25/11/18, to T. Moroney, Sec. QRU, Brisbane, Item 4/12/18, A6286, 1st Military Dt, 2/11/18–26/2/19.
39 Deputy Chief Censor, Department of Defence, Melbourne, 27/9/18, to the Chief of the General Staff, secret memorandum, AA Accession MP 367, File C512/1/618, Brighton, Farrell Collection.

40 (CA908, Investigation, Western Australia), Summary of Communism and Index, 1922–24, 'File WA1024A Summary of Communism vol.1 June to Dec. 1923', AA Accession AS1979/199, Item vol.1; J.S. Garden, Sec. OBUPL Sydney, 3/2/19, to J. Quinton, GPO Brisbane, Item 19/2/19; Items 27/11/18, 8/1/19, A6286, 1st Military Dt, 2/11/18–26/2/19.

41 Armstrong, 'Closer unity', p.209; N. Jeffery, 23/2/19, to Sec. Fed. Furnishing Trades Union, Brisbane, Item 26/2/19, A6286, 1st Military Dt, 2/11/18–26/2/19; N. Jeffery, 25/2/19, to F. Callanan, Sydney, Item 24/2/19, A6286, 2nd Military Dt, 5/8/18–28/4/19; *Prol*, 8/3/19, p.1; 15/3/19, p.3.

42 *Toiler*, 5/11/20, p.1; Hunt, 'Labour movement in north Queensland', pp.423–4; Armstrong, 'Closer unity', p.210.

43 *Ind Sol* (A), Dec. 1920, p.2; Sept. 1920, p.2; Feb. 1920, L, p.2; Feb. 1920, p.3; March 1920, p.1.

44 Roberts, 'The One Big Union', pp.3, 6–7, 9; Wilson, *All for the Cause*, p.110.

45 Rushton, 'The IWW in Sydney', p.22; SLP, *The Unity Question*, pp.14–15, 29; Ray Everitt, Gen. Sec.-Treas. WIIU, 16/10/17, to SLP, NL2576/4; Audley, 'A short history of the W.I.I.U.', p.6; no.5 Book, ABL N57/131; ABL N57/347.

46 NL3222/6; Local no.1, WIIU, NL3222/4.

47 'Manifesto of the Workers' International Industrial Union. To the workers, men and women, of South Australia', Adelaide, n.d. [c. April 1924], NL3222/3; NL3222/4.

48 A.S. Reardon, 10/11/18, to T. Laidler, Sec. WIIU Local no.1, ML772/11/163; Ray Everitt, 11/11/18, to Dear Fellow Worker, ML772/11/169; ABL N57/131, no.5 Book; Tom Audley, 17/12/18, 1/2/19, to T. Laidler, Sydney, ML772/11.

49 Wilson, *All for the Cause*, p.120; Dodds, *How One Big Union Works*, p.27; WIIU, 'Appeal to the rank and file of the trade unions', NL3222/4.

50 J.B. Scott notes, NL6206/62/3; Letter from J.A. Dawson, Melbourne, 22/5/18, to J. Vincent, WIIU Newtown, Item 27/5/18, A6286, 2nd Military Dt, 23/10/17–29/7/18; Item 13/8/18, 1st Military Dt, 3/7/18–30/10/18; ABL E164/7; Reeves, 'Yours 'til the war of classes is ended', p.21. In general, see Reeves, 'Industrial men, miners and politics in Wonthaggi'; Reeves, 'The rise and decline of industrial unionism'.

51 Wilson, *All for the Cause*, pp.120–1, 111; ABL E164/7; Tom Audley, 11/11/18, n.d., 10/2/19, 5/11/18, 31/3/19, to T. Laidler, ML772/11; J.B. Scott notes, NL6206/62/3; Typescript on WIIU, LT10772/3; May's notes, LT10882/8/22; Churchward, 'American influence', p.272; Audley, 'A short history of the W.I.I.U.', p.6.

52 Churchward, 'American influence', p.272; J.B. Scott notes, NL6206/62/3; Wilson, *All for the Cause*, pp.125–8; WIIU, 'Appeal to the rank and file of the trade unions', NL3222/4.

53 Typescript on WIIU, LT10772/3; May's notes, LT10882/8/22; Wilson, *All for the Cause*, pp.165–6; Murray, 'The Kalgoorlie woodline strikes', pp.31–5; *OBU Herald*, Nov. 1920, Dec. 1920, Jan. 1921, cited in Bedford, 'The One Big Union', p.26; Oliver, 'For only by the OBU', pp.1–13.

54 Corr. between Tom Audley and Sec. SLP, during 1924, NL2576/4; Wilson, *All for the Cause*, p.207; J.B. Scott notes, NL6206/62/3.

55 Quoted in Walker, *Solidarity Forever*, p.163.

56 *Ind Sol* (A), March 1920, p.1.

57 Bedford, 'The One Big Union', pp.33–4; Roberts, 'The One Big Union',
    p.19; Glynn, 'Industrial Union Propaganda League', ML772/21; *Common
    Cause*, 24/5/22, p.11; 12/5/22, p.6.

58 Hinton, *Labour and Socialism*, p.92; Dubofsky, *We Shall Be All*, p.288; Bedford,
    'The One Big Union', pp.39, 41.

59 Monty Miller, 20/3/18, to Mrs Annie Craig, Item 10/4/18, A6286, 1st
    Military Dt, 26/12/17–29/6/18; Monty Miller, 26/3/18, to Annie Craig,
    Qld, Item 17/4/18, A6286, 1st Military Dt, 26/12/17–29/6/18.

60 *Ind Sol* (M), 27/9/19, L, p.2; Sept. 1920, p.4; Roberts, 'The One Big Union',
    pp.17–18.

61 Claimed by the CPA in *A Comm*, 18/3/21, p.4; Childe, *How Labour Governs*,
    p.169; Lane, *Dawn to Dusk*, p.242; Bedford, 'The One Big Union', esp. p.27.
    Recently, Joan Simpson has defended the AWU from such charges in
    '"Radicals" and "Realists"'.

62 Armstrong, 'Closer unity', pp.227, 224, 210; Young, 'The NSW One Big
    Union', blames the ill-considered tactics of the OBU militants; Bongiorno
    attributes the WIUA's failure to 'the incompatibility of syndicalism . . . with
    the Australian environment', of which the AWU was merely a product ('The
    AWU', pp.53–4).

63 Bongiorno, 'The AWU', pp.34–6.

64 Roberts, 'The One Big Union', pp.2, 11, 17–21.

65 Hagan, *The History of the A.C.T.U.*, pp.18, 39; Hagan, 'The A.C.T.U.' in Fry
    (ed.), *Common Cause*, pp.42–4; NL6206/62/3.

66 Conlin, *Bread and Roses*, p.90; Renshaw, *The Wobblies*, p.265; De Caux, *Labor
    Radical*, p.546; David De Leon, *The American as Anarchist*, p.97. See also
    Preston, 'Shall this be all?', p.449.

67 Earsman, 13/12/21, to M. Francis, LT10882/5/9; T. Audley, 1/7/24,
    11/10/24, to Sec. SLP, NL2576/4; Playford, 'Left-wing of the South
    Australian labor movement', pp.40–1.

68 Olive, 'Struggles in the canefields', p.21; on the PWIU, see Moore, 'The
    Pastoral Workers' Industrial Union'; *The Constitution of the O.B.U. of
    Unemployed*, pp.7–8; Wheatley, 'The unemployed who kicked', pp.85–6,
    213–18.

69 Premier, 31/10/22, to Prime Minister, A3932 SC292 Pt.3; Inspector
    Weddell, Perth, 19/10/22, to Melbourne in (CA908, Investigation, Western
    Australia), Summary of Communism and Index, 1922–24, 'File WA1024A
    Summary of Communism vol.1 June to Dec., 1923', AA Accession AS1979/
    199, Item vol.1.

70 Wilson, *All for the Cause*, p.197; Playford, 'Left-wing of the South Australian
    labor movement', p.48.

71 T. Audley, 28/7/24, 6/8/24, to Sec. SLP, Sydney, NL2576/4; VSP Exec.
    Minutes, 22/9/24, 22/10/24, 1/7/25, NL564/1/7; Walker, *Solidarity
    Forever*, p.132; Garvey interview; J.B. Scott notes, NL6206/62/3; Mark
    Feinberg notes, NL6206/62/3; Playford, 'Left-wing of the South Australian
    labor movement', pp.56, 67; IWW, 'Hello, America', ABL N57/347;
    Howells, *Against the Stream*, pp.18–22.

72 Moss, *Sound of Trumpets*, p.268; McGillick, *Comrade No More*, pp.44–5, 37;
    Playford, 'Left-wing of the South Australian labor movement', p.57; *WW*,
    8/1/26, cited in Morrison, 'The Communist Party', pp.245–6; Wilson, *All
    for the Cause*, pp.197–9, 201, 203; Morrison, 'The Communist Party',
    pp.245–6.

73 Wilson, *All for the Cause*, p.206; Playford, 'Left-wing of the South Australian labor movement', pp.67, 137.

74 Wright Collection; *DA*, 20/5/28, p.4; 21/7/28, p.4; 17/11/28, p.4; 22/5/29, p.4; *SMH*, 27/1/30, p.9, cited in Wheatley, 'The unemployed who kicked', p.86; Howells interview.

75 Howells, *Against the Stream*, pp.18–22, 25–7.

76 *DA*, May 1928, p.2; Inglis, *Australians in the Spanish Civil War*, p.121; McGillick, *Comrade No More*, p.36; *DA*, May 1928, p.2; 23/6/28, p.2; 25/8/28, p.1; 11/8/28, p.4.

77 McNeill, 'IWW', pp.60–1; Wait, 'Reactions to demonstrations', pp.81–4.

78 Wilson, *All for the Cause*, pp.208–23; *DA*, Strike edn no.1, 30/9/28, p.1; Wait, 'Reactions to demonstrations', pp.55–6, 202–3; Moss, *Sound of Trumpets*, p.321.

79 *DA*, 11/8/28, p.4; 25/8/28, p.1.

80 Morrison, 'The Communist Party', pp.417–21; Police Department Records, cited in Wait, 'Reactions to demonstrations', pp.89–90; Playford, 'Left-wing of the South Australian labor movement', pp.57, 80, 96; *WW*, 13/2/31, p.6, quoted in Playford, 'Left-wing of the South Australian labor movement', pp.96–7; Ted Moyle, notebook no.3, Moyle Collection; Garvey interview.

81 *DA*, 11/8/28, p.1; Morrison, 'The Communist Party', pp.417–21; *WW*, 13/2/31, p.6, quoted in Playford, 'Left-wing of the South Australian labor movement', pp.96–7; McGillick, *Comrade No More*, pp.35, 44; Moss, *Sound of Trumpets*, p.317; *Weekend Australian*, 5–6/7/86, Magazine p.2; NL2576; Inglis, *Australians in the Spanish Civil War*, p.122; Legislative Assembly, New South Wales, *Communists*.

82 *WW*, 19/6/31, ABL N57/793; Wright interview; Morrison, 'The Communist Party', pp.295–6, 417–21.

83 *Annals of the A.C.P.*, pp.25–6; *WW*, 21/11/30, 9/10/36, cited in Morrison, 'The Communist Party', pp.417–22.

84 Wilkins, 'Yes, we have a Labor government', pp.7–8.

85 Minutes, Perth IWW, 28/8/39; Violet Clarke Wilkins, Sec.-Treas. Perth Branch IWW, 4/9/39, to Clark Kellor, Editor, *Industrial Worker* (IWW Collection, Box 18, Folder 14, ALHUA).

86 IWW, *One Big Union of All Workers*; *Southern Socialist International Digest*, Sept. 1946, p.1, quoted in Wright, 'Left Communism in Australia', pp.51–2; Garvey interview.

87 Wright, 'Left Communism in Australia', p.55; A. Westbrook, 28/3/48, to FW; Wilkins, 17 Gladstone St, Burwood, 13/1/48, to W.A. Unger; Minutes, 8/2/48; Wilkins, 11/2/48, to Unger (IWW Collection, Box 97, Folders 1–15, ALHUA).

88 14/3/48, to Unger, IWW Collection, Box 97, Folders 1–15, ALHUA.

89 Minutes, IWW Sydney Branch, 8/2/48, 7/3/48, IWW Collection, Box 97, Folders 1–15, ALHUA; Wright, 'Left Communism in Australia', p.59.

90 A. Westbrook, 3/3/48, 26/2/48, to A. Farley, Chicago, IWW Collection, Box 97, Folders 1–15, ALHUA.

91 J.B. Scott notes, NL6206/62/3; Emmet Larkin, *James Larkin*, pp.281–3; Fox, *Jim Larkin*, p.160; *WW*, 18/3/32, p.2; 7/12/34, p.6.

92 Modjeska, 'Introduction', pp.23–4, 30.

93 *SMH*, 4/1/35, p.6; Gibson interview; King, 'My six years in the Soviet Union', pp.9–11.

94 *A Comm*, 18/2/21, p.7; *WW*, 4/1/35, p.6; 30/10/36, p.16; Barker, 29/2/21, to Glynn, in *Comm*, 13/5/21, p.6; Barker, 'Self-portrait', pp.18–27;

Hampstead and Highgate Express, 17/4/70, p.10; Fry (ed.), *Tom Barker*, pp.37, 39.

95 Burn, *Rent Strike*, pp.3–4; Barker, 'Self-portrait', p.18; *Hampstead and Highgate Express*, 12/11/71, 15/6/73; Fry, 'Tom Barker', p.175; Barker, 26/1/68, to Matti, Barker Collection, NL.

96 CA908, File WA1024A, AA1979/199; *SMH*, 12/6/70, p.4; Ross interview; National Association, *The Unpopular Comrade*; National Association, *Donald Grant*; McNamara, 'Donald Grant', pp.63–4; Newspaper clipping, c. 1931; Evatt, 10/4/46, to Grant; *Inverness Courier and General Advertiser*, 13/9/46, pp.5–6 (ML2005/1/1); Farrell, 'Donald Grant', p.76; *Socialist Comment and Review*, Sydney, 1/6/45, cited in Rushton, 'Revolutionary ideology', p.445; *Tribune*, 6/8/49, p.4; E. Ross, *The Coal Front*, p.125; ABL P43/8/6.

97 Wilson, *All for the Cause*, pp.228–9; Gen. Sec. SLP, 3/1/33, to F. Aguis, NL2576/2; T. Gilmore, Preface to Wilson, *All for the Cause*.

98 Corr. between Sawtell and Henry Boote, NL2070/1/184–241; McGillick, *Comrade No More*, pp.177–81; *Daily Mirror*, 15/11/71, p.26; *Australian*, 26/2/69, p.22; *SMH*, 2/10/71, p.10.

99 A6122 [132]; Thomas, 'Two veterans', p.7.

100 Kelly interview; Lang, 'The I.W.W.', p.35; Farrall, 'The Wobblies'; Howells, *Against the Stream*, pp.21–3.

101 Kelly interview; *Tribune*, 17/6/42, p.4; Sendy, 'The founders', p.1; McGillick, *Comrade No More*, pp.37–8; W.A. Wood, *The Life Story of L.L. Sharkey, Fighter for Freedom*, Sydney, 1950, p.4, cited in Morrison, 'The Communist Party', p.291.

102 Charles Reeve, State Penitentiary, 20/9/1919, to Dear Little Mother, p.4, ML5653.

103 Charles Reeve, State Penitentiary, 29/1/21, pp.1–2, ML5653.

104 Mackie interview; IWW file, Riley Collection, LT; Matteson interview; *Rebel Worker*, 1, 5, Oct.–Nov. 1982, p.1.

105 *Burning Issue*, 7, Autumn 1993, p.15; *Industrial Worker*, 90, 1558, April 1993, pp.4, 2.

Select Bibliography

Primary Sources

Manuscript Collections

Archives of Labor History and Urban Affairs, Walter P. Reuther Library, Wayne State University, Detroit, Michigan: IWW Collection, Boxes 18, 23, 97, 139
CPGB, London: Tom Mann Collection
In possession of author: Fred Farrall, assorted papers; Jim Garvey, assorted correspondence; Norman Jeffery, Notes taken from Baracchi Papers; Tom Payne, assorted letters; Mary Wright Collection
In possession of Sally Bowen: Jock and May Wilson Papers
In possession of Jim Moss: Ted Moyle Collection
In possession of Ann Turner: W.P. Earsman diaries
La Trobe Library, State Library of Victoria (LT): A.T. and May Brodney Collection, LT10882; F.J. Riley and Ephemera Collection, LT; Bertha Walker Collection, LT10772; Women's International League for Peace and Freedom Papers, LT9377
London Borough of Camden Local History Library: Tom Barker Collection
Mitchell Library, Sydney (ML): ASL Papers, ML2042; John Dwyer Papers, ML2184; De Groot Papers, ML; D.M. Grant Papers, ML2005; Fred Hancock Papers, ML772; IWW literature seized by police, 1917, ML; IWW Papers, ML A1333–4; IWW Scrapbook, ML; IWW Stickers etc., ML Ai8; IWW, Sydney Branch, Correspondence, 1902–1921, ML262; Charles Reeve Collection, ML5653
National Library of Australia, Canberra (NL): Frank Anstey Papers, NL512, 579, 966, 4636; Guido Baracchi, Manuscript of paper read to the Fellowship of Australian Writers, Sydney, 9/11/41, on the publication of *The Poems of Lesbia Harford*, Baracchi Papers, NL5241; Tom Barker Collection, NL (unaccessioned, received 16/9/87); H.E. Boote Papers, NL2070; E.J. Brady Papers, NL206; Herbert Brookes Papers, NL1924; Don Cameron Papers, NL1005; Mary Gilmore Papers, NL1948, 727; Duncan Hall Collection, NL5547; IWW Correspondence, chiefly inwards to Australian Clubs, 1897–1919, NL3516; E.E. Judd Papers, NL2873; Patrick O'Farrell Collection, NL6265; Political Labor Council, Victoria Minute

Book, NL131; F.J. Riley Papers, NL759; Lloyd Ross Papers, 1900–1970, NL3939; Lloyd Ross Oral History Tape, NL TRC 236; R.S. Ross Papers, NL3222; SLP of Australia Records, NL2576; Ian Turner Collection, NL6206; VSP Minute Books and Papers, 1908–1931, NL564
Noel Butlin Archives, ANU, Canberra (ABL): Australian Boot Trade Employees' Federation, Minute Books, 1906–1946, ABL T49; Australian Coal and Shale Employees Federation, Wonthaggi Minutes of general, special and stop-work meetings, Nov. 1911–Nov. 1921, ABL E164/1; Australian Coal and Shale Employees Federation Central Executive and Central Council Minute Books of meetings, Oct. 1917–Nov. 1929, ABL E165/2; Australian Mercantile Land and Finance Co. Records, ABL 162/3132; AWU, Queensland Branch Records, ABL M50; Australian Workers Union, Head Office Records, ABL E/154/47–53; Les Barnes Collection, ABL P8; Coal Miners Association, Victoria, Minutes, 1913–1930, ABL E164/4; Coal Miners Union, West Moreton, Minutes, 1906–1940, ABL E165/42–3; Federated Coopers of Australia, Minute Books, 1912–1956, ABL T50; Graziers' Association of New South Wales, Records, ABL E256/363; W.J.H. Harris Collection, ABL P43; Hotel, Club and Restaurant Employees Union of NSW, Records, 1913–1935, ABL T12; James Normington Rawling Collection, ABL N57; Harry Scott Bennett Collection, ABL P77; Tooths Brewery Ltd Legal Decisions, ABL N20/2268; Workers' Industrial Union, Local No.3, Wonthaggi Minutes of meetings, May 1918–Feb. 1920, ABL E164/7; Waterside Workers' Federation, Federal Council, Correspondence with AWU re One Big Union, 1922–1924, ABL T62/26/1–3; Waterside Workers Federation, Sydney Branch General Minutes, 1889–1957, ABL M70
Nuffield College, Oxford: Jack Tanner Papers

Interviews

Unless otherwise specified, interviews are with the author.
Tom Audley, June 1982; Tom Audley (with Pat Gowland and Norm Saffin), 17/2/78; Fred Coombe, 15/5/84; Lloyd Edmonds, 25/6/93; Fred Farrall, 1/6/84; Jim Garvey, 11/6/84; Bill Genery (with Ken Mansell), c. May 1969; Ralph Gibson, 26/9/85; Frank Hardy, 18/1/94; Frank Hardy (with Paul Adams), 16/9/89; Frank Hardy (with Paul Adams), 12/9/90; A.F. 'Bluey' Howells, 4/10/85; Bill Ivey, 27/8/86; Leo Kelly, 20/1/86; Bill Laidler, 28/5/86; Pat Mackie, 21/7/88; Michael Matteson, 27/1/94; Jack Mundey, 25/6/93; Tom Payne, 25/10/85; Lloyd Ross, 20/2/86; Jimmy Seamer, 29/8/85; Dick Surplus (with Jim Beatson), 1972; Judah Waten, c. Feb. 1984; Mary Wright, 27/10/85

Newspapers

Advertiser (Adelaide); *Age* (Melbourne); *Argus* (Melbourne); *Australian*; *Australian Communist*; *Australian Independent Workers' Gazette*; *Australian Worker* (Sydney); *Barrier Daily Truth* (Broken Hill); *Common Cause*; *Communist* (CPA); *Co-operator* (ARTSA); *Daily Mirror* (Sydney); *Daily News* (Perth); *Daily Telegraph* (Sydney); *Direct Action* (IWW, Sydney, 30/1/14–18/8/17); *Direct Action* (IUPL, Sydney, 1/12/21–April 1922); *Direct Action* (IWW, Adelaide, 1/5/28–17/11/28); *Empire Gazette*; *Evening News* (Sydney); *Herald* (Adelaide); *Industrialist* (Newcastle Industrial

Council); *Industrial Pioneer* (IWW, Chicago); *Industrial Solidarity* (IIW, Adelaide); *Industrial Solidarity* (IIW, Melbourne); *Industrial Worker* (IWW, Chicago); *Industrial Worker* (Spokane, Washington); *International Communist* (ASP); *International Socialist* (ASP); *International Socialist Review* (International Socialist Club); *Industrial Syndicalist* (Britain); *Knowledge and Unity* (CPA, Brisbane); *Labour News* (ALP, New South Wales); *Militant* (QRU, Brisbane); *New Order* (CPA, Brisbane); *New South Wales Review; Northern Territory Times* (Darwin); *One Big Union Monthly* (Chicago); *Pastoral Review; Pastoral Workers Bulletin* (PWIU); *People* (SLP); *Punch* (Melbourne); *Proletariat* (IIW, Sydney); *Railways Union Gazette; Rebel Worker* (Anarcho-Syndicalist Federation); *Register* (Adelaide); *Revolutionary Socialist* (SLP); *Social Democrat* (Social Democratic League, Sydney); *Socialist Standard* (SPGB); *Solidarity* (Industrial Labour Party); *Soviets To-Day; Sun* (Sydney); *Syndicalist* (London); *Sydney Morning Herald; The New Guard; The Publicist* (Australia First Movement); *Toiler* (CPA, Brisbane); *Toiler* (Newcastle); *Tribune* (CPA); *Truth* (Sydney); *Vanguard* (ALP, Victoria); *Westralian Worker; Worker* (AWU, Queensland); *Workers Weekly* (CPA)

Pamphlets

Anderson, Norman C., *One Big Union for Australia*, Will Andrade, Melbourne, [1922]
Barker Defence Committee, *Barker Defence Committee*, IWW Print, Sydney, 20 Sept. 1915
Boote, H.E., *The Case of Grant. Fifteen Years for Fifteen Words*, Worker Print, Sydney, [1918]
Boote, H.E., *Guilty or Not Guilty? An Examination of the I.W.W. Cases*, Worker Print, Sydney, [1918]
Boote, H.E., *Set the Twelve Men Free*, NSW Labor Council, Sydney, [1918]
Brown, A.E., *The Case for a Shorter Work Day*, IWW, Sydney, [c.1917]
Burn, Dave, *Rent Strike. St Pancras 1960*, Pluto Press, London, 1972
Clearly, P.S., *The One Big Union. Will it Emancipate the Worker?*, Sydney, 1919
Communist Party of Great Britain, History Group, *Tom Mann in Australasia – 1902–1909*, Pamphlet no.38, Summer 1965
Conroy, Charles, *Fools or Traitors?*, Sydney, 1920
Conroy, Charles, *Political Action*, Brisbane, 1918
Considine, M.P., *The Strike-Breakers, The Truth about the Tramway Fiasco*, H.E. Holland, Printer, Sydney, n.d.
Constitution of the Industrial Workers of the World Club of Australasia & New Zealand, est. 1907 under 1905 Preamble, People Printery, Sydney, 1912
Craig, Will and Alexander, J.M., *The Workless Army and the Army of Labor*, Ruskin Press, Melbourne, 1927
Defence and Release Committee, *A Challenge to the People Who Malign the Industrial Workers of the World*, Sydney, [1917]
De Leon, Daniel, *Socialism Versus Anarchism*, Sydney, n.d.
De Leon, Daniel, *Socialist Reconstruction of Society: the Industrial Vote*, New York, 1905
Dodds, A.D., *How One Big Union Works. An Australian Example*, WIIU Literature and Education Bureau, Melbourne, [c.1919]
Draft Resisters' Union, *Stop Conscription*, [c.1967]
Glynn, Tom, *Industrial Efficiency and its Antidote*, IWW, Sydney, [c.1915]

Greer, J.H., *The Social Evil. Prostitution: Its Cause and Cure*, IWW, Sydney, n.d.

Groupe D'Etudes Scientifiques, *Manifesto-Protest, Jesuitism of the IWW*, Communist Anarchist Press, Sydney, March 1914

Hade, M.J., *Justice Raped; Exposure of the I.W.W. Frame Up*, Sydney, 1920

Hagerty, T.J., *Economic Discontent and its Remedy*, Australasian Socialist Party, Sydney, n.d.

Hickey, P.H., *Solidarity or Sectionalism? A Plea for Unity*, AWU, Qld Branch, Brisbane, 1918

Holland, H.E., *Labor Leg-Ironed*, Wellington, 1912

Holland, H.E., *Labor Sledgehammered or Arbitration, Wages Boards, and the Socialist Alternative – Industrial Unionism*, SFA, Sydney, 1908

Holland, H.E., *The Crime of Conscription*, ASP, Sydney, 1912

Holland, H.E., *The Tramway Spy! An Exposure of Mr Kneeshaw's Pimp System and a Call to the Organised Workers to Down Tools in Aid of the Tramway Men*, International Socialists, Sydney, n.d.

Hutchinson, M.L. and Andrade, Will, *Billy Hughes and his Critics*, Progressive and Economic Association, Melbourne, [c.1918]

Industrial Labor Party. Its Formation and Growth since 1919, n.d.

Industrial Union Propaganda League, Sydney, 12 Oct. 1921

I.W.W. Appeal to Unionists and the General Public, Melbourne, [1916]

IWW, Constitution, *By-Laws*, Chicago, 1910

IWW, *One Big Union of All Workers*, IWW, Hawthorn, [c.1947]

IWW, *Preamble and Constitution*, Chicago, 1910

IWW, *Rebel Songs*, Melbourne, 1966

IWW, *Songs of the Industrial Workers of the World*, 3rd Australian edn, Sydney, [c.1916]

IWW, *Songs of the Workers to Fan the Flames of Discontent*, 34th edn, Chicago, 1973

IWW, *Songs to Fan the Flames of Discontent*, Sydney, n.d.

IWW, *The Immediate Demands of the I.W.W.*, Melbourne, n.d.

IWW Publishing Bureau, *I.W.W. Songs*, Sydney, n.d.

IWW, Australian Administration, *I.W.W. Songs and Poems to Fan the Flames of Discontent*, 5th Australian edn, Adelaide, [1925]

IWW, Sydney Local, *Direct Action*, Sydney, n.d.

IWW, Sydney Local, *How Capital has Hypnotised Society*, Sydney, [1913–14]

IWW, Sydney Local, *Songs of the Industrial Workers of the World*, Sydney, [1912]

IWW, Melbourne Branch, *The Wobbly*, Carlton South, [c.1970]

IWW, NSW Branch, *Object and Preamble*, Sydney, [1925]

IWW Club, *An Open Letter to the Australian Working Class*, People Print, Sydney, 1909

IWW Club, Sydney, *Anti-Militarism, An Appeal from the I.W.W. Clubs to the Australian Working Class*, State Executive of the IWW Clubs, Sydney, June 1911

IWW Club, *Constitution*, People Printery, Sydney, March 1909

IWW Club, *Constitution of the Industrial Workers of the World Club of Australasia and New Zealand*, People Printery, Sydney, 1912

IWW Club, *'Dear Fellow Worker'*, Sydney, 1 Sept. 1911

IWW Club, *The Literature for the Times*, Sydney, [c.1912]

IWW Club, Sydney, *Industrial Unionism and Politics*, People Print, Sydney, [1911]

IWW Club National Executive, *The Two Wars; The Worker and Militarism*, People Printery, Sydney, n.d.

IWW Prisoners Release Committee, *Breakers of Men or Torturing the Twelve. An Exposure of the Brutal and Coercive Treatment of the Twelve I.W.W. Men in the Gaols of N.S.W.*, Melbourne, [c.1919]

Judd, E.E., *The Case for the O.B.U.*, Exec. NSW OBU Congress, May 1919, 2nd edn, Sydney, 1919

Judd, E.E., *The War and the Sydney Labor Council*, SLP of Australia, Sydney, 1917

Kerr, George, *Solidarity Sentenced. The Conscription Aftermath. Labour Agitators get 150 Years Gaol. Sensational Disclosures*, AMA, Broken Hill, Marxian Press, Sydney, [1917]

Lafargue, Paul, *The Right to be Lazy*, IWW, Sydney, [c.1917]

Mann, Tom, *The Way to Win: An Open Letter to Trade Unionists on Methods of Industrial Unionism*, Broken Hill, 1909

Miles, J.B., *Who are the Communists? The Result of an Investigation*, Supplement to *International Communist*, 24 Sept.1921

Mulvogue, B.A., *Proposed Schemes for Closer Unionism in Victoria*, Labor Call Print, Melbourne, [1917]

National Association, *Donald Grant*, Sydney, [1925]

National Association, *The History of Donald Grant*, Sydney, [1925]

National Association, *The Unpopular Comrade*, Sydney, [1925]

Nilsson, B.E. *Political Socialism or Capturing the Government*, IWW, Sydney, [c.1915]

One Big Union Propaganda League, *I.W.W. Cases. Sensational Disclosures*, Melbourne, n.d.

Pease, Frank Chester, *Revolution and the I.W.W.*, Australian Administration of the IWW, Sydney, n.d.

Progressive and Economic Association, *The Second Maritime Strike*, Melbourne, [c.1919]

Release and Defence Committee, *I.W.W. Commission, 1918. Mr Windeyer's Great Indictment*, Worker Print, Sydney, [1919]

Release Committee, Brisbane, *Workers of Queensland, Attention! Short Resume of the Evidence Against the I.W.W. Members*, [1917]

Release Committee, Melbourne, *15 Reasons Why the 12 Victims of the 1916 Conscription Referendum Should be Released*, [1919]

Ross, Edgar, *The Coal Front (An Account of the 1949 Coal Strike and the Issues it Raised)* Sydney, n.d.

Ross, Edgar, *The Russian Revolution – Its Impact on Australia*, Socialist Party of Australia, Sydney, 1972

St John, Vincent, *Industrial Unionism and the I.W.W.*, IWW, Sydney, [1917]

St John, Vincent, *The I.W.W., Its History, Structure and Methods*, IWW Publishing Bureau, Pennsylvania, 1917

'Secret Service', *Queer Queensland. The Breeding Ground of the Bolshevik*, Brisbane, 21 Oct. 1918

Sinclair, D.W., and Duncan, J., *Justice Outraged. The Case for the Twelve*, ILP, Sydney, [1918]

SLP of Australia, *The Unity Question and a Brief History of the Socialist Labor Party*, SLP, Sydney, 1917

SLP, Adelaide Branch, *Alf W. Wilson and His Calumniators*, [April 1927]

Smith, Walker C., *Sabotage*, Australian Administration of the IWW, Sydney, [1915–16]

The Constitution of the O.B.U. of Unemployed, Proletarian Press, Annandale, 1927

The Industrial Socialist Labor Party, Industrial Print, Sydney, [c.1919]

The New Democracy, Literature and Education Bureau of the WIIU Australian Administration, South Melbourne, [c.1920]

To the I.W.W. A Special Message from the Communist International (Moscow), Foreword by Tom Glynn, Proletarian Publishing Association, Melbourne, [1920]
Trades and Labor Council of NSW, IWW Release Committee, *Speeches from the Dock of NSW and West Australian I.W.W. Members*, Worker Trade Union Print, Sydney, 1920
Trautmann, W.E., *New Industrial Methods. Education, Organisation, Emancipation*, IWW Organisation, Sydney, Worker Trade Union Print, 1927
Trautmann, W.E., *One Great Union*, Literature and Education Bureau of the WIIU, Melbourne, n.d. [c.1919]
Walker, Bertha, *How to Defeat Conscription, A Story of the 1916 and 1917 Campaigns in Victoria*, Anti-Conscription Jubilee Committee, Oct. 1968
WIUA, *One Big Union. Industrial Unionism*, Marxian Print, Sydney, [1919]
WIUA, *Preamble, Classification and Rules*, Melbourne, 1919
WIIU, *A Manifesto to Wage Workers*, WIIU Australian Administration, Newtown, [c.1917]
WIIU, *Appeal to the Rank and File of the Trade Unions*, WIIU, Melbourne, [c.1921]
WIIU, *Job Control*, Literature Bureau of the WIIU and the SLP, Australian Administration, Adelaide, 1928
WIIU, *Preamble and Constitution*, Australian Administration, Newtown, Sydney, [c.1918]
WIIU, *The Workers' International Industrial Union. Preamble and Constitution*, Detroit, 1919
WIIU, *Revolutionary Industrial Unionism. Tactics and Plan of the Workers' International Industrial Union*, Melbourne: Literature and Education Bureau of the WIIU, September 1919
WIIU, *We Can and We Will Own the Workshops*, WIIU Local no.1, Sydney, [c.1917]
Williams, *Eleven Blind Leaders*, IWW, Pennsylvania, 1910
Wilson, Alf, *Jeremiades of Jeroboam Judd*, Adelaide, [c.1926]
Wilson, Alf, *Manifesto of the Workers' International Industrial Union, To the Workers, Men and Women, of South Australia*, WIIU, Adelaide, [April 1924]
Woodruff, Abner E., *The Advancing Proletariat, A Study of the Movement of the Working Class From Wage Slavery to Freedom*, IWW Publishing Bureau, Sydney, [c.1914]

Memoirs and contemporary commentary

Anon., 'The iron heel in Australia', *International Socialist Review*, 17/18, Feb. 1917
Audley, Tom, 'A short history of the W.I.I.U.', *Recorder*, 3, 2, Feb. 1968, pp.2–6
Barker, Tom, 'How I did my time at Albury, and was deported to Chile', *Overland*, 34, May 1966, pp.43–4
Farrall, Fred, 'The Wobblies – I.W.W.', unpublished notes, copy in possession of the author
Feinberg, Mark, 'The Industrial Workers of the World', *Recorder*, 74, Feb. 1975, pp.9–14
Fitzgerald, J.D., 'The I.W.W. crimes', in J.D. Fitzgerald, *Studies in Australian Crime*, 1, 1924, pp.144–76
Fry, E.C. (ed.), *Tom Barker and the IWW*, Canberra, 1965
Howells, A.F., *Against the Stream: The Memories of a Philosophical Anarchist, 1927–1939*, Melbourne, 1983

Jeffery, Norman, 'Robin Gollan and the I.W.W.', *Common Cause*, 3 Aug. 1963, p.2

King, J.B., 'My six years in the Soviet Union', *Soviets To-Day*, Dec. 1936, pp.9–11

Lane, E.H., Dawn to Dusk, *Reminiscences of a Rebel*, Brisbane, 1939

Lossieff, V., 'Industrial Workers of the World', *The Communist International*, n.d.,
     [c.1921], pp.111–16 (Mary Wright Collection)

Mann, Tom, *Tom Mann's Memoirs*, London, 1967

McGillick, Tony, *Comrade No More: The Autobiography of a Former Communist
     Leader*, Western Australia, 1980

McNeill, Jim, 'Industrial Workers of the World', in Lowenstein, Wendy (ed.),
     Weevils in the Flour, Melbourne, 1978, pp.59–63

Moss, Jim, 'Communist Party formation in South Australia', in *Sixty Years of
     Struggle, A Journal of Communist and Labour History*, 2, pp.21–6

Olive, Doug, 'Struggles in the canefields and for control of the AWU', in *Sixty
     Years of Struggle, A Journal of Communist and Labour History*, 1, pp.19–26

Payne, Tom, 'Contribution to human progress', *Soviet Woman*, April 1970, pp.9, 12

Reed, John, 'The fighting I.W.W. in America', *The Communist International*, n.d.,
     [c.1920], pp.88–98 (Mary Wright Collection)

Sawtell, Michael, 'Occultism & Aborigine welfare', *Quest*, 21, April 1952,
     pp.11–12

Sawtell, Michael, 'To who may not belong', *Quest*, 31, Mar.–Apr. 1953, pp.11, 14

Sinclaire, F., 'An unjust judgment. Persecution of the I.W.W.', *Fellowship*, III, 5,
     Dec. 1916, pp.43–45

Williams, Vic (ed.), *Eureka and Beyond, Monty Miller, His Own Story*, Willagee,
     W.A., 1988

Walker, Bertha, *Solidarity Forever*, National Press, Melbourne, 1972

Wilkins, Violet Clarke, 'Yes, we have a Labor government', *One Big Union
     Monthly*, Chicago, Jan. 1938, pp.7–8

Government records and official publications

Australian Archives, ACT Branch:

AA 1979/199, Item WA1024A, Vol.I, Investigation Branch Reports, Summary of
     Communism, Vol.1. Summaries 1–25, Period June 1922–Dec. 1923

A3932 SC292: PM's Dept, Corr. Files, 1918–26, 'Suspected and Undesirable
     Persons'

A3932 SC295: PM's Dept, Corr. Files, 1918–26, 'The I.W.W.'

A6122 [132]: Australian Security Intelligence Organization, Central Office,
     NSW Trades and Labor Council (Sept. 1925–Jan. 1948)

A6286, 1st Military District, 26/12/17–2/9/19

A6286, 2nd Military District, 23/10/17–8/9/19

A6286, 3rd Military District, 25/10/17–10/9/19

A6286, 4th Military District, 6/12/17–30/8/19

A6286, 5th Military District, 3/1/18–30/8/19

B197 File 202/1/495. Defence Secret 2021/1/270. Summary of Ryan's Disloyal
     Associations

CP 78/22: G-G's Office, Gen. Corr., 1912–27

CP 407/1, Bundles 1–3, 3rd Military District Intelligence Reports: Brief
     Summary of Information Disclosing Enemy Trading or other suspicious
     action

CRS A3934: PM's Dept, Corr. Files, 1926

CRS A456: A-G's Dept, Corr. Files, War Series, 1914–27

CRS A456, Item W26/148 PH.B, Industrial Workers of the World. Statement giving a brief outline of the activities of the above organisation in Australia

CRS A3934, Item SC 5 [1], Reginald Hayes for Deputy Chief Censor, Department of Defence, Melbourne, 27/9/18, Memorandum for the Chief of the General Staff. SECRET

CRS CP404/1, Item Bundle 1, List No.1, compiled from documentary evidence found at the headquarters of the organisation by the police on 23 September 1916 (Inspector General of Police, Sydney, 7/11/16 to Major J.B. Wilson, Intelligence Officer, General Staff, 2nd Military District, Victoria Barracks, Sydney)

CRS CP404/1, Item Bundle 1, List No.2, contains the names of men believed to be at present members of the organisation (Inspector General of Police, Sydney, 7/11/16 to Major J.B. Wilson, Intelligence Officer, General Staff, 2nd Military District, Victoria Barracks, Sydney)

CRS CP404/1, Item Bundle 1, IWW Sydney Branch Only, Total 1546

CRS CP404/1, Item Bundle 1, List of I.W.W. Correspondence in Queensland

MP 367 File C 512/1/618, Censor, 1st Military District, Commonwealth Military Forces, Brisbane, 21/9/18, Memorandum to Deputy Chief Censor, Victoria Barracks, Melbourne, SECRET

Commonwealth Archives, Melbourne Branch:

CRS B 197: 1997/1/139, Members of IWW in NSW, 1916; 1997/1/144, IWW Leaflets, 1916; 1997/1/161, Prohibited Publications, IWW, 1916

MP 95/1: RE981; RE836; RE853; RE1798; RE1968; MF2437; 2604; 2719

MP 707/1: V/232, IWW Propagandists in Victoria 1919; V/236, Clothing Factory Fitzroy, Melbourne IWW, Dec. 1916; V/247, J.A. Dawson, IWW

Commonwealth Parliamentary Debates

Legislative Assembly, New South Wales, Report of Royal Commission of Inquiry into the Matter of the Trial and Conviction and Sentences Imposed on Charles Reeve and Others, Government Printer, Sydney, 11 August 1920

Legislative Assembly, New South Wales, Communists (List of Names of Certain, in New South Wales) 23 December 1931, Government Printer, Sydney, 1932

Melbourne Public Records Office:

Report of Det. Coonan: Victorian Commissioner of Police: File No.W6331; W4840; W10416; V5446; V10457

NSW Commissions, Police, Royal Commission to inquire into certain charges... in the case the King v. Reeve, Aug.–Nov. 1918 (ML1548)

NSW Courts, Supreme Court, Transcript of proceedings in the case of the King v. Reeve and others, 7/11/16–1/12/16 (ML1696)

New South Wales Parliamentary Debates

State Archives of New South Wales:

NSW Police Department, Special Bundles, re IWW: Box 7/5543; 7/5588; 7/5590–93; 7/5595–98; 7/6720; A/17952

Police Files: 32097.75.F 16/40351

Police Files: 47/78.1

Secondary Sources

Books

Bedford, Ian, *The Shell of the Old*, Adelaide, 1981

Below, C., *The Vedgymight History of Australia*, Melbourne, 1983

Bottomore, T.B., and Rubel, Maximilien, *Karl Marx. Selected Writings in Sociology and Social Philosophy*, Harmondsworth, 1986

Brissenden, P.F., *The I.W.W., A Study of American Syndicalism*, New York, 1957

Brissenden, P.F., *The Launching of the Industrial Workers of the World*, New York, 1971, [1913]

Brooks, J.G., *American Syndicalism: the I.W.W.*, New York, 1969, [1913]

Burgmann, Verity, *'In Our Time': Socialism and the Rise of Labor, 1885–1905*, Sydney, 1985

Cain, Frank, *The Wobblies at War, A History of the IWW and the Great War in Australia*, Melbourne, 1993

Campbell, E.W., *History of the Australian Labour Movement, A Marxist Interpretation*, Sydney, 1945

Child, John, *Unionism and the Labor Movement*, Melbourne, 1971

Childe, Vere Gordon, *How Labour Governs, A Study of Workers' Representation in Australia*, Melbourne, 1964, [1923]

Conlin, J.R., *Bread and Roses Too: Studies of the Wobblies*, Westport Conn., 1969

Conlin, J.R., (ed.), *At the Point of Production, The Local History of the I.W.W.*, Westport Conn., 1981

Cornford, Daniel A., *Workers and Dissent in the Redwood Empire*, Philadelphia, 1987

Damousi, Joy, *Women Come Rally: Socialism, Communism and Gender in Australia 1890–1955*, Oxford, 1994

De Caux, Len, *Labour Radical: From the Wobblies to CIO, a Personal History*, Boston, 1970

De Caux, Len, *The Living Spirit of the Wobblies*, New York, 1978

De Leon, David, *The American as Anarchist, Reflections on Indigenous Radicalism*, Baltimore, 1978

Derfler, Leslie, *Socialism Since Marx, A Century of the European Left*, London, 1973

Diggins, J.P., *The American Left in the Twentieth Century*, New York, 1973

Dowell, E.F., *A History of Criminal Syndicalism Legislation in the United States*, New York, 1969

Dubofsky, Melvyn, *'Big Bill' Haywood*, New York, 1987

Dubofsky, Melvyn, *We Shall Be All: a History of the Industrial Workers of the World*, Chicago, 1969

Evans, Raymond, *Loyalty and Disloyalty. Social Conflict on the Queensland Homefront, 1914–18*, Sydney, 1987

Evatt, H.V., *Australian Labour Leader, The Story of W.A. Holman and the Labour Movement*, 3rd edn, Sydney, 1945

Farrell, Frank, *International Socialism and Australian Labour. The Left in Australia 1919–1939*, Sydney, 1981

Ficken, Robert E., *The Forested Land: A History of Lumbering in Western Washington*, Seattle, 1987

Fitzhardinge, L.F., *William Morris Hughes, A Political Biography*, I, *That Fiery Particle 1902–1914*, Sydney, 1964

Fitzhardinge, L.F., *William Morris Hughes, A Political Biography*, II, *The Little Digger 1914–1952*, Sydney, 1979

Fitzpatrick, Brian, *A Short History of the Australian Labor Movement*, Melbourne, 1944

Fitzpatrick, Brian, *The British Empire in Australia, An Economic History 1834–1939*, Melbourne, 1941

Fox, R.M., *Jim Larkin, The Rise of the Underman*, London, 1957

Fry, Eric (ed.), *Common Cause, Essays in Australian and New Zealand Labour History*, Sydney, 1986

Gambs, J.S., *The Decline of the I.W.W.*, New York, 1966

Gollan, Robin, *The Coalminers of New South Wales: a History of the Union, 1860–1960*, Melbourne, 1963

Hagan, Jim, *The History of the A.C.T.U.*, Melbourne, 1981

Hagan, Jim, and Turner, Ken, *A History of the Labor Party in New South Wales 1891–1991*, Melbourne, 1991

Hardy, Frank, *Power Without Glory*, Realist Printing and Publishing Co., Melbourne, 2nd edn, October 1950

Hobsbawm, E.J., *Worlds of Labour, Further Studies in the History of Labour*, London, 1984

Hyman, Richard, *Marxism and the Sociology of Trade Unionism*, London, 1971

Iman, R.S., and Koch, T.W., *Labor in American Society*, Glenview Ill., 1965

Inglis, Amirah, *Australians in the Spanish Civil War*, Sydney, 1987

Iremonger, John, Merritt, John, and Osborne, Graeme (eds), *Strikes, Studies in Twentieth Century Australian Social History*, Sydney, 1973

Jauncey, L.C., *The Story of Conscription in Australia*, Melbourne, 1968, [1935]

Kennedy, Brian, *Silver, Sin, and Sixpenny Ale, A Social History of Broken Hill 1883–1921*, Melbourne, 1978

Kornbluh, Joyce L. (ed.), *Rebel Voices. An IWW Anthology*, Ann Arbor, 1964

Larkin, Emmet, *James Larkin, Irish Labour Leader, 1876–1947*, Cambridge Mass., 1965

Lehning, Arthur (ed.), *Michael Bakunin. Selected Writings*, London, 1973

Luxemburg, Rosa, *The Mass Strike, the Political Party and the Trade Unions*, in Mary-Alice Waters (ed.), *Rosa Luxemburg Speaks*, New York, 1970, pp.153–218

Mackie, Pat, *Mount Isa. The Story of a Dispute*, Hawthorn, 1989

McQueen, Humphrey, *A New Britannia*, Ringwood, 1970

Martin, David E., and Rubinstein, David, *Ideology and the Labour Movement, Essays presented to John Saville*, London, 1979

Marx, Karl, and Engels, Frederick, *Selected Works*, Moscow, 1970

Modjeska, Drusilla, and Pizer, Marjorie (eds), *The Poems of Lesbia Harford*, Sydney, 1985

Moss, Jim, *Sound of Trumpets. History of the Labour Movement in South Australia*, Adelaide, 1985

O'Farrell, P.J., *Harry Holland, Militant Socialist*, Canberra, 1964

Olssen, Erik, *The Red Feds. Revolutionary Industrial Unionism and the New Zealand Federation of Labour 1908–1913*, Oxford, 1988

Parker, C.H., *The Casual Laborer and Other Essays*, New York, 1967

Peterson, H.C., and Fite, G.C., *Opponents of War 1917–1918*, Seattle, 1957

Renshaw, Patrick, *The Wobblies, The Story of Syndicalism in the United States*, New York, 1967

Ridley, F.F., *Revolutionary Syndicalism in France, the Direct Action of its Time*, Cambridge, 1970

Ross, Edgar, *These Things Shall Be! Bob Ross, Socialist Pioneer – His Life and Times*, Sydney, 1988

Salerno, Salvatore, *Red November, Black November: Culture and Community in the Industrial Workers of the World*, Albany, 1989
Saposs, D.J., *Left Wing Unionism, A Study of Radical Policies and Tactics*, New York, 1967, [1926]
Sharkey, L.L., *An Outline History of the Australian Communist Party*, Sydney, 1944
Scott, Ernest, *Australia During the War*, Sydney, 1936
Spargo, John, *Syndicalism, Industrial Unionism and Socialism*, New York, 1913
Stearns, Peter, *Be a Man! Males in Modern Society*, New York, 1979
Stearns, Peter, *Revolutionary Syndicalism and French Labor*, New Brunswick, N.J., 1971
Sutcliffe, J.T., *A History of Trade Unionism in Australia*, Melbourne, 1967, [1921]
Torr, Dona, *Tom Mann*, London, 1944
The Founding Convention of the IWW. Proceedings, New York, 1969
The Poems of Lesbia Harford, Melbourne, 1941
Throssell, Ric (ed.), *Straight Left. Katharine Susannah Prichard*, Sydney, 1982
Tripp, Anne Huber, *The I.W.W. and the Paterson Silk Strike of 1913*, Urbana and Chicago, 1987
Turner, Ian, *Industrial Labour and Politics, The Dynamics of the Labour Movement in Eastern Austraia, 1900–1921*
Turner, Ian, *Sydney's Burning*, Melbourne, 1967
Tyler, Robert L., *Rebels of the Woods: the I.W.W. in the Pacific Northwest*, Eugene, Oregon, 1967
Ward, Russel, *The Australian Legend*, Melbourne, 1958
Waten, Judah, *Scenes of Revolutionary Life*, Sydney, 1982
Waten, Judah, *The Unbending*, Melbourne, 1972, [1954]
Williams, Justina, *The First Furrow*, Willagee, W.A., 1976
Winters, Donald E., *The Soul of the Wobblies: The I.W.W., Religion and American Culture in the Progressive Era, 1905–1917*, Westport, Greenwood, 1985

Articles

Bedford, Ian, 'The Industrial Workers of the World in Australia', *Labour History*, 13, Nov. 1967, pp.40–6
Bedford, Ian, 'The One Big Union, 1918–1923', in Spann, R.N. (ed.) *Sydney Studies in Politics*, 3, Melbourne, 1963, pp.5–43
Beilharz, Peter, 'John Anderson and the syndicalist moment', *Political Theory Newsletter*, 5, 1, April 1993, pp.5–13
Brody, David, 'Radical labor history and rank-and-file militancy', *Labor History*, 16, 1, Winter 1975, pp.117–126
Brody, David, 'The old labor history and the new: in search of an American working class', *Labor History*, 20, 1, Winter 1979, pp.111–26
Brodney, May, 'Militant Propagandists of the Labor Movement', *Labour History*, 5, Nov. 1963, pp.11–17
Brown, Geoff, 'Introduction', in *The Industrial Syndicalist*, 1, 1, July 1910–11, 11, May 1911, *Documents in Socialist History*, 3, Nottingham, 1974, pp.5–29
Buhle, Paul, 'The Wobblies in perspective', *Monthly Review*, 22, 2, June 1970, pp.44–53
Burgmann, Verity, 'Betsy Matthias', *Australian Dictionary of Biography*, 10, p.449
Burgmann, Verity, 'Racism, socialism and the labour movement, 1887–1917', *Labour History*, 47, 1984, pp.39–54
Cain, Frank, 'The Industrial Workers of the World. Aspects of its suppression in Australia, 1916–1919', *Labour History*, 42, May 1982, pp.54–62

Churchward, L.G., 'The American influence on the Australian labour movement', *Historical Studies*, 5, 19, Nov. 1952, pp.258–77

Coates, Roger, 'Note on the Industrial Workers of the World', *Labour History*, 6, May 1964, pp.25–8

Coates, Roger, 'Tom Barker: last of the self-taught socialists', *Tribune*, 17 June 1970

Conlin, J.R., 'Introduction', in Conlin (ed.), *At the Point of Production*, pp.3–24

Coward, Dan, 'Crime and punishment: The great strike in New South Wales, August to October 1917', in Iremonger, Merritt and Osborne (eds), *Strikes*, pp.51–80

Cuthbert, Catherine, 'Lesbia Harford and Marie Pitt: forgotten poets', *Hecate*, VIII, 1, 1982, pp.32–48

Cutler, Terrence, 'Sunday, Bloody Sunday: the Townsville meatworkers' strike of 1918–19', in Iremonger, Merritt and Osborne (eds), *Strikes*, pp.81–102

Daniel, C.E., 'In defence of the wheatland Wobblies: a critical analysis of the IWW in California', *Labor History*, 19, 4, Fall 1978, pp.485–509

Dixson, Miriam 'The first Communist "united front" in Australia', *Labour History*, 10, May 1966, pp.20–31

Dubofsky, Melvyn, 'Dissent: history of American radicalism', in Alfred F. Young (ed.), *Dissent: Explorations in the History of American Radicalism*, De Kalb, Ill., 1968, pp.176–213

Dubofsky, Melvyn, 'Film as history: history as drama', *Labor History*, 22, 1, Winter 1981, pp.136–40

Farrell, Frank, 'Donald Grant', *Australian Dictionary of Biography*, 9, pp.75–6

Fewster, Kevin 'The operation of state apparatuses in times of crisis: censorship and conscription, 1916', *War and Society*, 3, 1, May 1985, pp.37–54

Ficken, R.E., 'The Wobbly horrors: Pacific Northwest lumbermen and the Industrial Workers of the World, 1917–1918', *Labor History*, 24, 3, Summer 1983, pp.325–41

Fitzpatrick, Brian, 'Comments on *The Unbending* by Judah Waten', *Meanjin*, XIII, 1954, pp.459–60

Fry, Eric, 'Australian worker, Monty Miller', in Eric Fry (ed.), *Rebels and Radicals*, Sydney, 1983, pp.178–93

Fry, Eric, 'Tom Barker', *Australian Dictionary of Biography*, Vol.7, pp.174–5

Gollan, Bob, 'Has the Australian labour movement ever been radical?', *Arena*, 21, 1970, pp.40–4

Gomez. J.A., 'History, documentary, and audience manipulation: a view of "The Wobblies"', *Labor History*, 22, 1, Winter 1981, pp.142–45

Greenwood, Gordon, 'Australia at war, 1914–18', in Gordon Greenwood (ed.), *Australia, A Social and Political History*, Sydney, 1955

Haley, Martin, 'The I.W.W. and conscription', *Meanjin*, 14, Winter 1955, pp.268–70

Hector, Chris, 'The carnival at the Beaufort Street temple of forensic wisdom', *The Review*, 15–21 July 1972, pp.1116–17

Lake, Marilyn, 'The politics of respectability: identifying the masculinist context', *Historical Studies*, 22, 86, April 1986, pp.116–31

Lang, J.T., 'The I.W.W., the judge and cement', *Truth*, 13 June 1954, pp.34–5

LeWarne, C.P., 'On the Wobbly train to Fresno', *Labor History*, 14, 2, Spring 1973, pp.264–89

Macintyre, Stuart, 'Foundation. The Communist Party of Australia', *Overland*, 132, Spring 1993, pp.6–12

McKee, D.K., 'Daniel De Leon: a reappraisal', *Labor History*, 1, 3, Fall 1960, pp.264–97

McNamara, W.J., 'Donald Grant – a tribute', *Labour History*, 19, Nov. 1970, pp.63–4

McQueen, Humphrey, 'Laborism and socialism', in Richard Gordon (ed.), *The Australian New Left*, Melbourne, 1970, pp.43–65

Mitchell, Bruce, 'Embers of Protest. Ian Turner's *Sydney's Burning*', *Arena*, 14, Spring 1976, pp.70–72

Modjeska, Drusilla, 'Introduction', in Modjeska and Pizer (eds), *Lesbia Harford*, pp.1–39

Modjeska, Drusilla, 'Lesbia Harford and her work', *Overland*, 98, April 1985, pp.18–21

Moore, Andrew, 'The Pastoral Workers' Industrial Union, 1930–1937', *Labour History*, 49, Nov. 1985, pp.61–74

Murray, J., 'The Kalgoorlie woodline strike 1919–1920: a study of conflict within the working class', in Lenore Layman (ed.), *Studies in Western Australian History*, V, Dec. 1982, pp.22–37

Nairn, N.B., Review of Turner's *Sydney's Burning* in *Historical Studies*, 13, Oct. 1967, p.131

O'Connor, Harvey, 'From Wobblies to CIO', *Monthly Review*, 22, 11, April 1971, pp.47–52

O'Farrell, P.J., 'The trial of the Sydney Twelve', *Quadrant*, 16, 75, Jan./Feb. 1972

Oliver, Bobbie, ' "For Only by the OBU Shall Workmen's Wrongs be Righted". A Study of the One Big Union Movement in Western Australia, 1919 to 1922', in Charlie Fox and Michael Hess (eds), *Papers in Labour History*, 5, Perth Branch, Australian Society for the Study in Labour History, pp.1–17

Osborne, Graeme, 'Town and company: The Broken Hill industrial dispute of 1908–09', in Iremonger, Merritt and Osborne (eds), *Strikes*, pp.26–50

Peterson, Larry, 'The intellectual world of the IWW: an American worker's library in the first half of the 20th century', *History Workshop*, 22, Autumn 1986, pp.153–72

Preston, William, 'Shall this be all? U.S. historians versus William D.Haywood et al', *Labor History*, 12, 3, Summer 1971, pp.435–53

Reeves, Andrew, 'Anti-war repression; so what's new', *Farrago*, 1 Sept. 1971, pp.18–19

Reeves, Andrew, 'Percy Laidler', *Australian Dictionary of Biography*, 9, pp.645–6

Reeves, Andrew, 'Yours 'Til the War of Classes is Ended: OBU Organisers on Western Australian eastern goldfields', *Labour History*, 65, Nov. 1993, pp.19–25

Rushton, P.J., 'The revolutionary ideology of the Industrial Workers of the World in Australia', *Historical Studies*, 15, 59, Oct. 1972, pp.424–46

Rushton, P.J., 'The trial of the Sydney Twelve: the original charge', *Labour History*, 25, Nov. 1973, pp.53–7

Saville, John, 'The radical left expects the past to do its duty', *Labour History*, 18, 2, Spring 1977, pp.267–74

Schofield, Ann, 'Rebel girls and union maids: the woman question in the journals of the AFL and IWW, 1905–1920', *Feminist Studies*, 2, Summer 1983, pp.335–58

Segal, Naomi, 'Who and what was Siebenhaar: a note on the life and persecution of a Western Australian anarchist', Studies in Western Australian History Occasional Papers, No.1, University of Western Australia, 1988

Sheldon, Peter, 'System and strategy: the changing shape of unionism among NSW construction labourers, 1910–19', *Labour History*, 65, Nov. 1993, pp.115–35

Shor, Francis, 'Masculine power and virile syndicalism: a gendered analysis of the IWW in Australia', *Labour History*, 63, Nov. 1992, pp.83–99

Simpson, Joan, ' "Radicals"and "realists": the Australian Workers' Union response to the One Big Union challenge', in *Traditions for Reform in New South Wales. Labor History Essays*, Sydney, 1987, pp.38–52

Sims, R.C., 'Idaho's Criminal Syndicalism Act: one State's response to radical labour', *Labor History*, 15, 4, Fall 1974, pp.511–27

Taft, Philip, 'The federal trials of the IWW', *Labor History*, 3, 1, Winter 1962, pp.57–91

Taksa, Lucy, 'Defence not defiance: social protest and the New South Wales strike of 1917', *Labour History*, 60, May 1991, pp.16–33

'The I.W.W. – An exchange of views', *Labor History*, 11, 3, Summer 1970, pp.355–72

'The I.W.W.', *Recorder*, 47, Aug. 1970

'The I.W.W.', *Recorder*, 48, Oct. 1970

Thomas, Pete, 'Two veterans look back to IWW and earlier', *Tribune*, 22 July 1970, p.7

Turner, Ian, 'The One Big Union, 1918–1923', *Labour History*, 5, Nov. 1963, pp.65–8

Veblen, Thorstein, 'Farm labor and the I.W.W.', in Thorstein Veblen, *Essays in our Changing Order*, New York, 1954, pp.319–37

Walker, Bertha, 'Salute to Tom Barker', *Recorder*, 46, June 1970, Supplement

Walker, Bertha, 'Tom Barker: one of the greats passes', *Tribune*, 3 June 1970, p.6

Walker, Louise, 'The IWW: fanning the flames of discontent', *Socialist Action*, 35, Nov. 1988, p.13

Woiral, G.P., 'Observing the I.W.W. in California, May–July 1914', *Labor History*, 25, 3, Summer 1984, pp.437–47

Wright, Steven, 'Left Communism in Australia: J.A. Dawson and the "Southern Advocate for Workers' Councils"', *Thesis Eleven*, 1, 1980, pp.43–77

Young, Irwin, 'The NSW One Big Union, 1918–1919', *Journal of Industrial Relations*, 6, 1964, pp.226–38

Young, J.D., 'Daniel De Leon and Anglo-American Socialism', *Labor History*, 17, 3, Summer 1976, pp.329–50

Young, J.D., 'The problems and progress of the social history of the British working classes, 1880–1914', *Labor History*, 18, 2, Spring 1977, pp.257–66

Zieger, Robert, 'Workers and scholars: recent trends in American labor historiography', *Labor History*, 13, 2, Spring 1972, pp.245–66

Theses and unpublished manuscripts

Armstrong, J.B., 'Closer unity in the Queensland trade union movement 1900–1922', M.A. thesis, University of Queensland, 1975

Barnes, D.M., 'The ideology of the Industrial Workers of the World: 1905–1921', Ph.D. thesis, Washington State University, 1962

Birch, Anthony, ' "The Wobblies vs the rest": the Industrial Workers of the World in Australia during the Great War', B.A. Hons thesis, History, University of Melbourne, 1991

Bongiorno, Frank, 'The Australian Workers' Union and the One Big Union 1918–1924', B.A. Hons thesis, History, University of Melbourne, 1990

Burgmann, Meredith, 'A new concept of unionism: the New South Wales Builders Labourers' Federation 1970–1974', Ph.D. thesis, Macquarie University, 1981

Burgmann, Verity, 'Revolutionaries and racists: Australian socialism and the problem of racism, 1887–1917', Ph.D. thesis, ANU, 1980

Cain, Francis, 'The origins of political surveillance, 1916–1932: reactions to radicalism during and after the First World War', Ph.D. thesis, Monash University, 1979

Damousi, Joy, 'Socialist women in Australia, c.1890–c.1918', Ph.D. thesis, ANU, 1987

Evans, Ray, 'Radical departures. Paul Freeman and political deportations from Australia following World War One', paper presented to the Australian Historical Association Conference, Sydney, 1988

Fewster, Kevin, 'Expression and suppression: aspects of military censorship in Australia during the Great War', Ph.D. thesis, University of NSW, 1980

Hayden, Bill, '*The Wobblies At War*. Book launch by the Governor-General, Newcastle, June 25, 1993'

Healy, Chris, 'The Australian Peace Alliance, Melbourne, 1914–1924', B.A. Hons thesis, History, University of Melbourne, 1982

Hewitt, Geoffrey, 'A history of the Victorian Socialist Party: 1906–1932', M.A. thesis, La Trobe University, 1974

Howard, J.M., 'Industrial relations in Broken Hill mining 1903–1925', M.A. thesis, University of Sydney, 1955

Hunt, D.W., 'A history of the labour movement in north Queensland: trade unionism, politics and industrial conflict, 1900–1920', Ph.D. thesis, James Cook University, 1979

Karabogias, Michael, 'Fanning the flames of discontent. The success of the Industrial Workers of the World in Australia', B.A. Hons thesis, History, ANU, 1984

Kiek, L.E., 'The history of the South Australian labour unions', M.A. thesis, University of Adelaide, 1948

Macintyre, Clement, 'Winning a battle, losing the class war: the Wobblies on trial in Western Australia, 1916', unpublished undergraduate essay, School of Social Inquiry, Murdoch University, c.1979

Mansell, Ken, 'The east is red: the New Left', M.A. thesis, University of Melbourne, 1994

Metcalfe, Andrew, 'Sex and solidarity', paper presented verbally to Labour History Conference, Melbourne, July 1991

Morrison, Peter, 'The Communist Party of Australia and the Australian radical-socialist tradition, 1920–1939', Ph.D. thesis, University of Adelaide, 1977

O'Farrell, P.J., 'The Industrial Workers of the World in the USA. Revolutionary industrial unionism', paper presented to the Department of History, Research School of Social Sciences, ANU, September 1956

Osborne, Graeme, 'Tom Mann: his Australasian experience 1902–1910', Ph.D. thesis, ANU, 1972

Playford, John, 'History of the left-wing of the South Australian labor movement, 1908–1936', B.A. Hons thesis, History, University of Adelaide, 1958

Reeves, Andrew, 'Industrial men, miners and politics in Wonthaggi, 1909–1968', M.A. thesis, La Trobe University, 1977

Reeves, Andrew, 'The rise and decline of industrial unionism – the Workers' International Industrial Union in Australia', B.A. Hons thesis, University of Melbourne, 1973

Riedlinger, Peter, 'The red north recalled: radical perspectives on working class life in north Queensland', paper presented to Labour History Conference, Newcastle, June 1993

Roberts, Miriam, 'The One Big Union', Work in Progress Seminar, ANU Institute of Advanced Studies, 27 March 1962

Rushton, Peter, 'The Industrial Workers of the World in Sydney, 1913–1917: a study in revolutionary ideology and practice', M.A. thesis, University of Sydney, 1969

Sheldon, Peter, 'Failure of the IWW: an industrial explanation', paper presented verbally to Labour History Conference, Melbourne, July 1991

Shepherd, Michael, 'Compulsory military training: the South Australian debate, 1901–1914', B.A. Hons thesis, University of Adelaide, 1976

Segal, Naomi, 'Westralian Wobblies: the Industrial Workers of the World in Western Australia, 1914–1917', paper presented to the Department of History, University of Western Australia, 6 October 1986

Seggie, Kevin, 'The role of the police force in New South Wales and its relation to the government 1900–1939', Ph.D. thesis, Macquarie University, 1987

Sendy, John, 'The founders', unpublished manuscript

Taylor, Kerry Allan, 'Worker's vanguard or people's voice?: the Communist Party of New Zealand from origins to 1946', Ph.D. thesis, Victoria University of Wellington, 1994

Wait, R.N., 'Reactions to demonstrations and riots in Adelaide, 1928–1932', M.A. thesis, University of Adelaide, 1973

Wheatley, Nadia, 'The unemployed who kicked: a study of the political struggles and organisations of the New South Wales unemployed in the Great Depression', M.A. thesis, Macquarie University, 1975

Index